# NĀGĀRJUNA'S PHILOSOPHY
as presented in
THE MAHĀ-PRAJÑĀPĀRAMITĀ-ŚĀSTRA

Dedicated to the memory of

Dr. P. C. Bagchi

# NĀGĀRJUNA'S PHILOSOPHY

as presented in

# THE MAHĀ-PRAJÑĀPĀRAMITĀ-ŚĀSTRA

K. Venkata Ramanan

Reissued with permission of
Harvard-Yenching Institute

MOTILAL BANARSIDASS PUBLISHERS
PRIVATE LIMITED • DELHI

*Reprint: Delhi, 1975, 1978, 1987, 1993, 1998, 2002*
*Originally Published in 1966 by Charles E. Tuttle Company*
*of Rutland, Vermont & Tokyo, Japan*



ISBN: 81-208-0159-8 (Cloth)
ISBN: 81-208-0214-4 (Paper)

*Also available at:*
MOTILAL BANARSIDASS
41 U.A. Bungalow Road, Jawahar Nagar, Delhi 110 007
8 Mahalaxmi Chamber, 22 Bhulabhai Desai Road, Mumbai 400 026
236, 9th Main III Block, Jayanagar, Bangalore 560 011
120 Royapettah High Road, Mylapore, Chennai 600 004
Sanas Plaza, 1302 Baji Rao Road, Pune 411 002
8 Camac Street, Kolkata 700 017
Ashok Rajpath, Patna 800 004
Chowk, Varanasi 221 001

*Printed in India*
BY JAINENDRA PRAKASH JAIN AT SHRI JAINENDRA PRESS,
A-45 NARAINA, PHASE-I, NEW DELHI 110 028
AND PUBLISHED BY NARENDRA PRAKASH JAIN FOR
MOTILAL BANARSIDASS PUBLISHERS PRIVATE LIMITED,
BUNGALOW ROAD, DELHI 110 007

# TABLE OF CONTENTS

Foreword .......... 9
Preface .......... 13

I. Introduction .......... 25

life and work of nāgārjuna
basic conceptions in the philosophy of nāgārjuna
nāgārjuna and the buddha
nāgārjuna and the buddhist schools

II. Concepts and Conventional Entities (*Nāma* and *Lakṣaṇa*) .......... 70

nature of convention
modes of convention

III. Ignorance .......... 89

nature and function of ignorance
the sense of "I"
the false sense of self

IV. Ignorance and Knowledge .......... 111

ignorance and knowledge
kinds of knowledge
levels and perspectives of understanding

V. Knowledge *(Prajñā)* as the Principle of Comprehension .. 127

THE MIDDLE WAY: THE NON-EXCLUSIVE WAY
THE WAYS OF TEACHING

VI. Extremes and Alternatives .......................... 151

THE EXTREMES
THE ALTERNATIVES

VII. Criticism of Categories .............................. 171

THE MUNDANE AND THE ULTIMATE TRUTH
CRITICISM OF CATEGORIES

VIII. The World and the Individual ...................... 209

NON-SUBSTANTIALITY OF THE ELEMENTS OF EXISTENCE
THE NOTION OF SELF AS A SUBSTANTIAL ENTITY (SOUL)
THE COURSE OF PERSONAL LIFE

IX. Reality................................................ 251

THE INDETERMINATE GROUND
THE UNDIVIDED BEING

X. The Way ............................................ 276

THE WAY OF COMPREHENSION
THE GREAT WAY AND THE SMALL WAY *(Mahāyāna* and *Hīnayāna)*
THE FACTORS OF THE WAY AND THE GATES OF FREEDOM

XI. Consummation ..................................... 297

THE BODHISATTVA
THE BODHISATTVA AND THE BUDDHA

TABLE OF CONTENTS

# FOREWORD
## (TO THE ORIGINAL 1966 EDITION)

As one of the few Indian scholars of philosophy who in modern times have lived and studied in China, Dr. Krishniah Venkata Ramanan is unusually qualified to undertake the study here presented, based on the Chinese version of a *sūtra* commentary of which the Sanskrit original has long since vanished. He has left for another occasion his reasons for accepting the traditional but questionable ascription of the commentary to Nāgārjuna, believing the identity of the author immaterial to the present purpose—"to give as far as possible an objective and complete picture of the Mādhyamika philosophy as it can be gathered from the whole of this text."

Dr. Venkata Ramanan has produced a well-documented account of a difficult but important system of thought. His scholarly approach to his materials, his intellectual discrimination, and his command of Chinese sources (by no means confined to the *Ta-chih-tu-lun*) will surely earn him wide respect in India and abroad. This enterprising scholar is also well versed in modern Japanese Buddhist studies, and has lectured at Ohtani University and elsewhere in Japan.

The present work, begun in China and substantially completed in India, was revised while the author was in residence at Harvard University as a Visiting Scholar under auspices of the Harvard-Yenching Institute. One of the last instructions given me by the Institute's Director, Professor Edwin O. Reischauer, before he went on leave to assume his post as American Ambassador to Japan, was to carry out his plan to publish Dr. Venkata Ramanan's book—in the interest of furthering scholarly relations between East and South Asia, as well as deepening the understanding of Asia's cultural traditions wherever the book is read.

GLEN W. BAXTER
Acting Director
HARVARD-YENCHING INSTITUTE

*Cambridge, Massachusetts*

*March*, 1965

# ABBREVIATIONS

AAA — *The Abhisamayālaṅkārāloka of Haribhadra* (the Commentaries on the *Prajñāpāramitās,* vol. I), ed. G. Tucci (Gaekwad's Oriental Series LXII), Baroda, 1932.

*Aṅgu.* — *Aṅguttara Nikāya,* edd. R. Morris, E. Hardy, 5 vols. Pali Text Society, London 1885–1900.

Aspects — *Aspects of Mahāyāna Buddhism and Its Relation to Hīnayāna* by Nalinaksha Dutt, Luzac & Co., London, 1930

*Aṣṭa.* — *Aṣṭasāhasrikā Prajñāpāramitā,* ed. Rajendralala Mitra (Bibliotheca Indica), Calcutta, 1888.

*Bareau* — *Les Sectes Bouddhiques du Petit Vehicule,* by André Bareau, École Française d'Extreme-Orient, Saigon, 1955.

CCB (*Central Conception*) — *The Central Conception of Buddhism and the Meaning of the Word "Dharma,"* by Th. Stcherbatsky, Royal Asiatic Society, London, 1923 (Prize Publication Fund, Vol. VII).

*Dīgha* — *Dīgha Nikāya,* edd. T.W. Rhys Davids, J. E. Carpenter, W. Stede, 3 vols. Pali Text Society, London, 1908–1911.

*Fa-Ren* — *Yi-pu-tsung-lun-lun shu-chi-fa-ren* (異部宗輪論述記發軔) Oyama, Kyoto, 1891. This includes K'uei-chi's *Shu-chi* (述記)

GOS — Gaekwad's Oriental Series, Oriental Series, Oriental Institute.

*Kārikā* — *Mūlamadhyamakakārikās de Nāgārjuna avec la Prasannapadā* Commentaire de Candrakīrti), ed. Louis de la Vallée Poussin (Bibl. Buddhica, IV), St. Petersbourg, 1915.

| | |
|---|---|
| *Kimura* | *A Historical Study of Hīnayāna and Mahāyāna and the Origin of Mahāyāna Buddhism,* by Ryukan Kimura, Calcutta University, 1927. |
| *Majjh.* | *Majjhima Nikāya,* edd. V. Trenekner and Lord Chalmers, 3 vols. Pali Text Society, London, 1888–1899. |
| *Masuda* | *Origin and Doctrines of Early Indian Buddhist Schools* (a translation of Vasumitra's Treatise with annotations), Asia Minor, vol. II, 1925, pp. 1–78. |
| *Pañcaviṃśati* | *Pañcaviṃśati-sāhasrikā Prajñāpāramitā,* ed. Nalinaksha Dutt (Calcutta Oriental Series, No. 28), London, 1934. |
| *Prasannapadā* | see *Kārikā.* |
| *Saṃyu.* | *Saṃyutta Nikāya,* ed. L. Feer, 5 vols. Pali Text Society, London, 1884–1898. |
| *Śāstra* | *The Mahā-prajñāpāramitā-śāstra* of Nāgārjuna (tr. Kumārajīva), T. 1509, vol. 25, pp. 57A–756C. |
| T. | *Taishō-shinshū-daizōkyō* (大正新修大藏經) ed. Takakusu and Watanabe, Tokyo, 1922–1933. |
| *Vibhāṣā* | *Abhidharma-mahā-vibhāṣā-śāstra* (tr. Hsüan-tsang), T. 1545, vol. 27, pp. 1–1004. |

(JOURNALS):

| | |
|---|---|
| JBORS | Journal of Bihar and Orissa Research Society (later, since 1943 Journal of Bihar Research Society), Patna. |
| JPTS | Journal of Pali Text Society, London, published for the Society of the Oxford University Press. |
| JRAS | Journal of the Royal Asiatic Society of Great Britain and Ireland, London. |

# PREFACE

The present work as indicated in the title is devoted primarily to a study of the *Mahā-prajñāpāramitā-śāstra* (大智度論, T. 1509, vol XXV, pp. 57a–756c) (abbreviated in the present work as the *Śāstra)* which is a commentary on the *Prajñāpāramitā-sūtra of* 25,000 *gāthās,* the *Pañcaviṁśatisāhasrikā Prajñāpāramitā.* The *Śāstra* is the most comprehensive work of those traditionally attributed to Nāgārjuna, the well known teacher of the Mādhyamika philosophy or the philosophy of the Middle Way. This work is lost in its original and is preserved only in its Chinese translation. Professor Étienne Lamotte has rendered into French the first eighteen of the one hundred chapters *(chüan)* of this text *(Le Traité de la Grande Vertu de Sagesse,* vols. I & II, publ. 1944 and 1949, Bureaux du Muséon, Louvain). It is a magnificent work that Professor Lamotte has done, which he has furnished with copious literary and historical notes. This work of Professor Lamotte has been of great help to me. My present work, however, is a philosophical study intended to give as far as possible an objective and complete picture of the Mādhyamika philosophy as it can be gathered from the whole of this text.

Professor Lamotte has advanced arguments to doubt Nāgārjuna's authorship of the *Śāstra.* These arguments have not persuaded me and I believe that cogent arguments can be made in favour of the traditional view. I prefer, however, to postpone such arguments to a later date as they could not aid but would detract from the aim of the present work, which is to set forth the basic philosophical conceptions found in the *Śāstra.* I hope that it will appear to the reader as it has appeared to me that the basic conceptions of the *Śāstra* constitute a natural continuation and development of those found in the well known works of Nāgārjuna like the *Mādhyamika-kārikā* (abbreviated in the present work as *Kārikā*) and the *Vigrahavyāvartanī*. If so, my retaining of the traditional attribution can be justified even if one cannot settle the tangled question of its authorship.

As Professor Demiéville has observed, this text seems to have sunk into oblivion in India, supplanted by the texts of the quickly rising school of Yogācāra-vijñānavāda.[1] Perhaps the height of metaphysics to which the *Śāstra* rises was felt to be too great for lesser minds. Anyway the constructive metaphysics which the Yogācāra-vijñānavāda offered on absolutist lines based on the teachings of the Buddha seems to have grown in popularity. Hardly a reference to the *Śāstra* can be found in the Buddhist texts now available in their original Sanskrit versions. In China, during the two hundred years between Kumārajīva and Hsüan-tsang the *Śāstra* was much studied and was extensively in use. But after the time of Hsüan-tsang, with the introduction of Vijñānavāda it was little regarded as a source book of Buddhist philosophy of the Mahāyāna tradition. Even where it was in use it was mixed with the constructive metaphysical system of Yogācāra-vijñānavāda.

It was Kumārajīva who introduced Nāgārjuna and the Mādhyamika philosophy to China. Kumārajīva was a native of Kucha born in 343/344 A.D. of an Indian father and a mother who was a princess of the Kucha royal family.[2] It was Kumārajīva's mother who took him to Kaśmir for education in Buddhist lore, where he studied Sarvāstivāda under Bandhudatta; three years later he was introduced to Mahāyāna by Buddhayaśas in Kashgar. The fame of Kumārajīva as a Buddhist scholar induced the ruler of Ch'in to bring him to his country. However he was detained by the ruler of Liang (in modern Kansu) in his capital, Ku-tsang. Kumārajīva lived there for nearly seventeen years. Then in 401/402 A.D. he was brought as a captive to the Ch'in capital, Ch'ang-an, under the rule of Emperor Yao-hsing by whom he was received with great respect. Kumārajīva was fifty-eight when he came to Ch'ang-an. He remained in China the rest of his life.[3] The Emperor Yao-hsing not only held him in high esteem but himself took active part in the study and translation of Buddhist texts. Kumārajīva had a great number of disciples of whom there were ten chief ones. Among these were Seng-chao 僧肇 (384–414), Tao-sheng 道生 (d. 434) and Seng-jui 僧叡. He had also a famous Buddhist scholar as his friend, viz., Hui-yüan 慧遠 (334–416), who was a disciple of Tao-an 道安 (312–385). The correspondence between Kumārajīva and Hui-yüan is preserved in the Chinese Tripitaka: 大乘大義章, T. 1856.

As a scholar, Kumārajīva's principal work seems to have been the translation of Buddhist texts; he seems to have written scarcely any independent treatise of his own. We are told that he did write a text called *Shih-hsiang-lun* 實相論 (The Treatise on the Real Nature of Things) at the request of the Emperor Yao-hsing, but it is not extant. His oral explanations of the *Vimalakīrtinirdeśa* (T. 1775), however, have come down to us through Seng-chao. It is supposed that his influence was due not to his writings but to his oral explanations and winning personality.[4] Kumārajīva translated several recensions of the *Prajñāpāramitā-sūtras,* like the *Pañcaviṁśati-sāhasrikā,* the *Aṣṭa-sāhasrikā* and the *Vajracchedikā.*[5] He translated also such important Mahāyāna Sūtras as the *Vimalakīrtinirdeśa* and the *Śūraṅgama-samādhi,* which breathe the spirit of the Mādhyamika philosophy. He also translated the *Saddharmapuṇḍarīka.* All of these works have been cited in the *Śāstra* as authoritative. Kumārajīva translated also texts other than those connected with the *Prajñāpāramitā* or the Mādhyamika; *Satyasiddhiśāstra* of Harivarman was one such. But this he did very probably to provide a stepping stone to the mature philosophy of the Middle Way, through its criticism of Sarvāstivāda. Kumārajīva's appreciation lay in the philosophy of the Middle Way. He was through and through a man of the *prajāñpāramitā* and a follower of Nāgārjuna.

Kumārajīva translated also some texts on the method of *dhyāna* (meditation) and Tao-sheng, one of his foremost disciples, has been counted as a precursor of the Ch'an (or Zen) school. The roots of this school lay in the philosophy of *prajñāpāramitā* and that, principally through the Mādhyamika criticism of which Nāgārjuna was the unsurpassed master. Kumārajīva translated four of the principal works attributed to Nāgārjuna, viz., the *Madhyamaka-śāstra* (i.e., the *Mādhyamika-kārikā,* with the commentary of Piṅgaḷa), the *Dvadaśamukha-śāstra,* the *Daśabhūmi-vibhāṣā-śāstra* and the *Mahā-prajñāpāramitā-śāstra.* He translated also Deva's *Śata-śāstra.* We are told that he commenced the translation of the *Śāstra* in 402 and finished it in 405;[6] but it is possible that he began his work while he was still in Ku-tsang.

Although it seems that Kumārajīva did not himself write much, still under his influence this branch of Buddhist philosophy came to be much studied and some brilliant minds in China have left records of their deep study of this school. Seng-chao and Chi-tsang 吉藏 (549–623) are preeminent among these. Chi-tsang, an important Chinese master of the Mādhyamika philosophy, has left records of extensive use of the *Śāstra*. 大乘義章 (T. 1851) (Exposition of the Meaning of Mahāyāna) of Hui-yüan (523–92) also makes extensive use of this text. Hui-yüan has arranged his exposition of the topics so as to contrast the accounts of Abhidharma (Sarvāstivāda) and Satyasiddhi with the account of Mahāyāna and under the latter he cites throughout the relevant passages from the *Śāstra*. These works of Chi-tsang and Hui-yüan were of great help to me in coordinating and organizing my materials. We have also an analysis and notes on the *Śāstra* prepared by one Hui-ying 慧影 (600 A.D.).[7]

So far our understanding of Nāgārjuna's philosophy has been largely based on the *Kārikā*, which is all too abstract and overwhelmingly negative in emphasis and character. But the *Kārikā* contains not only negative arguments but also utterances of truth that speak of the Mādhyamika's outlook on life. Still, on the basis of the *Kārikā* alone it is difficult to get a clear picture of the Mādhyamika philosophy. In this the *Śāstra* is more helpful. It provides us with a complete picture of the Mādhyamika philosophy. In the light of the *Śāstra* the negative arguments of the *Kārikā* gain the much needed concrete setting by which one can fix it in its proper place in this total picture. Accordingly the *Kārikā* which is the most basic and the best known work of Nāgārjuna has been kept in view throughout the present study. The parallel passages from it have been noted and at times the negative arguments of the *Śāstra* have been amplified by it.

The Introduction contains a short account of the life and work of Nāgārjuna. I have tried to give there a detailed account of his works available in original Sanskrit and of those that are attributed to him in the Chinese and the Tibetan traditions, including their restorations and retranslations by modern scholars. While the primary source of the present study is the *Śāstra* itself, other works that can be reasonably attributed to Nāgārjuna have also been referred to wherever they are relevant.

As the present work is primarily a philosophical study, the historical sequence of Buddhist philosophy in its various aspects has hardly been touched. However, the Introduction contains a short historical account of its broad lines as an aid to lead up to the present topic. No reference is made to the general background of Indian philosophy, nor even to any non-Buddhist schools, with the exception of Sāṅkhya, Vaiśeṣika and Nyāya. References to these were necessary in order to discuss certain problems where the *Śāstra* itself has referred to their views. An exception is made in the case of Jainism and a short account is given of the Jaina non-absolutism of judgments contrasting it with the relativity of the Mādhyamika. The Conclusion summarizes (ch. XII) briefly the development of the philosophy of the Middle Way in India and in China in the early part of its career. But this account is admittedly an over-simplification intended only to assist further studies that may be conducted in this field. The Conclusion contains also a very brief account of the Advaitavedānta of Śaṅkara so as to show some lines of similarity and difference between it and the philosophy of the Middle Way, but even this is done only in a cursory way. In all these matters a certain self-imposed limitation was considered essential, although naturally it is hoped that the present work may lead to further historical, critical and comparative studies, by providing these with the necessary first acquaintance with the subject matter of which this is an exposition.

The present attempt is to provide the materials contained in the *Śāstra* as far as possible through direct citations from it replenished with interpretative statements. It was thought advisable to adopt this method for the reason that the entire text of the *Śāstra* has so far been a closed book to the English reading public. It is for the first time that an attempt is made to study the text extensively with a view to arriving at the comprehensive picture that it provides of the philosophy of the Middle Way, presented through direct citations from it in English translation. I have tried to collect all the passages of the *Śāstra* which are relevant to the study of the philosophy of the Middle Way. Of these passages I have treated in greater detail those which concern the problem of knowledge and the problem of reality. Thus chapters II–VI deal with problems concerning concepts, knowledge, ingnorance and with certain questions regarding the critical examination of categories. Chapters VII–IX deal with the actual critical examination, bearing out its import, with the roots of the life of conflict and suffering, and with the right understanding which leads to the realization of the highest truth namely, the undivided being (*advaya-dharma*), the ultimate end of man's thirst for the real (*dharmaiṣaṇā* 求法 [8]).

Chapters X–XI of the present work deal very briefly with the cultivation of the Way which leads to consummation, viz., the complete extinction of ignorance and passion and their transformation into wisdom and compassion. It is to be remembered that the wayfaring is the deepening of one's assimilation of the truth that one finds in the critical examination of things by means of reason or rational investigation, in the light of the sense of the real. The factors of the Way are the various stages and elements in this course of deepening and widening one's comprehension through the two phases: right understanding and the meritorious action that springs from compassion, *prajñā and puṇya*. It is to an expostition of this deeper implication of wayfaring that the two chapters, X–XI, are devoted. Throughout it is the skilfulness of nonclinging which springs from the proper understanding of things that is the pervading spirit of the philosophy of the Middle Way.

As the *Śāstra* abounds in repetition it was found necessary to gather together the relevant passages in the case of every topic, but to give usually only one of them in the text, and furnish references to others in the notes. In some cases where different passages seem to touch different aspects of the same problem, it was found advisable to present these passages in the text itself, eliminating repetitions as far as possible. Again, in addition to directly citing from the text in closely printed passages, at times paraphrasing has also been adopted; and in this latter case, the translation is at times somewhat free. Passages paraphrased have not been closely printed but at the end of a paraphrased passage a notation is given and the reference is given to its occurrence in the Chinese text. Parallel as well as other relevant passages, wherever they occur, have likewise been adduced. Attempt is made to give the Chinese characters in the case of technical or key terms where they were considered to be helpful. Sanskrit terms have been introduced. As far as possible attempt is made to give their equivalents in English at their first appearance. It is most difficult to convey the precise sense of the technical terms of one language in the technical terms of another; and within the same language, the senses that terms convey differ from system to system. It is necessary to paraphrase terms, to collect and compare their different uses within the same system, and in the same text in different contexts. Some terms indeed must just be kept untranslated. All these methods have been adopted in the course of this work. Some terms have been discussed, and their meanings distinguished within the body of the text. Such are, for example, terms like *nāma, lakṣaṇa, prajñā, tathatā, svabhāva, dharma-dhātu, bhūta-koṭi*. Of all these terms the *Śāstra* itself gives their different imports in different contexts and these have been mentioned in the body of the present work. Again, terms like *grāha, samjñā, smṛti, viparyaya* or *viparyāsa, kṣānti,* had to be mentioned specially and their different imports delineated in the notes. *Svabhāva,* literally self-being, has been rendered as "absoluteness" or "unconditionedness," specially in referring to *sasvabhāvavāda,* which has been rendered here as "the error of misplaced absoluteness." *Advaya* and *anutpāda* have been rendered as "undivided" and "unborn." In the case of such negative expressions it is not the not-yet-divided or the not-yet-born that is meant. The meaning is the *dharma* devoid of all divisions, the ult imate truth of birthlessness, unaffected by time. Similarly the term "indeterminate" as used here does not mean indistinct or vague; it stands for the ultimate reality beyond determinations.

To prepare myself for the understanding of the *Prajñāpāramitā-śāstra* I first read through and compared the Chinese translations of the *Mādhyamika-kārikā* and the *Pañcavimśati-sāhasrikā-prajñāpāramitā* with the Sanskrit originals. This has enabled me to furnish Sanskrit equivalents in many cases for the Chinese technical terms in the *Śāstra*. In some cases a single Chinese word is used in many meanings, often representing more than one Sanskrit term. I have given special care to collecting and comparing occurrences of such terms, e.g., 住, 行, 著, 取, 見 and 觀.

The entire work is presented as a Mādhyamika would present it. Thus I have used such terms as "the hearers" *(śrāvaka)*, "the Small Way" (Hīnayana) and "the Great Way" (Mahāyāna) as a Mādhyamika would use them. I hope that this will be understood as an expedient intended simply to give a more vivid account of the system which is being described. *Śāstra* itself uses these terms. But it should be remembered that though the *Śāstra* speaks caustically of some teachers of the Small Way, its author need not be supposed to have any animus against the Small Way as such. He might well have said, "Those who are followers of the Great Way will become small if they shall cling. On the other hand, even the elements that are called factors of the Small Way, if they are cultivated non-clingingly, may lead to final consummation in the Great Way. What matters in both ways is the understanding and the attitude."

My study and translation of the *Śāstra* were based on the woodcut edition of 姑蘇刻經處, 光緒九年, (1883/1884 A.D.). But in the final revision of the work, the references have been made to the Taishō edition of the Chinese Tripiṭaka.

The beginnings of my study of the Mādhyamika philosophy date back to my undergraduate days in the Mysore University in the years 1942–1943, and are due in particular to the incentive of Professor Radhakrishnan's presentation of the philosophy of Nāgārjuna in his *Indian Philosophy,* vol. I, (George Allen and Unwin, 1923), pp. 643–669. I continued my studies at the Benares Hindu University under his guidance. I wish to acknowledge here my deepest sense of gratefulness to this great teacher for the immense help and encouragement I have obtained from him. I found Professor Stcherbatsky's *Conception of Buddhist Nirvāṇa,* which embodies a translation of Chapters I and XXV of the *Kārikā* with Candrakīrti's *Prasannapadā,* of considerable help in my early stages. My study of the Chinese Buddhist texts began in China, when I was a Government of India Research Scholar at the National University of Peking in the years 1947–1949, under the guidance of

Professors T'ang Yung-t'ung 湯用彤 and Wang San-ti'en 王森田. Professor Wang San-t'ien was particularly helpful to me in my study of the different commentaries on the *Mādhyamika-kārikā,* preserved in the Chinese Collection. My work on the *Prajñāpāramitā-śāstra* started in Visvabharati University, early in 1950, under the encouragement and guidance of its late Vice-chancellor, Dr. P.C. Bagchi. The major portion of my work was done under him and I regret that this work could not be completed during his life-time. I was able to give further shape to this work when Professor S.N. Bose who succeeded Dr. Bagchi as the Vice-chancellor of the Visvabharati University, very kindly took the initiative to get me relieved of my teaching work for several months until I left for the United States for study as a Visiting Scholar at the Harvard-Yenching Institute. I am deeply grateful to Professor S.N. Bose for his very kind help. Also my sincere thanks are due to the members of the department of philosophy of the Visvabharati University, including its chairman Dr. Kalidas Bhattacharya, for the readiness and goodwill with which they shared among themselves the teaching work that should have been allotted to me during those months.

I express hereby my sincerest gratitude to the authorities of the Harvard-Yenching Institute for the splendid opportunity they provided for me to work in this Institute. I found here able professors eager to render all the help I needed. Professor Yang Lien-sheng gave me unstinted help by going through my entire translation from the *Śāstra* and gave suggestions to improve its presentation. Professor Daniel H.H. Ingalls, Chairman of the Department of Sanskrit and Indian Studies, read the whole work, gave clarity to my thought and improved my expressions. At the request of the Harvard-Yenching Institute, Dr. A. K. Reischauer, the author of *Studies in Japanese Buddhism,* read the MS twice, trimmed its language and suggested changes in the organization of the Introduction.

This work was originally submitted and approved for the degree of Doctor of Letters of the Visvabharati University. I am most thankful to Prof. W. Liebenthal who was till recently the Visiting Professor at the Visvabharati University, to Prof. W.T. Chan of Dartmouth College, New Hampshire and to Prof. T.R.V. Murti of the Benares Hindu

University for their valuable suggestions for improvement. I owe to Prof. Murti's book, *The Central Philosophy of Buddhism,* (George Allen and Unwin, 1955), the impetus to rethink the central problem of the philosophy of the Mādhyamika school of Buddhist thought. I am also indebted to him for his valuable bibliographical account (*ibid.* pp. 87–103). I wish to convey my indebtedness to Prof. D.M. Datta (Retd. Prof. of Philosophy, Patna University) with whom I had the privilege to have many conversations; the chapter, *Extremes and Alternatives* is chiefly the outcome of these. Of others who read the MS and suggested improvements mention must be made of Prof. E.A. Burtt of Cornell, Prof. J.R. Ware of the Harvard-Yenching Institute, Prof. Nagao Gadjin of Kyoto University and Father Casey (Maryknoll Fathers, Boston). I am thankful to Prof. Tsukamoto Zenryu of the Research Institute for Humanistic Studies of Kyoto University for drawing my attention to the bibliographical account of Hui-yüan and Hui-ying in 續高僧傳 (T. 2060).

In regard to my approach to the Pali Nikāyas I have derived much help from Ananda K. Coomaraswamy and I.B. Horner: *Living Thoughts of Gautama the Buddha* (Living Thoughts Library, Cassell & Company Ltd., London, 1948).

I cannot adequately state how deeply grateful I am to the authorities of the Harvard-Yenching Institute, especially to its Director, Dr. Edwin O. Reischauer, for his interest in my work from the beginning of my stay at Harvard and for extending to me every kind of help culminating in the acceptance of this work for publication.

Thanks are also due to the library authorities of the Visvabharati University and to those of the Harvard-Yenching Institute and Widener's Library.

I wish to acknowledge with a deep sense of gratitude the unfailing encouragement and cooperation I have constantly received from my wife.

K. VENKATA RAMANAN

# NĀGĀRJUNA'S PHILOSOPHY

## AS PRESENTED IN

## THE MAHĀ-PRAJÑĀPĀRAMITĀ-ŚĀSTRA

*CHAPTER I*

# INTRODUCTION

*Section I*

## LIFE AND WORK OF NĀGĀRJUNA

*Life of Nāgārjuna:* While Nāgārjuna as a Buddhist philosopher has few equals in the history of Buddhism, there has been harldly another personality so elusive as his. The tendency to mystify and build stories of embellishments around a momentous personality seems to have reached its zenith in his case. It is therefore not strange that eminent scholars like Professor Max Walleser should strike a very skeptical note not only in regard to the different and sometimes conflicting traditional accounts of the life and work of this Buddhist master but also in regard to the very question of his having ever existed.[1] However, works like the *Mādhyamika-kārikā* testify by their very existence to the historicity of their author who is undisputedly known as Nāgārjuna, the great Buddhist philosopher who trod the path of *prajñāpāramitā*[2] and wrote even the *Kārikā* in order to expound the basic teachings of the *Prajñāpāramitā-sūtras.*[3] Furthermore the recent archaeological discoveries at Amarāvatī[4] corroborate to some extent certain broad facts about Nāgārjuna's life on which his traditional biographies agree,[5] these facts being his friendship with a Śātavāhana king and his having spent the latter part of his career in the monastery built for him by this king at Bhramaragirī (Śrīparvata).[6]

All the biographical accounts of Nāgārjuna, including the one attributed to Kumārajīva which differs from the rest in certain respects, mention that he was born as a Brahmin in South India. In regard to his boyhood and youth, the Tibetan sources state that he had to leave his home even as a child because his parents sent him away being unable to bear the sight of his premature death at the age of seven which the astrologers had predicted of him. However, the boy escaped from this fate, so these sources say, by entering the Buddhist Order and practising the *aparimitāyurdhāraṇī* according to the instructions of his teacher Rāhulabhadra (or Sarāha) at Nāḷanda.[7] Kumārajīva is at variance with this account. He tells us that Nāgārjuna was overpowered with lust and passion in his early days, seduced women in the royal court by the use of the art of invisibility and only narrowly escaped death at the hands of the guards at a touching moment. This stirred him deeply and awakened him to the truth that the origin of suffering is passion. Thereupon he entered the Buddhist Order and studied all the Buddhist texts that were available to him; and not being satisfied with them, he wandered in search of other texts.[8] The 'prevailing' tradition which he could readily obtain was presumably Sarvāstivāda and Nāgārjuna's deep study of it is beyond doubt. This is amply borne out by his penetrating understanding and searching criticism of this school in his *Kārikā*.[9] All the accounts of his life, speak of his having obtained the *Prajñāpāramitā-sūtras* (Kumārajiva's *Vaipulya-sūtras)* from a Nāga[10] and these texts satisfied so deeply his quest for "other teachings" of the Buddha that he devoted his whole life to teach and propagate the profound truths contained in them.

The Tibetan sources state that Nāgārjuna was a teacher at Nālanda and they speak of his all-embracing compassion and intense care for the whole community.[11] Kumārajīva however does not mention Nālanda.[12] The accounts of Nāgārjuna's passing away though differently told amount to his having himself put an end to his life or having given his consent to his own death at the hands of another, viz., the son of the king with whom he was tied in life and death.[13] The different accounts of Nāgārjuna's life, though briefly told, bear out certain broad facts of the life of a master-mind of Buddhist lore and these could be hardly said to be too incongruous to be credible. However, the one point of great divergence is about the circumstances of his younger days leading to his accepting the Buddhist Order. Perhaps in this regard Kumārajīva's account merits consideration more than the rest if only for its being presumably earlier than that of the Tibetan sources.[14]

*Nāgārjuna and the Nāgas:* As regards the Nāga from whom Nāgārjuna is said to have obtained the *Prajñāpāramitā-sūtras,* Kumārajīva speaks of the Nāga chief *(Mahānāga)* who led him into the sea and opened up for him the *"Treasury of the Seven Jewels" (Saptaranakośa).* Nāgārjuna read the *Vaipulya (Mahāyāna) Sūtras* which the *Mahānāga* selected for his reading, and having read them he deeply penetrated into their meaning. He told the *Mahānāga* that what he already read there was ten times of what he had read in Jambudvīpa and eventually brought away with him a boxful of them.[15] The Tibetan sources are more specific with regard to what he brought from there, for they tell us that there was among these texts, the *Prajñāpāramitā-sūtras* of 100,000 *gāthās.*[16] The tradition that Nāgārjuna brought these *Sūtras* from the country of the Nāgas may be taken as pointing to the preservation of another tradition of the Buddhist teaching in the South, different from those that were prevailing in his time in the North, and it bears on the fact that from his time onwards the *Prajñāpāramitā* teaching came to overshadow more and more the other lines of Buddhist philosophy.

*Nāgārjuna and the Śātavāhanas:* The Śātavāhana king who is stated to have been the great friend of Nāgārjuna and to have built the monastery for him in Śrīparvata seems to have been a breakaway from the faith of his forefathers, viz., the Buddhist faith; and to him Nāgārjuna wrote letters of admonition.[17] This royal friend is reputed to have been the "lord of the three seas."[18] The king was presumably Gautamīputra Śātakarṇī who is called the only *"brāhmaṇa"* in his lineage as well as "the lord of the three seas" in the Nasik Edict issued by his mother Bālaśrī.[19] This is the king that won a victory over Kṣaharāta Nahapāna, and this victory was proclaimed in the Edict issued from the king's victorious camp in the year 18 of his reign.[20]

Two dates are held out for Gautamīputra Śātakarṇī who ruled for twenty-four years, viz., the first quarter of the second century or the last quarter of the first century of our era, depending among other things, on the question whether the year 46 in the reign of Nahapāna with which the year 18 of Gautamīputra coincides is taken as referring to the Śaka era or simply to one of his regnal years. Those who accept the year 46 as referring to the Śaka era assign this Edict of victory to 124 A.D. and consider Gautamīputra to have reigned from 106 A.D. to 130 A.D.[21] While the earlier date is upheld by Professor K.A.N. Sastri who places Gautamīputra in 80–104 A.D.,[22] the later date is upheld among others by Dr. H.C. Raychaudhuri.[23] And those who subscribe to the later date of Gautamīputra subscribe also the later date of Hāla. As to the intervening years between the two kings, the Purāṇas mention it as fifty-five or sixty years.[24]

*Nāgārjuna and Kaniṣka:* Hsüan-tsang mentions Nāgārjuna as a contemporary of Aśvaghoṣa who is himself mentioned as a contemporary of Kaniṣka.[25] He recounts a tradition according to which Nāgārjuna is considered as the sun shining in the west, one of the four suns that illumined the world from the four directions.[26] A late Indian text, *Rājataraṅgiṇī* of Kalhaṇa, speaks of Nāgārjuna as a contemporary of Huṣka, Juṣka and Kaniṣka.[27] Huṣka and Juṣka are probably Huviṣka and Vajeṣka, the contemporaries of Kaniṣka II, who was ruling in the years 41 after the accession of Kaniṣka I.[28] If the latter's accession be assigned to 78 A.D., then Kaniṣka II should be considered as ruling in 119 A.D.; and if the later date be accepted for Gautamīputra he would be a contemporary of Kaniṣka II.

The *Śāstra* mentions several times the *Abhidharma-vibhāṣā-śāstra* (or simply *Vibhāṣā*), a fundamental text of the Sarvāstivādins.[29] It is Hsüan-tsang who tells us that there was a Council in the period of Kaniṣka, that it was intended to put into order the then prevailing currents of Buddhist thought and that it composed three huge commentaries, one of which was the *Vibhāṣā*, which is a commentary on the *Jñānaprasthāna* of Kātyāyanīputra.[29a] The Council, he tells us, met at the initiative of king Kaniṣka and under the leadership of Pārśva.[30] A slightly earlier authority, Paramārtha, gives us a different account. The Council, according to him, met at the initiative of Kātyāyanīputra and it accomplished the work of not only composing the *Vibhāṣā* as the commentary to *Jñānaprasthāna* but also of compiling the latter text. On the suggestion of Kātyāyanīputra, the then reigning king consented to take steps in order to preserve these great works. Paramārtha tells us that the Council was constituted of five hundred arahats and five hundred bodhisattvas and worked for twelve years even to achieve the composition of *Vibhāṣā*. Aśvaghoṣa is said to have participated in the Council.[31] Paramārtha was conveying to his readers a tradition about an event that happened at least four hundred years before him but with this the tradition of Hsüan-tsang is at variance. It is possible that a Council was held during Kaniṣka's time, and it is possible that there was a gathering of the teachers of Sarvāstivāda who worked for many years and composed *Vibhāṣā* as a commentary of the text that was already there before them, viz., the *Jñānaprasthāna*. It could hardly be that the same Council composed of five hundred Arahats and five hundred bodhisattvas sat for several years to compile *Jñānaprasthāna* and sat again for twelve years and composed the *Vibhāṣā*. Paramārtha may have been mixing up the later work of the disciples of Kātyāyanīputra with the work of Kātyāyanīputra himself. That this was in all probability the case is borne out all the more clearly by what the *Śāstra* has to say. It tells us that a hundred years after the Buddha, in the time of Aśoka (it must be Kālāśoka) there was a Council and thereafter there grew up the different schools. From then on gradually the dissensions grew and when it came to the time of Kātyāyanīputra who was himself a very clever and well read brahmin, he attempted to interpret the teachings of the Buddha and so he wrote the *Jñānaprasthāna*. Later his disciples wrote the *Vibhāṣā* in order to make the text clear to the less intelligent.[32] In this account of the *Śāstra* we have the sequence of *Jñānaprasthāna* and *Vibhāṣā* which is missing in Paramārtha while at the same time we have the advantage of not having to suppose that a thousand people sat together for over twenty years working on these two texts. We have no reference to Kaniṣka at all. This does not deny the possibility of a Kaniṣkan Council, but this bears out that the mention of the *Vibhāṣā* in the *Śāstra* need not by itself lead us to think that it is posterior to the Kaniṣkan Council. It is possible that a *Vibhāṣā* was there already which came to be redacted and recognized there.

Still we may not doubt Nāgārjuna's contemporaneity with Kaniṣka I. And if the later date be accepted for Gautamīputra, it is possible that a considerable part, if not the whole of his reign, coincided with the later years of Nāgārjuna. How much advanced in age was he when Gautamīputra came to power? If Hāla is also to be considered as a contemporary of Nāgārjuna and if the intervening period between Hāla and Gautamīputra is to be accepted as fifty-five or sixty years, certainly Nāgārjuna must have been quite advanced in age when Gautamīputra came to power, well beyond eighty. And if we have to reckon with the fact that there is ground in the Tibetan sources, with which Hsüan-tsang seems to agree, to hold that Nāgārjuna was a friend for a long time with the same king to whom he wrote the letters of admonition, notwithstanding the possibility of his having been contemporaneous and friendly with a number of Śātavāhana kings, then he might have well lived up to the end of the reign of Gautamīputra. In such a case it may be surmised that he lived a fairly long life, perhaps a hundred years. Even so, it seems that nothing definite could be said about the date of Nāgārjuna at least as long as the dates of the kings in the Śātavāhana lineage remain unsettled, especially of those kings with whom he could be reasonably held to have been contemporaneous. Accepting tentatively the later date for Gautamīputra and reckoning with the possibility of Nāgārjuna's being contemporaneous not only with him but also with Hāla, it could perhaps be taken as a highly probable working hypothesis that the upper and the lower limits of the philosophical activity of Nāgārjuna lay somewhere between 50 A.D. and 120 A.D. If the earlier date is to be accepted for Gautamīputra, these limits have to be pushed back by about twenty years. The period between 50 A.D. and 120 A.D. would be synchronous also with the reigns of Kaniṣka I and Kaniṣka II. This corroborates the other tradition that Nāgārjuna was a contemporary of these kings.

*Nāgārjuna's sources:* We have seen that it is to the exposition of the teachings of the *Prajñāpāramitā-sūtras* that Nāgārjuna set himself. These *Sūtras* embody the central teaching that the ultimate nature of the determinate is itself the unconditioned reality—that in the ultimate truth, the undivided being, there is no division of conditioned and unconditioned—and that the wisdom that consists in and is itself the same as this ultimate truth of things has, in regard to determinate existence, which is the mundane truth, the essential import of the skilfulness of non-clinging, not clinging to the determinate as ultimate in its determinate nature. Undivided being *(advaya-dharma)* and the skilfulness of non-clinging *(anupalambha-yoga)* constitute practically the heart of the *Prajñāpāramitā-sūtras*, and in them *śūnyatā*[33] becomes the overarching concept as the most felicitous means of conveying their basic teachings in all their different aspects. The universal compassion of the wise comes to be emphasized as the necessary import and hence the invariable accompaniment of the wisdom that is *śūnyatā*. Perfect wisdom and universal compassion come to be emphasized as the two inalienable phases of the integral course of the life of the wise. The skilfulness of non-clinging as the way of *śūnyatā*, in life and in understanding, comes to receive great emphasis.

The earliest recension of these *Sūtras* may have been in existence about a century before Nāgārjuna;[34] and the credit of bringing them to prominence by laying bare their profound teachings belongs to him.[35] The depth of insight, the rigour of logic and the felicity of expression which he brought to bear upon his work as a teacher of the Great Way *(Mahāyāna)*, the way of the perfection of wisdom *(prajñāpāramitā)*, made a revolution almost startling in the history of Buddhist philosophy and influenced profoundly the subsequent philosophical thinking both within and outside the Buddhist fold. Although he is said to have brought from the country of the Nāgas the *Prajñāpāramitā-sūtras* in 100,000 *gāthās*, the recension of which the *Śāstra* is the commentary is that of 25,000 *gāthās* which seems to have been an abridgement of the former.[36] It is possible that he himself had a hand in settling the reading of the abridged version. Nāgārjuna must have taught these *Sūtras* for many, many years, practically till the very end of his career.

Besides the *Prajñāpāramitā-sūtras*, Nāgārjuna had quite a number of other *Mahāyāna-sūtras* before him, some of which must have influenced him profoundly in sharpening and giving shape to his philosophical thinking.[37] One such is that small but exceptionally profound and extraordinarily absorbing *Sūtra*, the *Vimalakīrti-nirdeśa*.[38] This *Sūtra* is full of the spirit of the philosophy of the absolute, the *advaya-dharma*. It is equal in profundity to the *Prajñāpāramitā-sūtras* and at the same time free from the repetitions and the excessive emphasis on the negative import of *śūnyatā* in which the latter abound. The *Vimalakīrti-nirdeśa* has a deep touch of humanity about it which speaks of the essence of the Great Way. It sets forth the import of the ultimacy of the undivided or non-dual *dharma* with regard to the determinate modes of thought and life. Life in the world, when lived in the light of the highest truth, is itself Nirvāṇa. Again, while the speakable is the determinate, silence is the highest truth for the wise, who yet speak of the unspeakable, by virtue of their skilfulness of non-clinging and lead people by means of the determinations of thought to what lies beyond them. The *Śāstra* quotes several times from this grand *Sūtra*.[39] *Saddharmapuṇḍarīka*, *Akṣayamati-paripṛcchā*, *Śūraṅgama-samādhi* are some of the important *Mahāyāna-sūtras* which find frequent mention in the *Śāstra*. All these *Sūtras*, in one way or another, set forth the basic teaching of the Great Way, viz., the ultimate truth of the undivided being and the wayfaring by non-clinging. One has to note also the influence on Nāgārjuna of the *Kāśyapa-parivarta* which has for its central theme the Middle Way *(madhyamā-pratipat)*, the Way that transcends the extremes which are falsifications and sees things as they are *(dharmāṇām bhūta-pratyavekṣā)*.[40] We have a commentary attributed to Nāgārjuna on *"The Sūtra on the Ten Bhūmis" (Daśabhūmika-sūtra)*. Only a fragment of this text has come down to us in its Chinese translation.[41] The commentary has citations from the *Kārikā* and breathes the spirit of the philosophy of the Middle Way not only in its use of the negative arguments, but in laying bare how the factors of the Way come to be cultivated in the light of *śūnyatā*.[42] It may also be noted that the *Śastra* frequently uses citations from the *Āgamas*[43] which it considers, in keeping with the spirit of *Mahāyāna*, as genuine teachings of the Buddha and specially intended for those who tread the Way of the Hearers (the *Śrāvakayāna)*, the Small Way, and as not without the deeper truths of things.

Nāgārjuna's immediate interest seems to have been to set in order the spiritual life of the community of the Buddha's disciples by finding and providing for them a basis wider than the one to which each school clung, and thus to remove the ground of contention and quarrel. The synthesis that he achieved was essentially one of revivifying the original insight of the Master, viz., the insight of the Middle Way, the way that is all-comprehensive and hence above contention. It is the Buddhist schools, especially the Sarvāstivādins, that keep his attention engaged, and almost all that he wrote had an immediate, direct, bearing on their doctrine of elements. The *Śāstra* refers to the non-Buddhist schools but rarely. Of these, it is the Sāṅkhya and the Vaiśeṣika that provide the specimens respectively of clinging to identity and difference and the existence and the non-existence of the effect in the cause as well as of holding fast to the belief in the multiplicity of separate entities, I-substances.[44] The *Kārikā* refers to the imagination that there is an impervious core of personality, essentially unrelated to deeds and their consequences and yet somehow attached to them, eternal and all-pervasive and yet somehow migrating from one set of constituents to another.[45] It is these tenets of the Sāṅkhya and the Vaiśeṣika that become the objects of frequent criticism at the hands of the Buddhist thinkers and it is not difficult to see that their arguments are patterned after Nagarjuna's.

One of the important criticisms that the *Śāstra* levels against the substantialist theory of self of the non-Buddhists is with regard to the part that the latter assign to "soul" in the act of knowing. These criticisms are levelled with particular reference to the naïve belief of the Vaiśeṣika and the Nyāya that the soul which is not of the nature of knowledge or awareness can yet function as the ultimate ground of knowing[46] and with reference to their uncritical acceptance that the *pramāṇas,* the ordinary means of knowledge, viz., sense-perception and the inference that is based on it, yield us the understanding of the ultimate truth of things.[47] The criticism that the *Śāstra* offers amounts to a dismissal of the spurious "soul," the I-substance, and the revelation that a critical use of *pramāṇas* means an awareness of their having their ground in the undivided prajñā, even in their extending our acquaintance in the world of the determinate. Again, as determinate modes of knowing, they are not suited to deal with the ultimate truth, the indeterminate, non-dual, dharma. In the usual way of *prasaṅga*, the *reductio ad absurdum*, the *Śāstra* lays bare the inherent contradictions involved in the naïve belief of these schools with regard to the soul as well as the *pramāṇas* while at the same time making it clear that the import of the sense of "I" or subjectivity as well as the use of *pramāṇas* are not themselves rejected.[48]

*The works of Nāgārjuna:* Kumārajīva's biography of Nāgārjuna mentions five kinds of works as his: I) *Upadeśa* in 100,000 *gāthās,* II) *Buddhamārgālaṅkāra-śāstra,* the Treatise on the Factors of the Way of the Buddha in 5,000 *gāthās,* III) *Mahākaruṇopāya-śāstra,* the Treatise on the Skilfulness of Great Compassion, in 5,000 *gāthās,* IV) the *Madhyamaka-śāstra,* the Treatise on the Middle Way, in 500 *gāthās* and V) *Akutobhaya-śāstra,* the Fearless Treatise, in 100,000 *gathas.* The biography mentions that the *Madhyamaka-śāstra* is contained in the *Akutobhaya-śāstra.*[49] Of these the *Madhyamaka-śāstra* is the *Kārikā* which has come down to us in its original Sanskrit version in about 450 verses. The term *Upadeśa* meaning either scriptural instruction or oral instruction on the basis of scripture may refer to the *Śāstra.*[50] The *Buddhamārgālaṅkāra-śāstra* has by its title a clear suggestion that it has a bearing on the *Daśabhūmika-śāstra.* While it is difficult to say what the *Akutobhaya-śāstra* stands for, it may be noted that the Tibetan Collection has a commentary on the *Kārikā* by the name *"Akutobhaya"* attributed to Nāgārjuna.[51] Nothing can be said about the *Mahākaruṇopāya-śāstra.* It is quite likely that some of these titles refer more to classes of texts than to individual texts.

The Chinese Collection gives several works as Nāgārjuna's.[52] Of these T. 1572, *Akṣara-śataka,* is a work of Āryadeva and not of Nāgārjuna.[53] T. 1576, *Mahāyānaviṁśikā,* is considered to be probably a work not of our Nāgārjuna but of a later person of the same name.[54] T. 1616, *Aṣṭādaśa-śūnyatā-śāstra,* is a treatise of the later school, the Vijñaptimātratā Siddhi, and is definitely not by Nāgārjuna, the Mādhyamika Philosopher.[55] T. 1662 is the *Bodhicaryāvatāra* of Sāntideva and is not a work of Nāgārjuna. T. 1632, *Upāyahṛdaya,* is also considered not to be a work of Nāgārjuna;[56] it has hardly any bearing on or reference to the principal theme of Nāgārjuna's works, viz., *śūnyatā* and the Middle Way *(madhyamā pratipat)*. Nāgārjuna's authorship of T. 1661, *Lakṣaṇa-vimukta-bodhi-hrdaya (citta)-śāstra,* and of T. 1676, *Mahāpraṇidhānotpāda-gāthā,* is doubtful. T. 1668, *Mahāyāna-vyākhyā-śāstra,* is a work on Yogācāra-vijñānavāda and is not of Nāgārjuna, the Mādhyamika philosopher.[57] T. 1671, 福蓋正行所集經, a compilation of Sūtras attributed to Nāgārjuna, does not seem to be the work of a Mādhyamika. It has no bearing on the *Śūnyatā* or the Middle Way. It seems to be a collection of *sūtra* passages on moral precepts. T. 1420, *Nāgārjuna-pañcavidyā-śāstra,* is a late Tāntric text and is not a work of Mādhyamika philosophy.

Some of the texts listed as Nāgārjuna's in the Chinese Collection have already been referred to above. These are: 1) *Madhyamaka Śāstra (Mādhyamika Kārikā)* with three commentaries: I) *Prajñāmūla* of Piṅgala, II) *Prajñāpradīpa* of Bhāvaviveka and III) *Mahāyāna-madhyamakadarśana-vyākhyā-śāstra* of Sthiramati;[58] even *Madhyamakānugama-śāstra* of Asaṅga was in all probability intended by him as a commentary on this text;[59] 2) *Vigraha-vyāvartanī* which includes the author's own vṛtti;[60] 3) *Mahā-Prajñāpāramitā-śāstra* (T. 1509) and 4) *Daśabhūmi-vibhāṣā-śāstra.*[61] 5) *Suhṛllekhā* and 6) *Ratnāvalī* which as we have seen are Nāgārjuna's letters to his friend, the Śātavāhana king, have their translations in Chinese.[62] In addition, we have in the Chinese Collection these works which are attributed to Nāgārjuna and the nature of which seems to be in keeping with the attribution: 1) *Pratītyasamutpāda-hṛdaya-śāstra,*[63] 2) *Dvādaśamukha-śāstra,*[64] 3) *Mahāyānabhavabheda-śāstra (Bhava-saṅkrānti-śāstra),*[65] 4) *Yuktiṣaṣṭikā,*[66] 5) *Ekaśloka-śāstra,*[67] 6) *Bodhisambhāra-śāstra*[68] and 7) *Dharmadhātu-stava.*[69]

Of these some are available in their Tibetan versions in the Tibetan Collection of the Buddhist Canon.[70] Some of these are, as in Chinese, different commentaries of the same text separately listed. Of the three commentaries available in Chinese on the *Kārikā,* Bhāvaviveka's *Prajnāpradīpa* (3853, 3854) is available in Tibetan with a *Tīkā* (3859) that is not available in Chinese. In addition, the Tibetan Collection has two important commentaries on the *Kārikā* which are not available in Chinese: I) Buddhapālita's *vṛtti* (3842)[71] and II) Candrakīrti's commentary

(3860). Of these two, the latter is the Tibetan version of the original Sanskrit *Prasannapadā*.[72] Of the works available in Chinese, we have the following in Tibetan also: *Vigrahavyāvartanī* (3828) with its *vṛtti* (3832); *Pratītyasamutpāda-hṛdaya-kārikā* (3836) and its commentary (3837). *Bhavasaṅkrānti* (3840) is available in Chinese but its *Ṭīkā* (3841) is not there; similarly *Yuktiṣaṣṭikā* (3825) is available in Chinese but its commentary by Candrakīrti (3864) is not found there. But neither *Vaidalya* of which *Sūtra* (3826) and *Prakaraṇa* (3830) are separately mentioned, nor *Śunyatāsaptati*[73] (3827) of which there is a *vṛtti* (3831) is to be found in Chinese. Three of the texts listed in the Tibetan Collection belong to separate authors: *Akṣaraśataka* (3834) is of Deva and 3835 is its commentary; *Abodhabodhaka* (3838) is of a Nāgārjunagarbha.

In Sanskrit as already noted we have two of the aforementioned texts extant in their original, viz., *Mādhyamika-kārikā* with Candrakīrti's commentary, *Prasannapadā*, and *Vigrahavyāvartanī* with Nāgārjuna's own *vṛtti*. Besides, we have in Sanskrit, *Ratnāvalī* edited by Prof. G. Tucci who has also edited two of Nāgārjuna's devotional verses (stava), *Niraupamya-stava* and *Paramārtha-stava* in their original Sanskrit varsion.[75] One of these, *Niraupamya-stava*, along with three others, *Lokātīta*, *Acintya* and *Stutyatīta*, have been retranslated into Sanskrit from Tibetan by Prabhubhai Patel.[76] Recently Sjt. Sunitikumar Pathak of Visvabharati University has retranslated from Tibetan into Sanskrit a text, *Āryadharmadhātu-garbha-vivaraṇa*,[77] which is attributed to Nāgārjuna. It purports to expound the links in the course of phenomenal existence, and has close and unmistakable affinity with the relevant portion of the *Śāstra*. It is probably a work of Nāgārjuna. Nāgārjuna is known to have compiled a collection of *Sūtras (Sūtra-samuccaya)*[78] which of course is not extant.

The works that can be attributed to Nāgārjuna may be reclassified into these broad categories:

I. Texts that constitute chiefly a critical examination of other schools, especially of the Sarvāstivāda doctrine of elements:

1) *Madhyamaka-śāstra (Mādhyamika-kārikā)*; 2) *Vigrahavyāvartanī*; 3) *Ekaśloka-śāstra* and 4) *Dvādaśamukha-śāstra*. 5) *Śūnyatā-saptati* also perhaps belongs to this class.

II. Texts chiefly expository:

1) *Pratītyasamutpāda-hṛdaya-śāstra* is an exposition of the twelve-linked chain of the course of phenomenal existence, which constitutes the subject matter of *Kārikā* XXVI; 2) *Yukti-ṣaṣṭikā* is a short compendium on the basic tenets of Mahāyāna; 3) *Bodhisattva-pātheya-śāstra* is a short exposition of the factors of the Great Way.

III. Commentaries or/and Records of Oral Instruction *(Upadeśa)*:

1) *Mahāprajñāpāramitā-śāstra* and 2) *Daśabhūmi-vibhāṣā-śāstra* are the two important works that belong to this class; 3) *Bhavasaṅkrānti-śāstra* and 4) *Ārya-dharmādhātu-garbha-vivaraṇa* also perhaps belong here; 5) perhaps *Vaidalya* which has a *Sūtra* and a *Prakaraṇa* also belongs here.

IV. Devotional verses:

1) *Niraupamya-stava*, 2) *Lokātīta-stava*, 3) *Acintya-stava*, 4) *Stutyatīta-stava* 5) *Paramārtha-stava*, and 6) *Dharmadhātu-stava*.

V. Letters:

1) *Suhṛllekhā* and 2) *Ratnāvalī*.

VI. To these there can perhaps be added the *Collection of Sūtras (Sūtra-samuccaya)* on the authority of Śāntideva's *Bodhicaryāvatara;* the work is however not extant.[79]

*Section II*

## THE BASIC CONCEPTIONS IN THE PHILOSOPHY OF NĀGĀRJUNA

*Nonexclusive understanding as the root of the skilfulness of non-clinging:* It appears that, when Nāgārjuna approached the main philosophical teaching of the Buddha, he was confronted with a multitude of contending schools of philosophy, each making an exclusive claim, seizing the fragmentary as complete, clinging to the relative as absolute. That this tendency was quite prevalent then among the Buddhist schools is evidenced by the emphasis put in the works of Nāgārjuna on non-contentiousness *(anupalambha,)* which he regarded as belonging to the very heart of the Buddha's teachings. There is also the explicit reference in the *Śāstra* to the prevailing attitude of contention among the Buddha's followers which vitiated the atmosphere and constituted an obstruction to clear understanding.[80] To Nāgārjuna it must have appeared strange and sad that the very words of the Master who taught the non-contentious way should have been made the object of contention *(upalambha)* and clinging *(grāha)*.[81] By this His followers were practically shutting themselves out from the richness inherent in His teachings, and were hardly taking seriously the fact that He taught one and the same truth differently to different people. To be aware of the possibility of different formulations of one and the same truth from different standpoints is to rise above the exclusive clinging to any one of these formulations as absolutely true. This is the non-exclusive understanding that lies at the root of the Buddha's skilfulness. That he had this skilfulness His disciples readily agreed; but its significance they seem hardly to have appraised. On the contrary they had set aside this basic truth which belonged to the very heart of the Way He showed.

*The tendency to seize is the root of conflict and suffering:* This situation seems to have provided for Nāgārjuna but one instance of the inveterate tendency of the human mind, the tendency to cling, to seize. This tendency, which functions under a false imagination and not on right understanding, is the root of suffering in life and of dead-ends *(anta)* and conflict in understanding.[82] By seizing the relatively distinct as absolutely separate one is never able to regain the dynamic, organic relatedness in which the richness of life consists.[83] Again, setting out to provide an intelligible account of the meaningfulness of life he who involves himself in dead-ends really ends in self-contradictions.

The tendency to seize the relative as absolute is at root the thirst for the real in man but it is misapplied.[84] This misapplied drive toward the real has been called in the present work, the error of misplaced absoluteness. This is a false imagination that engenders the attitude of clinging and confines one to the level of fragmentariness. While the thirst for the real is indeed the root of all the activities of man, it is under ignorance, not knowing the true nature of things that one seizes hold of everything one comes across, clings to it as a safe refuge, as ultimately and fully satisfying the thirst for the unconditioned, only to meet with disappointment and frustration.

In right understanding *(dharmāṇām bhūtapratyavekṣā)* not only there is revealed the determinate as determinate but there is revealed also in it the indeterminate or the unconditioned as distinct from the determinate.[85] But if one were to seize in turn the distinction of the determinate and the indeterminate as an absolute separateness, that again would be to commit once more the error of clinging. The determinate is not a self-being; it is not only essentially related to all the other things in the world which are also specific determinate entities, but as a determinate entity it has its being only in dependence on the indeterminate. *Pratītyasamutpāda,* conditioned or dependent origination, which means the essential relativity of things, has its bearing on the determinate entity not only in regard to its arising from the complex of causal factors, but also in regard to its essentially dependent nature, viz., its dependence on the independent, ultimate, reality.[86] It is a basic conception in the philosophy of Nāgārjuna that while the indeterminate reality is the ground of the determinate entities, it is only the ultimate nature of the latter themselves and not another entity apart from them.[87]

*The ultimate nature of man is the undivided being:* In regard to the nature and destiny of the human individual, this has the profound significance that man as a specific, determinate individual is not absolutely confined to his determinate nature. As an individual, man is essentially related to the rest of the world. He is also not apart from the indeterminate reality which is the ultimate ground of his very being. And in his ultimate nature man is himself the indeterminate, unconditioned reality, the undivided being. The ultimate meaning of the sense of lack, the sense of devoidness *(śūnyatā)*, which is the thirst for the real, Nāgārjuna would say, lies in the realization of this real nature of oneself. The imagination that one is bound forever to one's fragmentariness alienates the conditioned from the unconditioned, reducing the relative distinction to absolute separateness. The thirst for the real in man is not bound to end in despair. What brings about despair is one's own imagination that one's limitedness is one's ultimate nature. A rise in one's awareness from the level of finiteness to the realization of one's ultimate nature is possible, Nāgārjuna would say, and in this rise consists the fulfillment of the thirst in man.

The way to this realization is prepared by one's awakening to the absurdities and self-contradictions involved in one's false imagination. Nāgārjuna's criticism of the categories, the basic factors of life and understanding, is intended to lay bare these absurdities, thereby to reveal the conditionedness *(śūnyatā)* of the conditioned as well as the further truth that the conditionedness of the conditioned is not unconditioned *(śūnyatā-śūnyatā)*.

*Prajñā as the principle of comprehension is the Middle Way:* The understanding that is the consummating phase of criticism is appreciative of the unique nature and value of every specific standpoint, and yet is not confined to any one point of view. This is a comprehensive understanding inclusive of the several standpoints on the same level as well as of the different levels of understanding.[88] Levels and perspectives need to be distinguished and this distinction needs to be appreciated as a relative distinction and not an absolute division. This comprehensive understanding is sought to be conveyed in the philosophy of the Middle Way by *prajñā.* As the principle of comprehension it is the Middle Way, the way that rises above exclusiveness. In it there is no rejection of anything except the imagination of absoluteness in regard to what is only relative. As Nāgārjuna says in the *Kārikā,* "Everything holds good in the case of one who is in agreement with *śūnyatā*."[89]

In this philosophy of the Middle Way, determinate entities as well as specific concepts and conceptual formulations are not only accepted but taken as essential to give expression to the real in man. These are essential also for the complete realization of the ultimate reality. "The ultimate truth cannot be taught," says Nāgārjuna, "except in the context of the mundane truth, and unless the ultimate truth is comprehended, Nirvāṇa cannot be realized."[90] But clinging to the specific concepts and conceptual systems as absolute is rejected. A view, a specific conceptual formulation is, at root a unique way in which one seeks to give expression to the sense of the unconditioned, on the plane of the determinate, by way of the ever-increasing, ever-enhancing, understanding of and the establishing of a unity with the rest of the world. This is the growth which one achieves in respect to one's being in the world. This everyone does in his own way, from his own specific standpoint which embodies its own perspective.[91] The rejection of views which is an essential point in the philosophy of the Middle Way means that no specific view, being specific, is limitless, and no view, being a view, is ultimate.[92] The ultimate truth is not any "view."[93] "Silence is the ultimate truth for the wise."[94] And yet, the ultimate truth can be and needs to be expressed from the mundane standpoint.[95] This is the standpoint of man as a self-conscious individual striving through thought and action to give expression to the deepest sense in him, viz., the sense of the real.

*To elucidate the sense of the real is the mission of the Mādhyamika:* The sense of the real, with its import that the conditioned is distinct from the unconditioned and further that the real, ultimate nature of the conditioned is itself the unconditioned reality is the minimum presupposition of all endeavour of man and its elucidation is the primary function of philosophy. All the specific formulations of conceptual systems are secondary to and are based on it. Even the attitude of refraining from constructing any system is ultimately based on this basic truth. However one may put it, this is the truth of the ultimacy of the unconditioned. This is the basic import of self-consciousness, the fundamental insight, the timeless truth, the eternal light in the heart of man.[96] It is there only to be "discovered," to be realized. This is not a presupposition put forth for later corroboration, but the insight that is the ultimate foundation of every "proposition" proposed of things. No one has any exclusive claim to this truth, but everyone, if he chooses, can discover it in himself as the bedrock, the foundation of his very being.

It is this ultimate truth that the Mādhyamika, the traveller on the Middle Way, has sought to lay bare. His claim that he has no position of his own[97] means that this basic truth, which he lays bare is not anything exclusively his own but is in the possession of every self-conscious individual. One can see it if one develops an eye to see it and it is his mission to enkindle this insight. His rejection of views does not mean that he is opposed to building systems; he would himself formulate specific systems, not to cling to them, but to use them as a help to those who are in need of them. That he does not have any position of his own means that he does not seize any specific formulation exclusively. This sense of non-exclusiveness enables him to keep himself *en rapport* with every system and to see the truth in every position. Non-exclusiveness *(śūnyatā)*, the Mādhyamika would say, is of the very nature of wisdom *(prajñā)*. Rejecting the error of misplaced absoluteness, he reveals the conditioned as conditioned and the unconditioned as unconditioned. In this he is doing just what the sun does; the sun does not make the high low or the low high, but just reveals the nature of things as they are, the low as low and the high as high.[98]

*The place of the Kārikā and the Śāstra in the total system:* In the *Kārikā* itself one finds practically all the principal conceptions in the philosophy of Nāgārjuna. But there these are obscured by its overwhelmingly negative character. The fact that there he is advancing arguments *reductio ad absurdum* needs to be kept in mind while one reads that text. The negative conclusions belong not to him but to those whose positions are under examination. The absoluteness of specific views and of particular entities is assumed for the sake of argument and the conclusions that naturally follow from such a position are exposed, which, on account of the absurdity of the initial assumption, are bound to be absurd. Thus the imagined absoluteness *(sasvabhāvatva)* of what is only relative is rejected and at the same time relativity *(naiḥsvābhāvya)* is revealed as its true nature. Relativity or non-ultimacy of views and conditionedness or non-substantiality of entities—this is the truth that is borne out by *śūnyatā* in reference to the mundane nature of things. In the *Kārikā, pratītyasamutpāda* (conditioned origination), *śūnyatā, upādāya-prajñapti* (derived name) and *madhyamā-pratipat* (the Middle Way) are expressly declared as synonyms.[99] Here one finds further that the relativity of the relative is not its ultimate nature; to cling to *śūnyatā* or relativity as itself absolute is the most serious of errors.[100]

Further, the *Kārikā* declares that the distinction of mundane and ultimate truth is basic to understanding the profound meaning in the teachings of the Buddha.[101] "That which is of the nature of coming and going, arising and perishing, in its conditioned (mundane) nature is itself Nirvāṇa in its unconditioned (ultimate) nature."[102] This means that the unconditioned reality is the ground of the conditioned, contingent entities; that is the reality and these constitute the "appearance." Throughout the *Kārikā,* there is implied the sense of the unconditioned, the thirst for the real in man; it is the misapplication of this sense of the real that results in the error of false realism *(sasvabhāva-vāda)*.

Thus we find all the essential elements constituting the basic framework of the philosophy of Nāgārjuna are actually provided in the *Kārikā*. This work, as we have seen, is known to have been written in order to expound the basic teachings of the *Prajñāpāramitā-sūtras*. But actually its chief purpose was not so much to give an exposition of their philosophy as to prepare the ground for such an exposition, viz., by clearing away misconceptions, especially the basic error of clinging to the elements of analysis, to which the Sarvāstivādins were subject. It is ignorance, says the *Kārikā,* to mistake the relative for the absolute, to hold fast to separateness of elements as ultimate and to cling to an unconditional denial of self.[103] It is significant that the *Kārikā* devotes a whole chapter (ch. XXIV) for explaining that *śūnyatā* is not nihilism but relativity and conditionedness, that it is not a rejection of the world of becoming and the meaningfulness of life but the very way mundane existence is appreciated as a course of conditioned becoming as well as the way the values of life become possible of realization. "For him who is in agreement with *śūnyatā* everything stands in harmony and for him who is not in agreement with *śūnyatā* nothing stands in harmony."[104] Under the circumstances it seems that there is not only nothing incongruous in the author of the *Kārikā* accepting things in their mundane truth but it becomes incumbent on him to do so. And it seems that Nāgārjuna set for himself a challenge to show how not only the unique nature of everything can go well with the ultimate truth of the undivided being, but, that the mundane existence itself becomes possible, conceivable, only on the ground of the unconditioned reality. Nāgārjuna meets this challenge by pointing, on the one hand, to the different levels of comprehension and, on the other, to the absurdity into which one would drive oneself by mistaking the relative for the absolute.

What we do miss in the *Kārikā* is an emphasis on and a detailed account of *prajñā* as the principle of comprehending the different levels of understanding. We do not have there an analysis of error and its ways in regard to the mundane and the ultimate truths. There is no specific attention drawn in the *Kārikā* to the thirst for the real in man nor any emphasis on the real as the ground or as the immanent reality of the determinate. We also miss in it an account of the course of wayfaring in the various aspects of the Way, with the skilfulness of non-clinging. It is precisely these that are brought to light in the *Śāstra*, the first thirty-four chapters of which practically set forth all the essential elements in the philosophy of the Middle Way with extraordinary vividness. Chapter VI of the *Śāstra* has a detailed analysis of illusion (ignorance);[104a] ch. XVIII has an account of *prajñā* as the all-comprehensive understanding[105] and as the very ultimate nature of all things;[106] ch. XXXI has an account of all the eighteen kinds of *śūnyatā;*[107] ch. XXXII has a brilliant and vivid account of the real as the ground of the world of the determinate as well as an account of the thirst for the real in man;[108] ch. XXXII gives also a very illuminating statement about the nature and purpose of the negative criticism, in connection with the criticism of causes and conditions, when it says that what is denied here is not the causes and conditions but the prevailing perversions about them;[109] these are the perversions of clinging to alternatives as extremes and arriving at distorted accounts about the mundane truth. It is significant that the *Śāstra* dwells at length (ch. XXXVI) on an exposition of the categories of the elements of analysis, preliminary to the criticism that lays bare their *śūnyatā.*[110] Logically analysis is prior to criticism; and *śūnyatā* is not the rejection of elements but the revelation of their conditionedness. Chapters XIX–XXIX again, significantly enough, set forth the factors of the Way according to *Abhidharma (Sarvāstivāda)* as well as according to *Mahāyāna,* and practically at the end of every topic in this connection, it shows how the elements of *Abhidharma* are to be assimilated into the Great Way. First there is the analysis and then there comes *śūnyatā* which is a revelation of their relativity and non-ultimacy, leading finally to comprehension.[111] The Great Way is the all-inclusive way. The *Śāstra* shares with the *Kārikā* and expresses in even stronger terms the emphasis on the need to overcome the error of clinging to which the analysts are victims. Chapters XXXIX–XL contain an account of the "Five Eyes,"[112] which are really the different levels of comprehension ranging from the eyes of the flesh to the eye of the Buddha, from the perversions of the common man to the Buddha's *sarvākārajñatā,* knowledge of all forms. Here again, it is not that with the rise of the eye of the Buddha the other eyes cease to function. They continue to function, now in a new light, with the width of understanding and the depth of insight that belong to the wise. This is significant as it has a direct bearing on the place of understanding with all its categories in the total comprehension of the wise. The chapters on *tathatā* (LXXII) and *bhūtakoṭi* (XC) are also worth special mention as the former makes clear the immanence of the real in every being[113] and the latter gives a brilliant account of *upāya,* the skilfulness of non-clinging.[114] In fact, the last twenty-five chapters of the *Śāstra* are repeated accounts of this skilfulness by virtue of which the wise teach through names and characters *(nāma* and *lakṣaṇa),* concepts and conventional entities, the ultimate truth that lies beyond these.[115] This is expressed in sum in the *Kārikā* when it says that except in the context of *vyavahāra* the ultimate truth cannot be taught.[116]

The *Śāstra* is not a systematic treatise with a logical sequence. It is a commentary. In it topics are discussed as and when they are occasioned either by the occurrence of the connected text in the *Sūtra* or by the inquiry of the listeners. The first thirty-four chapters constitute the commentary of only one of the eighty-nine sections *(prakaraṇas)* of the *Sūtra.*[117] The commentary, however, does not extend everywhere at the same length. In the later chapters the *Sūtra* is very often longer than the corresponding *Śāstra* portion. Further, there is much repetition of argument, sometimes almost verbatim, notwithstanding the occasional references to the previous chapters.[118] But the consistency of ideas, the integrity of thought is beyond doubt. Its intimate connection with the *Kārikā,* almost the whole of which is reproduced in fragments here and there throughout the text shows that it is not only of one piece with it but includes and exceeds it. In the light of the *Śāstra,* the *Kārikā* takes its proper place and bears out its function in the total system of the philosophy of *prajñāpāramitā,* as preparatory to and as a most essential stage in the wayfaring of the *bodhisattva,* the traveller on the Great Way. The realization of the non-ultimacy of specific views and the non-substantiality of specific entities is the essential first step in the wayfarer's realization of the ultimate truth as well as in his work in the world.

*Section III*

## NĀGĀRJUNA AND THE BUDDHA

*The two yānas (vehicles, ways):* The question of the relation of the philosophy of Nāgārjuna to the teachings of the Buddha had all its weight for those who doubted the authenticity of the *Sūtras* of the Great Way and chose to limit themselves for authority to their own "baskets." The fact that the *Śāstra* points out that even their "baskets" do contain the main philosophical teachings of the Great Way, although the followers of the Small Way had not the ability to see it,[119] shows that the authenticity of the teachings of Mahāyāna was questioned in its time.[120]

Traditionally the main philosophical distinction between the two chief lines of Buddhist philosophy lay in their view of the basic elements *(dharmāḥ)* of existence. To view these elements as substantial and possessed of self-being *(svabhāva)* amounted to accepting a pluralistic view based on the ultimacy of separateness. This view was held notably by the Sarvāstivādins and was rejected by those who tended to the absolutist line. The latter emphasized the ultimacy of the unconditioned reality and stood for non-exclusiveness in understanding.[121] It was their business to show that the baskets of the former also contained the crucial teaching of the non-substantiality of the basic elements of existence,[122] including as its necessary import, the deeper truth that the conditioned is itself in its ultimate nature the unconditioned reality, that the world is itself Nirvāṇa, when rightly seen.

It is necessary to remember that the text that is the subject of our present study belongs to and breathes the atmosphere of a time when the division of the community *(saṅgha)* was an accepted fact and the two lines were in a state of constant controversy in which those who trod the Great Way took it as their responsibility to show that what they taught was not only not foreign to but actually the essential, deeper, meaning of the teachings of the Buddha, even as contained in the "baskets" of the Small Way. The *Śāstra* frequently says, "The big contains the small, although the small cannot contain the big."[123]

Without entering into the question of the crucial difference between the two chief lines of Buddhist philosophy, we may briefly review here the few conceptions that were held basic to the teachings of the Buddha by all His followers. We may thereby see how even these lead to what constitutes the main teaching in the philosophy of Nāgārjuna.

*Conditioned Origination and the Middle Way:* The two most important conceptions for our consideration are "conditioned origination" and "the Middle Way." These two are treated as synonyms even in the Pali Canon.[124] With Nāgārjuna it is an essential point that they be seen as only different expressions of one and the same principle, the principle of relativity or conditionedness.[125] One can say that while "conditioned origination" emphasizes the import of relativity in regard to the entities or events that constitute the course of mundane existence, the Middle Way emphasizes the import of relativity in regard to views concerning the mundane nature of things. We may inquire into these conceptions as preserved in the Pali *Nikāyas* appraising what we find in the light of what has been set forth above as the main teaching in the philosophy of Nāgārjuna.

*The Four Noble Truths:* The eradication of suffering by tracing it to its roots constitutes the essence of the Four Noble Truths taught by the Buddha. They form the subject matter of His first preaching, the turning of the "Wheel of *Dharma*."[126] They constitute the foundation of

Buddhism. The first preaching makes it clear that the cause of suffering is craving, which is rooted in ignorance. The constituents of personality are painful precisely because of clinging, seizing, which is due to craving. If one destroys the root of suffering, suffering itself will be extinguished. This is the truth of "conditioned origination": "This being, that becomes, and with the extinction of this, that ceases to be."[127] As the teaching of the Buddha is mainly concerned with the origin and extinction of suffering, this truth of conditioned origination constitutes the very heart of the *dharma*. Conditioned origination is identified with the *dhamma* (*dharma*). "He who sees the *dhamma* sees the conditioned origination and he who sees the conditioned origination sees the *dhamma*."[128]

*The Middle Way:* The first preaching of the Buddha brings out also the truth of the Middle Way. Right views which are the first element in the Eightfold Noble Way consist in keeping free from extremes. These extremes, it must be borne in mind, are to be understood as applying not only to morals but also to correct understanding. In the case of morals the extremes are sensualism and asceticism.[129] In the case of correct understanding, the Middle Way is the way that is free from the extremes of "is" and "is not." While becoming, conditioned origination, is analysable as "is" and "is not," to cling to any one of these aspects exclusively is to turn them into extremes and extremes are falsifications; they then become the dead-ends of eternalism and annihilationism.[130] Actually nothing in the world exists absolutely and nothing perishes totally. By drawing the fact of arising to the attention of those who cling exclusively to non-being and the fact of ceasing to the attention of those who cling exclusively to being, the Buddha reveals that things here are neither absolutely being nor absolutely non-being, but are arising and perishing, forming a continuity of becoming.[131]

*The Buddha's silence as the revealer of truth:* In regard to the human individual, the errors of eternalism and annihilationism appear as extremes in conceiving one's mundane nature. When Vacchagotta asked the Buddha whether there is the self, the Buddha kept silent. When

Vacchagotta asked the Buddha whether there is not the self, the Buddha again kept silent. After Vacchagotta went away without an answer, Ānanda asked the Buddha why He had not answered the question. The Buddha replied that if He had answered that there is the self, He would have been subscribing to the view of eternalism; if He had answered that there is not the self, He would have been subscribing to the view of annihilationism.[132] That the question was asked by Vacchagotta with a clinging mind, with the deep-rooted tendency to seize "is" or "is not" exclusively, is clear.

What are old-age and death and what is it that has old-age and death? In regard to a question like this that tends to swing between the extremes of identity and difference of the self and the *skandhas,* the Buddha's answer would be that the question is not rightly put.[133] The views that sensation is myself, that sensation is not myself, that myself possesses sensation,[134] and the views that the body is the self, the self has the body, the body is in the self and the self is in the body,[135] all these are only different forms of exclusive views, formulated in terms of absolute identity and absolute difference which are themselves further reducible to the forms of eternalism and negativism. Again, if the Buddha would not answer such questions as, "Is suffering wrought by oneself or by another? Is suffering wrought both by oneself and by another? Or is suffering wrought neither by oneself nor by another?", it was because an aye or a nay to any of these would lead one either to eternalism or to annihilationism.[136] Not accepting these extremes the Buddha taught the truth *(dharma)* by the Middle Way, viz., "conditioned origination," as the right view in regard to the mundane nature of the individual.

Even the "fourteen unanswered questions," which the Buddha set aside and did not answer, are all formulated on the pattern of the errors of eternalism and annihilationism. They are all questions about the mundane nature of things.[137] These are set forth briefly in the *Udāna* where the Buddha gives an account of them as kinds of partial views, to which the ignorant cling as the whole and only view, and thereby give rise to quarrels. Then He proceeds to narrate the story of the six blind men that quarrelled as to what kind of a thing an elephant was, one saying that it was like a pot and the other like a winnowing fan, and so on. The Buddha proceeds to say that in a similar way the teachers belonging to the other sects do not know what is the goal and what is not the goal, do not know what is the way and what is not the way and so they "wrangle, quarrel and dispute." They have only a partial view of things, they do not have a comprehensive understanding.[138]

The views presented in these questions are about the world and the individual; and every one of these is based on a partial observation of things and consists in seizing a certain aspect and claiming completeness for it, even as he that touched the head of the elephant maintained that the elephant was like a pot, and he that touched only the ear maintained that the elephant was like a winnowing fan. Any answer to any of them would only lead the questioner to further clinging. And the Buddha's dismissal of them is understandable as due to the falsity of their initial assumption of exclusive division and the tendency of the questioners to cling to one of the alternatives as itself ultimate. The question whether the world is eternal or not eternal (evanescent), for example, is unanswerable because the assumption of the dichotomy is false. It assumes that a thing is either absolutely existent or absolutely non-existent and both these are false in regard to things that exist but conditionally. Is the self the same as the body or different from it? No answer can be given because the question assumes that the self is either absolutely identical with or absolutely different from the body. The relation that the self as a self-conscious dynamic organism bears to the constituents of personality is not describable in these absolute terms. Does the self exist after death or does it not exist? The question is not answerable in this form, for the assumption is that the self is either eternal or evanescent. To abandon these views is to give up the claim of completeness in regard to what is only fragmentary. Everyone of these views owes its being to lack of "direct, unimpeded comprehension" of the true nature of things, viz., the truth of the "conditioned origination," which is revealed by their rejection. The Middle Way is to see things as they are, to recognize the possibility of determining things differently from different standpoints and to recognize that these determinations cannot be seized as absolute. This is the way that realizes the relativity of specific views and of determinate entities. This becomes practically the central point in the philosophy of Nāgārjuna.

*The mundane and the ultimate nature:* With regard to the life of the human individual, "conditioned origination" bears the import that whatever is one's state of life is what one has worked out for oneself as one's self-expression. Impelled by thirst and conditioned by one's understanding, one does deeds which bear their results.[139] Shrouded by ignorance and impelled by desire one does deeds that bind one to the life of conflict and suffering. The way out of these is to eradicate their roots, viz., ignorance and passion. Free from ignorance and passion one may yet do deeds and not be subjected to suffering. Extinction of the root of suffering is the meaning of Nirvāṇa; it is also the eternal joy that one realizes with the extinction of passion. Nirvāṇa is the ultimate goal towards which all beings move seeking fulfilment. The Buddha drew the attention of the monks to the log of wood being carried along the stream of the River Gaṅgā and told them that if they, like the log, do not ground on this bank or on the other bank and also do not sink down in midstream, then they will "float down to Nirvāṇa, glide down to Nirvāṇa, gravitate towards Nirvāṇa" because "right view floats, glides, gravitates towards Nirvāṇa."[140]

The *Nikāyas* make out that becoming, the course of birth and death, itself is not anything unconditioned; there is the need to recognize that there is the unmade, the not becoming, which is the ultimate truth, the Nirvāṇa.[141] The Buddha declares that those who say that from becoming there is release are unreleased from becoming.[142] But if this should mean a literal abandoning of becoming, an absolute separation of the becoming from the not becoming, that again would be another extreme. The Buddha declares that even those who say that by the abandoning of becoming there is release from becoming are not free from it.[143] But if this should be taken to mean that the impermanent is as such permanent, even that would be to miss the distinction between the ultimate truth and the mundane truth; that would be to confuse the one with the other, which is clearly an illusion.[144] There is becoming and there is the release from becoming, there is *samsāra* (the course of mundane existence, conditioned becoming) and there is Nirvāṇa (the unconditioned reality); but *samsāra* is not as such Nirvāṇa and Nirvāṇa is not another entity apart from *samsāra.* And the being of *samsāra* is not of the same kind as Nirvāṇa. It is not difficult to see that we have here the basic truth about the course of mundane existence which the Mādhyamika expresses when he says that that which is contingent in its conditioned nature is itself Nirvāṇa in its unconditioned nature.[145]

The true being of the Tathāgata, say the *Nikāyas,* which, as Nāgārjuna would say, is also the true being of all, is not conceivable in any specific way.[146] The modes of conceiving simply do not hold there; they are irrelevant there. In the case of the Tathāgata whose "outflows" have become completely, residuelessly, extinct, the imaginations that he arises, that he does not arise, that he both arises and does not arise and that he neither arises nor does not arise, do not hold. When the fire that is burning in front becomes extinct, it cannot be said that it went to the east or to the west or north or south, for this way of speaking does not hold here. Just in the same way, all the determinate forms by which the ultimate nature of the Tathāgata could be predicated have all become extinct. In this ultimate nature, the Tathāgata is "deep, immeasurable, unfathomable, like the mighty ocean."[147] The ultimately real nature of the Tathāgata is indeterminable; it is the same as Nirvāṇa, and this the Tathāgata has realized.

It is necessary to note here an important distinction that has emerged from the above consideration, viz., the distinction between mundane and ultimate truth. The indeterminability of the ultimate nature is not of the same kind as the indeterminability of the mundane nature. The latter is the indescribability of things as absolutely existent or absolutely non-existent, etc. These are extremes as descriptions of the mundane nature of things and are as such falsifications. Their rejection reveals the conditioned, changing, nature of things. But the indeterminability of the ultimate nature is of a different kind. There the question of extremes does not arise; for it is not a case of seizing some one aspect and claiming absoluteness for it. There the rejection of the *koṭis* does not amount to a revelation of the Middle Way nor of "conditioned origination." The Tathāgata, in his ultimate nature, is not the conditionally born. With regard to this nature it cannot be said that he exists but conditionally. The indeterminability of the ultimate nature is really the inapplicability of the ways of concepts. This distinction of the mundane and the ultimate truth is basic to the philosophy of Nāgārjuna.[147a]

*Nāgārjuna and the Buddha:* Thus the conceptions of "conditioned origination" and the Middle Way, which were accepted by all the Buddhist schools as basic to the teachings of the Buddha and which must have found their place in all the "collections" of His teachings, were apparently worked out by Nāgārjuna along the lines suggested above. For him they yield the truth of the non-clinging way, the Middle Way; they bear the significance of the conditionedness of determinate entities and the relativity of specific concepts and conceptual systems; they bear again the all-important truth that the conditioned is not ultimate in its conditioned nature or that the conditionedness of the conditioned is not its ultimate nature, but that in its ultimate nature the conditioned is itself the unconditioned reality. And he finds in them what he considers as their most basic conception, viz., the distinction of the mundane and the ultimate. Thus he says in the *Kārikā:* "The teachings of the Buddha are based on two truths, the mundane and the ultimate. Those who do not know the distinction between these two truths do not understand the profound meaning in the teachings of the Buddha."[148] It is essential to bear this in mind as we go along with our present study.

*Section IV*

## NĀGĀRJUNA AND THE BUDDHIST SCHOOLS

*The basic ideas common to the Buddhist schools:* The transition from the Buddha to the Buddhist schools is a passing from the original insight of the Master to the subsequent elaborations by the disciples. It is important to remember that all the schools claim to base their systems on the actual teachings of the Buddha as they were handed down by their respective traditions and that every school claims to be completely within the scope of the Way He showed, following His words in letter and spirit. All the teachings of the Buddha are true,[149] says The *Śāstra*, whereby it means that there is no question of denying the claim of authenticity to the different traditions which preserved, and in their own ways developed, the original teachings of the Buddha with different emphases, and from different standpoints. The *Śastra* gives the striking example of the ring finger *(anāmikā)*, of which it can be truly said that it is short as well as long, but from different standpoints.[150] The basic thing is to rise above any exclusive claim, the claim which is dogmatic. In other words, Nāgārjuna's approach in this regard was one of finding, on the one hand, what constitutes the heart of the teachings of the Buddha and, on the other hand, appreciating the relative merits of the different currents of philosophical thinking within the Buddhist fold as the different expressions of the basic truth which all of them shared together.[151]

There was a nucleus, a common ground of ideas, which all the followers of the Buddha shared together.[152] All the Buddhist schools accept the teaching of the Four Noble Truths and as the very heart of the Way the Buddha showed, also the doctrines of "conditioned origination," and the Middle Way. Consequently all schools accept conditioned becoming as the true nature of composite things. All hold that among the basic constituents of personality there is no I-substance impervious to change. Craving is the root of human suffering and ignorance is the root of craving. Nirvāṇa is the extinction of the root of suffering and it is at the same time the eternal state in which there is no possibility of conditionedness or non-substantiality. Extinction of suffering is through extinction of its root and the way to it consists in the cultivation of the Eightfold Noble Path through personal effort. Again, all schools recognize the denial of views, and as in the case of the Buddha so in the case of His followers, the denial of views means the denial of such views as are based on extremes, especially the extremes of eternalism and negativism, both of which are traced back to the false sense of self. The denial of views means practically the denial of the false sense of self.[153]

However, one has to remember that the teachings of the Buddha allowed for different levels and standpoints, and thus, for different interpretations leading to different kinds of synthesis, in terms of the very conceptions that were accepted as basic to the *Dharma.* And the seeds of difference in understanding and interpreting the teachings of the Buddha must have been there from the very beginning. Immediately after His passing away a Council was called in order to come to an agreement concerning the principal points of the creed and discipline. The second Council that met a hundred years later saw the doctrinal differences expressed, but it is not difficult to see that the account that we have there is only their advanced phase.[154] The five points of Mahādeva[155] amount to emphasizing the need for putting an end to the deeper roots of ignorance and passion by a deeper penetration into the *Dharma* and the need for the realization of the ultimate truth in one's own person rather than accepting it from others. His five points could be appreciated as directed especially against those who appeared to have been clinging to the letter rather than penetrate into the spirit of the teachings of the Buddha. "Even a single word can serve to awaken one to the truth of things." What is essential is the maturity of mind. This points the way to appreciate how dissension, particularly in doctrinal matters, must have come up among the Buddha's followers when they came to deliberate upon His teachings. The tradition has it that within the second quarter of the second century after the passing away of the Buddha there was a division within the *saṅgha;* the differences by then must have become too pronounced for his disciples to hold together any more.

*The three broad lines:* It is a span of roughly five hundred years between the passing away of the Buddha and the rise of Nāgārjuna as a Buddhist philosopher. That this period was one of intense philosophical activity is evidenced not only by the emergence of several philosophically important branches from within the two main stems of the *saṅgha,*[156] but also by the amount of rich, penetrating, and profound literature that appeared at the end of this period.[157] The division of Hīnayāna and Mahāyāna is later than the breakup of the *saṅgha* into the Sthaviras and the Mahāsāṅghikas, later than even the further division of these main stems into the several different schools, the "Early Schools."

Among these early schools there were those which laid emphasis on analysis, held to a plurality of ultimate elements, and tended to a kind of mechanistic conception of personality; these were chiefly the Sarvāstivādins. And there were the Mahāsāṅghikas who tended on the whole to emphasize the distinction between the conditioned and the unconditioned. They seem to have held from the very beginning the non-ultimacy of the basic elements of existence and recognized the unconditioned as the ground of the conditioned, thus being in possession of all that is needed for a philosophical absolutism. This is true in general of all the schools of the Mahāsāṅghikas, and all these had already emerged even before the other stem, that of the Sthaviras, began to put forth branches. And between these two main lines of Buddhist philosophy during this period, one may notice a kind of logically unstable line, a line that tended to move away from the realistic, pluralistic and mechanistic conception of the Sarvāstivādins and did not quite reach the other, the absolutistic line.[158] These were the schools that chose to secede from the Sthaviras, dissent from the Sarvāstivādins and emphasize the concrete, integral, organic nature of life and personality. These were the Vātsīputrīyas,[159] the Sāmmitīyas,[160] and the Sautrāntikas.[161] To these one might add the Dārṣṭāntikas,[162] who were, according to one tradition, the forerunners of the Sautrāntikas and who figure very prominently in the *Vibhāṣā* as one of the formidable schools with whom the Sarvāstivādins had to contend, being in this respect second only to the Vibhajyavādins. These schools that fall in between the pluralistic and the absolutistic lines took becoming seriously and tried to reject the tendency to cling to the abstract as ultimate, which was the dominant tendency of the analysts (the Sarvāstivādins). Among these one finds the emphasis on the sense of unity and freedom as basic to self-hood. These tended to hold the non-ultimacy of difference between individuality and its constituents.

Not all schools were equally prominent in regard to doctrinal contributions and not all of them were secessions on the ground of doctrinal differences. But such schools as did have their own developments came to have them only after long philosophical thinking. Logically analysis comes prior to criticism, but this need not mean that historically it was so; both tendencies were presumably there from the very beginning. The tendency towards criticism holding the non-substantiality of the basic elements of existence *(dharma-śūnyatā)* was there perhaps even before the actual emergence of the school that emphasized difference as absolute. But, for the most part, all these tendencies worked more or less simultaneously and were developing together in different centres. Each of these had its own emphasis and all developments were founded on the words of the Buddha. Their methods were different, but they worked together by mutual criticism.

A. *The pluralistic line:* (I) *The basic doctrine of Sarvāstivāda:* The Sarvāstivādins derive their name from their doctrine of the unvarying, and therefore ultimate, nature of the fundamental elements, entities or essences *(dharmāḥ)*. This is an extreme form of the emphasis on the analysis and definition of elements. For the Sarvāstivādins "everything exists *(sarvam asti)*" means: I) all elements are real for they hold firmly their own essences which they never give up—each element has its own essence or is itself in its very nature that essence; II) again, all elements, all fundamental essences, always exist.[163] Of the essences themselves there is no arising or perishing; the arising and perishing are of their functions. Whether the elements rise to function or not, they are there all the same; they are real.[164] This doctrine of the timeless and underived character of the specific essences is unique to the Sarvāstivādins. For them *abhidharma* means a thorough analysis of the fundamental elements, in order to understand them clearly, so that there is no further illusion about them. The *dharmas,* the elements or essences, exist, and they exist by their own right. They are in this sense *"ātman,"* self-being. The *Vibhāṣā* admits *dharmātmā* while it denies *pudgalātmā;*[165] the latter refers to the individual, which is a name for the specific complex of the functions of these fundamental elements and it is this that is seized as "I" and "mine." In truth the self that is the object of the notion of "I" is a complex of the functions of elements that appear and disappear, but the ignorant hold to the self as a simple, substantial entity. This is an error. But the realization that the fundamental elements are self-existent and unchanging, not essentially dependent or relative, is not a perversion; it is the wisdom that is essential for the removal of bondage and the realization of freedom.

Although all the fundamental elements are alike self-existent and devoid of change, the Sarvāstivādins say that they are still distinguished into composite and incomposite. Such elements as have the possibility of becoming associated with the elements of birth and death, rise to function by this association, and have the possibility of giving rise to functions that constitute the members of a composite body, are called the composite elements; the incomposite elements have not this nature.[166] *Nirodha,* which is an incomposite element, is the same as Nirvāṇa; it is a positive element with its own nature. With the arising or appearing of this element in the series of elements that constitutes the course of an individual life, there ceases to be any further accumulation of deeds that bring about the continuation of that stream. This is the extinction of the course of birth and death. This element of *Nirodha* or extinction is of the nature of freedom; it is the highest good, it is the permanent.[167]

(II) *Time and change:* The Sarvāstivādins lay great emphasis on minute analysis of the causal factors that bring about every event in the course of mundane existence. While this is not the place to go into the details about the Sarvāstivāda analysis of causes and conditions, the essential thing to bear in mind here is that the work turned out by the causal functioning of the elements is the "thing" constituted of the functions that they give rise to by way of mutual association; the thing is therefore conditionally originated and destroyed, but the basic elements themselves rest in their own nature unaffected by temporality.[168] While the basic elements are non-temporal, their function is temporal; temporality consists in functioning.[169] The unit of time is the unit of function. A unit-function is the minimum conceivable period for the cycle of rising to function, carrying out the function and ceasing to function.[170] This minimum conceivable division of function or process is called a moment; it is the limit of compositeness. The functions are essentially conditioned by nature and it is these that constitute mundane things, including the individual self. This is the Sarvāstivādin's interpretation of "conditioned origination." As each unit of function is distinct from the others, it has a separate essence of its own and so, in essence, one moment is separate from another. Each moment has a separate essence as its ground which is changeless. This conception is basic to the Sarvāstivāda doctrine of elements. An atom, when identified with a moment, a unit-function, is obviously not timeless. But that essence of which it is the function is timeless. It is in this sense that the *Vibhāṣā* states that the atomic elements cannot be cut or destroyed or even tied to strings like beads.[171]

As time is synonymous with function, the distinction between the three times is based on the functioning of the elements: the composite element that has not yet been functioning is called the future; the element that is just functioning is called the present; and the element that has ceased to function is called the past.[172]

From the doctrine of the essential separateness of the basic elements of existence certain consequences follow. As each moment is separate from the others, belonging to an element which is essentially non-relational and independent, that a thing moves means that there happens a series of momentary flashings of these separate essences. As the appearances of separate essences, these flashings are themselves separate. Movement is divisible into a series of units and each unit is distinct and therefore separate from the rest. Movement really means a series of separate functions.[173]

Again, while answering the question whether the characters of compositeness are identical with the composite element or different from it, the Sarvāstivādins say that substance and character are essentially separate but they always function together, i.e., they rise to function only in mutual association. They never function apart and yet essentially they are always separate.[174] Again, accepting the fact of relativity they say that all things rest in their respective natures precisely because they are mutually dependent; because in the pairs that constitute the distinct, like light and shade, day and night, winter and summer, each is mutually opposed to the other, therefore each of these is real, substantial.[175] The essences or elements do not admit of change; the change of state that is mentioned as an essential factor of compositeness is simply another name for the element of oldness, which is also another substance. That a thing is old means that the function of the element of oldness has arisen in the series that constitutes the thing. It does not mean any decay of the essence.[176] As the function of an element, although not the element itself, admits of birth or decay, it can still be said that things change, which means that the associating elements of birth, oldness and decay function respectively in succession. Substances do not change; but functions arise and perish in sequence.[177]

(III) *The Middle Way:* The Sarvāstivādins admit *śūnyatā*. For them this means that among the basic elements of existence there is no *ātman*, no eternal substantial entity called "I". They interpret the Middle Way so as to make it agree with their doctrine of elements. The avoidance of the extremes is only in regard to the nature of the constituted entities, the "things," and this means that in regard to the constituted thing, there is no possibility of such views as absolutely existent and absolutely non-existent; this is to reveal the nature of existence as a series of arising and perishing events. But in this the question of the basic elements does not arise. The doctrine of elements is really their answer to the further question of the source or the ground of the events or functions that constitute existence. The Sarvāstivādins would say that the reality of the basic elements does not violate the principle of the Middle Way, for, they would assert, the domain of the former is different from that of the latter and the two doctrines, the conditioned origination of events and the self-existence of the basic elements are bound together. By this they seek to distinguish themselves from the eternalists who hold that the extinction of things means their latency and the production of things means their manifestation.[178]

B. *The line in between: Emphasis on becoming and selfhood:* The critics of the Sarvāstivādins point out that they tend to a kind of eternalism,[179] the absolute self-being of the multiple specific elements, and that with this they fail to make room for change or becoming, which was taught by the Buddha to be the essential nature of things. Again, the Sarvāstivādins cling to the distinct as separate and hold separateness to be absolute. With this they fail to provide for the organic nature of the course of phenomenal existence, and the difficulties in this regard become pronounced especially in connection with the problem of personality. The Sarvāstivādins have not swerved from the natural conclusion of their position, viz., of explaining away the sense of unity and freedom which is instrinsic to self-hood, and which is in fact the very basis of the moral endeavour of man.[180] Subjectivity or individual experience hardly claims their attention, and with it, negation and privation or error naturally need to be explained away. One could perhaps see here an instance of the objectivism of the analysts at its peak.

These considerations led the seceders from the main line of the Sthaviras to dissent from the Sarvāstivādins. All those who dissented from the Sarvāstivādins and made significant contributions to Buddhist thought were such as emphasized the meaningfulness of subjectivity, and the organic unity of personality. These they brought to the front as the cardinal elements in their interpretation of the basic conceptions of Buddhist philosophy, viz., "conditioned origination" and the Middle Way. And with these they sought to oppose the extreme kind of objectivism in which they found the Sarvāstivādins involved. The Vātsīputrīyas, the Sāmmitīyas, and the Sautrāntikas (Saṅkrāntivādins) are at one on this point. They maintain the actuality of becoming, change, development, and maintain the meaningfulness of the sense of self. They tend to hold that "conditioned origination" does not mean a super-addition of a world of unchanging elements to a world of functions, but the essentially conditioned and changing nature of the elements themselves. In contrast with the Sarvāstivādins, these interpret becoming as the arising and perishing of events essentially related in and through a common ground which persists while the particular events arise and perish. As the Sāmmitīyas say:

Momentary extinction is not (a total) extinction; It is a proceeding from moment to moment.[181]

The Vātsīputrīyas hold that there are *saṃskāras* that last for a while, and there are *saṃskāras* that perish every moment.[182] The Sautrāntikas, in denying the "reality" of past and future and in maintaining that the meaningfulness of "non-existence" does not mean the existence of the non-existent,[183] stood for the actuality of becoming, which as they show, is denied in the eternalism of the Sarvāstivādins. Even the Mahāsāṅghikas, who will be considered soon, maintained the actuality of becoming, as the later Mahāsāṅghikas held that the seed develops into the sprout[184] and the Prajñaptivādins, that *karma* (deed) develops into the result.[185]

Even as regards personality the Vātsīputrīyas, the Sāmmitīyas, the Sautrāntikas and the Mahīśāsakas[186] maintained the actuality of selfhood, implying the meaningfulness of personal life. They tended to emphasize the sense of unity and freedom as intrinsic to the sense of selfhood. As the Sāmmitīyas would say, it is an error of the analysts to reduce the constituted wholly to the terms of constituents, to miss the organic unity of the self, to split the organism into minute divisions, reduce it to a mere collocation of simple atomic elements and then imagine that the self is a mere name while the simple atomic elements are real and ultimate. They say:

Therefore absolute difference is a heresy. Therefore not to take the lead of absolute difference is not to follow heresy.[187]

C. *The absolutist line: The Mahāsāṅghikas:* The line of Buddhist thought that stressed the actuality of becoming and the meaningfulness of the sense of self-hood and denied the absoluteness of difference does not seem to have stressed the distinction between the mundane and the ultimate, the one as conventional and the other as transcendental or real and eternal. The credit of having kept alive the emphasis on the ultimacy of the unconditioned reality by drawing attention to the non-substantiality of the basic elements of existence *(dharma-śūnyatā)* belongs to the Mahāsāṅghikas. Every branch of these clearly drew the distinction between the mundane and the ultimate, came to emphasize the non-ultimacy of the mundane and thus facilitated the fixing of attention on the ultimate. The Bahuśrutīyas[188] distinguished the mundane from the transmundane teachings of the Buddha and held that the latter directly lead one to freedom from defilements. These were the teachings of the impermanence of the composite, the painful nature of the defiled, *śūnyatā* of the composite as well as the incomposite, the absence of self-being in things and the peace of Nirvāṇa. The Prajñaptivādins[189] maintained that the *skandhas* in their true nature do not consitute pain, that they are conditionally named "pain" only when they combine to constitute the complexes of defiled entities. They maintained also that the twelve *āyatanas* are not real entities. It is in the Ekavyāvahārikas[190] however, that one finds the full-fledged doctrine of the non-substantiality of elements. They maintained that all things, mundane as well as transmundane, the self as well as the elements, are only derived names and devoid of substantiality. Ekavyāvahārikas were the first to branch off from their main stem, the Mahāsāṅghikas, perhaps only geographically and not doctrinally, for Vasumitra puts them along with the latter and not separately. The Lokottaravādins[191] maintained the distinction between mundane and the transmundane and held the former as unreal and the latter as real. The doer and the deeds that are defiled are unreal for they spring from false notions, while the undefiled is the reality. Perversion consists in mistaking the non-self for the self and the impermanent for the permanent. K'uei Chi tells us that this school maintained that all *kleśas* in the world arise from perversion and the perverse is not a reality; therefore everything here is only a derived name and altogether devoid of substantiality, but the transmundane objects are real, and they are the Way and the fruit of the Way. Only these are real and all the objects of common experience are false.[192] This school, K'uei-chi tells us, derives its name from this distinction between the mundane and the transmundane.[193] The best-known doctrine of the Lokottaravādins is, of course, the distinction between the conventional self hood of the Buddha and the transcendental essence of Buddhahood.[194] Presumably this is a distinction which was accepted by all the branches of the Mahāsāṅghikas and there is no doubt that this was one of their most prolific ideas and at the same time most basic to their line of thought. The Kaukkuṭikas, again are said to have maintained that only *abhidharma,* enquiry into and comprehension of the ultimate nature of everything, is the true, essential teaching of the Buddha, while both *vinaya* (moral code) and *sūtra* (the discourses) are expedients.[195] Vasumitra puts even these along with their parent stem, the Mahāsāṅghikas, from whom, therefore, they do not seem to have differed in the essentials of the doctrine. Thus it is among the Mahāsāṅghikas that one finds the emphasis on the distinction between the conventional and the transcendental as well as the emphasis on the transcendental as the real, the substantial, the eternal. This is virtually the way of criticism. And if we can trust Kwei-chi, who, for the most part, followed Paramārtha in his interpretation of Vasumitra's treatise, the Mahāsāṅghikas seem to have maintained that the incomposite is not merely the goal but the ground, the source of composite elements, that *nirodha* is not mere negation but the permanent principle which is the ground of all that is composite.[196] With regard to the ultimate nature of the individual, the Mahāsāṅghikas held the view that *vijñāna* or *citta,* the self-conscious principle, the basis of personality, is in its very nature pure and that impurities are accidental.[197] In this view of the ultimate nature of the self, they are virtually one with the Sāmmitīyas[198] and the Sautrāntikas.[199]

*Nāgārjuna and the Buddhist schools:* It is too much to say that the Mahāsāṅghikas in their early stage of thought had already reached a full-fledged absolutism. But one can see that they were on the way. While the origin of this tendency toward absolutism which culminates in Mahāyāna can presumably be traced to the earliest times when the followers of the Buddha began to reflect on His teachings, it must have been quite a few centuries before they arrived at a fairly clear conception in this direction. The emphasis on the transmundane nature of the Buddha which is a stress on the transcendental, ultimate essence of the mundane, human Buddha, no doubt belongs here, viz., in the distinction between the mundane and the ultimate and in the emphasis on the latter as the true essence of things. The Buddha had himself said, "He who sees the *Dharma* sees me."[200] And there was the teaching which was no doubt included in all the collections, viz., whether there are the Buddhas or there are not the Buddhas the true nature of things ever remains the same. It is precisely teachings like these that come to be emphasized and developed in Mahāyāna, culminating in the absolutistic philosophy of the *Prajñāpāramitā-sūtras*. But it is to be remembered that the line of thought that came to a culmination in these *Sūtras* and obtained a systematic form in the works of Nāgārjuna had a history of its development from implicit beginnings and these beginnings are to be found in those who emphasized the transmundane over the mundane, the unconditioned over the conditioned, and stood for nonexclusiveness in understanding.[201]

One can appreciate the fact of Nāgārjuna's attention being focussed so much on the root of the Sarvāstivādins' doctrine of elements as a continuation of the old controversy between the Mahāsāṅghikas and the Sarvāstivādins which flows down through the *Prajñāpāramitā-sūtras*. To them he would say that while Mahāyāna would go all the way with them with regard to their analysis, definition and classification of elements, and would emphasize these phases of understanding as essential for a complete comprehension of the true nature of things, the traveller on the Great Way would keep free from the error of the analysts, viz., the error of clinging to the ultimates of analysis as ultimates in reality.[202] The imagination that the distinct, in being distinct, is separate and substantial, he would say, is the basic error in the doctrine of elements. Thus he says in the *Kārikā,* those who conceive the elements of existence as each separate from the other and reduce the self to the terms of these separate elements are not experts in understanding the teachings of the Buddha.[203] In rejecting the false notion of separateness of basic elements, Nāgārjuna would join hands with the line of Buddhist thought that emphasized the concreteness of becoming and the meaningfulness of the sense of self-hood. Subjectivity, the sense of unity and freedom intrinsic to self-hood, is the very fulcrum on which personal life rests; it is an error to ignore this and try to explain away self-hood as an illusion and the person as a collocation of essentially separate elements.[204] But Nāgārjuna would point out that while accepting and appreciating the actuality of becoming and the meaningfulness of subjectivity, it is not only necessary to recognize but essential to emphasize that the mundane truth is not the ultimate truth. For the ultimate meaning of the thirst in man consists in the realization of the unconditioned reality. The sense of the real in man needs to be put on its own. Not to emphasize it is to allow for the possibility of its getting ignored. And a failure to comprehend its complete meaning will inevitably lead to a substitution of false absolutes, resulting in dead-ends in understanding and suffering in life. For, the sense of the unconditioned which belongs to the very essence of self-hood can in no way be explained away.

But if this emphasis on the unconditioned were to lead one again either to imagine that the conditioned is separate from the unconditioned or to explain away the conditioned as a mere illusion, that would again be a case of clinging, clinging to the conditionedness of the conditioned as ultimate or clinging to the unconditioned as exclusive of the conditioned. The ultimate reality is devoid of significance for the mundane except as its very real nature; for, apart from the mundane there is no ultimate. In truth, the ultimate nature of the conditioned is itself the unconditioned reality. The world is itself Nirvāṇa when rightly seen. And while the realization of this truth sets one free from clinging to creatureliness as the ultimate nature of oneself, it reveals also a way of living the mundane life different from that which breeds conflict and suffering. It is this understanding, which is the deeper understanding of the mundane, Nāgārjuna would say, that distinguishes those who only hear from those who comprehend the teachings of the Buddha. In the Great Way, he would say, nothing needs to be abandoned except one's own perversion. "Everything stands in harmony with him who is in harmony with *śūnyatā*."

*Nāgārjuna on Hīnayāna and Mahāyāna:* We may perhaps refer here very briefly to what seems to have been the circumstance leading to the "origin" of Mahāyāna and how Nāgārjuna considered the question of the relation between the Small Way and the Great Way. As noted above, it was chiefly the Sarvāstivādins, on the one hand, and the Mahāsāṅghikas, on the other, that seem to have been the participants in the keenest controversy and even rivalry; and presumably the controversy began even before the actual emergence of the Sarvāstivādins as a separate school from the Sthaviras. The teaching of the Mahāyāna is understandable as a continuation of the early absolutistic tendency which was the chief characteristic of the Mahāsāṅghikas. Presumably it was they who later chose to call their way the Great Way in order to distinguish it from that of those whom they considered as falling short of the deeper insight contained in the teachings of the Buddha, and in order to show that they did not exclude the latter but included and transcended them.[205] From the beginning the Mahāsāṅghikas must have considered the Sthaviras not adequately advanced in the deeper understanding of the doctrine, even as the Sthaviras must have looked down upon the former as too liberal in matters of discipline. And yet the Mahāsāṅghikas must have from early times sought to incorporate the Sarvāstivāda analysis of elements into the body of their own doctrines without forsaking their own unique, fundamental, emphasis, and proving thereby that they accepted whatever is acceptable in the Sarvāstivāda while not getting stuck in the morass of analysis. The assimilation of the Sarvāstivāda analysis, far from making them deviate from their emphasis on the non-ultimacy of the elements of existence, seems to have enabled them to develop their absolutism on better grounds and make it richer in comprehension.

It is in some way like this that one can understand the emergence of the "new composition" of the *Sūtras* directly emerging among the Mahāsāṅghikas,[206] while at the same time incorporating all the categories of Sarvāstivāda, demonstrating them to be non-ultimate and non-substantial which the Sarvāstivādins themselves held to be ultimate and substantial. Thus they were only deepening and making more thorough the original insight which inspired them from the very beginning, the insight of the transcendental essence of the mundane as well as the sense of non-exclusiveness. The emergence of the new name Mahāyāna and the literature called the *Mahāyāna-sūtras* marked an epoch in the history of Buddhist philosophy; but although the literary compositions were new, the basic ideas that they embodied were still those found in the teachings of the Buddha as emphasized and elaborated by the Mahāsāṅghikas. The emergence of Mahayana was the arising of a new name for a fresh synthesis of the Master's teachings. It was a creative synthesis of the old. In this the Mahāsāṅghikas must have worked closely on the materials provided by the Sarvāstivādins who had much to contribute to this development of Buddhist philosophy.[207]

If the farer on the Great Way is asked to offer a basic point of distinction between the two ways, the "Great" and the "Small," he will no doubt point to all-comprehensiveness more than any other as characteristic of his way. Comprehension has its dimensions of depth and width and to the farer on the Great Way this means, on the one hand, the penetration into the deeper nature of things which culminates in the realization that the ultimate nature of the conditioned is itself the unconditioned reality. On the other hand, comprehension stands also for the realization of the essential relatedness of determinate entities. This is the mundane truth, and with regard to the human individual it has the all-important bearing of one's essential relatedness with the rest of the world. It is this insight of the true nature of things that is the basis of the universal compassion of the wise.

In practical religious life the most frequent and the most common criticism in regard to the farers on the Small Way is that they lack wisdom, lack compassion and lack skilfulness.[208] The farers on the Small Way are intent on seeking their own good, working for their own salvation.[209] Their wayfaring is conditioned by fear and not inspired by compassion. They seek to enter Nirvāṇa only too hurriedly.[210] They do not have the necessary patience, the capacity for forbearance *(kṣānti)*.[211] They are only too anxious to do away with their individuality, for they do not see that individuality, when rightly understood and rightly lived, can itself become the channel for unbounded love and unsurpassed joy with which to elevate and gladden the entire world. They do not have *sarvākārajñatā*, the knowledge of all forms, which is the knowledge of all things from all standpoints at all levels.[212] They do not need it as they are not interested to know the unique way of every individual and to help everyone to attain to perfection in one's own way, for this is the work only of the bodhisattvas and the Buddhas. The hearers *(śrāvaka)* are not interested in the extraordinary powers *(ṛddhi)* that are an aid to convert the minds of the common people and to turn them away from ignorance and passion and towards the ultimate good.[213] In their estimation of the nature of the Buddha they hardly get beyond His physical form.[214] They consider Him as only an ordinary being, subject to birth and death and do not rise to see the transmundane nature, the transcendental essence of Buddhahood. They do not have any idea as to how the Buddha, being Himself free from ignorance and passion, can yet function as an individual. To live in the world and yet be free from defilements, to retain individuality and yet be free from the false sense of self, to work for the world and yet be free from pride and passion—this is the skilfulness of the Buddha, and the *śrāvakas,* the hearers, do not rise to this level because they lack the deeper understanding of the true nature of things. In their anxiety to get away from the situation of conflict and pain, they fail to see that the course they adopt, viz., the course of fear and escape, is precisely the one that is condemned by the Buddha. They forget that if the attitude that they adopt were the only attitude possible, then even the Buddha, in whom they take refuge and whom they accept as their leader, would not have been there, for it is from the *prajñāpārāmitā* that the Buddha is born[215] and the *prajñāpārāmitā* is the very principle of comprehension, comprehensive understanding and all-embracing compassion.

The farer on the Great Way would add that if the *śrāvakas* would only deepen their understanding and widen their outlook, they could also tread the path of the bodhisattva.[216] The way of the Buddha is the wide way; it is non-exclusive, open to all.[217] It is always possible for one to deepen one's understanding. Truly, they would add, there is no rigid division between the careers of the *śrāvakas* and the bodhisattvas and between the analysis of elements and the philosophy of the absolute. It is the mission of those who have the deeper understanding of things to enliven a spirit of further enquiry in the minds of those whose understanding has suffered a setback. This is the mission of criticism, which is to lay bare the inherent inconsistencies in the positions of those who cling and hold fast to the relative as absolute.

# CHAPTER II

# CONCEPTS AND CONVENTIONAL ENTITIES

(*Nāma* and *Lakṣaṇa*)

## Section I

## NATURE OF CONVENTION

*The thirst for the real as the urge to build:* The thirst for the real in man[1] is the starting point as well as the foundation of the philosophy of the Middle Way. It is a basic fact about human thinking that it confronts everywhere an "other" to itself, which it endeavours to subsume into its own being. Growth in knowledge consists in a progressive assimilation of the object and an establishment of a unity with it.[2] The progressive extension of acquaintance as well as the progressive deepening of comprehension are ways in which man responds to the urge in him for the limitless, an urge which is basic to all his activities. The intuition of sense, the synthesis of imagination and understanding and even the appropriation of the different kinds of experience to oneself by which the otherwise mute becomes meaningful, all these are different ways in which the self-conscious person gives vent on the cognitive plane to his deepest urge, the thirst for the real. And man's accomplishment in the sphere of theoretic understanding cannot be sharply divided from his function as a person on the plane of action. In fact, knowledge is inefficient without action and action is blind without knowledge. They flow into each other and are essentially different phases of one and the same basic urge.[3]

*The self as the builder of the world:* The person is a unity, an integrated reality. He is not a collocation of several otherwise separate elements, as the analysts would imagine. The elements found in personality are what the person himself gives rise to as his self-expression in response to the urge in him. The thirst for the real is the basic fact about man. What we are and what we do depends on the way we respond to and interpret to ourselves this deepest urge. Thus says the *Śāstra,*

The bodhisattva constantly loves and delights in meditating on the Buddha and therefore while leaving the body and while assuming the body, he constantly realizes the presence of the Buddha. This is like the beings that constantly cultivate the sense of passion and in whom therefore the sense of passion is intense (重), taking up the body of a passionate bird like a peacock, . . . and those in whom anger is intense taking birth among poisonous insects. . . . (The bodhisattva) takes on the bodily (existence) according to what his mind intensely thinks and esteems high (隨心所重).[4] (276a)

The bodhisattva meditating on the Buddha realizes everywhere the presence of the Buddha . . . as he is collected and pure in his thought. This is like the person (standing before) a mirror (水鏡) having very well decorated his body; the mirror being bright and clean reflects all things (as they are); the image is not in the mirror itself. The person sees the image of his own body as the mirror is bright and clean. Everything, always, in its very nature is pure.[5] (276b)

The world around us is a reflection of the condition of our mind; we do deeds that build the world for us exactly in the way we interpret to ourselves the reality of things.

Whatever is in the three realms (三界), all that is the construction of mind *(citta)*. How is it so? It is in accordance with one's thought that one realizes all things (隨心所念悉皆得見). By mind does one see the Buddha and by mind does one become a Buddha. The mind itself is the Buddha, the mind itself is my body. (Under ignorance) the mind does not know itself; does not see itself; it is due to ignorance that one seizes the determinate nature of the mind (若取心相悉皆無智). (In this state), the mind (that is thus seized) is also false. All (these) things arise from ignorance. The bodhisattva penetrates into the ultimate reality of all things, viz., the eternal *śūnyatā,* through (his comprehension of) this nature of mind (因是心相即入諸法實相).[6] (276b)

That this is not subjectivism or subjective idealism is borne out here. What we are, what we make of ourselves depends on the way we interpret reality to ourselves, which is itself not denied.[6a] Even the Buddha as an individual cannot alter the course of things; it is only by rightly comprehending it that he becomes the Buddha. The truth of things is independent of anyone's subjective fancy; the Buddha does not Himself make it.[7] Our comprehensions are true exactly according to the measure to which they are reflective of the true nature of things.

*The world of convention:* The world of convention is the network of concepts and conventional entities,[8] the warp and woof, which, as the work of the ignorant, is a misinterpretation and misrepresentation of the true being, while as the work of the Buddha, it is a revelation of the unconditioned through the conditioned and the contingent. The wise realize the true being stripped of the modes of concepts and conventions and in their case these function as the channel for the free flow of the deeper truth and not as a veil that hides it.

The Buddha reveals (the true nature of) all things by means of *nāma* and *lakṣaṇa* (以名字相), in order to enable all to understand (解) (the truth of) things. (646a)

The common people dwell only in *nāma* and *lakṣaṇa,* the thought—constructions that are devoid of substantiality (虛妄憶想分別). (688a)

The ignorant do not get beyond *nāma* and *lakṣaṇa* to the real nature of things. They hold to these as ultimate and therefore cling to them. But the sense of the beyond is not wholly absent even while under ignorance. "Within the same mind there is knowledge as well as ignorance."[8a] Even the ignorant have the sense of the real. Thus the *Śāstra* says:

That men are ignorant does not mean that they are ignorant like cows and goats (非謂如牛羊等愚癡). (Even) these people seek the pathway to reality. But owing to perversion, they give rise to several kinds of misconstruction. (60b)

The ignorant pursue names while what they seek is reality (逐名求實).[9] (T92c)

In any case, whether it is the world of the Buddha or of the common man, it is what it is precisely as we make it.

All things are creations *(nirmāṇa)* (化); among these there are the creations of the *śrāvakas,* the creations of the *pratyekabuddhas,* the creations of the bodhisattvas, and the creations of the Buddha. There are also the creations of afflictions *(kleśa)* and of deeds *(karma)*. . . . Whatever thing there is (that is subject to birth and death), all that is a *nirmāṇa.*[10] (728c)

(Although all things are alike *nirmāṇa* and therefore) devoid of reality (still) there holds among them the distinction of one thing from another . . . even as the things seen in dream, despite their unreality, admit of distinctions.[11] (729c)

In fact all that is created is a creation of deeds; but there is a difference between the deeds that are undefiled and the deeds that spring from affliction and passion. The one is the world of the wise, and the other, the world of the ignorant. The creations of the ignorant that arise from impure deeds are prompted by affliction, while the creations of the sages spring from wisdom and compassion.

The world of convention is called *nirmāṇa* to indicate that it is a creation; it is called *samvṛti* to indicate that it veils the truth of things; it is called *vyavahāra* to say that it has mundane truth, "empirical validity," although devoid of ultimacy; it is called *prapañca* to show that it is an elaboration through concepts and conventional entities. The "builder" of the world is *vijñāna* or *citta* as a self-conscious principle of intellection.[12] And in this building of the world the two, *nāma* and *lakṣaṇa* names and what they stand for, constitute the warp and woof.

*Concepts and conventional entities (nāma and lakṣaṇa):* A) *Nāma: name, concept:* In analyzing aspects and apprehending their synthesis, discerning the ways of their combination in the unity of the thing, the thing is given a name. The name designates the object. The process of naming which is also the process of ideation or formation of concepts involves abstraction of characters from within the thing. The characters so abstracted may be either essential to the thing or accidental. Either way they belong to the content of the concept that designates the thing. Each of these aspects also has its own name; and each of the ways of their combination has also its own name. And "name" itself has its meaning as well as "meaning" has its name. In every case the name or concept, in so far as it is significant, conveys a certain meaning (content) for which it stands or which it represents. *Nāma* means the word as well as the concept or notion, while *lakṣaṇa* stands for the content, the character, essential or nonessential, as well as for the "entities" to which these characters belong and which they signify.

The synthesis of experience worked out by understanding is altogether constituted of *nāma* and *lakṣaṇa*. *Nāma* which means name or concept, means not simply the pure or formal categories of knowledge, for even the empirical content has a name; it is also *nāma.* Again, the content or *lakṣaṇa* covers not only the empirical content but the modes of their combination also. Thus relations are also called *lakṣaṇa* (conventional entities) with their own names.

*Nāma* and *lakṣaṇa,* concepts and their contents, the words and what they designate, constitute the entire world of experience. Thus the *Sūtra* says: "All things are . . . only *nāma* and *lakṣaṇa.*"[13] Speaking of *nāma,* the *Sūtra* says, "*Nāma* is the means by which one holds the thing (firmly in the mind) (以名取諸法是故爲名)."[14] Things exist in and through the functions they fulfill and "names arise," says the *Śāstra,* "as references to the (characters and) functions of things (隨事起名)."[15] The sixteen names of the individual, arise, e.g., as specific references to his particular characters and functions. The names of various officials, again, for example, arise from the offices they fulfill which vary according to their knowledge and ability. Even names like recluse, the obtainer of the way, arise from their references to the nature and function of their respective referents.[16]

B) *Lakṣaṇa* (I) *Sign:* Says the *Śāstra:*

*Nāma* is the word *(varṇa)* (字) (that designates) the thing. For example, "fire" is the word that designates the (complex) entity the nature of which is heat (and illumination). *Lakṣaṇa* (is the sign by means of which the thing may be cognized. Smoke, e.g., is the sign of fire). Seeing the smoke one understands that it indicates the presence of fire. (While smoke is the sign of fire) heat is the essential nature (體) of fire. Again, in reference to the complex of the five skandhas, "man" or "woman" is the *nāma* (name); the bodily features by means of which the person can be distinguished as man or woman, constitute the *lakṣaṇa* (sign). On seeing these signs, the name is given as man or woman. (691b)

Speaking almost in the same terms but referring to *"artha"* (義), the meaning, instead of *"lakṣaṇa,"* mark or sign, we have the *Śāstra* saying:

There are in all two things, *nāma* (名字) and *artha* (名字義), the name or the word and its meaning. For example, "fire" is the name and the meaning that it conveys is the complex entity composed of heat and illumination . . . It is the complex of these two elements, that is called "fire." If there were another "fire" apart from these two, then it should have had a third function apart from them but which is not the case. So it should be known that it is the complex of these two elements that is derivedly named "fire" (是二法和合名爲火).[17] (358a)

When it is said that smoke is the *lakṣaṇa* of fire, *lakṣaṇa* is taken as a mark, a sign. *Nāma* and *lakṣaṇa* are mutually dependent, and the perception of the *lakṣaṇa* is the condition for the naming of the thing.

First there is the perception of the features of man or woman and then the name is given as man or woman. *Lakṣaṇa* is the root and *nāma* is the branch.[18] (691b)

*Lakṣaṇa* is called *nimitta* or occasion with regard to its functioning as the occasion for the rise of ideas and emotions.

When one sees with one's eyes the (bodily) form one seizes with a bias (偏取) (only) such characters that one likes and clings to them (而生著); the others do not have the same interest in regard to these characters. As these (characters) are capable of giving rise to passion and clinging they are called *nimitta* (相), i.e., occasions (for the rise of passion).[19] (691b)

*Lakṣaṇa* (II): *Essential Character, Nature: Lakṣaṇa* meaning the sign or mark (accidental character) is distinguished from *lakṣaṇa* meaning the essential character or nature *(prakṛti)*. In answer to a question regarding the distinction between *lakṣaṇa* (character, 相) and *prakṛti* (nature, 性) the *Śāstra* observes:

Some say, in their meaning (其實) there is no difference, the difference is only in name. To speak of *prakṛti* is itself to speak of *lakṣaṇa* and to speak of *lakṣaṇa* is itself to speak of *prakrti*. For example, to speak of the nature of fire is itself to speak of its *lakṣaṇa* of heat, and to speak of its *lakṣaṇa* of heat is itself to speak of its *prakṛti*.

Some say, there is a little difference between *prakṛti* and *lakṣaṇa*. *Prakṛti* refers to the essential nature (體) of the thing, while *lakṣaṇa* refers to (the mark which is) the means to cognize it (可識). For example, of the *Śākya-putra, prakṛti* is the acceptance and the leading of moral life while the *lakṣaṇas* are the shaved head and the coloured cloth . . . Of the fire, heat is *prakṛti* while smoke is *lakṣaṇa*. The proximate is the *prakṛti* while the distant is the *lakṣaṇa*. There is no necessity about the mark that it should arise from the very nature of the thing, while *prakṛti* is the very essential nature of the thing. Thus, a metal may bear the mark of gold in appearing yellow in colour, while in essence it may be just brass. When the metal is burnt in fire or rubbed on stone, then it is known that it has not the nature of gold. Again, for example, when a person is respecting and worshipping he may appear to be a good man.

But when he becomes wild, scolding (people) without any sense of shame, becomes angry and frightful, then his true nature would come to light. Between *prakṛti* and *lakṣaṇa* there are these distinctions of being internal and external, proximate and distant, the first appearance and later revelation.[20] (293b)

In another context speaking of the ten powers *(bala)* of the Buddha the *Śāstra* draws the distinction between *dhātu* (nature) (性) and *lakṣaṇa* (mark) and says:

*Dhātu* is (the essence that is deepened by) cumulative cultivation (積習) and *lakṣaṇa* is (the sign or mark that is) born from *dhātu*.[21] (239b)

Again,

*Lakṣaṇa* becomes *prakṛti* (成性) by cumulative cultivation. Take anger, for example. In the case of a person who gets angry constantly, every day without a break, anger itself would become his nature and so he would become ill-natured.

In some cases *prakṛti* and *lakṣaṇa* are different. For example, seeing the smoke one would recognize the fire; smoke is the mark of fire, it is not itself fire; In other cases there is no difference between the two. For example, heat is the nature of fire and it is also the mark of fire.[22] (528b)

*Lakṣaṇa* (III) *Determinate Entity: Lakṣaṇa* also means determinate existent entity. This is understandable because the entity being determinate derives its being and maintains its uniqueness only through determination (specification by abstraction), which consists in dividing and setting apart the rest. Thus the *Sūtra* says:

All that is *lakṣaṇa* is dual, divided (一切相皆是二); all that is divided is a particular existent entity. All that is an existent entity is subject to birth and death.[22a] (661c)

The ignorant who attend only to the obvious miss the hinterland; they seize the specific as the self-contained. The wise are awake to the complete truth. Thus the *Śāstra* commenting on the above passage, says:

The things that constitute duality cannot be one without the other (不得相離). But common people speak of them as two, (i.e. separate and independent) and so what they say is a perversion. . . . Whatever is a case of seizing the *lakṣaṇa* is a case of faring in duality (取相皆是二).[23] (664a)

To seize the determinate (取相) is really to allow oneself to be misled by names; it is to imagine that different names mean separate essences; this is to turn relative distinctions into absolute divisions. When names are not seized as standing for separate substances, then they cannot be made objects of clinging.

A thing derives its significance only when specified and named. All things are spoken of only through name, determination.

It is only in name (但有名字) that the *bodhi* is spoken of. Even the bodhisattva is spoken of only through names . . . All these names (as well as the named) are born of the complex of causes and conditions and they are spoken of only through derived names, thought-constructions (但以分別憶想假名說).[23a] (318a)

When a determinate thing is analyzed into its constituent elements by virtue of the combination of which the thing derives its name, it cannot be placed either inside or outside or in between them. The composite thing is not one more thing in addition to its components. The thing is the components themselves in combination; the latter are the thing itself analyzed into different aspects. Between the constituents and the constituted there cannot be any such relation of inside or outside or in between which holds only among entities that are mutually apart.

(The referent of) the name "fire" for example is not itself inside the two elements of heat and light (which constitute the object called fire). But why? These elements are two while fire is one; one is not two and two is not one.

There can be no confusion (合) between the name and what it means (i.e., the thing named). In such a case when the word "fire" is being uttered, the mouth should get burnt. (Again, the name and the named are not completely apart.) If they were completely apart (離), then, having asked for fire one might get water. On account of these reasons, it should be known that the name fire is not itself inside these two elements.

But suppose fire is outside these two elements (unconnected with them in any way). Then, when one hears the name "fire," there should not be born in him the thought of fire in regard to these two elements. And if the name fire is in between these two elements (being vague in its significance), then it has not any fixed sphere of reference (依止處) . . . And in that case there cannot be any definite knowledge of fire (不可知).

Therefore it should be known that fire cannot be found in any of these three zones. Fire is only a derived name (and the thing designated by it is also only a conditioned entity).

Just the same is the case with the bodhisattva. Two elements, *nāma* and *rūpa,* combine and it is the complex of these two elements that is called the bodhisattva. *Rūpa* is different and *nāma* is different. And (apart from these two) if there is any entity called the bodhisattva, that should be a third entity (separate from these). But actually there is no such thing. Therefore it should be known that bodhisattva is only a derived name. And the name bodhisattva cannot be located either inside or outside or in between *(nāma* and *rūpa).*[24] (358a–b)

When we imagine the components to be separate and independent, we cannot get back to the unity of the thing. It is only the awareness of the determinate as determinate, the relative as relative that restores us to the original organic unity of the aspects in the thing, as well as to the unity of the thing itself with its larger setting.

*The name and the named:* It is necessary to bring to mind that this whole discussion on names and determinate essences or entities bears directly on the doctrine of elements of the Sarvāstivādins who base their pluralism on the separateness of names and argue from their meaningfulness to the reality of the entities they stand for.[25] Now the *Śāstra* points out that the presence of a name need not mean the actuality of the thing named and the existence of the name does not mean at all the reality or the self-being of the thing named.

It is not proper to say that (the thing) is a reality (a substantial entity) just because there is the name (有名故有). . . . Names are of two kinds, true (實) and untrue (不實), (or significant and non-significant). As an example of the non-significant (non-connotative) name, mention may be made of a grass called *"cauri."* Now, the grass does not steal. It is truly devoid of the character of the thief and yet it is called by the name (which has the connotation) of stealing. Again there are the non-significant, non-denotative) names like hare's horn, or hair of the tortoise which do not denote anything actually existent. Although cloth is not unreal in the same sense as the hare's horn, still, (it has only a conditioned being); it is there when its causal factors cooperate and it ceases to be when they become dispersed. Again, take for example a forest or an army; things like these have names, but there are no substances (or things in themselves corresponding to these). (Again,) for example, the wooden image of man has no doubt the name of man and yet in it one should not search for the nature of the actual human being. Similarly although there is the name "cloth", still, pursuing it one should not expect to find any substantial entity (眞實) called "cloth." (147b)

Again, the realists contend that the cloth is a reality for it has its characters and functions. A piece of cloth is either short or long, coarse or fine; it has its colour; it has its causes and conditions; it has its production and destruction; and it has its consequences. So, they contend, cloth should be recognized as a real, substantial entity.

(Surely) the cloth can function as the condition for the birth of different thoughts and emotions in the minds of the perceivers. For example, when one gets it, one feels happy and losing it one becomes sad. (147b) In reply the *Śāstra* points out:

Things that act as conditions for the rise of ideas are, again, of two kinds. Ideas arise from things that are true and they also arise from things that are false. The notions of the objects of dream, the moon in the water, the stump of wood in the dark mistakenly seen as man, are the ones that arise from false objects. So nothing definite can be said about the things that act as conditions for the birth of ideas (viz., whether they are real or unreal). Therefore, (being the condition for) the birth of ideas should not be taken as the (decisive) reason (for the reality of the objects seen). If the birth of the ideas were itself the criterion for the reality of the object, then there should not be the further search into the nature of the object whether it is really there or not (更不應求實有). Now the eyes see the moon in the water; the idea is born that this is the moon. And if that (moon) from which the idea of the moon was born were itself the real moon, then there would not be any other (moon as) the real moon. (i.e., the moon in the sky) at all. (147b–147c)

In other words, that things have names, that they have their respective natures and functions, that they serve as objects of cognition and as occasions for the rise of thoughts and emotions, these cannot be adduced as reasons for their reality. But to mistake the unreal for the non-existent is again to swing from the extreme of absolute existence to that of absolute non-existence. Absolute existence and absolute non-existence both are false as referring to things mundane. Things are unreal, i.e., conditioned and non-substantial but not non-existent. Again everything has its own nature but is not unconditioned. This is the truth of conditioned origination, the Middle Way.

*Section II*

# MODES OF CONVENTION

*Modes of determinate being:* The conventional entities that constitute the mundane existence can be distinguished as of three kinds: The complex thing, the subtle constituents and the ways in which the latter combine to constitute the thing. Every one of these has its own kind of being. Each is a kind of conventional entity with its own name. But this should not mislead one to imagine that these kinds of entities which are arrived at by logical analysis have all their own unconditioned and separate existence. Of course, as relative modes of being they not only hold good but are essential aspects of common experience.

Thus we find the *Śāstra* mentioning three modes of determinate being which can be called relational modes of being or relational entities, actual entities (subtle constituent elements of the complex objects) and the complex objects themselves.

Thus the *Śāstra* says:

(Determinate) being can be of three kinds (有有三種): that of relational entities (相待有), that of (complex things with) derived names (假名有), and that of the subtle constituents (法有).

(The first kind of being viz.,) that of relational entities, (stands for what is designated by such relational terms as) long and short, this and that. . . . (In themselves these are abstractions.) These designations refer to and derive their meaning from the mutual relations (that actual things bear to one another). "Long" derives its significance depending on the "short," and "short" derives its significance depending on the "long." (Similarly) "this" depends on "that" and "that" on "this." If one is to the east of a thing, then the thing is to one's west, and *vice-versa*. The thing is one and the same and not different (一物未異), and yet there are these distinctions of "east" and "west." All these ("long," "short" etc.) have names but are devoid of substantial referents, (有名而無實). Such names as these are called the names of mutual relations (among actually existent entities). They do not stand for any actual entities

(實法). Therefore these names are not like "form," "smell," "taste," "touch," etc. (which stand for actual entities, elements of existence). (147c)

It may be noted that the names of these relational modes arise as references to the ways in which things become, arise and perish in mutuality. They are in themselves not even actual things; these are mutual references that hold among actual things by virtue of the relations that the latter bear to one another. The *Śāstra* speaks in another context:

It is in reference to the birth and death of elements, viz., *skandhas, āyatanas* and *dhātus,* that there is the derived name "time" (見陰界入生滅假名爲時); there is no time (as substance) other than these. Even space and time, together and apart (i.e., whole and part), identity and difference, long and short are names that arise in a similar way (as references to the ways in which things function in mutual relatedness). Common people cling to them at heart and so they say that these are substantial entities. Hence one must abandon (one's clinging to) the conventional entities of the mundane truth.[26] (65c–66a)

Speaking of the modes of convention the *Śāstra* continues:

The being of (complex things with) derived names is like (the name) curd (and what it stands for). "Curd" is (a complex thing) constituted of form, smell, taste and touch; these four causal factors combine (and there is the complex thing) depending on which (i.e., as referring to which) there is the name, "curd." "Curd," of course, is an existent thing, but its existence (有) is not of the same kind as the existence of its causal factors (不同因緣法有). It is unreal (無) (dependent, derived being) and yet it is not unreal in the same sense as the hare's horn, or the hair of the tortoise, (which are just words without anything corresponding to them). It is only through the combination of the (subtle) causal factors (there is the thing and as its designation there is) the name "curd." The same is the case with "cloth." (The same is also the case even with the person, the individual).

(As to the being of the subtle atomic elements like form, smell, taste and touch,) these subtle elements combine and there are the subtle particles of hair. Through (the combination of) the subtle particles of hair there is the hair itself. Through (the combination of) several hairs, there is a lock of hair. And through the collections of locks of hair there are threads and from the threads there is cloth. From cloth there is the ready made dress. Now, in the absence of the particles of hair there would not be the hair; in the absence of the locks of hair, there would not be the threads; in the absence of the threads there would not be the cloth, and in the absence of the cloth there would not be the ready-made dress. (147c)

But are the subtle elements, being ultimate in analysis, themselves real? Speaking of the "subtlest" as only a name imposed, the *Śāstra* says:

The "subtlest" has nothing (substantial) as its referent. The name is simply imposed (on what is conceived by some as the subtlest) (至微無實強爲之名); because gross and subtle are only relative terms. From the standpoint of something "gross," there is something "subtle;" but this "subtle" thing itself has still subtler elements (as its constituents and there could be no end to this division). (147c)

Pursuing in this way, one finds that (subtle and indivisible and therefore real and imperishable) atomic elements cannot be found. (The name "atoms" meaning "indivisible" is only superimposed on some thing that is not truly indivisible.)[27] (148a)

*Stripping bare the true being: (I) The three modes of convention:* To strip reality bare of the veils of confusion consists not in the literal destruction or even abandoning of things of mundane existence but in giving up one's false imaginations in regard to the true nature of things. It is a progressive deepening of one's comprehension of reality. Corresponding to the grossness or subtlety of the conventional entities that become objects of clinging under ignorance, the *Prajñāpārmitā-sūtras* give two accounts of this stripping bare. These are really accounts of conventional modes of being meant to be of help to one in giving up one's false imaginations about the true nature of things.

Beguiled by names imposed on things the ignorant imagine everything to be real and nonrelational. By mistaking ultimates in analysis as ultimates in reality, the analysts miss the truly ultimate, the undivided being. It is essential to distinguish the unreal from the real, the conventional from the ultimate. The three kinds of convention *(prajñapti)* that are mentioned here stand for the kinds of conventional entities to which people at different levels of understanding cling as ultimate and unconditioned.

Speaking of the kinds of convention, the *Śāstra* says:

The subtle elements like the five *skandhas* are the kinds of entities designated by (the convention called) *dharma-prajñapti* (法波羅攝提). It is the complex entity constituted of these subtle elements that is called the individual. It is the combination of many single bones that is called the skull. It is the combination of the roots and branches, leaves and flowers that is called the tree. This is (the kind of convention called) *avavāda* (受)—*prajñapti*. By means of these names (individual etc.) the characters of the two kinds of (constituent) elements (viz., bodily and mental) are seized and spoken of as the two (basic) kinds (that constitute the composite entity called the ego). This is (the kind of convention called) *nāma-saṅketa* (名字)—*prajñapti*.

Again, it is by a combination of the many subtle elements that a gross thing is born. Take, for example, the gross physical thing; it arises as the result of the coming together of many subtle physical elements. This is *dharma-prajñapti* because from (the combination of) certain things certain other things are born (從法有法). When these gross things combine, there is (again another composite thing born, as referring to which) there arises yet another name. When the capacity to illuminate and the capacity to burn come together (there arises the complex thing as the designation of which) there arises the name "fire." (Here) based on *nāma* and *rūpa* (which are relatively basic elements) there is the "individual." *Nāma* and *rūpa* are (the basic, constituent) elements; "individual" is a derived name. This is *avavāda-prajñapti*. It is called *avavāda* because here *"nāma"* is seized and *"rūpa"* is seized (取色取名故名爲受). At the end of many names, yet other names arise, e.g., at the end of the names "rafter," "brick," etc. there arises yet another name, "house." At the end of the names "roots," "branches," "leaves" and "flowers," there arises yet another name, "tree." This is *nāmasaṅketa-prajñapti.* (358b–c)

The wayfarer in order to get at the truth of these conventional entities and thus to become free from clinging to them as absolute:

First denies the *nāma-saṅketa-prajñapti,* and reaches the *avavāda-prajñapti,* then he denies the *avavāda-prajñapti,* and reaches the *dharma-prajñapti,* and lastly he denies the *dharma-prajñapti* and reaches the universal reality (到諸法實相中). The universal reality is the *prajñāpāramitā* itself, devoid of all names and determinate essences.[28] (358c)

In other words, it might be said that common people cling at the level of gross things; further penetration by analysis puts one on the level of the different complex entities like matter, mind and life which are also as much open to clinging as the gross things themselves. Still further analysis leads one to the level of logical entities (like the *dharmas* of the Sarvāstivādins), the separate minute elements which one arrives at by logical analysis of concrete experience. Even the last are as much open to clinging as the other two kinds. It is by realizing that even the subtlest of things that one arrives at by analysis are not ultimate in reality that one becomes free from one's clinging to the products of analysis. The philosophy of *śūnyatā* seeks to bring about this realization by laying bare the inconsistencies to which one is led by imagining that the subtle and the separate are ultimate and absolute.

*(II) The three grades of essential nature:* The same process of stripping bare the essential nature of things, the ultimate reality, is contained in another account of the *Prajñāpāramitā,* viz., that of the three kinds or levels of *lakṣaṇa,* essential nature. It consists in starting with the *lakṣaṇa* of the complex, conditioned things, passing through the subtle elements

of analysis, and reaching finally the ultimate reality, the indeterminate *dharma* by a progressive deepening of one's insight into the true nature of things. This is to enable one to become free from clinging in regard to all objects starting from the gross objects of the common man down to the ultimate reality itself.

Thus the *Śāstra* says:

*Lakṣaṇa* (essential nature) is of three kinds: that of the derived names (假名相) (and the composite things designated by them), that of the subtle (constituent) elements (法相) and that of the indeterminate (*dharma*) (無相相). (The first kind, viz.,) the *lakṣaṇa* of derived names refers to (the determinate essences of the composite) objects like cart, house, forest, army and individual. On the complex of all (the constituent) elements there is imposed this yet another name (viz., "cart," or "house" or "individual"). Owing to the power of ignorance one seizes (these objects) which are by nature derived names (and dependent entities) and gives rise to all afflictions and deeds.

(The second kind), that of the subtle constituent elements (stands for) the subtle elements like the five *skandhas,* the twelve *āyatanas* and the eighteen *dhātus*. All (these) are seen as real when seen only with the eyes of flesh. But when seen with the eye of wisdom, they are known to be unreal. Therefore even these subtle constituent elements are unreal and the words (that speak of them as real) are deceptive. Therefore one should give up (one's clinging to) the subtle constituent elements.

Leaving these two kinds, there remains only the essential nature of the indeterminate (無相相) *(dharma)*. Some people seize (even) this indeterminate *dharma;* pursuing the characters that they thus seize (under ignorance), they again become subject to life in bondage. Therefore one should not cling even to the indeterminate *(dharma)*.

(The true comprehension of) the indeterminate *(dharma)* is that in which clinging to all these three kinds is given up (離三種相故名無相). When there is no character (or determinate nature) (that can be seized) then there is no seizing; when there is no seizing (and therefore no binding) there is also no coming out (from bondage) . . . To be devoid of (specific) nature (無性) is to be devoid of (specific) character. To be devoid of specific character (自相空) is itself to be eternally devoid of (all determinate) essence. To be devoid of (all determinate) essence is itself to be identical (同) with *dharma-dhātu, tathatā, bhūtakōṭi* (i.e., the ultimate reality).[29] (495b)

*The Middle Way:* The Middle Way is the way that rises above the two extremes in its comprehension of the mundane nature of things; it restores to the mind the undistorted understanding of the conditioned, dynamic nature of all entities, and in that very act it restores also one's awareness of the real nature of oneself as well as of all the rest as the unconditioned *dharma*.

"To speak is to determine" (若說即是有相);[30] and yet, the determinate is not exclusively so. A collection of bare particulars is not even conceivable. To cling exclusively to the determinate is to deprive life of its richness and dynamism, while to cling exclusively to the indeterminate is to reduce it to the level of the determinate and divest it of all its meaning and relevance to the dependent and the contingent.

"*Salakṣaṇa* (determinate) is one extreme, *alakṣaṇa* (indeterminate) is another; to reject these two extremes and to fare on the Middle Way is the true nature of the Buddha." (492c)

# CHAPTER III

# IGNORANCE

## Section I

## NATURE AND FUNCTION OF IGNORANCE

*Nature of Ignorance:* We have already noted that even the ignorant has the sense of the real. But in him the sense of the ground of things has been minimized to the limit; and the exclusive absorption in the specific and the obvious is at its peak. He does not distinguish the mundane and the ultimate. He imagines the conditioned as unconditioned. But this imagination of his does not alter the true nature of things; and this unalterability is the only hope for man, although of this he may not be always aware.[1] The *Prajñāpāramitā-sūtras* emphasize the fundamental truth that the true nature of things ever remains the same, unaffected by our imaginative constructions, and convey this truth by the illustrations of illusion.[2] We may note here a few points about illusion and its cancellation.

(I) With the cancellation of error, the character that is revealed to be false comes to be realized as something that has been superimposed on things by virtue of our own imaginative construction. It was in our ignorance that we imagined it to belong to the thing itself as its true nature. Unreflective belief in the reality of the imagined is cancelled as false in the light of reflective criticism: if it were true, it should not have been negated. While truth is revealed by rational criticism, falsity is imagined by ignorance.

(II) To deny false beliefs is not to deny the things themselves, nor does this denial necessarily amount to the actual negation of the "appearance".[3] The denial is of our uncritical belief in regard to things.

What was once conceived to be real is now realized to be unreal.

(III) With the realization of the falsity of the imagined characters, again, what was once conceived to be objective to and constraining the self is now revealed to be truly not so; the once believed ultimacy of the line of division between the "self" and the "not-self," the subjective and the objective, is rejected as untrue.

Defining ignorance, the *Sūtra* says:

> All things are devoid of substantiality (諸法無所有); they so exist that they are not absolutely existent. This (non-substantiality of things which is their true nature) people do not know, and this is ignorance . . . (All things are non-substantial) and in regard to these the common people, owing to the power of ignorance and the thirst of passion (無明力渴愛故), give rise to perversions and imaginative constructions (妄見分別). This is called ignorance. These people get bound by the two dead-ends; they do not know and have not seen the truth of the non-substantiality of things and so they give rise to imaginative constructions in regard to all things and cling to them (憶想分別著). On account of their clinging in regard to things that are non-substantial, they yet give rise to (perverted) cognitions, (perverted) understandings and (perverted) views. . . . So they are considered as common people, comparable to children. Such people do not get beyond (life in the limited spheres, viz., the realm of desire etc.); . . . they do not dwell (in the noble way); for this reason they are called the common people, comparable to children; they are called also "the clinging" (著者). . . . Because they lack the power of skilfulness, they give rise to imaginative constructions and cling (to things).[4] (374a–b)

*Kinds of error:* (I) *Error in regard to the mundane truth:* The passage cited above shows that ignorance consists in misconstruction, mistaking things for what they are not. In the context of the mundane nature of things preeminent in this passage, the misconstruction consists in mistaking the relative as absolute, the fragmentary as complete. This is *viparyaya* (perversion):

The common people owing to the poison of ignorance give rise to perversion (作轉相) in regard to everything. In regard to the impermanent they give rise to the thought of permanence. (171c)

This power of ignorance to generate perversion is compared to the power of a dream that creates illusory objects which one fondly believes to be real while still in the dream, only to laugh at one's own foolish imagination when one awakes.[5]

The thoughts and emotions that are thus built on perversions are crooked ones distorted by wrong notions.

Owing to the afflictions *(kleśas)* headed by ignorance, people give rise to perversion and (thus to) crooked (thoughts and emotions) in regard to the true nature of things (於實相中轉異邪曲).[6] (298c)

The passage which we have quoted above as defining ignorance (374a–b) makes out that it is by clinging that one gets bound to dead-ends. It is the unseasoned emotion that clings at every step, seizes everything that it lights upon. When the mind lacks the comprehensive awareness of the complete nature of things it sticks fast to the fragmentary as the complete. This is owing to the thirst working in blindness. The mind in this state swings from extreme to extreme; in its swinging to extremes, it clings to dead-ends. Extremes or dead-ends are the partial seized as complete, the relative seized as absolute.

The same passage on ignorance shows that it is by the power of skilfulness that one keeps oneself free from clinging. Wisdom consists in giving up dogmatism by widening the understanding, by deepening the penetration. The right comprehension in regard to the mundane nature of things consists in realizing that all things are *śūnya,* relative and non-substantial, conditioned and changing. This comprehension lies at the root of the skilfulness of the wise.

(II) *Error in regard to the ultimate truth:* If this comprehension of things as conditioned and non-substantial be taken as itself the comprehension of their ultimate truth, this again would be a case of clinging. This is a case of imagining that the conditioned nature of things is itself their ultimate nature, that everything is absolutely conditioned. Now, this would mean an absolute division between the conditioned and the unconditioned, the divided and the undivided, the permanent and the impermanent, and in this case the undivided would not be the truly undivided, as it would be divided from the divided. The undivided would not be the *bhūtalakṣana,* the true nature of things, as it would be absolutely different and completely separate from them. This is an error not in respect to the mundane nature of things but in respect to their ultimate nature. This is also a case of the error of misplaced absoluteness, for, while the conditionedness of the conditioned and the consequent division between the conditioned and the unconditioned are alike conditioned, they are here mistaken to be absolute and ultimate.

This error which one may fall into in regard to the ultimate nature of things consists in the imagination of determination and division in reference to it, by which one misses its unconditioned, undivided nature. Thus the *Śāstra* says:

As ignorance and other *kleśas* enter (and hide the truth of) things one misses their true nature; as one misses their true nature one's understanding of them becomes crooked and not straight. When the wise banish ignorance then the truth of things shines once again. For example, the thick dark cloud covers up the nature of *ākāśa* which is ever pure by nature. But when the clouds are blown away then the purity of *ākāśa* shines forth once again. (334a)

The Buddhas by virtue of their power of great merit, wisdom and skill, remove the perversions in the hearts of the common people and enable them to comprehend the *svabhāva-śūnyatā* (the ultimate reality) of things. *Ākāśa* for example is ever pure by its very nature; dirt and darkness do not soil it (不著垢闇). But sometimes with the blowing of the wind the clouds screen it. The common people simply say that *ākāśa* has become impure. But when the fierce wind blows once again and removes the clouds, people would say that *ākāśa* has become pure. But in truth *ākāśa* neither became dirty nor clean. Just in the same way do the Buddhas, by the fierce wind of their teachings of the *dharma*, blow away (from the minds of the common people) the screen of the clouds of perversion enabling them to get (back to) the (original) purity. But in truth, the ultimate nature of things itself neither (becomes) impure nor clean.[7] (698b)

*Error is not devoid of object:* It is to be noted that whether it is at the "mundane" level or at the "transmundane" level error is not devoid of object. While at the mundane level the object of error is the conditioned, changing, entity, the error in regard to the ultimate truth has for its object the unconditioned reality itself. While in the one case the error consists in the imagination of unconditionedness and substantiality in regard to the conditioned and non-substantial, in the other case it consists in the imagination of division and determination in regard to that which is undivided and indeterminate. The cancellation of error in the one case means the revelation of the conditioned and changing nature of things, and the cancellation of error in the other case means the revelation of the ultimate reality as the undivided being. And under all circumstances the root form of error still stands as the error of misplaced absoluteness, which always functions by way of seizing, clinging.

The *Śāstra* points out that it is not true that at any time cognition happens without an object. Thus it says:

If it is said that things are seen to be existent (purely) out of perversion (without any objective basis), then, where one sees a single person why does one not see two or three persons instead? For (is it not the contention here that) cognition happens without any object and that everything is seen purely out of perversion? (171c)

Even in a dream cognition is not devoid of an object, although it cannot be taken as true beyond the state of the dream. Those who argue that dream objects are as real as the objects of waking experience commit the same error as those who deny the object altogether, holding it to be totally non-existent. Both commit alike the error of clinging to dead-ends.

Posing the question whether it is not true that even in a dream there is cognition only when the mind confronts the proper object and how, in that case, it could be that the dream objects are unreal, the *Śāstra* proceeds to say that although in a dream we do see many things, still, they are not unconditionally true. For, the unconditionally true is undeniable, while the dream objects are denied beyond the state of dream, as they are private and inconsistent with the objects of normal, waking experience which is open to all. Thus the *Śāstra* says:

(In dreams) we see things that (are inconsistent with the things of waking experience and which therefore) should not be seen (as true) (不應見而見). In a dream (for example) one sees a man with horns on his head. Sometimes one sees in a dream that the human body flies in the sky. Actually, no man has horns on his head nor can the human body fly in the sky. Therefore (the objects seen in the dream) are not true.

But surely, says the inquirer, there is the human head and surely there are the horns although in different places. On account of the confusion in the mind (以心惑故) one just sees that the human head has horns. Again, surely, there is the sky and there are the things that fly, and simply out of confusion, one sees that one's body itself flies in the sky. It cannot be that the objects seen in the dream are false (非無實也). (For, is it not the very objects which we see in waking experience that constitute the objects in dream?)[8] (103c)

There is no doubt, says the *Śāstra,* that there is the human head and there are also horns; still, that the human head bears horns is false. But the inquirer would urge:

The world is wide and the fruits of the deeds done by men in their former lives are various. It may be that in some other country the human head bears horns; It may be that there men have only one hand and one leg and are only one foot high, or they may even be nine feet high. What is there to wonder if a man has horns on his head?

Now, if people in other countries have horns on their head, let them have; but in a dream we see that in this very country, the very person whom we know has horns on his head, and this cannot be true. Again, if one would see in a dream the end of space, the end of the regions, the end of time, how can this be true? Where is the place where there is no space, no region, no time? Therefore it is said that in a dream we see things as existent which are actually non-existent. (103c–104a)

In a dream we do experience objects, but they hold only there; they have no truth beyond that state. And when we judge that in a dream we experience as existent the things that are truly non-existent we are judging the dream-state from the standpoint of the waking state. But even in a dream, cognition is not without an object.

As to your question as to how there can be cognition even when there are no objects, now, although, (in truth), there are not in dream the five kinds of sense objects (as substantial entities), still, out of one's own thought (aided by) memory, (自思惟念力轉故) there arise (the diverse kinds of) things (that serve) as objects (法緣生). For example, some one might say men have two heads; by hearing these words, there arises (in some mind) the thought (that men really may have two heads). That in a dream one sees as existent things that are really nonexistent is also like this. The same is the case with all things. Although all things are devoid of reality, all the same, (they are objects of experience), they are heard and seen and known. (104a)

The things that are illustrated as illusory are indeed objects of experience, but they are not real and self-existent; there arises the sense of reality in regard to them only in the mind of the uncritical, who, in accepting these things as real and self-existent, allow themselves to be bound by them; but the wise, who have realized the illusoriness of these things stand beyond them, for they know the true nature of these.

(When for example) the ignorant (hear an echo) they would say that (inside the cave there is actually) a person making the sound. But the wise understand within themselves that this sound which is an echo is not produced by any person (inside the cave). The sound that emerges from the cave arises only on account of the contact (of the first sound with the cave) and only thus derives its name, echo. The echo is *śūnya,* devoid of substance, and yet it can deceive the ears (of the hearers). (103a)

Again, when a child sees an image in the mirror, it feels delighted at heart, and passionately seeks to seize it. When the image disappears, it breaks the mirror to pieces (out of rage), but attempts to seize (the image once again). The elders laugh at this. Now, this is just the case with (the ignorant, who) having lost the pleasaure (of the five senses), seek it once again. And these are laughed at by the wise who have realized the Way. (104c)

*The wise and the ignorant:* While the thing is one and the same, our attitude in regard to it differs according to the way we understand it. No one can alter the true nature of things, but everyone can improve his own conception of them. This is the idea that is sought to be set forth in the several illustrations of illusion.

The sharp in understanding grasp (without difficulty) this (central) idea of the Buddha's teachings, but those whose power of grasping is blunt give rise to clinging at every step. They cling to words and names. If they hear of *śūnyatā,* to this they cling. If they hear that *śūnyatā* is also *śūnya* even to this they cling. If they hear that all things in their ultimate nature are themselves the peace, (the Nirvāṇa), where the entire course of words stops, even there they cling. As their own mind is impure so, even the noble truths that they hear they mistake, seizing them in an impure way. When a person with his eyes covered with a coloured screen perceives the pure crystal, the *sphaṭika,* even there he perceives only the screen of his own eyes; (in his ignorance he imputes the colour of the screen to the crystal itself and) he just says that the crystal is itself impure. (722c–723a)

In reference to the elements (like the sense, the object and the contact of sense with object that arise by way of conditioned origination) one gives rise to all kinds of *kleśas* and sinful deeds as a result of one's perverse thoughts. But in regard to these very elements one who has the right thought (and right attitude) gives rise to elements of merit (that are of help to him in his way-faring).[9] (364c)

Difference, distinction, is essential to the mundane nature of things, where everything is a specific, determinate entity. The course of the world is an organic unity of the distinct and the unique. And yet if one clings to the determinate as itself the ultimate, then, neither the mundane nature nor the ultimate nature of things can be rightly conceived; one then fails to realize the good that the world is capable of yielding. If one clings to the divided, the determinate, as itself ultimate then one cannot enhance one's potency for merit.

But the bodhisattva, faring in the ultimate reality, viz., the undivided *dharma,* ever increases his potency for good from the very beginning up to the end of his wayfaring. There is no mixture of error (in his potency for merit, and so it stands invincible). (656c)

To repeat the central idea in the philosophy of Nāgārjuna, with which his works are replete:

When one fares by seizing, by clinging, then (in one's case) the world would be a (mass of) perversion; but when one fares free from seizing, free from clinging, then (the world itself) is Nirvāṇa.[9a] (644c)

When the Buddha specifies things and their relations, when He speaks of the conditioned entities and their ways of working, He is not violating the ultimate nature of things, for He is aware of them as conditioned and specific and He does not mistake their determinate nature itself to be their ultimate nature. Those who lack the sense of the beyond cling to the determinate while the wise have no confusion about things.[10]

*Section II*

## THE SENSE OF "I" AND THE FALSE SENSE OF SELF

*The rise of the sense of "I":* The sense of "I"[11] implying by contrast the sense of "not-I" naturally belongs to the world of the determinate. But the uniqueness of self-consciousness is that there is immanent in it the awareness of the unconditioned reality as its ultimate nature. The self-conscious intellect, having differentiated the undifferenced, identifies itself with the specific complex entity, the body-mind. And in this identification, the intellect, owing to the operation of ignorance, wrongly transfers its sense of unconditionedness which is its ultimate nature to itself in its mundane nature. The sense of self is due to self-conscious intellection, but the falsity in the false sense of self is due to ignorance. The sense of self or the sense of "I", according to the *Śāstra,* is the reflection of the unconditioned reality in the conditioned self-conscious intellect; it is the sense of the real in man.

The moon is really in the sky, but the image appears in the water (月實在虛空中影現於水). The moon of the universal reality is in the sky of *tathatā, dharma-dhātu, bhūtakoṭi,* while (its reflection, the sense of) "I" and "mine," appears in the water of the minds of men and gods.[12] (102b)

The sense of "I" in its true form is the sense of the real immanent in man; the true import, the ultimate, original meaning of "I" is self-being, unconditionedness. But the mind, the self-conscious intellect, under the influence of ignorance, comes to apply wrongly this sense of unconditionedness to itself in its mundane, i.e., conditioned nature, as well as to that with which it identifies itself and through that to all things that it lights upon.

A shadow appears only when there is a bright light; when there is no light there is no shadow. Similarly, when the *kleśas,* afflictions, and the *samyojanas,* factors of bondage, (products of ignorance) obstruct the light of *samyagdṛṣṭi* (or *prajñā),* then there arise the shadow of "I" and the shadow of all other things. (104a)

Moreover, it is in a still sheet of water that the image of the moon becomes visible. It is not visible in disturbed water. In the heart that is stupefied by ignorance, there become visible the sense of ego, the sense of pride and the consequent factors of bondage. But, when the water of the heart is beaten and disturbed by the staff of true wisdom, then the ego image (and the pride image) do not appear. (102b)

It is under ignorance that one misses the moon and sees only the image, and mistakes the image itself for the real moon. It is then that the sense of "I" comes to be applied exclusively to the object with which the self, viz., the self-conscious intellect has identified itself. And with this identification of the intellect with the specific object, the ultimate meaning of self, viz., self-being, underivedness, comes to be applied, only wrongly, to this very object, and thus the derived comes to be mistaken for the underived. The misapplication of this sense of unconditionedness then comes to be extended to everything that the differentiating intellect alights upon; every particular individual entity comes to be endowed with underivedness and substantiality, of which it is actually devoid. And thus there arises the clinging in regard to everything.[13]

This identification of the self-conscious intellect with the specific, conditioned, complex entity as one's own self would lead one to distinguishing all else as what is external to oneself in contrast to this specific entity which by virtue of its having been identified with the self-conscious principle, itself comes to be considered as internal. Thus there arise the distinctions of self and other, internal and external. While these distinctions belong to the very essence of the mundane nature of things, and constitute the very form in which the entire mundane existence appears, they are turned into falsity when they are treated not as relative distinctions but as absolute divisions. On the basis of this notion of the absolute exclusiveness of self, there proceeds the other tendency of the principle of intellection, viz., the tendency to unify but now in terms of "I" and that which "belongs to me," the "mine," i.e., in terms of possession. Thus there arise greed and anger, and the sinful deeds prompted by them.

From the sense of "I" there arises the sense of "mine." With the rise of the sense of "I" and the sense of "mine," there arises the sense of greed in regard to things that benefit the self, and there arises the sense of anger in regard to things that thwart (the interest of the self). Bonds of passions such as these arise not out of wisdom but out of madness and perversion. Therefore they are called (the products of) stupidity. These three poisons of greed etc. are the root of all *kleśas*.[14] (286c)

The false sense of "I" and the consequent sense of possession arise not only in regard to the entire individual entity, the body-mind complex as a whole, but they arise also in regard to each of the elements within the complex entity, i.e., in regard to each of the five *skandhas*.

Owing to the power of the false sense of self, one sees the self in four ways, viz., that "*rūpa* is I," "*rūpa* is mine," "in me there is *rūpa*" and "in *rupa* there is myself." (Similar kinds of views arise even in regard to the other four *skandhas)*. Thus there are altogether twenty kinds of false sense of self. When one realizes the awakening to true wisdom, then one understands the falsity of these.[15] (103c)

*Kinds of self-reference: the sense of "I" and the false sense of self:* It is in this self-conscious intellection that the crux of individuality lies. But the self-conscious intellection is not itself to be identified with the wrong notion of individuality. It becomes the wrong notion when it functions under ignorance. Functioning under the light of knowledge it would be the unerring sense of self. The sense of "I" is at cross roads, it has a double reference. It shares at once two orders of being, the conditioned and the unconditioned; it is at once a universalizing as well as a particularizing tendency. It can work as much for liberation as for bondage; it can work non-clingingly as well as by clinging. What makes the difference is the continuation or the extinction of the perverting force of ignorance. *Satkāyadṛṣṭi* is perversion at its root. This is to be distinguished from the unerring sense of self.[16]

The sense of "I" is not in itself false, although it belongs to the world of the determinate. As a mundane truth it refers to the complex of personality. Self-reference as a reference to the real self, i.e., the real nature of one's being, is only one side of the sense of " I." For, it is at the same time a reference to the divided, relative entity with which the being identifies itself as "I," and this entity, thus becomes the "self" of the being; the life of the being consists in the life of this entity with which it has identified itself. From the standpoint of this specific entity, the body-mind complex, the being differentiates itself from all the rest as the not-self. This is the ordinary empirical self. It serves to analyze and differentiate things as well as to reunify them from the standpoint of a specific center of experience as its own. This is the very way in which one brings forth one's hidden potencies to manifestation; appropriation of experience through the sense of "I" is what makes events in life meaningful. The entire world, the common man as well as the bodhisattva, even the Buddha, works through the sense of "I." Everyone has his own self (different from the self of others) in which he is interested and it is for the growth and fulfilment of this self of his that everyone works. And the sense of "I" is not rigidly fixed in respect to its objects, either in kind or in extent. In extent, it may vary from this specific individual, this body-mind complex, which is its self, to all individuals, the entire world. Again, in kind, it may vary from the divided, relative changing entity, to the undivided, absolute being, the real self.

In respect to the manner of its working, again, as a reference to the specific determinate entity, the body-mind complex as "I," the sense of self admits of different kinds. Firstly, there is the sense of self with the understanding in regard to the specific empirical self as neither exclusive of other selves nor anything ultimate and absolute; this is the unerring sense of "I," which comes with mature self-consicousness in which one is not blind to the meaning of the sense of the beyond, and therefore in which there is not the clinging to the determinate self either as absolutely determinate and therefore totally different from the undivided being or as itself an eternal independent substance. The wise use the sense of self and live their individual lives but ever keeping free from the error of clinging.

Secondly, one may understand one's individual self as divided and therefore determinate and yet may entertain the notion that the divided is absolutely so, and therefore completely divided from the undivided. This is to err in regard to its ultimate nature, for this would amount to carrying over transferring the division to the unconditioned reality; this is to confuse the mundane with the ultimate. This is to miss the comprehension of the truly undivided. This is, as it was seen above, the error in regard to the ultimate truth.

Thirdly, one's individual self, the ordinary object of the notion of "I," the body-mind complex, may be conceived as itself independent and ultimate; of the not "I" which is split, again, into many different entities each may again be conceived to be equally independent and ultimate. This is to err not only in regard to the ultimate nature of things, but even in regard to their mundane nature. For this is an imagination of ultimacy in regard to that which is in fact determinate. This is the error of misplaced absoluteness carried to its completion.

Strictly it is the last that is the complete form of *satkāya-dṛṣṭi,* the false sense of self, the error which is the root of all errors. It is a *dṛṣṭi* (view) in which the complex, conditioned entity *(kāya)* is imagined to be absolute and unconditioned *(sat)* and in which this imagination is extended to everything that the differentiating intellect seizes hold of. The whole of experience is first split into "I" and "not-I" and the "not-I" again is split into many different objects. First there is the imagination of absolute exclusiveness in regard to the "I," i.e., the entity that constitutes the object of the notion of "I," and then the same notion of absolute exclusiveness is imagined in regard to every other thing. Thus each of the divided entities is itself imagined to be absolute and exclusive of all the rest. It is this imagination of absoluteness and exclusiveness in regard to the things which are in truth determinate and relative that lies at the root of all error and evil. This imagination is precisely the way in which ignorance works. In respect to the mundane truth, where all things are *nāma* and *lakṣaṇa,* there is the error of imagining that everything is independent and absolute; in reference to the ultimate truth, which is the undivided being, the real nature of all things, there is the error of entertaining the notion of division and determination. This is the same thing as imagining, "I shall realize Nirvāṇa, Nirvāṇa shall be mine." For, here there is the entertaining of the notion that the "I" is one thing and Nirvāṇa is another. To take this notion seriously is to split the undivided being into "I" and "Nirvāṇa," into the realizer and the realized, subject and object. Even here one falls short of the truly undivided.

*The unerring sense of "I":* The wise use the sense of "I" unerringly, non-clingingly, i.e., not entertaining the notion of a real ego as a separate I-substance, nor clinging to the conditioned complex entity, the body-mind as itself ultimate.

In regard to this non-clinging use of "I," the *Śāstra* says:

Although the disciples of the Buddha understand (the truth in the teaching of) "no I," still, they speak in terms of "I" (and "mine") following the mundane way (隨俗法說我); it is not that they entertain the notion of a real I-substance (非實我也). This is like buying the copper coins for the gold ones; no one laughs at it for that should be the very way of business. The use of "I" is also like this. Even in regard to the things that are really devoid of self-hood, the "I" is still used; this is in line with the way of the world. There should be no difficulty here. (64a)

Further, the course of talk in the world springs from three roots: perversion (邪見), pride (慢) and names (or concepts) (名字). Of these, (the first) two are impure and (the last) one is pure. The common man combines in his discourse (and in all his mundane activities) all these three roots. The beginner in the way combines two kinds, viz., pride and names while the sages have only one kind, viz., names (or concepts). Although at heart (well established in) the truth of things and not violating it, they yet carry on their discourse by the use of names or concepts in keeping with the mundane truth. They do this with the intention of removing the perversion prevalent in the world, and they do not quarrel. So they abandon the two roots of worldly discourse that are impure and use only the one that is pure. The Buddha and His disciples use the sense of "I" in keeping with the ways of the world. And there is nothing wrong in it. (64a–b)

Names or concepts as well as their root, the principle of self-consciousness, are in themselves pure; they can be either rightly used or misused.[17] The root of our misuse lies in our ignorance. The basic error is to cling to the determinate as itself absolute. This holds good as much in the case of the affirmation of "I" as in its negation. The wrong affirmation of "I" is its absolute affirmation, the affirmation that the "I" as the principle of individuality, as the specific centre of personality is absolute and unconditioned. The wrong denial of "I" is its total denial, its denial even as a mundane truth, as a derived name, as a relative concept. A non-clinging affirmation of individuality is the one in which it is not affirmed as absolute but recognized to be relative and a non-clinging denial of "I" is the one in which the sense of "I" is recognized as a derived name, a relative concept, but is denied to be ultimate and underived. The *Śāstra* says that even in their teaching of no "I" and "mine" (the Buddha and) His disciples do not cling to this determination of no "I."

To him who would cling to the determination of no "I" (and "mine"), and would say that this alone is true and the rest is false, one should indeed object: "According to you, in the true nature of things, there is no I, and so how can you say, 'I have heard?' " But now, actually, while the Buddha and His disciples teach that all things are *śūnya, akiñcana,* (even) in regard to this they remain non-clinging at heart. They do not cling even in regard to the universal truth of things, how much less to the things that are devoid of self-hood. Therefore, there should be no difficulty of this kind, viz., as to how they can speak in terms of "I" (and "mine").[18] (64b)

When the sense of "I" refers to the mundane nature of the individual, i.e., the empirical self, it would be false if it should mean that the individual is a real eternal substance; it is an unerring sense, if it is recognized that the individual is *śūnya,* essentially conditioned and derivedly named. If one keeps this truth in mind, then there is no difficulty in understanding how the Buddha has sometimes taught of self and sometimes of no self. Thus the *Śāstra* says:

To him who understands the meaning in the teaching of the Buddha and grasps the truth of derived name, He has taught that there is "I"; but to one who does not understand the meaning in the teachings of the Buddha and does not grasp the truth of the derived name, He has taught, there is no "I."[19] (253c)

The teaching of no "I" is of two kinds: the one in which there is the seizing of the determination of "no I," clinging to the denial of "I," and the other is the denial of "I" while refraining from seizing "no I" and keeping free from (turning it into a *dṛṣṭi* by) clinging to it. (In the latter case) one naturally gives up (all clinging). The first kind of no "I" is an extreme, (a case of exclusiveness) while the second one is the Middle Doctrine (the non-exclusive way). (253c)

*Section III*

## THE FALSE SENSE OF SELF

*The false sense of self as the root of afflictions and dṛṣtis: Tṛṣṇā* as the origin of *kleśa* stands for thirst, passion, as the root of seizing and clinging. *Kleśa* is the painful state of emotional conflict which results from the failure to fulfil the thirst, from the disparity between the expected and the realized. Ignorance, functioning again through *tṛṣṇā,* gives rise to *dṛṣti,* which is to seize the specific concepts and the conceptual systems that embody them as themselves absolute and limitless. This is dogmatism, claiming absoluteness for the relative, completeness for the fragmentary. This is perversion. Both *kleśa* and *dṛṣti* have their origin in the false sense of self, the root-error.

The common people, out of ignorance and perversion, and (the consequent) seizing of the determinate (as ultimate) give rise to all kinds of *kleśas* viz., *tṛṣṇā,* etc.; from these in turn there arise the different kinds of deeds, leading to different kinds of bodily existence and the experiencing of different kinds of pain and pleasure. For example, the silkworm emits silk from within itself and becomes caught within it, and in consequence suffers the pain of being boiled and burned. (This is just the case with the ignorant). But the wise with the power of their pure wisdom analyze and distinguish everything, root and branch, (and find that) all things are *śūnya* (non-substantial). In order to help all people, they speak to everyone about the nature of the objects of their clinging, viz., the five *skandhas* etc. They tell them: "You have yourselves given rise to all this simply out of your ignorance, and having yourselves given rise to them you yourselves cling to them (自作自著).[20] (294b)

*The false sense of self as the root of afflictions:* Ignorance working through the false sense of self is thus at the root of our being limited to the rounds of birth and death, and thus at the root of all our hankering and suffering.

Ignorance is the root (of all *kleśas).*[21] (696b)

Out of perversion people do deeds that bind them to a limited life. . . . Of all that they do, passion, greed, is the root. Simply being shrouded by passion, they give rise to the clinging mind. (611c)

Craving is the root of clinging. (200a)

People really do not know that essentially things are non-substantial. Therefore, they follow their (perverse) thoughts, seize the characters of things and give rise to clinging (隨心取相生著). From clinging there arises attachment *(rāga)* (以著故染). Due to attachment they pursue the five kinds of the objects of desire. Due to this pursuing of the objects of desire they become shrouded by greed. Due to greed there arise jealousy, anger and quarrel. From anger there arise sinful deeds. But they do not have any knowledge about this course of things. Therefore, at the end of their life, they follow their deeds which function as the conditions for their birth in another sphere for the next span of life.

Again they continue to do deeds that prepare for them lives of birth and death. Thus they revolve for ever in the six states of existence (thus making the cycle) that knows no end.[22] (720a)

If one would seek to become free from suffering, he should then first put an end to *tṛṣṇā*; when *tṛṣṇā* has been ended, suffering will just become extinct. (720b)

The root of suffering is clinging, the root of clinging is craving, and the root of craving is ignorance.

*The false sense of self as the root of dṛṣṭis:* In regard to understanding, ignorance working through the false sense of self generates in us the belief of limitlessness in regard to the specific concepts or determinate conceptual systems. We select from out of the presented only the aspects of our interest and neglect the rest; to the rest that is neglected we become first indifferent and then blind; in our blindness, we claim completeness for the aspects that we have selected. We seize them as absolute, we cling to them as the complete truth, we become dogmatic. The dogmatic views that thus develop can all be traced back to their root, viz., the tendency to seize the conditioned as unconditioned, which is the error of misplaced absoluteness. This error consisting in seizing hold of aspects of things as self-complete and absolute, swings from extreme to extreme, from the extreme of being to the extreme of non-being, from the extreme of (complete) self-possessedness of things to the extreme of absolute devoidness of selfhood. The extremes are completely exclusive of each other: either wholly being or wholly non-being, either wholly self-possessed or wholly devoid of selfhood. While the intellectual analysis of the presented content into its different aspects is conducive to and necessary for a comprehensive understanding, analysis is miscarried if the fragmentary is mistaken for the complete, the relative is mistaken for the absolute. Existence and non-existence, when held as absolute characters of things, become extremes.

If one would (exclusively) see the arising and enduring of things, then that would (result in) the wrong view of the absolute existence of things.

Again, if one would (exclusively) see the decaying and perishing of things, then that would (result in) the wrong view of negativism. People in the three realms mostly cling to these two extremes. But both these are perversions and not true. If things are absolutely existent then they should never become non-existent. Formerly it was there (absolutely) and now it is not there (absolutely), to hold this view is to fall into negativism. To take one's stand on negativism is not right.[23] (171a)

While contrast or polarity is an indispensable and essential mundane truth, it is turned into falsity when the determinate is seized as absolute. Thus we find the *Śāstra* giving accounts of several kinds of extremes which are really relative distinctions turned into absolute divisions.

Eternal is one extreme, evanescent is another. Abandoning these two extremes to fare on the Middle Way, this is *prajñāpāramitā*. Similarly permanence and impermanence, pain and pleasure, non-substantial and substantial, self and not-self etc. (also become extremes when exclusively embraced). Materiality is one extreme, immateriality is another. Visibility is one extreme, invisibility is another; resisting is one extreme, non-resisting is another; composite is one extreme, incomposite is another; defiled is one extreme, undefiled is another; mundane is one extreme, transmundane is another. The same is the case with all forms of duality. (All these could be turned into extremes when exclusively embraced). Ignorance is one extreme, extinction of ignorance is another; birth and death is one extreme, cessation of birth and death is another; that all things are existent is one extreme, that all things are non-existent are another. Abandoning these two extremes to fare on the Middle Way, this is *prajñāpāramitā*. Bodhisattva is one extreme, the six *pāramitās* is another; the Buddha is one extreme, the *bodhi* is another. Abandoning these two extremes to fare on the Middle Way, this is *prajñāpāramitā*. To put the matter briefly, the six internal senses are one extreme, the six external objects are another; abandoning these two extremes to fare on the Middle Way, this is *prajñāpāramitā*. That this is *prajñāpāramitā* is one extreme; that this is not *prajñāpāramitā* is another extreme; to abandon these two extremes and to fare on the Middle Way, this is *prajñāpāramitā.* (370a–b)

The false sense of self gives rise to the extremes of eternalism and negativism and breeds through them all the other wrong views concerning the world and the individual. They have all as their essential nature the seizing of the determinate as ultimate, the clinging to the fragmentary as complete. The conceptions that are relative and complementary become in that way absolute and exclusive. The conflict of these absolute and exclusive views thus leads one to denying or accepting uncritically all the contending views, ending in a superficial eclecticism, an external combination rather than inner harmonization of conflicting views, or in scepticism and agnosticism. Speaking of the false sense of self as the root of all these views, the *Śāstra* says:

Although each view has its own distinctness, the false sense of self is the root (of all other false views). People, out of ignorance, give rise to the false sense of self in reference to the five *skandhas* which are *śūnya.* With the false sense of self arising, (influenced by it), some say that when this body dies the (person) moves on while others say that he does not move. The view that a person moves on (to another body) would result in *eternalism,* and the view that the person does not move on would result in *negativism.* Holding negativism, if one would (blindly) indulge in the pleasures of the present life, cling to the five kinds of objects of desire, and take the sinful deeds as themselves the best, then there results the false view of *dṛṣṭi-parāmarśa.* On the contrary, if one would hold to eternalism, renounce the home life and cultivate the way to ultimate liberation (from bodily existence), accept moral precepts and indulge in (self-torture and) painful penances, then there would result the false view of *śīlavrata-parāmarśa.* Sometimes, seeing that eternalism and negativism are both wrong, one would hold the view that things just happen without any cause or condition and that is *mithyā-dṛṣṭi.* Dwelling in these five kinds of views, (one would give rise to) further false views, viz., that the world is eternal or evanescent, that the world had an end in the past or it will have an end in the future etc., and in this way there arise the remaining fifty-seven views. Therefore it is said that *satkāya-dṛṣṭi* comprehends all the sixty-two kinds of *dṛṣṭis*.[24] (607b)

If one avoids these extremes of absolute existence and absolute non-existence, one will realize the Middle Way, the true view of the nature of things—and then one will see things as the bodhisattva or the Buddha sees them; then one will not cling either to the particular, the specific or to the universal, the indeterminate.

The Buddha cancels (遮) the two extremes and teaches the Middle Way, viz., the way of neither duality nor non-duality; "duality" here means the particular, unique natures of all things (conceived exclusively), and "non-duality" means the one (universal) nature of *śūnyatā* (again conceived exclusively). Here by means of *śūnyatā* is denied (the false sense) that every thing is (absolutely) unique and separate. When this cancellation is accomplished, even the sense of non-duality is given up (lest it might itself be exclusively embraced). (727a)

*CHAPTER IV*

# IGNORANCE AND KNOWLEDGE

*Section I*

## IGNORANCE AND KNOWLEDGE

*Ignorance is not ultimate:* If ignorance were ultimate, it could never be extinguished. But if it were a complete non-entity, totally non-existent, then it would be a mere name devoid of reference; and the giving up of it would be devoid of meaning.[1] Besides, then, it would not have any nature or function of its own.

Speaking of the nature of ignorance, the *Śāstra* quotes a *Sūtra,*[2] in which the Buddha tells a *therī* that ignorance is not an entity (with an independent nature of its own) residing either inside or outside; it does not have a coming nor going, neither a birth nor an extinction, for there is not anywhere any definite entity with an ultimate nature of its own called ignorance. The *therī* asks the Buddha as to how, in that case, it could be said that "the *saṃskāras* (the formative forces in the life of the individual), depend on ignorance," and that "the entire mass of suffering *(duḥkha)* thus comes into existence." How can there be a tree without any root? The Buddha replies that although all things are in truth devoid of substantiality, because the common people have not heard and have not known this true nature of things, they give rise to all kinds of *kleśas* in regard to these, and the *kleśas* give rise to deeds and the deeds, to birth in the next span of life; but in these there is no element that is really, in its own right, ineradicably, of the nature of producing *kleśa* (無有實作煩惱). This is like the magician producing the things of magic. The magically created things cannot be said to be either inside or outside or anywhere. There is not a single entity that is magically created, of which it could be said that it has a real being. All the same the magically created things are undoubtedly objects of experience; and they do indeed produce the various feelings of jealousy, pleasure, etc. But how could it be that although they do not have any real being, they are all the same capable of functioning as objects of experience and capable of giving rise to pleasure, etc.? The *therī* tells the Buddha:

Such is the very nature of magical creation (是幻相爾). Although devoid of (any real) being at root, they are yet objects of sight and objects of hearing. (102a)

The Buddha adds:

Such is the nature of ignorance too. Although, of it, it cannot be (said) that it is inside or outside, . . . although it is devoid of any ultimate nature of its own (亦無實性), . . . still, ignorance does indeed function as the condition for the birth of the *saṃskāras* . . . When the magical power of creation ceases, the magically created objects also come to an end; (even so) when ignorance comes to an end, (the products of ignorance), the *saṃskāras* (etc.), also come to an end.[3] (102a)

Ignorance is indeed a power that creates objects of experience; it has its nature and function; but it cannot be held on that account to be an ultimate entity. Ignorance is not wholly determinable as either existing or not existing; it shares in this respect the nature of all mundane entities, itself being in fact "the root of all things as the common people conceive them." But there is a very important difference between the mundane entities and ignorance which is the root of misconstruction. While ignorance, when realized as ignorance, has itself totally disappeared, the mundane entities, even after being realized as unreal may continue to be experienced. This is to say that the conditioned nature of things which is their mundane nature need not itself be bound up with ignorance. The mistaking of the conditioned as itself the unconditioned pertains not to the continuation or the extinction of the objects of experience, but to one's belief in regard to their reality or unreality. It is not that even with the realization of the ultimate truth the mundane things necessarily disappear; they continue to appear but the wise do not entertain the notion of ultimacy in regard to them, nor do they entertain the notion of any ultimate division between the determinate and the absolute.

*The ultimate nature of ignorance:* The sense of the real is our ground for cancelling illusion; it is made more vivid by the revelation of the falsity of our beliefs. And it is only in the case of one who is aware of ignorance that a critique of ignorance has sense. It is intended to trace illusion to its root, in order to root it out completely. But in the case of one who is already wholly beyond ignorance it has no use. Again, if ignorance as concealment and misconstruction were ultimate, then it would be ineradicable; but in that case there would not be any awareness of ignorance at all. That there is such an awareness and that ignorance is experienced to have once functioned and then become extinct in some cases is the only ground for man's cultivation in the path of knowledge. The wise institute devices whereby they bring the meaning of certain cases of disillusionment to bear upon the entire network of ignorance in which the common people are caught. They thus enliven in them the sense of the real, reveal to them its true meaning and help them to realize the true nature of things.[4]

The extinction of ignorance does not leave us in a blank; it is not an act separate from the arising of knowledge. The two are simultaneous; they are two different sides of the same act, two phases of one principle. The *Śāstra* observes that in their ultimate nature there is no difference between ignorance and knowledge, even as there is no difference in the ultimate truth between the world of the determinate and Nirvāṇa, the unconditioned reality.

When the myriad streams (flowing in myriad different places), each with its own colour, its own taste, enter the great ocean, they blend and become of one taste and derive one name. In the same way, stupidity and wisdom enter *prajñāpāramitā* and blend and become of one essence (and then) there would be no difference between them. Again, when the five colours approach Mt. Sumeru, they automatically lose their own colours and all blend into the one golden hue. In the same way, when all things internal and external enter *prajñāpāramitā,* they blend and become of one essence. Why is it so?

Because *prajñāpāramitā* is by nature completely pure.

Moreover, the real nature of stupidity is itself *prajñā.* But if one would mistake and cling to this *prajñā,* then this itself would be stupidity. Thus, (in truth), what difference is there between stupidity and wisdom?

When one first enters the Way of the Buddha, then there is the distinction that this is stupidity and this is wisdom. But later, when one's penetration gradually becomes deep, then, (at last), there would be no difference between stupidity and wisdom. (321a–b)

This is to deny not the presence of ignorance but its ultimacy. With the correction of error the wrong notion does not persist; ignorance does not coexist with knowledge in regard to the same thing in the same mind.[5] When the bodhisattva, with the intention of putting an end to ignorance, seeks to know its true nature (體), then:

Ignorance would just become knowledge itself (即時是明) (for it is then seen to be in its ultimate nature) the universal reality *(bhūtalakṣaṇa),* the *bhūtakoṭi,* itself. (697a)

Even of the products of ignorance, the true nature is purity, which is another name for the ultimate reality, the undivided being. So the *Sūtra* says:

(In its ultimate nature) ignorance is purity itself; and so even the *saṃskāras* (etc., the products of ignorance) are (in their ultimate nature) purity itself.[6] (505b)

Commenting on this, the *Śāstra* says that the Buddha is speaking here about the ultimate nature of the three elements of poison, which as lewdness etc., owe their being to ignorance, while in their ultimate nature they are purity itself (三毒實性清淨).[7]

This holds good even of the mind, the self-conscious principle of intellection, the centre of personality, as well as of all that it gives rise to.

In the ultimate truth, even mind and mental elements cannot be obtained, how much less the further distinction of the mind with passion or the mind devoid of passion? (543b)

The fact that in its ultimate nature ignorance is itself *prajñā* has an important bearing on the nature of knowledge. While a total ignorance of ignorance is impossible, a complete knowledge of knowledge is not only possible but essential. This is the same as saying that while denial of ignorance is possible, knowledge knows no denial. While extinction could be significantly spoken of in respect to ignorance, this is not the case with knowledge; for the ultimate principle of knowledge knows no end, although the particular acts of knowing arise and perish. *Prajñā* as the ultimate principle of knowledge is not itself anything conditioned. When one speaks of the rise of wisdom, strictly, from the standpoint of the ultimate *prajñā,* it is to the extinction of ignorance that one refers. Non-ultimacy of *avidyā* is the sufficient ground for one's endeavour to remove it.

*Section II*

## KINDS OF KNOWLEDGE

*Prajñā as reality and prajñā as knowledge: Prajñā* as knowledge is to be distinguished from *prajñā* as reality. *Prajñā* as reality is the unconditioned *dharma,* the undivided being, the unnameable that is yet spoken through names.

*Prajñāpāramitā* is the real nature of all things, the undeniable, indestructible *dharma.* Whether there is the Buddha or there is not the Buddha, this real nature of things eternally is. This eternal nature of things *(dharma-sthāna)* is not any thing made by the Buddha (or any one else).[8] (370a)

*Prajñā* is the ultimately real nature of the divided and determinate. The ultimate reality is called *prajñā,* the basic principle of knowledge, only by imposing a name and that, in the mundane truth, on the plane of the relative, i.e., when it is contrasted with the objects and systems of objects that arise and perish. In the ultimate truth it is the reality in which there is not even the distinction of knowledge and reality, knowing and being, or even of knowledge and ignorance. It is the real which is the ultimate end of all our seeking. *Prajñā* as reality pertains to the later part of the present work. It is with *prajñā* as knowledge that the present part is concerned.

*Prajñā as the ultimate principle of knowledge and prajñā as the act of knowing: Prajñā* as knowledge is significant only in reference to the world of the determinate, where there is the distinction of knowledge and reality, of knowing and being as well as of knowledge and ignorance. According to the *Śāstra, prajñā* as knowledge can be distinguished into two kinds which can be called the eternal (substantial) and the functional (impermanent). While the eternal *prajñā* is the ultimate reality itself only derivedly called *prajñā,* i.e., as contrasted with the "objective" world of relativity and change, the functional *prajñā* is the function of the mind, the self-conscious intellect contrasted with ignorance and in regard to the objective reality which it confronts.

There are two kinds of *prajñā*. The one is the eternal *prajñā*. The other is (the impermanent *prajñā)* which functions along with the five *pāramitās*. (The latter is) the functional *prajñā-pāramitā* (有用般若波羅密) (while the former could be called the substantial or the stable *prajñā)*. . . . The functional *prajñā* can put an end to the darkness of ignorance, and can fetch the true (eternal) *prajñā*. . . . In the eternal *prajñā* (the undivided reality) there cannot be found (even the distinction of) ignorance and knowledge. (521b)

The eternal *prajñā* is the ultimate, permanent principle of knowledge which is the "eternal light in the heart of man." The *prajñā* itself ever remains unextinct while the particular objects arise and perish. It is the permanent principle in the light of which alone the critical judgement of things as impermanent is meaningful. Nothing, not even Nirvāṇa (as set against *samsāra)*, can claim absoluteness in the light of the criticism instituted with the principle that the ultimate reality is the undivided being.

The *prajñāpāramitā* (the ultimate principle of knowledge) can cancel all things, it can cancel even Nirvāṇa; it straightaway transcends all things, unimpeded. (While all things perish) the power of wisdom does not itself perish, (as) it transcends all and there is nothing else that can deny it. Therefore it is said that if there is anything excelling even Nirvāṇa, even that the power of wisdom can deny. (But *prajñāpāramitā* itself remains undenied).[9] (449b)

The functional *prajñā* is really the act of knowing which can be said to consist of I) analysis, II) criticism and III) comprehension.[9a] These acts of knowing, as modes of the power of *prajñā,* have their ground in the permanent principle of knowledge.

*The knowledge of the unconditioned reality:* The act of knowing that has for its object the unconditioned reality is in its basic form the judgement that the real is the unconditioned, which is carried out in the light of the highest knowledge that is completely free from all distorting elements of ignorance and passion. It is a knowledge (judgement) regarding the ultimate nature of things, the highest reality, and hence it is called the highest knowledge, *prajñā* par excellence. This act of knowing which is also called *prajñāpāramitā* is, however, impermanent and it should be recognized as such, despite the fact that it is called permanent. In this regard the *Śāstra* points out:

*Prajñāpāramitā* is of the nature of knowledge; it is a seeing of things; it arises from the combination of causal factors. . . . Of the *prajñāpāramitā,* the object is *tathatā, dharma-dhātu, bhūtakoṭi,* the incomposite *dharma;* therefore it is (called) permanent. (521a)

Although (this) knowledge arises from the combination of causes and conditions, still, it takes for its object the *dharma* which is devoid of birth and is by nature *śūnya.* Therefore (even this knowledge) is called

the *dharma* that is devoid of birth and by nature *śūnya*.[10] (321a)
Knowledge derives its name in accordance with its object. (321a)

It is this knowledge of the unconditioned reality that enables the bodhisattva to enter the non-dual *dharma*, and transcending all divisions and distinctions to comprehend fully the undivided being. Thus he can comprehensively fare in the *prajñāpāramitā* (the integral experience or the undivided reality).

The *Śāstra* mentions three different kinds of knowledge prevalent in the world and points out that the *prajñāpāramitā*, the knowledge of the ultimate reality, is the highest kind, wisdom par excellence; it is superior to all of them.

There are three kinds of knowledge in the world: firstly there is the skilful knowledge of mundane things, the wide acquaintance with things like literature and arts, the knowledge of benevolence, religious rites etc.; secondly, there is the knowledge that leads one to freedom from birth (in inferior spheres) like the realm of sense-desire, etc.; thirdly there is the transmundane knowledge (that sets one) free from the sense of "I" and "mine," and puts an end to all elements of defilement. This is the knowledge of the *śrāvakas* and the *pratyeka-buddhas* whose *āsravas* have become extinct. But *prajñāpāramitā* is the highest kind and superior to all of these. It is completely pure and free from clinging. It is the knowledge that benefits (爲饒益) all people (一切衆生).[11] (370c)

This highest kind of knowledge is an integral principle that comprehends the aspect of cognition as well as emotion, comprises truth as well as compassion. As the knowledge of the ultimate nature of things it completely destroys ignorance, puts an end to passion, purifies the eye of wisdom, and turns the attention of people away from the ordinary objects of pleasure and fixes it in the highest source of peace and joy.

The *dharma* that is called *prajñāpāramitā* is most profound, difficult to comprehend. (In their real nature which is the same as *prajñāpāramitā)* all things are completely devoid of all determinate natures, therefore *prajñā-pāramitā* (the real nature of things) is most profound. In it all thoughts and all activities of mind come to an end, therefore it is difficult to see. In it there is not the clinging even to *prajñāpāramitā* and therefore it is said to be difficult to comprehend. In it all the three kinds of poison and all kinds of *prapañca* come to an end and therefore it is called Peace. With the realization of the excellent taste of this *prajñā,* one realizes a permanent fulfilment (of heart), and there is no more any hankering left (常得滿足更無所求). All other kinds of *prajñā* are gross, rough, devoid of joy. Therefore this *prajñā* is called excellent.[12] (450a)

People have various misconstructions of *kleśas* and false notions, making their minds turbid. But when they realize the *prajñā,* then their minds become pure and of one form (清淨一色). . . . *Prajñāpāramitā* can illuminate the darkness of ignorance that is associated with all elements of affliction as well as the ignorance that is not so associated; (it can brighten up) the darkness of stupidity in regard to all things. . . . *Prajñāpāramitā* can cure (the disease of) the eye of wisdom and then the eye of wisdom would itself change into *prajñā.* . . . It can turn (能轉) the attention of people's minds from the usual objects of desire and pleasure (towards the object of eternal fulfilment and joy). (478c–479a)

*Section III*

## LEVELS AND PERSPECTIVES

*The five eyes: Levels and perspectives of understanding:* The fact that *prajñā* in its purest form is ever there as the very nature of the self-conscious individual is a point that should not be missed. But in ordinary people it is covered up with the dirt of ignorance and passion. It is not only possible but essential to wash away this dirt; then the original brightness of *prajñā* shines forth once again. The five kinds of eyes that the *prajñā-pāramitā-sūtras* speak of[13] are really the different levels of comprehension, the different degrees of removal of this dirt from the mirror of mind, enabling it to reflect the true nature of itself as well as of all things. The eyes yield views; but the views differ not only in range, but in depth and in the quality of illumination.

The bodhisattva already has the eyes of flesh and has partially even the other four kinds of eyes. But these eyes are covered up with (the dust of) the limitations of sin (i.e., ignorance and passion) (諸罪結使覆) and are therefore unclean. For example, the mirror is by its nature bright, but due to the dust (垢故) on it, (its brightness) cannot be seen; but if the dust is washed away, then it shines bright as ever before (照明如本) (347a)

The eye is the faculty or power of sight, yielding a view, an idea, a judgment, of the nature of things. As kinds of the power of sight the eyes are always in themselves pure, although there are differences among them of depth and extension, as well as of the mode of comprehension. The deepening of the sight consists in realizing the relative nature and value of the different levels and perspectives; and this naturally implies a level of complete comprehension. To persist in the limited levels and perspectives and cling to them as themselves limitless is an error. The ultimate sight is the sight of the ultimate, the unconditioned. Nothing short of that can yield the ultimate "view." But the ultimate view is not any "view," not any definite view exclusive of all the rest. It is a view in so far as it is an awareness, a comprehension; but it is an awareness that is complete, an understanding that is comprehensive of all other levels and entirely free from errors and shortcomings.

*The eyes of the flesh and the deva eye:* The eyes of flesh and the *deva* eye see only partially. By confining oneself to these eyes one commits the error of seizing the determinate as itself the absolute. But it should be borne in mind that none that is self-conscious is bereft of the sense of the real; in fact all eyes, as kinds of sight, have their origin in *prajñā*. Thus the *Sūtra* says:

All the five eyes of the Buddha arise from *prajñāpāramitā*. (467c)

In the light of the sense of the real one puts an end to the factors of ignorance and passion that limit one's vision; by the cultivation of the sense of the beyond one purifies one's eyes. Thus the *Sūtra* says:

The bodhisattva while cultivating *prajñāpāramitā* purifies his five eyes. (347a)

In themselves the eyes are not such as to constrain one to cling to characters. The "view" is due to the eyes; but the clinging to the view is due to ignorance. The Buddha also sees through the eyes of flesh, but He does not cling to the "view."

The objects of sight for the eyes of flesh or the physical eyes are the gross objects of ordinary experience; with the purification of the physical eyes "the bodhisattva can see (the whole of) visible *rūpa*,"[14] "all the three thousand great thousand worlds."[15] While the eyes of flesh become pure through one's (moral) deeds, the *deva* eye becomes pure through *dhyāna* and *samādhi*, contemplation and meditation, as well as by the leading of moral life.[16] The objects of sight for the *deva* eyes are "birth and death, good and bad and the causal factors of the good and evil deeds of all beings" in all the worlds, which lead them to different kinds of existence in different spheres.[17]

The eyes of flesh cannot see things that lie even beyond a wall; they cannot see distant objects.[18] These are the eyes with which common people see things.

(The eyes of the common people are capable of only a partial seeing). They see the near but not the distant; they see the external but not the internal; they see the gross but not the subtle. (If) they see the east they cannot see the west; (if) they see this, they cannot see that; (if) they see the combination they cannot see the dispersion; (if) they see birth, they cannot see extinction.[19] (350c)

These eyes see everything as having its own nature and different from all the rest. The sight that these eyes yield is not different from that of animals.[20] Therefore the "view" of the eyes of flesh cannot be uncritically accepted as yielding comprehension of the ultimate nature of things. Even the objects of sight for the *deva* eye are only the determinate characters like identity and difference, the unreal, composite entities formed of causal factors. If one would see merely through these eyes, one would be prone to cling to the determinate as itself the absolute. There is need for enlivening one's sense of the real through a critical assessment of the true nature of things. There is need for the sight of the eye of wisdom.[21]

*The eye of wisdom:* The eye of wisdom is free from the errors (of the eyes of flesh and of the *deva* eye).[22] The eye of wisdom and the other two eyes become pure through the cultivation of the limitless *prajñā* as well as through acts of merit, viz., of love and compassion.[22a] The object of the eye of wisdom is the true nature of things, Nirvāṇa, the unconditioned *dharma,* the universal reality. It can see all things, and it can put an end to all perversion. It is the eye of wisdom that yields us the sight of the highest truth, viz., that

Stupidity and wisdom are neither identical nor different, that the mundane is not different from the transmundane and vice versa, that the mundane is itself (in its real nature) the transmundane and the transmundane is itself (what appears as) the mundane . . . that in (the ultimate) truth there is no difference between them.

(In the ultimate truth) all the different views disappear, all the activities of mind return (and enter the *dharmatā)* and there is no other sphere (for the mind) to reach. There all words cease: the world is itself (beheld in its true nature) as Nirvāṇa and not anything different. It is this wisdom (by means of which one realizes this ultimate truth) that is called the eye of wisdom.[23] (348a)

It is by virtue of the power of the eye of wisdom that one keeps oneself free from clinging exclusively either to the composite or to the incomposite, either to the mundane or to the transmundane, either to the defiled or to the undefiled. Non-clingingly one fares in all things. One does not cling to the determinate when one does not lose sight of the truth of the non-exclusive *dharma* which the eye of wisdom yields.

If the bodhisattva should see (exclusively) the composite, the worldly, the defiled, then he would just fall a victim to the false notion of existence (卽墮有見中); but if he would see (exclusively) the incomposite, the transmundane, the undefiled, he would just fall a victim to the false notion of non-existence (卽墮無見中). Abandoning these extremes, by means of the unerring wisdom (以不戲論慧), he fares on the Middle Way. This is the eye of wisdom. . . . Realizing this eye of wisdom one puts an end to all elements of perversion (破邪曲諸法), to all elements of ignorance, general or particular, to every thing (that owes its being to ignorance). (348a–b)

People lose their eye of wisdom through ignorance, doubt and repentance, perversion and false notions. But when they realize the *prajñā,* then the eye of wisdom just becomes clear (again). (478c)

The common people owing to perversion see (only) through the eyes of flesh which yield the six kinds of sense-cognition. Thus they see things as each (with its own nature and) different (from all the rest and thus they cling to them). But if one will see things through the eye of wisdom, then one will realize that all these determinate entities are unreal, and that Nirvāṇa is the only true reality. (495c)

*The eye of dharma:* While the eye of wisdom is the eye that is fixed on the universal reality, on Nirvāṇa, the eye of *dharma* is fixed on the diverse ways in which the minds of people function. While the eye of wisdom has no direct reference to the compassionate heart of the bodhisattva, the eye of *dharma* is directly inspired by his universal love and his original oath to save all beings. The eye of *dharma* yields one the knowledge of the diverse ways in which the minds of people work, the knowledge that is essential in order to help every individual so that one intensifies one's sense of the real, gives up one's clinging to the determinate, fares on the way with insight and compassion, helping all others also to realize the true nature of things. It is this knowledge of the definite ways suited to specific individuals *(mārgānvayajñāna)* (道種

智), a knowledge which enables the bodhisattva to help everyone according to one's need, that is called the eye of *dharma*.[24]

(By means of this knowledge the bodhisattva) understands in what way, by what means, each individual should be helped (according to his own mental capacities and aptitudes) to realize Nirvāṇa. (521b)

Referring to the bodhisattva's cultivation of way-faring, the *Śāstra* speaks of an order of the way in which he gradually realizes the different kinds of eyes. Thus when he first sets his mind in the pathway to reality, he sees with his eyes of flesh that people in the world experience suffering. He gives rise within himself to the heart of compassion, cultivates meditation and realizes the *deva* eye, by means of which he sees how everywhere beings suffer various kinds of bodily and mental suffering. With his sense of compassion for all beings grown more intense, he seeks the eye of wisdom in order to know the truth of things, mundane and transmundane, relative and absolute. He sees the unique nature as well as the basic pattern of the mind of every individual and then sets his thought to consider how he can help all to realize the truth of things. Accordingly he seeks the eye of *dharma*.[25]

The eye of *dharma* is so called because it leads everyone, enabling all to enter the *dharma*, the unconditioned reality (each in his own way).[26] (349b)

*The eye of the Buddha:* All these four different eyes, or powers of sight, are limited. The eyes of flesh and the *deva* eye hardly penetrate beneath the surface-view; they have hardly any element of criticism or reflection in them. The eye of wisdom no doubt yields the highest knowledge, the knowledge of the relative as well as of the absolute, of the conditioned as well as of the unconditioned. But in it the element of compassion is not prominent, an element which is so basic to the career of the bodhisattva. In order that the eye of wisdom and the eye of *dharma*, in fact in order that all the four eyes may function together in unison, an integration of them is essential. The highest "eye" is that which is not exclusive of or confined to any of these and yet comprehends all in a basic integration; in this eye the other eyes find their consummation.

When (the bodhisattva) becomes the Buddha, (all the other four eyes, viz.,) the eyes of flesh, the *deva* eye, the eye of wisdom and the eye of *dharma* (enter the Buddha eye where they) lose their original names and are called only the eye of the Buddha. This is like the four great rivers of Jambudvīpa (India), losing their original names when they enter the great ocean.[27] (348b)

Speaking of the inadequacies of the eyes other than the Buddha-eye, the *Śāstra* observes that of ordinary people even when the eyes of flesh are functioning the *deva*-eye may not have been functioning. For, although the faculty of the physical sight may be mature, as the common people have not yet given up the sense of desire they do not as yet have the *deva*-eye. Of people whose deva-eye functions, the eye of wisdom may not as yet be functioning. Although a common person may have obtained the extraordinary power of the *deva*-eye, still he will not as yet have obtained the eye of wisdom. Even when the eye of wisdom functions, the eye of *dharma* may not function. For example, the *śrāvakas*, who have not yet abandoned their sense of desire, do not know the expedient ways of helping people to cross the ocean of birth and death, therefore they do not have the eye of *dharma*. Even when the eye of *dharma* functions, the eye of the Buddha may not as yet function. For example, even when the bodhisattva realizes the knowledge of the diverse ways of all people, still, as he has not yet become the Buddha he will not have the eye of the Buddha.[28]

The eyes of flesh (of the common people) are born from deeds, associated with defilements and prompted by afflictions, and therefore these are false, untrue. . . . Even the *deva*-eyes arise from the combination of causes and conditions like the states of trance, and therefore even these are false and cannot see things as they are.

Even the eye of wisdom and the eye of *dharma* are not completely pure, as in them the traces of *kleśa* are not extinguished, and therefore even they should be abandoned, transcended. But in the eye of the Buddha there is no error, no perversion, (for in it) all perversion has been completely extinguished—extinguished to its very end. (348b)

The eye of the Buddha is the eye that is completely free from passion and is saturated with unbounded compassion for all beings everywhere.[29] It is the eye of wisdom itself come to consummation.

(When the bodhisattva) becomes the Buddha the eye of wisdom itself comes to be called in turn the eye of the Buddha. As ignorance and other *kleśas* including even their traces, will all have been concluded, (he gains) a clear comprehension in regard to every thing. . . . (When one gains the eye of the Buddha) nothing remains unseen, unheard, uncomprehended and unrecognized. (348b)

The highest knowledge that the Buddha achieves is also called the knowledge of all forms;[30] it is the knowledge of every specific way of every determinate entity. It is the comprehension that is non-exclusive, neither exclusive of the mundane nor of the ultimate. It is the comprehension in which the true nature of things is clear as daylight; it is at the same time the bearing of limitless love and compassion toward all beings. It is the comprehension in which ignorance and passion have been concluded and which is aware that the true nature of ignorance is itself wisdom, that the true nature of passion is itself compassion. It is the true wisdom. This is the goal of the wayfaring of the bodhisattva. In the Buddha all the five eyes function and that in perfect unison. His comprehension is altogether saturated as much with compassion as with wisdom.

*CHAPTER V*

# KNOWLEDGE AS THE PRINCIPLE OF COMPREHENSION

*Section I*

## THE MIDDLE WAY: THE NON-EXCLUSIVE WAY

*Prajñā compared to the principle of accommodation:* In regard to being all-comprehensive, *prajñāpāramitā* is compared to *ākāśa,* the principle of accommodation,[1] which has room for everything. It is not itself anything, and yet all things live, move and have their being in dependence upon it. *Prajñā* as the sense of the unconditioned is the ground of all conditioned specific views, while it is not itself any specific view. All views derive their being from *prajñā,* for it is in response to and as expressions of the sense of the unconditioned that views are built, in order to satisfy the specific needs. These needs are the specifications or canalizations of the one basic urge, the urge to realize the real. While this is so, it is under ignorance that one claims absoluteness for one's own view. This is to lack in comprehension; this is exclusiveness, dogmatism. The non-exclusive understanding is the all-comprehensive *prajñā.* This is the same as the Middle Way that rises above extremes and hence above exclusiveness, reveals the mundane nature of things and leads one also to their ultimate truth. A middle way that does not open up the truth of things ceases to be the middle and ceases also to be the way. It would itself be an extreme and hence a dead-end.

Speaking of *prajñāpāramitā* as the comprehension that is non-clinging *(anupalambha),* the *Śāstra* points out that it cannot itself be conceived as anything specific nor can it be confined to any specific level or perspective;

*Prajñāpāramitā* is non-clinging *(anupalambha,* 不可得相). It cannot be seized either as existent or as non-existent, either as permanent or as impermanent, either as unreal (空) or as real (實). This is *prajñāpāramitā.* It is not (any specific entity) comprised in the (classifications), *skandhas, āyatanas* or *dhātus;* it is not anything composite or incomposite; not any *dharma* (非法) nor *adharma* (非非法); it is neither seizing (無取) nor abandoning (無捨), neither arising nor perishing; it is beyond the four *koṭis* of "is" and "is not"; getting at it one does not find in it anything that can be clung to, being comparable in this regard with the flame that cannot be touched from any of the four sides. . . . *Prajñāpāramitā* is also completely beyond the possibility of clinging, and any one who would attempt to cling to it would be burnt by (his own) fire of perversion.[2] (139c)

Transcending all determinations it is yet not exclusive of anything determinate, and is therefore itself undeniable;

*(Prajñāpāramitā* is truly) undeniable, indestructible. If there is anything existent even to the smallest extent, all that is determinate and is therefore deniable. If one speaks of non-existence, even that is deniable. In this *prajñā,* there is not any existence, nor any non-existence, not even neither existence nor non-existence; even such a description as this is also not there. This is the *dharma* which is peace, illimitable, indescribable. Therefore it is undeniable, indestructible. This is the true, real, *prajñāpāramitā.* It is the highest truth, there is nothing beyond it. Even as the highest emperor subdues all enemies and yet does not think highly of himself, just in the same way *prajñāpāramitā* can put an end to the entire network of words *(prapañca)* and yet it has not put an end to anything. (139c–140a)

*The root of contentions:* Speaking of the nature of the all-comprehensive understanding in a negative way, stating what it is not, the *Śāstra* quotes from the *Arthavargīya-sūtra*[3] the following stanzas:

Everyone takes his stand on his own view and by his own constructions gives rise to disputes; "To know this is to know the truth," he holds, "and not to know this is to be condemned."

(Truly) one who does not accept the view of another is devoid of wisdom. He that clings to his own construction is devoid of wisdom.

To stand on one's own view of truth and give rise to false constructions, if this is pure wisdom, then there is none who does not have it[4]. (60c–61a)

In these three stanzas, says the *Śāstra,* the Buddha has spoken of the ultimate truth. The *Śāstra* continues:

Common people take their stand on their own points of view, on their own doctrines and on their own thoughts and hence there arise all the contentions. *Prapañca* is the root of all contentions and *prapañca* is born from (wrong) notions. (61a)

*Prapañca* is the root of all contentions and *prapañca* is the clinging to words. The ignorant pursue names while what they seek is reality.[4a] They misapply the sense of the real; they mistake the specific for the ultimate, the relative for the absolute. In this they follow their own fancy instead of the nature of things as they are. Hence the contradictions which they meet at every step.

From clinging (受) to things there arise disputes; but if there is no clinging, what dispute will there be? He who understands that all *dṛṣṭis,* clinging or non-clinging, are in truth of the same nature, has already become free from all these.[5] (61a)

The wayfarer that can understand this does not seize, does not cling to anything, does not imagine that this alone is true (and not that). He does not quarrel with anyone. He can thus enjoy the flavour of the nectar of the Buddha's doctrine. Those teachings are wrong which are not of this nature (i.e., non-contentious and accommodative). If one does not accommodate other doctrines, does not know them, does not accept them, he indeed is the ignorant. Thus, then, all those who quarrel and contend are really devoid of wisdom. Why? Because every one of them refuses to accommodate the views of others. That is to say, there are those who say that what they themselves speak is the highest, the real, the pure truth; that the doctrines of the others are words, false and impure. (61a)

Thus every one of these contending teachers clings to his own standpoint and does not accommodate the views of others. "This alone is right all else is wrong" he says. If one accepts one's own doctrines, honours and cultivates one's own doctrines and does not accommodate and honour others' doctrines, and just picks up faults in them, and if this kind of conduct is the pure conduct, fetching the highest good, then there is none whose conduct is impure." Why? Because everyone accepts his own doctrine. (61b)

*Words are vehicles:* The Buddha exhorts all to take their stand on the *dharma* and not on any individual, to take their stand on the meaning and not just on words, on *jñāna* and not on *vijñāna,* on (the *sūtras* of) direct meaning and not on (those) of indirect meaning.[6] To take one's stand on words is to give rise to quarrels; this is to miss the fact that the one truth has been expressed in diverse ways in different words.

(One should) take one's stand on what the words (ultimately) mean (and not on any particular expression), because in regard to the ultimate meaning there can be no quarrel that this is good and this is bad, that this is sin and this is merit, this is false and this is true. Words are (just) a means to get the meaning (語以得義). But the meaning is not the words themselves (義非語也). For example when a person points to the moon with his finger in order to enable the confused to see the moon, if the latter would see only the finger, the person would ask: "While I point to the moon with my finger in order to enable you to see it, how is it that you see only the finger and miss the moon?" The case is the same even here. Words are pointers to, indicators of, meaning (語爲義指); words are not themselves the meaning. It is therefore that one should not take one's stand simply on words.[7] (125a–b)

Again, to take one's stand on *jñāna* is to accept the lead of critical understanding whereas to take one's stand on *vijñāna* is to follow one's own individual hankerings.[8]

*Vijñāna* deprived of the right understanding is the self-conscious principle seeking the real but in the wrong direction, under the error of misplaced absoluteness; the seeking would then be self-seeking, seeking one's own good and that in a perverse way, exaggerating the demands of the ego and hypostatizing abstractions.

*What is to be abandoned?*

In the *dharma* of the Buddha one abandons all passion, all wrong views, all pride of self; one puts an end to all (these) and does not cling (to anything). (63c)

Referring to the *Sūtra on the Raft,*[9] the *Śāstra* says that the Buddha has taught there that one has to abandon one's clinging even to good things, how much more to bad ones! He does not encourage any fond notion even in regard to the *prajñāpāramitā* or any leaning on it or clinging to it. How much less should one lean on or cling to other things![10]

The *Śāstra* proceeds:

The intention of the Buddha is this:

My disciples (must be) free from passion for *dharma,* free from attachment to *dharma,* free from partizanship. What they seek is only the freedom from (passion and) suffering; they do not quarrel about the (diverse) natures of things. (63c)

In the *Arthavargīya Sūtra*[11] Mākandika puts a difficulty before the Buddha:

(It may be that) in the case of rigidly fixing (and holding on to) things, there directly arise all sorts of (wrong) notions. But if all is abandoned, the internal as well as the external, how can enlightenment *(bodhi 道)* be realized at all? (63c)

The questioner commits the mistake of imagining that the determinate in itself leads to clinging, and that the indeterminate nature *(śūnyatā)* of things means a literal abandoning of them. These are only different phases of the error of clinging, the error of imputing the limitations in our approach to the nature of the things themselves. If the determinate in itself leads one to clinging, then, certainly, there is no way of realizing the *bodhi;* then, it would follow that to abandon clinging would be to abandon the determinate itself, and the "indeterminate" would mean a total denial of the determinate. These are the wrong notions that arise from the initial mistake of imagining that the determinate is in its very nature such as to lead one to clinging. But this is a view which leads one to self-contradiction at every step. For how can one speak and convey his meaning through specific concepts and yet say that the determinate leads one by its very nature to clinging? The Buddha's answer amounts to saying that what is to be abandoned is not the determinate itself, but one's clinging to it. One can realize freedom by abandoning the false sense of self, which is the root of all clinging:

*Bodhi* is not realized by seeing or hearing or understanding, nor is it realized by the (mere) observance of morals; nor is it realized by abandoning hearing and seeing and it is (definitely) not realized by giving up morals.

Thus what one should abandon is disputation as well as the (false) notion of "I" and "mine"; one should not cling to the diverse natures of things. It is in this way that *bodhi* can be realized. (63c)

Mākandika clings again. He imagines that the Buddha means a literal denial of thought and speech and of every course of mundane activity.

Then, as I see it now, (just) by an acceptance of the way of the dumb (持啞法) one can realize the way. (64a)

He misses the meaning in the words of the Buddha as his clinging to the determinate, his imagination that the root of suffering lies in the determinate itself, shuts him out from the truth that it really lies in his clinging to it. So the Buddha summarily replies:

You take your stand (依) on the path of wrong notions; I know your foolish way. Now, when you are not able to see (your own) wrong notions, you are yourself the dumb. (64a)

Words, concepts, are in themselves pure; what makes the difference is the way in which we use them. Views constructed of concepts need not all be false; there is the right view as well as the wrong view.[12]

*Section II*

## THE WAYS OF TEACHING:

### *A. The Direct and the Expedient Ways*

*The one dharma taught in many ways:* As the all-comprehensive understanding of the wise is not exclusive of anything, they are capable of putting into use any one of the specific standpoints and its corresponding judgement when it is called for in a specific situation. This is how the Buddha teaches. He draws the attention of people to aspects of things they have missed and He thus helps them to overcome their clinging and widen their understanding. When He sees the need to correct the error in one's approach He does so with skilfulness and understanding, by observing one's specific tendency and mental capacity and helping each in a way suited to him. The Buddha teaches the one *dharma* in numberless ways.

The *dharma* of the Buddhas is limitless like the great ocean. In accordance with the diverse mental capacities and aptitudes of the people they teach the (one) *dharma* in a variety of ways. Sometimes the *dharma* is taught (through) existence, sometimes it is taught (through) non-existence, sometimes (through) permanence and some other times (through) impermanence, sometimes (through) pain and some other times (through) pleasure, sometimes (through) self and some other times (through) "no self." Sometimes it is taught that one should exert oneself in cultivating the three kinds of deeds and should collect all elements of merit, while some other times it is taught that all things are devoid of construction (and impossible of collection). In this way, (the one *dharma)* has been taught in several ways.[13] (192a)

The Buddha taught that the self exists and He also taught that there is no self. Again He taught that all things exist and He also taught that all things are *śūnya,* that everything is devoid of existence. The *Śāstra* observes that while for a superficial view there seems to be mutual contradiction in these, there is no contradiction in fact, for these are different ways of expressing one and the same truth. By nature things are such that they are neither absolutely existent nor absolutely non-existent; they are conditionally existent and by nature becoming. In the becoming of things the aspects of "is" and "is not" are distinguishable though not separable. And a thing is describable from the standpoint of any one of these aspects but only relatively and not absolutely. It is this truth of the relativity of descriptions, the possibility of describing any given thing from several standpoints in several ways, that the Buddha uses in order to reveal the one-sidedness of the ignorant who cling exclusively to some one specific aspect and ignore the rest.[14] And there is no contradiction in making different statements about the same thing from different standpoints. That the self exists and that the self does not exist, both are true, even as the statements that everything exists as well as that all things are non-existent are equally true. There is no mutual contradiction among them, for they do not clash.

Both these teachings are true. Take for example, the ring finger; it is both long and short. From the standpoint of the middle finger it is short, and from the standpoint of the little finger it is long. That it is short and that it is long—both are true. The same is the case with the teaching of existence and non-existence. The teaching of existence is sometimes meant as the mundane truth and sometimes as the highest truth. The teaching of non-existence is also sometimes meant as a mundane truth and sometimes as the ultimate truth. The Buddha's teachings that the self exists and that the self does not exist, both are true.[15] (254a)

The *Śāstra* observes that the teaching that all things exist, that the self exists is meant for householders, as they mostly do not aspire to realize Nirvāṇa but just seek to reap the fruits of their deeds in their future spans of life. To those who have abandoned the home-life and have taken to a life of renunciation, it is taught that things do not exist, that the self does not exist. This is because those who have renounced the family life mostly aspire to realize Nirvāṇa. Those who seek Nirvāṇa do not seize anything and therefore their clinging naturally dies out and this death of clinging is itself Nirvāṇa.[16]

Again, the *Śāstra* states that when the power of faith etc. have not become ripe, people first seek the way through clinging, and later when their power of faith and understanding has become mature, they will be able to give up their clinging. For the sake of these the Buddha has taught concerning all the good elements in order that depending on them people will be able to give up their clinging to the bad ones. There are some in whom the power of faith etc. are already mature; they do not seek anything in a clinging way. They seek only the way to freedom from the course of birth and death. For the sake of such people, the Buddha has taught that all things are *śūnya*.[17]

*The direct and the expedient ways:* There is the distinction of the teaching of the ultimate nature of things and the teaching of their relative nature. Again, there is the distinction of direct *(nītārtha)* teaching, viz., that all things are *śūnya* and the indirect, expedient *(neyārtha)* teaching, viz., that the self does not exist.[18] And it is necessary to note that both these kinds of teaching are true statements, statements of things as they are. While the direct teaching sets forth in a direct manner the basic and the complete truth regardless of the specific tendencies of the hearers, the indirect, expedient, teaching emphasizes precisely such aspects of things as are suited to the specific tendencies of the individuals. But whether direct or expedient, whether of the ultimate truth or of the mundane truth, all the teachings of the Buddha have one single aim, viz., to enable all to destroy their ignorance, overcome their clinging and realize freedom from suffering. Again all these teachings are comprehended in the all-inclusive *prajñā,* which is not itself any specific view but the ground of all views.

In the teachings of the Buddha the ways that lead to Nirvāṇa are all equally one pointed (皆同一向); there are no divergent paths (無有異道). (254a)

Of these different teachings all are true, and yet none is true.[19] Every one of them has its respective, relative significance; and yet none of them is absolutely true. Even to cling to *śūnyatā* (relativity) as itself absolute would be a case of exclusiveness, and hence of blindness, dogmatism. It is to shut oneself out from the truly absolute, the non-exclusive, in the light of which relativity is itself seen to be non-ultimate.

If one does not cling to the *śūnyatā* of all things one's mind does not give room to quarrel; one just abandons all limitations (但除結使). This is the true wisdom. But if one clings to the *śūnyatā* of things and thus gives rise to quarrel, his bonds are not cut; then one would lean on (and cling to) this knowledge. But this is not the true knowledge.

As the Buddha has said, all His teachings are intended to help all people to cross (the ocean of birth and death). There is nothing in these that is not true. Whether any teaching is true or not depends solely on whether one is non-clinging or clinging in regard to it. (但衆生於中有著不著故有實不實). (254b)

The ultimate truth, the reality that is not itself anything specific *(akiñcana)* is the heart of the teaching of the Buddha. All the statements of the Buddha carry the ultimate significance of the unconditioned reality.[20] One who understands this does not contend.

### B. *The Four Siddhāntas*

*The two truths and the four siddhāntas:* The distinction in the teachings of the Buddha between those that pertain to the mundane truth and those that pertain to the ultimate truth, which we discussed in the preceding section, is set forth, again, in another form, viz., as the four *siddhāntas.*[21] These represent four different statements of one and the same truth but from different standpoints, the mundane and the individual, the remedial and the ultimate. In fact, the individual and the remedial kinds are only restatements of the mundane form; they are the kinds of indirect or expedient teaching suited to the individual needs of the people as they promote the good in them and serve as "remedies" for the specific kinds of "diseases" in their minds. Thus the primary distinction is still between the mundane and the ultimate. The *Śāstra* says:

All these are true and there is no mutual contradiction among them (皆是實無相違背). (59b)

It is to be noted that the scheme of the four *siddhāntas* as well as that of the direct and indirect teachings, and even the distinction of *abhidharma* (analysis) criticism *(śūnyatā)* and moral code *(piṭaka* or *vinaya)*, are all intended to bring out the intrinsic consistency and harmony in the teachings of the Buddha. To bring this to light the *Śāstra* emphasizes the need to penetrate beneath the apparent contradictions in His different teachings, and gives as an illustration His teachings about the self. A certain *Sūtra,* for example, says:

From different kinds of deeds (one) is born in different kinds of life in the world and experiences different kinds of touch and feeling. (60a)

Again in the *Phalgunasūtra*[22] it is said that there is no individual who experiences touch, and there is no individual who experiences feeling. (60a)

There is an apparent contradiction between what these two *Sūtras* say. Those who do not penetrate deep enough into the inner meaning in these teachings would condemn these two statements as contradictory; but in fact, these are only different expressions of the mundane nature of the "self" of the individual which is a ceaseless becoming, and in which the aspects of arising as well as perishing are distinguishable. It is in reference to these distinguishable aspects that the different statements are made. As "is" and "is not" are opposed to each other so, these statements that the self exists and that it does not exist are opposed to each other; but again, as the opposed concepts "is" and "is not" hold good equally of the conditioned, changing, entity from different standpoints, so do these opposing statements. There is no intrinsic contradiction in the mundane entity's being conceived as a complex of "is" and "is not"; similarly there is no inherent contradiction in the two teachings equally holding good in regard to the individual viewed from two different angles.

*The mundane truth:* Essential conditionedness *(pratītyasamutpāda)*, is the direct teaching of the mundane nature of things.

The mundane truth is that things exist as the result of the combination of causes and conditions, and that they have no separate essences of their own. A cart for example exists as a complex entity composed of wheel etc.; there is no cart (with a being of its own) apart from its components. Such is also the nature of the individual. The individual is there as the complex of the five *(skandhas)* (groups of material and mental elements); there is no individual apart from (and independent of) these five groups.[23] (59b)

That there is the individual is the mundane truth and not the highest truth, and *tathatā* as unconditioned and unchanging nature is not true in regard to the mundane nature of things.[24] The being of the individual is a dependent being as it is a complex of the five *skandhas,* and it is not anything unconditioned or independent. Milk, for example, is a complex of colour, smell, taste and touch; it is not anything in itself. Nor is it a non-entity, purely illusory like the second head or the third hand.[25] In that case there could not have been any such thing as the components of milk. But there is such a thing as the components of milk; this is admitted even by those who tend to dismiss individuality as a mere name without anything corresponding, not recognizing the individual even as a conditioned entity. To hold that there are only the *skandhas* and no individual at all is an error in regard to the mundane truth.

*The truth taught from the individual standpoint:*

The teaching that is from the individual standpoint is in accordance with the specific tendencies (and the mental capacities) of the different individuals (觀人心行). Even to the same thing some listen and some do not. (60a)

The Buddha's teachings that there is the self and that there is no self are of this kind. The intention in the former teaching is to remove the doubt of the people in regard to the next birth, in regard to sin and merit, and it is intended to save them from committing evil deeds and falling into the heresy of negativism. The other statement that there is no individual is intended to remove the wrong notion that the self exists as an absolute entity, that the individual is an unconditioned being, which is a false notion, a fall into the heresy of eternalism.[25a] In regard to the question as to who is the receiver of deeds, we have the following:

If the Buddha had answered that such and such a person is the receiver then the questioner would have fallen into the heresy of eternalism and then his heresy would have become reinforced, hardened, and made ineradicable. Therefore (the Buddha) did not say that there is the individual who experiences (pleasure and pain). (60a)

This is teaching each individual in accordance with his mental capacities and tendencies.

*The truth taught as a remedy:*

For every specific (mental) state (法) (conditioning the individual) there is always a remedy (對治). (And this mental state as well as its remedy are both) devoid of reality (unconditionedness). (60a)

Even as each specific disease in the body has its antidote, just so every disease of the mind has its remedy in the Buddha's *dharma*.

Observing and contemplating on the impurity (of the body) is a good remedy for lewdness and passion. But it is not so for anger . . .

For those who are full of anger cultivation of a compassionate heart is the proper remedy. . . . Contemplation on the causes and conditions of things is the proper remedy for stupidity. (60a)

But the truth taught as remedy is not the ultimate truth. If for example impermanence were the ultimate truth, i.e., if things were absolutely impermanent, then it would mean that the thing that is here, now, would perish and become totally lost; and in that case there would not be the causal continuity which is a fundamental truth of the mundane nature of things. The rotten seed does not give birth to any sprout; similarly if there is no fruit-bearing deed how can there be any fruit? Now, all the factors of the Noble Way do bear their fruits, they are the objects of the faith and knowledge of the wise and these cannot be denied. So, it is not true that everything is absolutely impermanent.[26] That all that is composite is impermanent is a relative truth.

(In the ultimate truth) the composite entities should not be (conceived as) having the feature of birth, duration and death, for, these features are not unconditioned. (60b)

*The ultimate truth:* While all the kinds of mundane truth are relative, conditioned and specific, it is only the ultimate truth that is unconditioned and hence undeniable.

The nature that is conceived as the self-nature of every element, of every discourse and of every word, of everything good and bad, the nature of every one of these can be analyzed, dispersed and cancelled. The truly real *dharma* in which the Buddhas . . . fare cannot be denied or cancelled. The above three kinds of truth are not comprehensive while this alone is comprehensive (通).

What does this comprehensiveness mean? To be comprehensive here means to be completely free from limitations (離一切過失) and hence immutable (不可變易) and unsurpassable (不可勝). How is it so? It is so because except the ultimate truth all other standpoints and all other discourses are subject to cancellation (皆可破故). (60c)

The speakable is the deniable, for it is the determinate. The ultimate truth which is indeterminate is the unutterable *dharma*.

As it is said in the *Stanzas setting forth the meaning of Mahāyāna* (摩訶衍義偈):

(There) the sphere of the speakable ceases, the activities of mind come to an end; the unborn, the undying *dharma* is of the nature of Nirvāṇa.

The sphere of the speakable is the domain of the determinate; the sphere where the words do not reach is the highest *dharma*.[27] (61b)

The comprehensive knowledge is not only of the relativity and compatibility of the many determinate views, it is also an awareness of their underlying unity; in what they ultimately mean they are not anything specific. Concepts which hold among the specific and the relative are irrelevant in regard to the ultimate truth of things. But at the same time the ultimate truth is not exclusive of specific concepts, not absolutely unutterable.[28] The wise teach through names and characters, the *dharma* that lies beyond these but this they do in a non-clinging way.

### C. *Analysis and Criticism*

*The three doors to the dharma: Analysis, criticism and cultivation of moral life:* The distinction of *Abhidharma* (analysis), *Śūnyatā* (criticism), and *Piṭaka* (or *Vinaya,* the moral code) is also meant to bring to light the basic harmony in the teachings of the Buddha.[29] The *Abhidharma* embodies an exposition of the distinct, unique, nature of every specific entity; here the method is analysis; and the emphasis is on what every specific thing is in its own nature. *Śūnyatā* (criticism) lays bare the non-ultimacy of the specific entities as well as their essential conditionedness or relativity; it lays bare also the conditionedness of even the conditioned nature, thereby enabling the mind to get at the truly unconditioned. The method here is criticism, a critical examination of the elements that are found by analysis to be constitutents of experience. The practical side of the wayfaring is brought to light in the cultivation of the moral life which consists in putting an end to the factors of privation and pain and enhancing the elements conducive to the realization of the undivided being. Elements of disintegration are terminated and the factors of integration are brought to birth. This harnesses both analysis and criticism, the knowledge of the unique nature of every specific entity as well as the sense of their conditionedness and contingency. Now, although there is an apparent conflict between analysis which emphasizes distinction and individuality of things and *śūnyatā* which emphasizes their inadequacy, relativity and contingency, still, for one who penetrates beneath the surface they become the revealers of the inner harmony in the teachings of the Buddha.

When the ignorant hear (the different kinds of teachings) they say that it is all a perversion.

But the wise enter the three gates *(Abhidharma, Śūnyatā* and *Piṭaka)* and comprehend that all the words of the Buddha are true and there is no contradiction among them. (192a)

Analysis is not in itself opposed to criticism; the knowledge of the unique nature of specific things or the specific systems of things is not in itself in conflict with the knowledge of the essential relativity of every specific thing or of every specific system of things. And the knowledge of their basic unity, the unity of origin and the unity of purpose, enables one to deal with them and bring them to their natural fulfilment; this is the strength and skilfulness of the wise. Again, while the cultivation of the moral life, bereft of the knowledge of the true nature of things, is apt to land one in the errors of clinging, these errors are not inevitable, nor are they inherent in analysis or criticism or even in the cultivation of the moral life itself. They owe their being to our ignorance and hence to our clinging to the fragmentary as complete.

*Analysis and the error of the analysts:* The ideal representation of the world of becoming in terms of the relative notions of "is" and "is not," "self" and "other," "identity" and "difference" is the very means by which its different aspects are distinguished and their mutual relations in the whole are appreciated; this is the mission of thought. It is this way that speech, communication, is possible. Thought and speech or communication require a certain fixity which is a fixity of designations, names, concepts. This fixity means that the same representation stands for the same meaning in a given context. This is the foundation and the basic form of the laws of thought. But this fixity of designations is not in itself opposed to change or to the becoming of things. The basic error in construing concepts consists in mistaking the unvaryingness of their import to stand for the ultimacy or absoluteness of the entities for which they stand. This is the error of the analysts. Now, if the basic constituent elements are essentially unrelated to one another, as the analysts hold, then all relatedness which is a matter of experience and to explain which even they have set out, becomes an unbased illusion. Again, if the basic elements do not admit of change, if they ever remain in their own essence, then becoming, change, which is the essential nature of things in the world, itself turns out to be an unbased illusion. This is the *reductio ad absurdum* of the doctrine of elements.

*Criticism and the error of the negativist:* On the contrary if one were to cling to the total non-existence of things by exclusively clinging to their aspect of ceasing to be and holding that the passing away of things means their total extinction, that would again mean an impossibility of mundane existence, as it amounts to a complete denial of causal continuity. To entertain this view is to mistake *śūnyatā* (non-substantiality) for total non-existence. This is to miss also the important truth that conditionedness is not itself unconditioned. This is also to mistake the unconditioned as apart from and exclusive of the conditioned.

Again, devoid of the comprehension of the true nature of things if one would exclusively cling to the code of moral discipline expounded in the *Vinaya,* one would fall a victim to the wrong notion of both existence and non-existence. The *Śāstra* observes in another context that an enquiry into the ultimate nature of things is not the concern of the *Vinaya.*[30]

*The principle of comprehension:* All these: the analysis of things, the criticism of elements as well as the cultivation of the moral life are in fact the inseparable aspects of the spiritual life of the wayfarer. In him who fares rightly on the Way, all these three blend in a unison, for they are united at root as the different expressions of the one urge, the urge for the real, and they are united also at the end as they blend and become of one essence in that which is the ultimate end of the wayfaring, viz., the realization of the undivided being. It is the power of *prajñāpāramitā,* which is the power of comprehension, that keeps one aware of their essential unity. To fare in these devoid of this power is to be devoid of the sense of their true nature.

Thus the *Śāstra* says:

> Without (the power of) *prajñāpāramitā* if one enters the door of *Abhidharma* (analysis), one falls into (the wrong notion of) existence; if one enters the door of *Śūnyatā* (criticism) one falls into (the wrong notion of) non-existence; and if one enters the door of *Piṭaka* (moral discipline) one falls into (the wrong notion of) both existence and non-existence.[31] (194a–b)

But if one would rightly comprehend things, and would not lose the sense of the beyond, then in his case these three constitute not hindrances but "doors" which open upon the profound meaning in the teachings of the Buddha.[31a] The building of views as systematic presentations of the constitution of things from different levels and standpoints is legitimate and natural. The views would be of help to one who does not cling. To one who clings they are a hindrance, for they are then perversions; they cease to be "doors" they become dead-ends. The wise, the non-clinging, formulate concepts, construct systems as well as alternate them freely, as freely as they would dismiss them.

> Although the bodhisattva faring in *prajñāpāramitā* understands the universal natures of things, he understands also their unique natures; although he understands the unique natures of things, he knows also their universal natures.[32] (194b)

The bodhisattva sees the many-sided natures, twofold, threefold and even the innumerable characters, of things.

Having known all these (diverse characters), he is capable of comprehending how all of them enter *śūnyatā,* the *śūnyatā* of essential nature; and so he remains non-clinging in regard to everything.[33] (195c)

It is this non-clinging knowledge of things, of which he is capable by virtue of his sense of the real, that enables him to achieve the status of the bodhisattva.

Having achieved the status of the bodhisattva, by virtue of his great compassion, by means of his power of skilfulness, he (once again) analyzes all things, their diverse names, (their respective natures and their mutual relations) in order to set people free (from ignorance and passion). Thus he enables all to realize (any of) the three vehicles. In this he is like the skilful alchemist who by virtue of the power of his chemicals can change silver into gold and gold into silver.[34] (195c)

That he does not entertain the notion of their absoluteness or ultimacy is because he understands that

The internal is like the external and the external is like the internal in that (both are relative entities and) none can be seized (as absolute). They are of one nature, born of causes and conditions, and are in truth *śūnya.* (In their ultimate nature) all things are eternally pure; in that nature (they are themselves) the *tathatā, dharmadhātu, bhūtakoṭi.*

(All things) enter the non-dual *(dharma).* Although things are not two, they are not one either.

When (the bodhisattva) comprehends things in this way his mind acquires (the power of) faith; it does not revert. This is the ability to bear the truth of things *(dharmakṣānti).*[35] (168b)

But if things are in truth devoid of determinations, it may be asked how one could distinguish different kinds of entities and form different concepts. Why should one not straightaway speak only of *śūnyatā,* the ultimate nature? To speak only of *śūnyatā* is to cling to it exclusively; this amounts to the view that the ultimate truth is exclusive of and apart from the determinate. This is a difficulty that arises from want of the power of comprehension and skilfulness.

The bodhisattva does not say that *śūnyatā* (the indeterminate nature) is anything that could be seized or clung to. If *(śūnyatā* were itself anything that) could be seized or clung to, then the bodhisattva should not have spoken of the diverse characters of things. The non-clinging *śūnyatā* is completely unobstructing; if there is any obstruction in it, then it is the clinging and not the non-clinging *śūnyatā*. Having comprehended the non-clinging *śūnyatā* (the bodhisattva) can again analyze and distinguish things (as well as set forth alternative systems of understanding) and he can, in this way, help all to realize freedom. This is the power of *prajñāpāramitā.* (195c)

### D. *The Four Ways of Answering*

*The silence of the Buddha:* The Buddha adopted different ways of answering the questions that were put to Him. Silence was His way of answering certain kinds of questions that clearly indicated the state of the questioner's mind as one that was steeped in the tendency to cling and therefore not conducive to see things as they are. The fourteen questions[36] in regard to which the Buddha kept silent are the kinds of difficulties in which men get entangled on account of clinging to the conditioned, seizing the relative as itself ultimate. Although the constructions to which men give rise are of various kinds, still all these pertain in the last analysis to the five *skandhas,*[37] the basic factors of the world of the determinate, which are all relative and devoid of absoluteness. These questions are based on the notions of absolute existence and absolute non-existence, as well as of absolute identity and absolute difference. These are different forms of the basic extremes, the extremes of eternalism and negativism or annihilationism, and are asked with a clinging mind. They are questions about the world or the body and the self or its constituents conceived either as ultimate, independent, entities ever existing in their own right or as evanescent elements which perish as soon as they appear, where the perishing is total and hence the arising, uncaused. Conceived in this way the views expressed in these questions constitute a direct denial of the mundane nature of things where everything arises but not devoid of conditions and perishes though not absolutely, and where all things are mutually related. Interrelatedness as well as becoming and change, constitute the essential nature of things here, and it is exactly this nature that these views deny.

Now, when the questions are framed in such a way that any answer to them would lead the questioner to one or other extreme on account of his deep tendency to cling, wisdom consists in keeping silent. Or, if the questioner is in a position to understand the truth of the essential conditionedness of things, the answer would be to deny all these positions which are only different forms of exclusiveness, and to set forth the relative, conditioned nature of things. If the questioner is so perverse as to persist in his pressing for an answer the only course is to chide him, to ask him to give up his perversions and attend to things of fundamental importance. The Buddha adopted all these modes of answering in regard to these questions.[38]

Speaking specifically of the fourteen questions and giving reasons for the Buddha's silence, the *Śāstra* says:

The Buddha did not answer these because the points of these questions, (viz., absolute existence and absolute non-existence of the world and the soul) are untrue, false (此事無實).

It is devoid of reason to hold that every thing is eternal (and self-existent); it is also devoid of reason to hold that all things are evanescent. Therefore the Buddha refused to answer (these questions which are framed on these false notions of absolute existence and absolute non-existence). Suppose someone asks, how much milk does one get by squeezing the horn of the cow? It would be a wrong question and should not be answered.

The course of the world is endless, being comparable in this with the wheel of a cart, which has no (absolute) beginning or (absolute) end.

Even a reply to these questions would be of no use; (but when clung to, the reply) could lead one to errors and make one fall into wrong notions.

The Buddha knows that these fourteen questions always (by their very nature) cover up and conceal the Four Noble Truths which constitute the true nature of things (viz., conditioned origination). If in the spot where one has to cross over to the other side there is any venomous creature, no one should be allowed to cross there; one should (on the contrary) be shown a safe, secure place where one can cross over (without any difficulty).

Some say that these questions are not intelligible to one who is not all-knowing and that the Buddha did not give any answer to these as people would not understand. (74c–75a)

*The revealer of the Middle Way:* It is necessary to note that the *Śāstra* leaves no doubt that the range which is covered by the fourteen questions is the range of conditioned origination. What they assume is a perversion as they cling exclusively to being and to non-being and thus they constitute the extremes of eternalism and negativism. What is revealed by their rejection is the Middle Way, the truth of *pratītya-samutpāda.*

(The bodhisattva who has obtained the ability to bear the truth of things) investigates unimpededly the subject-matter of the fourteen unanswered questions which are all based on the extremes of eternality and evanescence, (i.e., unconditioned existence and total perishing of things). (By virtue of this investigation) he never loses the Middle Way (不失中道).[39] (170a)

*The non-clinging use of concepts:* Still, to the non-clinging the truth may be told that

Beings are endless and even the knowledge of the Buddha is endless. This is the (mundane) truth. But if one would cling to this teaching, seize this character and give rise to contention and quarrel, then the

Buddha would say that it is perversion. For instance, that the world is permanent and that the world is impermanent, both these (become) perversions when these enter the fourteen questions (入十四難中) (and thus come to be seized as absolute being and absolute non-being). (266a)

Spoken non-clingingly "is" and "is not" or permanence and impermanence are true of things; it is as such that the Buddha makes use of them in His teachings.

He mostly taught through impermanence (and that in a non-clinging way, not conceiving it as absolute); this He did in order to help people to get rid of their perversion; He rarely used the teaching through permanence. But if one would cling to (the teaching of) impermanence, seize the character, and give rise to contention, then the Buddha would say, it is a perversion, a falsity. If one would not cling to impermanence (then it would open up the truth of things, it would be the first door to *śūnyatā;* for) then one would understand that impermanence is the same as pain, pain is the same as the devoidness of selfhood and devoidness of selfhood is itself *śūnyatā.* In this way one can enter the *śūnyatā* of all elements (入諸法空) through the comprehension of impermanence; (in this way "impermanence") is just the truth of things. Therefore it should be known that (in this way) impermanence enters the true nature of things (入真諦中); and this is the true (understanding). But impermanence becomes an object of clinging in the fourteen questions and so (there) it is a perversion.[40] (266a)

*The Right Way:* It is essential to note that the points raised in the fourteen questions are not in themselves unanswerable; but they become unanswerable when the aspects are clung to as absolute, when the conditioned is seized as unconditioned. In regard to all these fourteen questions the answer is *pratītyasamutpāda* or the Middle Way, the way that sees things as they are.[41] It is through the Middle Way that the Buddha met these questions whenever He answered them. The wise see things in their true nature and teach it to everyone just as they have themselves seen.

If any one would speak of the non-existent as existent and of the existent as non-existent, then he would not be the all-knowing person. The Buddha, the all-comprehensive in understanding, speaks of the existent as existent and of the non-existent as non-existent. He does not speak of the existent as non-existent nor of the non-existent as existent; He just speaks of things as they are in their true nature (但說諸法實相) . . . (In this regard He is comparable to the sun). The sun for example does not make anything tall or short nor does he level (all things) down to the ground. It illumines all things equally. This is the case even with the Buddha. He does not make the non-existent existent nor the existent non-existent. He always speaks the truth; and by the light of His wisdom He illumines all things.[42] (75a)

## CHAPTER VI

# EXTREMES AND ALTERNATIVES

### Section I

## THE EXTREMES

*Extremes and clinging:* Extremes are species of blindness, kinds of dogmatism. They are of the form: "This alone is true, all else is false." The aspects singled out in the concrete becoming are exclusively clung to and held as ultimate; they are not appreciated as mere aspects. The relative distinctions within the natural polarity of the self-conscious intellection are turned into absolute divisions. Contrasting concepts of "is" and "is not," "identity" and "difference," etc., constitute the very form in which rational comprehension of the conditioned entities is worked out and by which the world of the determinate is appreciated as a system. This is the essence of the doctrine of conditioned origination. But under ignorance which functions by way of clinging, concepts are seized and an ultimacy is imposed on one of the sides in the pair of the contrasting terms and this ultimacy is then transferred to the entity to which the term refers and from which it derives its import. Thus what has only relative being is mistaken as a substantial entity; the fragmentary is seized as complete. While the relative alternatives are true of things as their different perspectives from different standpoints, under clinging the alternatives are turned into extremes and the original integrity of the thing and the essential relativity of the aspects are lost sight of.

*Criticism: Its principle and purpose:* The primary purpose of criticism is to lay bare the truth that the entities to which the different philosophical schools cling as ultimate are in truth relative, conditioned, that the specific perspectives to which they cling as limitless are in truth determinate. That the specific is not the ultimate, the relative is not the absolute, is the principle that underlies criticism. It is intended to help people to overcome the basic confusion of the real and the unreal, the absolute and the relative. In this the one way which Nāgārjuna frequently adopted was of showing up the self-contradiction and absurdity to which the holders of exclusive views would lead themselves on their own grounds.[1] The most convincing way of enlightening people on the limitation of their position is to bring to light the natural consequences to which they are led by their own exclusive claims.

*Criticism: Its procedure:* The *modus operandi* of criticism consists in assuming the particular view in question as right and drawing the conclusions to which one is led by following its natural consequences which, on account of the falsity of the initial assumption, turn out to be false. By the falsity of the conclusions the falsity of their ground is revealed and the exclusive claim of dogmatic thought is thereby shown to be absurd. What is most essential to bear in mind is that the absurd conclusions do not belong to the critic himself; they belong to the upholders of exclusive claims. Again, the conclusions by which the holders of views stand contradicted on their own grounds, are negative, neither of the mundane entities nor of the relative validity of the specific views, but of the exclusive claims of absoluteness in regard to them.

In the critical examination the several possible alternatives of a position are tried not as relative positions but as absolute views with exclusive claims. For, that is the way in which they are held by their upholders. The arguments leading the different positions to their natural conclusions are all framed in reference to absolute concepts. Being is total being, non-being is total non-being, a complete extinction; self is wholly self-contained, other is wholly other, totally different. Identity is absolute identity, and difference is total separateness. The holders of views swing from extreme to extreme, from one exclusive position to another exclusive position. So, it is as extremes, exclusive positions, that the alternatives are tried. These are truly the relative and distinct falsely seized as absolute and divided.[2] The purpose of criticism is to expose the absurdities and the self-contradictions to which the upholders of the exclusive views lend themselves. The demonstration consists in showing that if things were of such nature as they are conceived in these extremes, then the world would be an utter blank, or a jumble of confusion and chaos devoid of meaning. The intelligible world of conditioned becoming and orderly growth, the world that provides for moral and spiritual endeavour, the very thing which the holders of these extreme views mean to uphold thus stands denied. This is the basic self-contradiction. Rejecting the truthfulness of absolute positions, the validity of exclusive views, criticism reveals the essential relativity, the intrinsic conditionedness as the mundane truth of things.

*The four extremes: How they are conceived:* Out of the contrasting pairs of the natural polarity of intellection one side is clung to as absolute and the other is explained away, or both are placed together in a mechanical combination, i.e., without the necessary correction of the initial assumption that they are ultimate and unrelated particulars and their combination as a complex of independent exclusives is itself held to be the truth; or driven by the sense of impossibility of such a combination, even that is totally denied, while yet the imagination of the independent reality of the object still stands undenied; or the denial of both "is" and "is not" is taken as absolute or total, i.e., as a denial even of the relative existence and relative non-existence.

In regard to "being," for instance, if one would start with the natural attitude of simple acceptance and affirmation, the one-levelled experience of the common man, and that, with a clinging mind, one would exclusively hold to being, viz., that everything has absolute being. This is eternalism.

The thing that is there in its own right never becomes non-existent, this is eternalism.[3]

But in confronting the passing away of things, which is opposed to the position that everything is an absolute being, one tends to the other extreme and holds to absolute non-being.

That the thing was there absolutely but is now totally lost, this is the view of annihilationism.[4]

Ordinary thought would stop at being and non-being taken one at one time. Either a thing is a being or it is a non-being; if it is not the one it should be the other. And being as well as non-being are taken as absolute, total. It is the swinging between the two extremes that is the cycle of ignorance in which common people are caught. But reflective thought, the reviewer of views would see the partiality, the incompleteness of each of these positions of being and non-being. The reflective mind feels the need to put the fragments together which were taken apart by the ordinary unreflective thought. But while seeking to arrive at the togetherness which constitutes the thing, the imagined absoluteness of what are only distinguishable aspects is yet accepted without question. Being and non-being are taken as absolutes, reals, ultimates, although it is held that these are always found together and never alone. Being is an ultimate, a real and so is non-being. Experience is a combination of ultimate reals, being and non-being. Certainly being is different from non-being. How can the one be the other? But despite their being intrinsically different, absolutely independent, still they form a combination and the one is never found apart from the other. The dualism of the Sāṅkhya is an instance of such a view.

The attitude engendered by the sense of impossibility either of the two exclusive characters residing in the same thing as its absolute nature or of the effective togetherness of two independent entities that are total exclusives gives rise to the fourth extreme. But the attitude of the fourth extreme is one in which all the possible alternatives, here conceived as absolutes, are exhausted. It is therefore an attitude of despair, a total rejection of all possibility of expressing the nature of the thing. This is an attitude which either rejects reason altogether and clings to chance *(ahetuka)*, or one which rejects even that and accepts a position of complete negation of any certain knowledge while accepting the reality of the thing (agnosticism). Or, again one denies even that and ends in a state of utter doubt (scepticism). The agnostic or the sceptic does not question the initial assumption of absoluteness in regard to what are only the distinguishable aspects. He sees the difficulty in the combination of the intrinsically opposed, but he does not question the veracity of the absolute division of the thing nor of the ultimacy of the aspects; to these he remains blind.

*The formulation of extremes (koṭi): Extremes exemplified:* It may be noted that there are two or three ways of formulating the four *koṭis:* (A) existence *(asti, bhāva, sat)*, non-existence *(nāsti, abhāva, asat)*, both *(sadasat, bhāvābhava)*, and neither—nor *(naivāsti, na ca nāsti)*; (B) self *(sva)*, other *(para)*, both *(ubhaya)* and neither—nor *(anubhaya)*; one *(eka)*, many *(nānā)*, both *(ubhaya)* and neither—nor *(anubhaya)*; identical *(tat)*, different *(anyat)*, both *(ubhaya)* and neither—nor *(anubhaya)*; and (C) self *(sva)*, other *(para)*, both *(ubhaya)*, and chance or devoid of reason) *(ahetuka)*.[5] What these *koṭis* deny and what their rejection reveals is the conditioned origination of things.

(1) The first *koṭi* in all the three forms stands for the naïve acceptance of things as they appear to be and that as absolutely so; this is the case of the common people. In the case of the philosophers, the first *koṭi* stands for the position of the analysts who mistake the simple elements which are the ultimates in analysis to be ultimates also in reality. This is the position of the Vaibhāṣikas and we may add here even the Vaiśeṣikas. This amounts to holding that every element is an absolute self-being *(svabhāva)*, an ultimate. This is eternalism; it is practically a denial of negation, and even the negative is accepted to be a kind of positive entity. This amounts to ignoring the aspect of cessation altogether.

(2) The second position holds firmly to the very aspect that was neglected or explained away in the first, viz., the aspect of cessation, and it is held to be the absolute nature of things, i.e., cessation is a total cessation. This amounts to ignoring the aspect of being which figures clearly as continuity in the stream of becoming; as denial of continuity, this amounts to a denial of becoming itself. Of the sixty-two *dṛṣṭis* seven kinds of annihilationism are mentioned, all of which are exemplifications of the doctrine of the total cessation of personality after death. Those who hold this view are termed 'nihilists' in Buddhist literature. The Vaipulyakas, who cling to *śūnyatā* as an extreme, also belong here. In regard to the problem of causation, particularly in regard to the ques-

tion of the relation between cause and effect or of the relation between the preceding and the succeeding moments in the causal series, the Buddhists always considered the Sāṅkhya as holding the view of identity and the Vaiśeṣikas as holding the view of difference, identity and difference being alike conceived as total identity and total difference.

(3) The third *koṭi,* that of both "is" and "is not" or both "identity" and "difference" may be compared with the position of the Nirgranthas, the Jainas. It is to be noted that the Jainas are epistemologically non-absolutists (relativists), but metaphysically pluralists. Their position is by its very nature unstable; to take relativism seriously is to deny ultimacy of difference and with the denial of the ultimacy of difference pluralism cannot stand. On the contrary, if they take pluralism seriously, they cannot be relativists. However, the Jainas do combine in them both these features and for the Buddhist who fares on the Middle Way this position seems to involve two difficulties. These are:

I) In regard to the mundane truth, while relativism is not only valid but essential, to hold that relativism is an ultimate feature of reality is to conceive the relative phases as absolute, or to seize the specific as ultimate. This is to miss the true import of "absolute." Is division or difference ultimate? The relativism of the Jainas amounts to saying both "yes" and "no"; their pluralism amounts to a categorical "yes." But to the farer on the Middle Way, who rises above exclusiveness, the mundane truth is describable in terms of difference as much as identity, plurality as well as unity. The ultimate truth, which is not anything specific or determinate, is neither describable as identity nor as difference, although the Buddha taught of it mostly through identity or unity[5a] and that, in a non-clinging way, i.e., not clinging to either identity or unity as itself ultimate. The ultimate is strictly *niṣprapañca,* non-conceptual; all conceptual formulations belong to the relative and hence to the mundane level.

II) Again, the pluralism of the Jainas lends itself to an interpretation that their relativism is really a syncretism, a mechanically putting together of the different elements. Every view as much as every thing, should have to be viewed as a complex of many independent reals, a view which is in this respect similar to that of the Vaibhāṣikas and the

Vaiśeṣikas. The *reductio ad absurdum* in that case is that the dynamic, organismic, nature of life and personality, and the nature of the world as a system stand denied; for to hold difference as absolute is to contradict the mundane nature of things as well as their ultimate nature. In the case of the extreme of both being and non-being it may be noted that when being as well as non-being are alike held to be absolutely, wholly true of one and the same thing, then one really cancels the other and there is nothing further that remains as the true description of the thing. But is not this absolute blank itself, the utter impossibility of all description itself, the absolute nature of the thing? With this question one is already in the fourth extreme.

It may be noted that in the extreme of neither being nor non-being, one could revert and say that "neither being" asserts non-being and "nor non-being" asserts being and thus it would be an assertion of both being and non-being. But as this kind of reversion would not constitute a new position it would not be worth considering; it stands condemned with the condemnation of the third extreme, viz., of both "is" and "is not." Further the kind of denial of the third extreme that makes way for the fourth is one in which the "being" and "non-being" are taken not severally but conjointly. Taking them severally would be to make them indistinguishable from the first and the second (severally or serially) and to miss the significance of the third extreme which is a conjoined assertion of being and non-being.

(4) The fourth *koṭi* is different in nature from the first three. The first three are forms of assertion. Even non-being is an assertion inasmuch as it is not only a negation but also a conceiving as "other than," "exclusive of," "wholly different from," being. It is only in this way that it becomes an extreme. To be an extreme, it must be a position which is clung to, which means that it is an assertion, and at the same time, exclusive. An extreme is thus an exclusive position, an absolute assertion, an unconditional view, which is an object of clinging. It is in this way that *śūnyatā* (indeterminate) itself is sometimes made an object of clinging by the uninformed. Now, all the first three *koṭis* are forms of assertion in which an ascription of absolute being or absolute non-being or both being and non-being is maintained. But the fourth *koṭi* is one

in which there is no ascription of any specific character, viz., of being or non-being, or both being and non-being, of identity or difference or both identity and difference; but all the same it is a position, an exclusive assertion, an object of clinging. It is a position in which the possibility of all description in terms of being etc. is totally denied. In being negative it is similar to the second *koṭi*. But while in the second *koṭi*, there is the scope for moving to the third, viz., of syncretic combination of both "is" and "is not," in the fourth even the possibility of this combined ascription is altogether denied. Here the clinging is to the total denial of all ascriptions, a denial even of relative description, holding the thing to *be* of such a nature that it is absolutely indescribable, that no statement, not even the conditioned statement, can be made of it. This is really to deny the possibility of all statements, of whatever kind, and hence of all thought, of all knowledge. In this case, first of all, not even the statement that the thing is not describable is possible. Secondly in the assertion that the thing is such that it is utterly indescribable the notion of the being of the thing is at the same time entertained, which must here be a total being as it is a case of clinging. This amounts to saying that while the thing is absolutely there, no knowledge of it is possible; this is clearly the position of agnosticism and is inconsistent with itself inasmuch as there must be, as the ground of such a statement, the knowledge of the thing as existent and as beyond or opposed to all description. Further in the case of a total denial of all statements, even of a relative statement, there would be no scope for any knowledge of anything. To quote the *Śāstra,* "it is fool's talk."[6]

The above account of the fourth *koṭi* is representative of the agnostic. With slight modification, it may be taken as representative of the eel wriggler, a case of mere quibble, sophistry, evasion. Instead of there being "no knowledge of anything," it would be no definite or certain knowledge of anything. This could be either "both is and is not," or with its denial, "neither is nor is not."[7] Dīrghanakha figures prominently as a sceptic who accepted no position, and when asked by the Buddha, he went to the extreme of not accepting even this position that he does not accept anything, whereupon the Buddha easily remarked that he was then no better than a common man and that he had no reason to consider himself superior. He was not worth listening to at all.[8]

The Jaina position of indeterminateness *(avaktavya)* viz., the impossibility of a thing being absolutely describable as either is or is not, where the description that "the thing both is and is not" is also denied, seems near to the Mādhyamikas' relativism of judgements in respect to mundane truth. But as it is already noted above, the import of indeterminateness is not taken seriously by the Jainas. To take it seriously is not only to admit the possibility of different standpoints and correspondingly different judgements all of which are equally true in respect to the determinate, which is clearly what the Jainas maintain, but it is also to admit that the ultimate truth is not anything determinate, that even the distinction between the determinate and the indeterminate is not ultimate. This amounts to saying that the ultimate reality is not anything determinable. This means for the Jainas to give up their pluralism and recognize the ultimate as indeterminate. But the very relativism of the Jainas also implicates the denial of even this description of the ultimate as the indeterminate, meaning for the Mādhyamika that the ultimate reality is not absolutely indeterminate, i.e., not exclusive of the determinate, but at the same time, not also the determinate as such. The determinate as such is relative, not absolute. But the absolute is not exclusive of the relative, nor is the relative anything apart from the absolute. The relative is itself the absolute, not as such, but in its ultimate nature.

In other words what is needed here is the recognition of the distinction of appearance and reality, the conditioned and the unconditioned.

To cling to indeterminateness as an absolute character in reference to the mundane is an error; this is to deny even the possibility of relative judgement. This is the error that arises by clinging to *śūnyatā* as a total negation. Indeterminateness in regard to the mundane nature of things means the impossibility of absolute statements, i.e., statements taken in an ultimate sense. It, however, leaves room for relative statements. This is the non-clinging *śūnyatā*. The basic judgement that "the real is the unconditioned" which is the fundamental prius of all criticism is undeniable on the plane of the mundane truth and is not denied there. What is denied is one's clinging to it by which, on the one hand, one tends to divide the conditioned from the unconditioned and on the other, tends to do away with the conditioned. This is an error. What makes the difference is not the presence or absence of statements but whether one is clinging or non-clinging in regard to them.

*Section II*

## THE ALTERNATIVES

*Relative judgements and absolute statements:* The farer on the Middle Way has no scope for contention. The Middle Way is non-contentious precisely because it is non-clinging. This is the all-embracing comprehension which is inclusive of all specific views. It is not a denial of anything; it is a rejection only of the dogmatic, exclusive claims. Thus the wise understand the origin of eternalism and understand also the grain of truth in it as well as its exaggerations. There is the aspect of "is" in becoming into which it can be analyzed and of which it cannot be denied. But the eternalist clings to "is" and leaves out or explains away the other aspect, "is not." Clinging to the aspect of arising and continuing, one ends in eternalism and clinging to the aspect of perishing, ceasing to be, one ends in annihilationism. To start with "is" and "is not" as reals and thus to get becoming out of their combination is absurd.

How can being and non-being be together in the same thing at the same time?

And to deny all possibility of understanding, just because one has failed to understand in the way in which one has started, is a still greater folly. This would be a "fool's talk," or a surrender to chance.

The farer on the Middle Way is free from these errors, for he keeps himself free from clinging to "is" and "is not;" he recognizes these as essentially relative aspects distinguishable in the fact of becoming; as such they are not ultimate; and being essentially relative, they are not mutually exclusive. From one standpoint "is" is true of things, from another, "is not" is true. Similarly both "is" and "is not" are true of one and the same thing simultaneously from different standpoints. To the reflective minds that analyze the many distinguishable aspects of things and review them in an intellectual synthesis, "is" is as much true of the thing as "is not"; they do not find any difficulty in appreciating the original unity of "is" and "is not" in the concrete becoming. They are thus above mere "is" and mere "is not." But this very awareness of the describability of the thing as both "is" and "is not" from two different standpoints which are themselves correlative, opens up also the other possibility of describing the thing as "neither is nor is not;" for in respect to its being it is not non-being and in respect to its non-being it is not being. This amounts to the denial of the absolute describability of the thing in term of "is" and "is not"; that it is relatively describable is implied.

The alternative statements are different from the extremes precisely because the former are specific judgements made with the unmistakable awareness of the other possibilities from other standpoints, as well as with the awareness that the relative standpoints and their reflective judgements are pertinent only to the mundane truth, the level of the relative. The skilfulness of the wise consists in their ability to keep themselves *en rapport* with any situation and see it rightly in order to give it the direction which is proper to its growth and fulfilment. This is possible because the wise are on a level above fragmentariness. This is the sense in saying that the Buddha has no view of His own. It is precisely because He has no view of His own that He has the ability to appreciate fully the nature of every specific view, understand its need and guide it accordingly, even as He is capable of having compassion for all, able to appreciate the need of every self, every being, and extend His help to everyone precisely because He has no "self" of His own.

We have seen the *Kārikā* saying:

The Buddha has taught of (the existence) of self as well as of the non-existence of self; He has also taught of neither self nor no self. (XVIII:6)

and,

Everything is true, nothing is true; everything is both true and not true; everything is neither true nor not true. This is the teaching of the Buddha. (XVIII:8)

These are cases where, if clinging were to operate, every one of these "positions" would become an extreme and hence false; but now, as these are positions free from clinging, they are not wrong; these are not extremes; they are alternatives, of which each is true and all are true.

Regarding the fourth alternative, an observation is necessary. As expressive of the indeterminate nature of the mundane truth, i.e., as a denial of the possibility of absolute statements in regard to the relative, this alternative suits best to the purpose of the farer on the Middle Way as it is his intention to point to the error of clinging. When there is no clinging in regard to it, then it is quite admissible for the Mādhyamika. Thus, commenting on the statement of the *Sūtra* that the bodhisattva's realization of the *bodhi* cannot be conceived even in terms of "neither by cultivation, nor by non-cultivation," the *Śāstra* observes that the Buddha denies even the fourth alternative because this question, whether it can be said that the bodhisattva realizes the *bodhi* by "neither cultivation nor non-cultivation" was asked by Subhūti with a clinging mind. Therefore the Buddha replies in the negative.

It is by (the former) clinging to the position of both cultivation and non-cultivation, that there arises (through its rejection) (the fourth position) that of "neither by cultivation nor by non-cultivation;" but if this position is mentioned with a non-clinging mind, without seizing the determinate, then there is nothing wrong in it.[9] (644a)

To cling to the fourth position amounts, on the one hand, to clinging to the denial of the describability of the fact of realization, i.e., even of its describability in conditioned terms, and, on the other, it amounts to mistaking the distinction between bodhisattva and the *bodhi*, which is only a relative distinction holding only in the mundane truth, as an absolute division, thereby removing the very possibility of this realization. So we have there itself in the *Sūtra* a further clarification in regard to the way the bodhisattva realizes the *bodhi*. The question is asked, if none of these four ways are proper in understanding the fact of realization, how else should one understand it. And the *Sūtra* replies:

The bodhisattva realizes the *sarvākārajñatā* in accordance with the true nature of things. (641c)

It is by refraining from seizing, it is by non-clinging, that the bodhisattva cultivates the *prajñā*.[1c] But what does non-clinging mean? To cling is to conceive in terms of two (i.e., division) (諸有二者是有所得); the undivided is the non-clinging (無有二者是無所得).[10a]

The denial is not of the fact of realization, nor of its understandability, but of the possibility of understanding it in terms of duality, or extremes.

As noted in the beginning of this work, while extremes are falsifications in regard to the mundane nature of things, they are irrelevant in regard to their ultimate nature. Actually in regard to the latter they have no special significance; for it is as contrasted with the Middle Way that they make sense. The Middle Way is not the ultimate truth. As a synonym of conditioned origination it belongs to the mundane level. As the awareness of the essential relativity of all views and of the essential conditionedness of all entities, i.e., as the non-exclusive way, it is significant only on the plane of the relative. As the remover of dogmatism, again, it is significant as distinct from and as the remedy for dead-ends. In short, the Middle Way is, in terms of the *Śāstra,* truth taught as remedy. It is as a remedy to dogmatism that *śūnyatā* as criticism has sense; and *śūnyatā* as criticism is the Middle Way.

*Rejection is of extremes:* There are several places in the *Prajñāpāramitā-sūtra* where extremes are stated and rejected as views that spring from the clinging mind. The rejection of these extremes is clearly shown as intended to reveal that it is impossible to understand the mundane truth, the conditioned origination, by seizing concepts, by clinging to characters. The rejection of extremes is again intended to reveal the ultimate identity or undividedness of the bodhisattva or the Buddha and the *bodhi,* i.e., of the individual and the ultimate reality. This is the non-duality of the way and the goal, of the conditioned and the unconditioned. The faring on the way as well as the realizing of the goal are accepted as mundane truth, but the clinging to them as ultimate in that nature is denied.

Whatever is a case of seizing duality all that is a case of clinging; to be free from seizing duality is to be non-clinging. Duality means clinging to the division that this is the eye and this is the form, this is the *bodhi* and this is the Buddha.[11]

The (truly) non-clinging *dharma* is the (ultimate) sameness *(samatā)* of clinging and non-clinging. (642b)

Even the distinction between clinging and non-clinging may itself be clung to; then also the comprehension of the ultimate reality, the undivided being, is missed. The Buddha has realized the *bodhi*, but not halting in the ultimate reality, nor stopping in the mundane. Neither of these is the right view. Did not the Buddha realize the *bodhi* at all? The Buddha says:

I did indeed realize the *bodhi*, but not halting either in the composite or in the incomposite. (645c)

The *Sūtra* points out that by halting in the way there is no realization of reality; and even by halting in the not-way there is no realization of reality. Even by halting in both the way and the not-way there is no realization of reality. Not even by halting in "neither the way nor the not-way" there is any realization of reality. One should realize the reality by not halting anywhere, not even on the Way.[12]

The *Śāstra* explains that in this passage halting means seizing the determinate, clinging to characters (住名取相).[12a]

There is the realization of Reality but not as it is imagined in these four extremes . . . Neither anything nor nothing, devoid of all *prapañca*—this is what is called realization of the Way. (658c)

The *Śāstra* observes;

If one is free from these four extremes, then the *prapañca* itself would be the Way. (662a)

As we have been observing, *prapañca,* in the sense of conceptual construction and elaboration, is not in itself opposed to the truth of things; on the contrary that is the very way in which the true nature of things could be set forth, expressed, communicated; this is essential for wayfaring. *Pratītyasamutpāda* is itself such a system of concepts, setting forth the nature of things as they are.

By the cultivation of the way, one does not realize the goal, nor by not cultivating the way does one realize the goal. By giving up the way one does not realize the goal, nor by staying in (or sticking to) the way does one realize the goal. (686a)

"It is by not imagining an ultimate division between the composite and the incomposite that one realizes all the fruits of wayfaring."[13] The *Śāstra* observes that this statement in the *Sūtra* is occasioned by the fact that Subhūti asked the question about the way and the goal with a clinging mind:

He means to extract the fruit from the way even as (ordinary people conceive the fact of) oil being squeezed from the hemp . . . If one would cultivate the way free from seizing characters, free from the clinging mind, then in his case there is the way, and there is the goal. (687b)

Is the *bodhi* realized by the way of origination or by the way of non-origination, or by both or by neither? None of these is true because there is not that division between the *bodhi* and the way which is here conceived and clung to.

The *bodhi* is itself the way, the way is itself the *bodhi.* (706b)

The Buddha does not realize the *bodhi,* for in the ultimate truth, there is not that division between the Buddha and *bodhi* which is here conceived and clung to as ultimate.

> The Buddha is Himself the *bodhi*, the *bodhi* is itself the Buddha. (706b)

Interpreted in the context of the mundane truth this means that

> Of all things, cause and effect are neither identical nor different. (708a)

Although both identity and difference are false as absolute characters of the relation between cause and effect, still, as relative characterizations, the wise use both identity and difference in this context, and that in the non-clinging way. The Buddha mostly used identity in conveying the ultimate truth, but He did not cling to it.[14]

In regard to this question of the relation between cause and effect we have in the *Sūtra* a very interesting passage which considers whether the *bodhi* is attained by the first moment of thought or by the subsequent moment of thought. If the first moment is unconnected with the next, and the next moment is unconnected with the first, how then can the bodhisattva cultivate the way and collect the elements of merit? The example of the flame of the burning lamp is given. It is asked whether the wick is burnt by the first moment of flame or by the next moment of flame. Neither by the first itself nor without the first, nor by the next itself nor without the next. But is the wick burnt or not? Indeed it is burnt. This is just the case even with the moments of thought in regard to the cultivation of the way. Neither by any of the moments of thought themselves nor completely without any of these, is the *bodhi* realized. But the *bodhi* is indeed realized by the bodhisattva. Exclaims the *Sūtra:*

> Profound indeed is this *pratitya-samutpāda!* (585a)

It should not be difficult to get at the import of this discourse in the

*Sūtra*. What is denied here is not the fact of realization, not even the understandability of its course, as it is clearly expressed as conditioned origination; what is denied here is its intelligibility in terms of absolute, non-relational, entities corresponding to the ultimates of analysis seized as self-being, in which

> The first moment of mind does not reach the next moment, and the next moment is not contained in the first moment. (584c)

Commenting on this passage of the *Sūtra*, the *Śāstra* observes:

> If merely by the first moment of thought one could become the Buddha, even independently of the succeeding moments, then with the very first thought of *bodhi*, the bodhisattva should have become the Buddha. But if there is not the first thought at all, (if it totally ceased to be) then how can there be the successive moments, the second, the third (etc.)? Of the successive moments, the second, the third (etc.) the first moment is (in fact) the very root . . .
>
> (Again) even the next moments are not (totally) apart from the first moment. If there is not the first moment, then there are not also the subsequent ones. It is only when from the first moment (onwards) there is the collection of the different kinds of merit, that the last moment becomes complete; and when the last moment is complete, it can put an end (completely) to *kleśas* and their residues and fetch the unexcelled *bodhi*. (585c)

The difficulty arises here on account of conceiving that the earlier and the later moments of thought are not related. Being not related, the past is conceived as totally extinct, and does not provide for any relatedness. In the absence of relatedness between the first and the next, there is no possibility of collecting the roots of merit. And in the absence of the collection of the roots of merit, how can there be the realization of the unexcelled *bodhi*?[15]

The *Śāstra* observes that by the example of the lamp the Buddha means to say:

You see actually with your very eyes that the wick is burnt; although it is neither (exclusively) by the first moment nor is it (exclusively) by the next, still the wick is indeed burnt. Even so I see with the eye of the Buddha that the bodhisattva does indeed realize the *bodhi*. Although it cannot be that it is by the first thought itself nor completely apart from the first thought that the realization is accomplished, still, the bodhisattva does . . . indeed realize the *bodhi*. (585c)

*The negative criticisms: Their significance:* The above account of the *Sūtra* shows a way to understand the negative criticisms of the farer on the Middle Way. These criticisms are intended to lay bare the absurdities in exclusive clinging, clinging to the specific as the ultimate. The fundamental *reductio ad absurdum* is the impossibility of mundane existence if everything is as the upholders of exclusive views conceive it to be. It is a rejection not of "is" or "is not" as the distinguishable aspects of becoming, but of eternalism and negativism, the false views built on relative truths, which are truths turned into falsity by exclusive clinging. It is again not a denial of the possibility of understanding the truth of things, but its revelation by means of criticism or rational investigation. So, far from being a denial of the mundane truth, criticism reveals it as *pratītyasamutpāda.*

It is to be noted that *śūnyatā* as criticism is not an end in itself; as revelatory of the non-substantiality of mundane things it is the means to the further realization of the ultimate reality. *Śūnyatā* as criticism lays bare on the one hand the conditionedness of the things to which we cling in our ignorance as unconditioned and on the other, it lays bare the truth that the entities that are seen to arise and perish in their conditioned nature are themselves in their ultimate nature the unconditioned reality, the Nirvāṇa. Those who cling in mind conceive *śūnyatā* as total negation. Actually, total negation is false in reference to the mundane truth, while negation and affirmation are irrelevant in regard to the ultimate truth. In the mundane truth:

It is the change *(anayathābhāva)* of the existent that people call negation.[15a]

Absolute existence and absolute non-existence are species of falsehood in regard to mundane truth which is relativity. We have seen above that even the extinction of ignorance or *avidyā*, is not an absolute negation that ends in a complete blank; the ceasing of *avidyā* is the arising of *prajñā;* the world is itself beheld as Nirvāṇa.

The doctrine of *pratītyasamutpāda* is indeed a systematic presentation of the basic constitution of things in their mundane nature. The denial of the laws of thought or of the *pramāṇas* is not implied in the rejection of extremes. The basic principle of thought, that no two contradictory judgements can hold good in regard to the same thing in the same respect is indeed accepted by the *Śastra.* This we have already seen. This is appreciated all the more when we see that this basic law of thought is upheld as essential in mundane experience. That the same man cannot both have and not have the horns on his head[16] and that the ring finger is both long and short from different standpoints,[17] are only different ways of stating the fundamental law of thought. Says the *Śāstra:*

If one does not pursue one's enquiry in accordance with reason (若不以理求) one cannot understand anything; but by pursuing the enquiry of things in accordance with reason, there is not anything that one cannot know. (138c)

Nāgārjuna does indeed defend himself against the charge of the opponents that he is contradicting *vyavahāra,* when he says in the *Kārikā:*

"Everything stands in harmony in his case who is in harmony with *śūnyatā;* but nothing stands in harmony with him who is not in harmony with *śūnyatā.*"

It is needless to say that whatever holds good in the case of the world of the determinate holds good also in the case of the *pramāṇas,* the determinate modes of knowing. What is rejected in the case of the determinate modes of knowing is the erroneous notion of their self-sufficiency or absoluteness, and what is revealed is their limitedness to the sphere of the determinate and the relative nature of the knowledge they yield, as well as their ultimate dependence on *prajñā* to which they owe their being and with which they are identical in their ultimate nature. It is the *prajñā* itself that functions as the eyes of flesh and as the knowledge of all forms.

*CHAPTER VII*

# CRITICISM OF CATEGORIES

*Section I*

## THE MUNDANE AND THE ULTIMATE TRUTH

*The disclosing of the mundane and the ultimate truth:* To cut at its root the tendency to cling to the specific as ultimate is the deepest truth of the denial of self which the Buddha taught. It is a denial not of the self itself but of the falsely imagined self-hood in regard to the body-mind complex. The basic meaning of self is underivedness, unconditionedness. The self-being *(svabhāva)* is the independent, unconditioned being which does not depend on anything to come into existence.[1] Even the "coming into existence" is not relevant in regard to it, for it never goes out of existence. That which was not existent before, is existent now, and will cease to be later is not the self-being. But arising and perishing are the very nature of the elements that constitute the body-mind complex. So the Buddha declared that the entities that are subject to arising and perishing are not fit to be considered as the self, for they are devoid of the nature of self, viz., self-being. It is this imagination of self-being or absoluteness in regard to the conditioned and contingent that is the root of error and suffering. It is this that the Buddha exhorts everyone to dispel. In its general form this is the error of misplaced absoluteness. We have already seen that for Nāgārjuna the Sarvāstivādins' doctrine of elements becomes an important and glaring instance of this basic error. It is the categories of the Sarvāstivādins that become the primary object of criticism in his works. He points out that the Sarvāstivādins cling at every step; they seize the relative as self-being and commit the very error against which the Buddha warned all His disciples, viz., the extreme of eternalism.

The extreme of negativism takes a minor place in the works of Nāgārjuna, although its mention and criticism become necessary for him for at least two reasons: I) Criticism of categories culminating in the revelation of their non-substantiality may itself tend in the case of one who follows the way of *śūnyatā* but with a clinging mind to end in the extreme of negativism, denying even the relative being of things and thus denying the very possibility of causal continuity. II) Again, the clinging in mind who are not the followers of the way of *śūnyatā* might easily tend to mistake it as a negativism that ends in an utter blank, a complete nothing.[2] While the latter is the false imagination that criticism puts an end to things themselves, making them non-existent, the former is the error of imagining that the non-being of things indicated by their passing away is total. The latter mistakes the nature of criticism and the former, the nature of the course of things. Both these are really forms of the same kind of clinging, viz., the clinging to negation or non-being. The way out of these lies in realizing relativity as the essential nature of things. Criticism or critical examination of the categories is a means to lay bare this true nature by putting an end to the false imagination of absoluteness in regard to the relative. Further, the very relativity of "is" and "is not," being and non-being, removes the notion of an absolute cessation of things. What is called relative non-being is only difference or change, which is not unconditioned.

It must be noted that the charge of negativism brought against the Mādhyamika is occasioned partly by the circumstance that he does not always make the distinction clear between the rejection of unconditionedness that reveals conditioned becoming as the mundane truth and the rejection of the ultimacy of the conditionedness of the conditioned that reveals the unconditioned, the undivided being as the ultimate reality. The primary meaning of *śūnyatā* is devoidness which is a direct reference to the truth of things, mundane and ultimate; but it refers also to the method (criticism) by which *śūnyatā* as truth is brought to light, viz., by rejecting the imagination of ultimacy and absoluteness in regard to what is only relative and non-ultimate. *Śūnyatā* as the mundane truth is relativity and conditioned becoming; this is brought to light by rejecting the supposed ultimacy and absoluteness of particular entities and specific concepts and conceptual systems. *Śūnyatā* as the ultimate truth is the unconditioned, undivided being which is the ultimate nature of the conditioned and the contingent; this is brought to light, again, by rejecting through criticism the imagination of the ultimacy of the conditionedness of the conditioned and consequently, of the division between the conditioned and the unconditioned. The first kind of criticism and the truth it brings to light are just called *śūnyatā,* whereas the second kind is, strictly speaking, *śūnyatā* of *śūnyatā (śūnyatā-śūnyatā).* But usually both these kinds are bracketed within *śūnyatā* without always making the distinction explicit. This is no doubt a source of confusion for all those to whom the distinction is not clear. And the charge that the Mādhyamika contradicts experience and lands in a blank draws its roots from here. However this distinction is made explicit by him when he is challenged with this charge. He will then point out that far from disavowing or even contradicting the mundane truth, *śūnyatā* is the only way in which the truth of things can be brought to light, and the cultivation of wayfaring be made possible.[3] Between the denial of absoluteness in the case of mundane things and the realization of the ultimate truth as the unconditioned reality, the undivided being, there is the most important intermediary, viz., the recognition of the mundane truth as conditioned origination. It is here that all mundane activities belong. The primary purpose of criticism is to set free the thirst for the real from its moorings in abstractions, its illusions about the nature of things, and to direct it to the truly unconditioned.

*Section II*

# CRITICISM OF CATEGORIES

## *A. Being, Non-being and Becoming*

*Being and non-being as extremes:* That in reference to the mundane nature of things, absolute being and total non-being are extremes and are therefore falsifications of concrete becoming is noted above in several places. This is enough in principle to demonstrate the inconsistencies involved in the imagination of absoluteness in regard to what is only relative. What follows here is a somewhat detailed account of the Mādhyamika's criticism, chiefly of the Sarvāstivāda categories instituted in order to lay bare the inconsistencies involved in the supposition of self-being *(svabhāva)* in regard to the specific and the relative. Everywhere what is denied is not the categories themselves but their supposed absoluteness.

The *Śāstra* points out that when one sees only the birth and endurance of things, then there arises the existence-view, and when one sees only the decay and death of things, then there arises the non-existence-view.[4] Speaking of how these views arise, the *Śāstra* observes that those who pursue the course of birth and death mostly cling to the notion of existence; those who work against it in order to terminate it mostly cling to the notion of non-existence. Those who cling to the sense of "I" cling to the notion of existence, while those who cling to the wrong notion that there is not the next span of life etc. cling to the notion of non-existence. Those in whom the two poisons (of hatred and passion) are in excess cling to the notion of existence and those in whom ignorance is in excess cling to the notion of non-existence. Those who do not know that the five *skandhas* arise by way of the cooperation of causal factors cling to existence, while those who do not know that the collection of deeds (leads to birth in the next span of life) cling to non-existence.[5] Again,

There are some who would say everything is *śūnya,* and would cling in mind to this *śūnya*-nature of things. They are said to hold the wrong view of non-existence because they cling to *śūnyatā* (non-ultimacy) (as itself the ultimate nature of things). There are some others who would say that everything that forms the object of the six kinds of sensation is real, and this is the existence view.

Again, they in whom *tṛṣṇā* is more cling to existence, and they in whom *dṛṣṭi* is more cling to non-existence. Such people cling to existence-view and non-existence-view. Both these kinds of views are false, not true; they reject the Middle Way.[6] (331b)

*Criticism:* What these extremes amount to is a complete denial of conditioned origination, becoming, change as well as its necessary principle, viz., causal continuity. Says the Śastra:

If everything has an absolute being of its own (定實有), then all things are devoid of causes and conditions. But if anything is born of the connectedness of causes and conditions, then it is devoid of (absolute) self-being (無自性). To be devoid of (absolute) self-being is itself to be *śūnya*.

Further, if (absolute) non-existence (無法) were true (實) of things then there would be neither sin nor merit, neither bondage nor freedom; there would not also be the varied natures of things (無諸法種種之異).

Further, those who cling to the existence view stand opposed to those who cling to the non-existence view. On account of this opposition there arise (the contentions of) right and wrong (是非); on account of such contentions there arise disputes (共諍). On account of disputes there arise the elements of bondage (結使). On account of the elements of bondage there arise deeds (that bind creatures to states of suffering). From such deeds ways of evil become open. In the true nature of things there are not these oppositions nor these (contentions of) right and wrong nor (the consequent) disputes.

Further, in the case of those who cling to things as (eternally) existent, there arise grief and affliction when things are (revealed to be) impermanent; and those who cling to (the passing away of things as absolute) non-existence, commit all kinds of sinful deeds and (despite their disbelief in causal continuity) they fall into hell and suffer pain.

Those who do not cling to existence or non-existence keep themselves free from errors and evils such as these. One should (indeed) give up (one's clinging to) these (views) and then one will realize the true nature of things.[7] (331b)

The existence view affirms that everything rests for ever in its own nature and is essentially non-relational. But if everything rests in its nature in its own right, then what thing can change?[8] As the *Kārikā* says, the absolutely self-same thing does not take on another's nature, nor can it be said that the other takes on the other's nature. For the absolutely self-same could never change and the other has no nature other than its self-nature which it can be said to take on.[9] That which has its nature as absolutely its own would never become another. If it would become another, then its nature is not absolutely its own.[10]

If the self is absolutely itself and the other is absolutely the other, if the division between the thing itself and the other is absolute, how can there be any change? For, to change is to become another.[11] Again, if all nature is an absolute (non-relational) nature how can there be any self-nature of anything in distinction from the other-nature? In the absence of self-nature, how can there be any other-nature? And what thing can be conceived to have a being which is neither of these? In the absence of existence, how can there be any non-existence? For is not non-existence, the non-existence of something? How can there be any absolute non-existence? In truth what is meant by non-existence is becoming, change.[12]

Those who wrongly conceive *śūnyatā* lend themselves to the kind of negativism that denies causal continuity. To hold that things are absolutely nothing is wrong. As the *Śāstra* would say, that which is utterly nothing is not even speakable. To say that this thing is not is itself to speak of its existence.[13]

What thing can undergo change if it has no nature at all? Everything has its own nature but not unconditioned. There is nothing which is utterly devoid of all nature, and therefore things are relatively existent, *śūnya*, and not nothing. The distinct essences which are the determinate natures of specific entities are not ultimate and unconditioned. We have already seen the *Śāstra* warning that the presence of names does not mean the reality of the things named. The names themselves arise depending on the distinct essences and so they cannot serve as the ground to prove the unconditionedness of these essences themselves. The *Śāstra* further draws attention to the fact that cognitions and their contents again are correlatives; it is by cognitions that the specific things are known to exist and it is depending on the nature of the specific things that cognitions arise; they are distinguishable but cannot be supposed to have any independent being.[14] To say that while all is utterly non-existent, it is only out of perversion that things are seen as existent is to reduce normal perception to baseless illusion.[15]

That things were existent formerly but are now totally lost, that they are existent now but will be wholly lost later on, this is the view of negativism. This is to deny the very possibility of causal continuity and along with it the very possibility of change or becoming, and this is to contradict the very nature of mundane existence.

*Rejection and revelation:* The rejection of absoluteness is the revelation of relativity. It is not that things are utterly non-existent nor that they have no nature of their own. Everything has its own nature but this nature of the thing is not absolute, not unconditioned.[16] This is the non-substantiality of things, conveyed by the teaching that things are impermanent. Impermanence is not their ultimate nature; when rightly appraised as reference to the passing away of things it leads one to the comprehension of *śūnyatā*.[17] But when clung to as an absolute character it would mean their total extinction and would thus become the wrong view of annihilationism. Impermanence as the relative truth means change or becoming; it is not a denial of the causal continuity but a step towards bringing it to light. In that way it puts an end to the wrong notion of permanence, absoluteness and self-being with regard to things in their determinate natures; it is the remedial kind of teaching and not a teaching of the ultimate truth.[18]

*B. Causes and Conditions*

*Critical examination: (A) The Sāṅkhya and the Vaiśeṣika:* With the problem of causal relation there is bound up the question of the relation of being and becoming. The world of becoming is conceived by philosophers to have one or several principles as its ground. While particular things arise and perish, their ground remains ever in its being, it knows no change. While the Mādhyamika would agree that the world of becoming is essentially conditioned and has for its ground the unconditioned reality which is eternal being, he would point out that the unconditioned ground of the conditioned cannot be anything short of the indeterminate reality, the undivided being, and that while in respect to the mundane nature of things there can be no one definite way of describing their relation to their ultimate ground, still, every description is true from its own standpoint and each has its own relative merit. In respect to the ultimate nature of things there can be no question of any description, for there is no division there between the conditioned and the unconditioned. Strictly, the ultimate truth is non-conceptual. Even the statement that the ultimate nature of the conditioned is itself the unconditioned reality is relevant only to the way of the self-conscious intellect on the plane of mundane truth. The wise who comprehend the relative truth contained in specific determinations are able by their power of skilfulness to put into use any of these under a particular situation. All their varied statements are one-pointed, viz., to help people to overcome ignorance and suffering. And so when philosophers cling to specific points of view and assert not only that the ultimate ground of the world of becoming is of a specific nature and of a specific number but that even the relation between the contingent entities and their absolute ground is of a specific kind, the Mādhyamika would point out that they commit the error of seizing the determinate as ultimate, cling to the relative as absolute. It is in this way that the *Sūtra* as well as the *Śāstra* mention that the specific views prevalent in the world pertain only to the constituents of the world of the determinate; they do not touch the unconditioned reality.

The non-Buddhistic schools that are most often referred to in Buddhist works in this connection are two: the Sāṅkhya and the Vaiśeṣika, the one holding that the ultimate principles are two and the other, many; the one holding that identity is the true relation between cause and effect and the other, difference; the one holding that the effect is contained (as a potency) in the cause and hence as "existent" in the cause and the other that the effect is wholly different and "non-existent" in the cause.[18a] These two provide for the Mādhyamika eminent examples of the extremes of existence and non-existence, identity and difference, one and many.

When he says that,

> Neither by itself nor by another nor even by both is anything produced; and the birth of the thing is not also devoid of conditions,[19] (104b),

what he refers to is the impossibility of conceiving the conditioned origination of things under the imagination that self and other are absolute, non-relational, totally separate.

The birth of a thing by itself would mean that the thing is there even before its birth and that having been there it brings itself to birth. This view of the self-origination of things is presented by the Buddhist as the view of the Sāṅkhya, who holds that the effect is "existent" in the cause *(sat-kārya-vāda)*. And the Mādhyamika's criticism is that the birth of an existent thing is devoid of sense. Again, the Sāṅkhyas maintain that identity is the true relation between cause and effect. The criticism of this is that in the case of total identity, there could be no question of any relation, for relation holds only between two distinguishable entities.

The Sāṅkhyas would no doubt bring in the conception of manifestation *(abhivyakti)*.[20] They would say that it is not that the effect is non-existent in the cause but that it is unmanifest. Thus their distinction between the cause and the effect is one of potency and actuality. Even then, the Mādhyamika would say that they will have to accept that there is an element of novelty in the causal production; that which was non-existent has come into being; this is true at least of manifestation. This means to give up the position of absolute identity between cause and effect, for they will have to distinguish between the cause and the effect, the potential and the actual, the unmanifest and the manifest, although as different states of one and the same principle. When *prakṛti* is undistinguished from its products there does not arise the question of identity or difference for there is just one principle, the *prakṛti*, and not it as well as its products. And when *prakṛti* is distinguished from its products then the relation between them cannot be total identity, for there is distinction; the two are different, though not absolutely so.

But proceeding to bring forth and to emphasize the distinction between cause and effect, the ground and the consequent, if one would swing to the extreme of total difference, and hold to total non-existence of the effect in the cause, as the Vaiśeṣikas do, even that, the Mādhyamika would say, would be to deny all causal relation.[21] How can this relation or any relation be conceived between things that are absolutely separate? "If the other is wholly another, how can it be productive of this thing?" Further, in order that there may be this relation of otherness, there must already be this thing, the effect, and if it is already there, how is it conceivable that it is produced by this "other," the cause? There is difference no doubt between the cause and the effect but not an absolute difference, even as there is identity or sameness but not totally so. The distinction is relative and it must be appreciated as such; and the one-sidedness, the exclusive clinging, needs to be abandoned. Without this necessary correction if one proceeds to place together mechanically the self and the other, the cause and the effect, and thus tries to conceive their relation, one will only incur the errors of both these extremes. Having failed to arrive at the right understanding of causal relations, to resign oneself to chance is a still greater folly. Of what thing can there be a production without the necessary causal factors?[22]

*Critical examination: B) The Ābhidharmika:* The *Abhidharma* analyzes causal relations in terms of *hetu* (causes) and *pratyaya* (conditions). Of the latter there are four, the productive, the objective, the immediately preceding and the decisive.[23] In regard to the basic question of the relation between the cause and the effect, the causal factors that cooperate to bring the effect into birth and the product that is thus brought into birth, *hetu* and *pratyaya* stand on the same ground. What is sought to be driven home by means of criticism is the absurdity involved in conceiving that the ultimates of analysis are ultimates also in reality. Causal relation stands denied in the case of those who commit this error and the doctrine of elements is an eminent example of it. The same will be the result even in the case of the negativists who cling to the passing away of things as their total extinction.

In regard to the condition of the first kind, the productive, *hetu,* the Mādhyamika raises the question, what is produced? Is it the existent or is it the non-existent? The production of the existent is devoid of sense, and the production of the non-existent is impossible; and there is no third thing which is both existent and non-existent. So, what is it that is produced? In the absence of anything produced, how can there be anything called productive?[24] In regard to the second kind of condition, *ālambana,* the object of cognition, is it the condition of the existent cognition or of the non-existent? Either way condition is inconceivable. In the one case there is no need for it and in the other case condition is devoid of sense.[25] In regard to the third kind, *samanantara,* the immediately preceding, the condition is said to be extinct before the production of the thing; but if the condition is thus absolutely extinct (都滅) how can it function as a condition?[26] It may be added, in the case of there being no origination either of the existent or of the non-existent, either by itself or by an other, how can there be any extinction? In the absence of extinction, how does the definition of the immediately preceding condition hold?

Does the product arise after the extinction of the condition or before its extinction? If the product arises after the extinction of the condition, that would mean again a negation of all causal relation between them. The condition is extinct and hence non-existent and the product has come into being and is existent. What relation can there be between something completely non-existent and an entity completely existent? But if the product should arise before the extinction of the condition, then the condition and the product would be simultaneous and hence causally independent.[27]

Suppose the condition becomes extinct after having given a part of its being to the product. In that case the condition would have a double being, the extinct and the existent.[28] What is the relation between the two? Thus, whether the product is related or unrelated to the condition, there can be no production of the thing by the condition.[29]

The condition is not there simultaneously with the product, for if it were, then the two would be mutually independent. The condition, again, is not prior to the product since that would mean the existence of the condition even when the product is non-existent. To suppose so would be to remove all necessary relation between them. And how can one conceive that the condition is there posterior to the product? Of what thing can the condition come into existence after the product has come into being?[30]

In regard to the fourth, the decisive kind of condition, *adhipati,* the Mādhyamika would ask, of the things that are (utterly) devoid of self-nature when there can be no existence *(sattā),* when nothing has any being of its own, how can it hold good that "this being, that becomes"?[31] Again, when things possess absolute self-nature and exist by themselves, how can it be that certain things function as conditions for certain other things?[32]

Again, the condition derives its name by virtue of its capacity to bring the thing into existence. But where is this capacity to function *(kriyā)* and how is it related to the condition? Is it some thing that "belongs to" the condition *(pratyavatī kriyā)?* Either it is the same as the condition itself or it is different from the condition. Either way the capacity of the condition cannot be established. If the two are wholly identical, then it is incorrect to say that it "belongs to" the condition. If it is totally different from and entirely unconnected with the condition, even then it is incorrect to say that the capacity is "of" the condition. The capacity cannot belong to the condition, nor can it remain in itself, unconnected with the condition. And where else can it belong? What capacity is there which is not of anything? It cannot be that the conditions are devoid of the capacity to produce things, for it is only by virtue of this capacity that they are called conditions. In the absence of this capacity, what thing can be a condition and how can the condition be productive? And how can there be a condition which is devoid of the capacity to produce?[33] The non-productive is not a condition.[34]

Again, if any thing is the product of its condition, the conditions are themselves in turn the products of their conditions. And so there is no question of any final and absolute link in this causal chain.[35]

*What is denied?* The above account is of the impasse to which one comes by clinging to extremes. The *Śāstra* raises the question whether the teaching of *śūnyatā* in *prajñāpāramitā* does not amount to denying the four conditions and points out that it is not correct to think that *prajñāpāramitā* is an absolute denial of the causes and conditions. In truth, *prajñāpāramitā* does not give up anything, does not deny anything. It simply lays bare the nature of things as they are; for it is completely pure, devoid of imaginative constructions.

As the Buddha (Himself) has taught, there are the four conditions. Only because people of little wisdom cling to these (著於四緣) and give rise to perverse disputes (而生邪論) so, in order to destroy their clinging, it is taught that all things are really *śūnya* (devoid of absoluteness). (But truly) nothing is denied. (296c)

This is not a denial of the four conditions themselves but of the false imaginations of people in regard to them. The bodhisattva does indeed cultivate the analysis, definition and classification of elements; he does indeed learn and understand the distinct nature and function of every one of these different kinds of conditions; but he comprehends also their *śūnyatā*, their non-ultimacy. The *Śāstra* observes that the four conditions are taught in order to enable one to analyse and understand that all things to which common people cling are truly devoid of reality; and this is a teaching not of the ultimate truth but of the mundane truth. In their mundane nature things are essentially relative.

Everything must have (its own) causes and conditions. It is only due to one's stupidity that one does not understand (this basic truth). For example, people seek fire from wood, water from earth and wind from a fan. (104c)

Everything arises from its own causal factors. Therefore it must not be held that either there is the product in the causal factors or that there is not the product, or that there is and is not, or that neither there is nor there is not the product. (105a)

The causally born is devoid of substantiality, self-being. The exposition of the four *pratyayas* as set forth in the *Abhidharma* is only what the beginners learn.

In one's search for (the deeper) truth if one would seize (determinate natures as expounded in the *Abhidharma* as themselves ultimate then one's clinging in regard to things) would become deep and thus one would enter into the wrong notions. (297b)

It is in order to destroy this clinging and remove this perversion that the criticism of categories is instituted, whereby the absurdities that would arise from clinging to the ultimates of analysis as ultimates in reality are exposed.

On account of one's misconstruction (戱論) about the true nature of the four conditions, there arise all such errors. But (if one understands them) in the light of the non-clinging *śūnyatā* of the *prajñāpāramitā,* then there will be no such error. People in the world take all that they hear or see, (and even) birth, old age, and death, as real and underived. But when the nature of these things is minutely examined (細求其相) then these (are found to be) unobtainable. It is therefore that in the *prajñāpāramitā,* only the perverse notions are cancelled, the four *pratyayas* (themselves) are not rejected (但除邪見而不破四緣). (297b)

### C. *Motion: Activity*

*Introduction:* In regard to motion and activity in general, it is to be noted that the Mādhyamika not only recognizes these as essential mundane truths but proceeds also to show the only way of conceiving them. He points out that it is the way of "sticking" to the fragmentary as complete, seizing the relative as non-relational that contradicts the facts of mundane activity. While the analysis of motion into minimum "units" is the way of conceptually presenting it, those who seize these fragments as themselves fundamental and try to understand motion by mechanically placing these units together as a series of momentary flashings of separate essences are bound to miss the original, integral, movement. What they would have instead is the abstract "moments" seized as ultimate. Again, in regard to the causal factors of movement, viz., the act, the agent and the object, an imagination of ultimacy of difference would mean their total separateness. This is to swing to an extreme. Not being able to establish movement on the basis of complete separateness, to cling to the notion of the complete identity of these elements is to swing to the other extreme. The same kind of swinging from extreme to extreme is found even in regard to the being or non-being of the factors of movement. The position of the extremists virtually amounts to a denial of the very possibility of movement. Having attempted to provide its only possible ground they virtually do away with it altogether. This is the self-contradiction inherent in their position. They enter an impasse. The way out is to correct the initial error, the error of imagining that the constituent factors of motion which are the ultimates of analysis are ultimates also in reality and that movement is derived from their mechanical combination. The error lies not in analysis itself but in clinging to the elements of analysis.

*Criticism: (A) Motion:* Of motion there can be three kinds of object (locus) from the standpoint of time, viz., the space that is already traversed (*gata*), that which is not yet traversed (*agata*) and that which is presently being traversed (*gamyamāna*). Similarly the agents (*gantā*) can be of three kinds, the no longer moving, the not yet moving and the presently moving. Now, of any one of these agents motion cannot be predicated in regard to any one of these objects.[36]

It cannot be that the already traversed or the not yet traversed is being traversed. Since both are alike devoid of movement, how can movement be predicated of them? The same is the case even with the moving body, the agent. It cannot be that the not yet moving body moves, nor that the no longer moving body moves.[37]

Of the presently moving (agent) or of the presently being traversed (locus) also no movement can be predicated. A statement that "the moving body moves" or that "the presently being traversed object is traversed" involves a duplication of movement, for in both movement is predicated of the "moving."[38] The duplication when literally clung to engenders the notion of there being two separate entities, the moving body and the movement it makes. The "moving body" is there as such in its own right and a movement is predicated of it. In the case of duplication of movement, there being two acts, there should be two agents, for, every act should have an agent.[39] This argument that movement cannot be predicated of (any object) whether past, present or future, holds good also in the case of the objects of all types of activity, like birth, stay and death, production, destruction and maintenance, etc.[40]

Again, to add to the above from the *Kārikā,* how can one conceive the relation between the act and the agent? Are they identical or different? It cannot be that the act is totally different from the agent.[41] Again, the agent does not cause that very movement by virtue of which he is called the agent, nor can he make any movement totally different from and therefore totally unconnected with himself.[42] The statement "the mover moves" predicates the movement of the mover. And in predicating a movement of the mover, either we predicate of him the same act of movement by virtue of which he bears the name "mover," or we predicate of him a movement different from that. In the former case, strictly, there can be no predication, for, if our statement is to be significant, one thing must be predicated of another, and of the same thing the same thing is not predicated. But if it is a movement separate from the mover, then how can that be predicated of him? On the one hand the subject and the predicate are separate, unrelated to each other, and on the other hand the "mover" cannot be supposed to have another movement in addition to that by virtue of which he bears the name "mover." How can we understand this relation of movement to the mover? Neither identity nor difference can be predicated of them. When the two cannot be established either by way of identity or by way of difference, what other way is there of establishing them?[43]

Again, of the same agent two different acts cannot be predicated, e.g., it cannot be that "the mover is resting," or that "the existent is extinct."[44] It is as absurd to say that "the existent is born" as to say that "the existent is extinct." Again, it cannot be that the existent agent does the existent act, or the non-existent agent does the existent-non-existent act. Nor can it be that the non-existent agent does the existent, the non-existent or the existent-non-existent act. And where is the agent other than the existent and the non-existent?[45]

*Criticism: B) Birth, decay and death:* As in the case of motion, so even in the case of birth etc, it cannot be held that the born is born, nor that the unborn is born nor even that the born-not-born is born.[46] The analysts conceive that birth, decay and death are all comprised in a unit of function and are yet different and so belong to separate essences which are ultimate and independent.[47]

If every element for ever rests in its own nature what makes it rise to function? Again, how is the element related to the function? And how to explain this relatedness of functions on the ground of the essential separateness of the basic elements? While the analysis of becoming into arising and perishing is the intellect's way of representing it, and while this representation is essential for the appreciation of the orderly procedure and the richness and variety of the conditioned becoming that constitutes the mundane nature of things, to seize these aspects as themselves basic and independent entities and to attempt to derive the becoming of things from the putting together of these abstract elements now imagined as ultimate is a perversion that is bound to end in an impasse.

Birth, decay and death are distinguishable aspects in the dynamic whole which is the composite thing. When these distinguishable aspects are themselves imagined to be entities, like form, smell etc. they are themselves to be treated as either having or not having the characters of compositeness.

Of birth, stay and death, the three characters of compositeness, either there are further characters of birth, stay and death, or there are not. If there are these further characters, then there will be an endless regression. If there are not, then these characters are not themselves composite, and not being themselves composite, how can they be the characters of compositeness?[48]

The question is: How is a thing born? It is said that a thing is born by being related to birth, being brought to birth by birth. When we conceive that the thing to be born is an entity in itself and that birth is another entity in itself, and yet say that the thing is to be born by being originated by birth, then there arise difficulties. Could we not say the same thing about birth also? If birth is also to be brought to birth,[49] then what brings it to birth? Another birth will not do, for there also the same question arises. We have entered a *cul-de-sac*. We have left the thing behind and taken up many other and subtler entities in its place and each of these is in turn given up and in its place many more elements appear. The stream of life is congealed into many disconnected entities and the abstract is imagined to be absolute. The invention of primary and secondary birth is of no avail. If birth is itself a thing to be brought to birth doubling the birth would be only to double the issue. On the supposition of many ultimately separate elements there cannot be any organic system of happenings.

Again, as the *Kārikā* asks, how can birth etc., which are elements opposed to one another, happen together?[50] How can they be in one and the same thing and at one and the same time? And if they are to happen one by one, how can one happen without the other? How can there be anything at any time with only birth without duration and extinction? If it could be so at any time, why should it not be so at all times? On this score either together or separately, birth and death cannot happen to things. If birth is itself one thing and death another, each mutually opposed to the other and both different from the thing, how can we conceive the relation of birth to death and of both to the thing itself? When we cannot see how a thing arises, how can we conceive its extinction?

It has been already observed that things by themselves cannot come to birth nor can it be conceived that certain things are brought into existence by certain other things. And how can we conceive birth and death to be there except as belonging to something? How can this something be conceived without birth and death?[51] Birth and death do not happen to an absolute being. Again birth and death are not either totally identical, or utterly different and disconnected. As the *Kārikā* puts it,

To him who conceives (absolute) existence in regard to things there happen the two views of eternalism and negativism, for the things then should be either absolutely existent or utterly evanescent.[52]

But can it not be that existence is a stream of elements which are really completely evanescent? In that case, there would happen on the one hand a complete negation of causal connection, and on the other, there would result the position that the thing having been absolutely existent now becomes totally non-existent. Again, even granting that there is a causal link, how is the last moment of one span of existence related to the first moment of the next? Whether the last moment of the preceding span of existence be conceived as already extinct, or not yet extinct or being presently extinct, in any case it cannot be related to the first moment of the succeeding span of existence.[53]

*What is denied?* Here again the negative criticism is a denial not of motion or birth or any other activity but of the possibility of understanding these on the supposition of the reality and separateness of the ultimates of analysis. It brings to light the truth of conditioned origination; that is not itself denied.

Speaking of right deeds, the *Śāstra* recounts practically all the arguments of the *Kārikā* (ch. II) and concludes:

In this way all deeds are *śūnya* (relative and contingent); and the deeds (that are done with this understanding) are called the right deeds (是名正業). (The farer on the Great Way), the bodhisattva, comprehends (入) the (ultimate) sameness of all deeds; and he does not take the good deed as meritorious and the evil deed as devoid of merit. (For, in the ultimate truth there is not this distinction of good and bad.) In the ultimate truth there are no deeds, good or evil. This is the true *prajñā*. But this is itself also the right deed (for it issues in the deed that is done with the right understanding). . . . Having achieved the true understanding of deeds, one neither does deeds nor desists from them (for one is devoid of clinging and so one does not consider oneself as the doer of deeds). And such a wise man always does the right deeds and never any wrong ones. This is the right deed of the bodhisattva.[54] (205c)

Rejecting on the one hand the clinging in regard to deeds and, on the other, the consequent sense of pride and passion, here is revealed the true understanding which is the basis of right deeds. The deeds themselves are not denied.

### D. *Beginning and End*

*Beginning and end as absolute concepts:* One of the outcomes of the discussion on the characters of compositeness is the impossibility of conceiving any absolute beginning in regard to the course of birth and death which is essentially conditioned becoming.

The world, whether of the constituted being or of the constituent elements, is devoid of beginning (and devoid of end).[55] (290c)

To conceive absolute beginning and absolute end in regard to the course of existence is to see them as devoid of conditions, which means a denial of causal continuity. Origination would then be uncaused and extinction, total. This predicament of beginning and end in fact confronts one at every step, in the case of every unit of becoming. In order to avoid the error of absolute beginning the clinging mind would swing to the other extreme of conceiving the course of existence to be absolutely beginningless; but this is again to think that it is unconditioned.

Actually when beginning means the root-principle, i.e., the root of error and evil which are the basic forces of the world of the ignorant, the beginning is ignorance itself and we have already observed that ignorance is not anything unconditioned. And when beginning means the beginning in time, there is always a beginning for every moment even as there is always an end. So, even in this sense, the course of existence is devoid of (absolute) beginning; but this consideration should not lead one to think that it is absolutely beginningless, devoid even of relative beginning. The course of existence in which the ignorant revolve has its root in ignorance which is not a total non-entity. Again, no event in the course of existence is devoid of its own relative beginning in time.

The *Śāstra* raises a question: Does not a denial of the devoidness of beginning mean an assertion of beginning? And does not an assertion of beginning lead one to the wrong notion of absolute beginning and (absolute) end? It answers:

Now, by means of the *śūnyatā* (non-ultimacy) of the devoidness of beginning (以無始空), the position that the cycle of existence is (absolutely) beginningless is denied and there is also no falling into the position that the cycle of existence has (an absolute) beginning (有始見). Having saved a man from fire, one should not put him again into deep waters. Now, here, the position that the cycle of existence is beginningless is denied and there is no clinging even to the position of there being a beginning. This is the faring on the Middle Way. (291a)

Again, it is by seizing individuality (取衆生相) and the characters of identity and difference (一相異相) and by pushing the imagination back from the present span of life to the span previous to it, that there arises the notion that neither of the individuals nor of their constituent elements can any beginning be found. This creates the notion of beginninglessness in regard to the cycle of birth and death. But this notion is false and is based on clinging to identity and difference (以一異爲本)[55a]. Actually,

Even as the *śūnyatā* of the composite negates (the clinging to) the composite things and when the *śūnyatā* of the composite itself turns out to be a perversion (是有爲空即復爲患) (giving rise to a clinging to the incomposite) then, by means of the *śūnyatā* (indeterminate nature) of the incomposite (the clinging to) the incomposite is also denied (復以無爲空破無爲法), just so, now, by means of (the idea of) beginninglessness of the cycle of existence the position of the beginning is denied and when beginninglessness is itself turned into (an extreme and when it thus turns out to be itself) a perversion (患), then by means of the *śūnyatā* of beginninglessness, even beginninglessness is denied. This is the *śūnyatā* of beginninglessness. (291a)

That all beings revolve in the cycle of birth and death of which the prior end cannot be found was mentioned by the Buddha only to impress on people the unmeasured length of the time of their revolving in the cycle, so that there might arise in them a sense of disgust (生厭患心) in regard to things of passion and clinging.[56] It is not a teaching of the ultimate truth (非爲實有).[57] It is a teaching of the remedial kind.

When one sees things with one's eye of wisdom then one comprehends that the individuals and the constituent elements are really completely *śūnya* (conditioned and relative). Hence the teaching of the *śūnyatā* of beginninglessness. (291b)

*Beginning and end as relative notions:* Although permanence and impermanence are not absolutely true of things, (常觀不實無常觀亦不實), still, the Buddha has often taught that the ideas of permanence and pleasure are perverse (倒), while the ideas of impermanence and suffering are true (諦). This He did because He saw that

People mostly cling (多著) to permanence and pleasure while they do not cling (不著) (so much) to impermanence and suffering. Therefore through (the relative truths of) impermanence and pain the perversion of permanence and pleasure is rejected. (291b)

Therefore the teaching that impermanence and suffering are true is only a remedial teaching which holds good in the everyday world.

But if people would cling even to impermanence and suffering, then the Buddha would teach that even these are *śūnya,* not ultimate. The same is the case even with having a beginning and being beginningless. The notion of beginninglessness can negate the perversion of clinging to beginning. But if one clings to the position of beginninglessness itself, then even that is taught to be *śūnya* (non-ultimate).[58] (291b)

That things have an absolute beginning is a great perversion (大惑). Because,

If (the course of life) has an (absolute) beginning then it should be that the very first birth of a being in a good or an evil state was without any conditioning factor of merit or sin. But if his birth was due to (his own) merit or sin, then that body of his was not his very first body, for one in the later embodiment must have received the results of one's own deeds, good or evil, done in one's previous span of life. That the course of life has no (absolute) beginning does not give room to this error. Therefore the bodhisattva will have already given up this gross perversion (麁惡邪見) (viz., that the course of life has an absolute beginning). He always cultivates the thought of beginninglessness in reference to the course of the life of all beings, and therefore he speaks of the course of the life of beings as beginningless. He always cultivates the comprehension of the causal law, and therefore he speaks of the elements constituting composite things as devoid of (absolute) beginning. (291b–c)

That the course of existence is not absolutely beginningless is the teaching meant to remove the error in regard to the devoidness of beginning. Even as the devoidness of beginning can negate the notion of having a beginning, so the notion of beginning can also negate the devoidness of beginning. Still, there is a difference between them. The notion of things having a beginning creates further perversion while the notion of the devoidness of beginning can function as a reason for the right view and the loving attitude (起慈悲及正見因緣) towards all. The thought that beings suffer pain from beginningless times gives rise to compassion (生悲心) for all and by the knowledge that from one span of bodily life there arises another span of bodily life, one can further know that deeds good or evil flow in unbroken continuity bearing results. Thus there arises the right attitude (生正見) in regard to all things. So,

If one does not cling to the notion of the devoidness of beginning then in his case this is a good thing, helpful in his wayfaring (助道善法). But if one seizes the character of devoidness of beginning and clings to it, then it is a perversion. (邪見). (291c)

### E. *Time: Past, Present and Future*

*Time as a substance:* The *Śāstra* makes clear that the wrong views about the beginning and end of the course of existence owe their being to a lack of right understanding of the nature of the three times:

Some give rise to wrong notions about the three times and make (unconditional) statements that the individuals and the constituent elements of the past have an (absolute) beginning or that they do not have (absolutely) any beginning. (255b)

Even as the wrong view of the beginning is concerning the past, so the wrong view of the end is concerning the future. The one remedy to these wrong views is the right understanding that all things are essentially conditioned and constitute the stream of events, every phase of which has a before and an after relative to it, and that neither the phase itself nor its before or after can be seized as absolute. Priority and posteriority are not absolute; these have significance only relatively to each other, and relatively to a specific event in its concrete setting. Prior and posterior as well as past, present and future belong to what have been considered above as relational concepts or concepts of mutual relation.[59] There is not anything like past in itself, present in itself or future in itself. And yet this is what is found on examination to have been the notion of those who assert that past, present and future always exist, as well as of those who conceive time as an immutable substance or a changeless reality.

There are some who say that all things, heaven and earth, good and bad, arise from time *(kāla)*, and that therefore time is the source of things.

> When time comes beings mature; when time approaches they hasten (toward extinction); time can awaken men; therefore time is the source of all things.[60] (65b)

There are others who say that although things are not made by time, still time is an essential condition (因) for the being of things. Time itself is an immutable substance (不變); it is a reality (實有) *(vastusat* or *dravyasat)*, but as it is subtle it cannot be seen (細故不可見) with physical eyes or known (不可知) in the way in which gross things are known. Still, from its effects (果故) like flowers and fruits, it can be known that there is time as their condition. Again, we see also the features (相) of time like past and present, slow and fast etc. and through its features we can know that there is time. Seeing the effect we know that its necessary condition is there (見果知有因). Therefore time is there as a reality (有時法). Time has no decay (不壞) and so time is eternal.[61]

But then, the *Śāstra* observes that if time is eternal, its features should be eternal too; this means that the past does not make the future. Again, if time is one and integral, there can be no question of the past producing the present or the future. And further, within the past there cannot be the future as this would lead to a confusion of times. So, if this view were right, then there would be no past or future and similarly there would be no present.[62] The holders of the view that time is a reality would justify the reality of the past as the necessary condition of the present. Thus, e.g., the subtle particles of earth are the necessary condition of the birth of a pot. Granted the reality of the past, present and future must be real also. Thus, time should be accepted as a reality.[63] Now, granting that the pot is future and the subtle particles of earth are past, still the past cannot make the future. For, on this view both the past and the future should have to be eternal. Again, if the past could make the future or if the future could arise from the past, then the past would be within the future. But then, how could it be called the past? So, even the past would then have to be denied.[64]

*Do past, present and future always exist?* An objector like the Ābhidharmika might argue:

> How can it be that there is no time? Time must be accepted (as a reality). The present has the character of presentness, the past has the character of pastness and the future has the character of futurity.[65] (65c)

To this, the *Śāstra* replies:

> But if it is held that all the three time-divisions have (already, even now) their respective characters, then all of them must be equally just present (應盡是現在世). Then there would not be any past or future. If the future is here even now (若今有未來) then it is just present and not future. (It should not be the not yet come. It should be the already come). (65c)

> But can it not be that while the past and the future do not function in the present, the past functioned in the past and the future will function in the future, that although all these have their respective characters even now, still every element has its own time of functioning?[66]

The *Śāstra* replies:

Now, either the past is past or it is not. If the past is past (若過去過去), then it is already extinct, and if it is not past (若過去不過去), then it has not the character of pastness. But why? Because it has given up its own character (of pastness). The same is the case with the future. (None of these can be said to have any own nature or self-being.) Therefore time itself is not a substance, not a reality (時法無實). And how can it bring to birth all things, the beautiful and the ugly, flower and fruit? (65c)

*Time as a derived notion:* The denial of time as a substance is not a total denial of time but is a revelation of time as a derived notion. As a means of referring to the course of events time is essential in the everyday world. The *Śāstra* says,

If there were absolutely no past or future, if there were only the present lasting for a moment, then even the Buddha could not have striven in the path and achieved the immeasurable merits (which He did indeed achieve). . . . So it must be known that the past and the future are there indeed. (254c)

But the statement that the past and the future are there does not mean that all the three times are just present. To those who hold that view, the objection may be raised that if past, present and future are all existent what is non-existent? Has not the Buddha taught that there are the four Noble Truths? Is not the truth of suffering *(duḥkha)* the foremost among them? And is not the cultivation of the truth of impermanence the foremost factor in the cultivation of the first Noble Truth? If the past, which is truly the not any more existent is also existent as well as the present, then, surely, the past cannot any more be said to be impermanent, lost, impossible to obtain?[67] Again, to hold that a thing is existent in all the three times, and that in passing from one state to another it has ever remained as it was, and is not lost, would be to fall into the wrong notion of eternalism.[68] Then,

This thing which is there really in the future would pass from there and enter the present and pass from there and enter the past even as a person, for example, passes from one room to another and in this movement he is not said to be himself lost. (254c)

But what is wrong if the thing is not lost in this passage from future to present and from present to past?

That in this passage the thing is not lost means that it ever remains self-identical which means that it is not impermanent. A denial of impermanence would amount to a denial of birth and death, of sin and merit and of bondage and liberation. (254c)

But these objections do not arise in the case of those who accept time as a derived notion. So the *Śāstra* observes that all the three periods of time do have their respective characters. The past has the character of pastness, the future has the character of futurity, the present has the character of presentness. The difficulties urged occur only if one holds that past and future have the character of being present. But now, past and future have each its own character (各自有相) but not the character of being present.[69]

That the past and the future are equally present would be to end in eternalism, while that they are absolutely non-existent (實無), would be to end in negativism. To hold that past and future are absolutely non-existent would be to deny causal continuity, which would render impossible the cultivation of moral life. If one is at the present moment dwelling in evil thought, and if all the moral worth that one has achieved from past deeds is now totally extinct, then one cannot now be considered as a wayfarer in *dharma*.[70] Again, on this supposition of total non-existence of past and future if the mind of a sage were at any time directed to worldly activities, then at that time he would be simply and wholly a common man, for all his former cultivation of the way would be completely non-existent now. Similarly, there would be no committing of the five deadly sins, nor would there be any cultivation of moral worth. This indeed is a perverse notion.[71]

The *Śāstra* continues,

We do not say that past and future are there in the same way in which the present is said to be (如現在相有); we say that although the past object is not any more existent, still it can be revived in memory (可生憶想) (consequently) giving rise to the mental states. For example, the fire of yesterday (is certainly not here now), it is extinct; (still) its impressions can be revived in memory (可生憶想念). Just because the thought (of the fire of yesterday) is (now) in mind, revived through memory, it cannot be held that the fire itself is here. Similarly, seeing the bundle of firewood one anticipates the fire of the future (知當然火), which also gives rise to the thought of the fire of tomorrow. As in the case of (the thought of) yesterday's fire so in the case of the fire of tomorrow, the presence of the thought of fire does not mean the actual presence of the fire itself. (255a)

Although the present mind does not endure even for a moment, still, as the stream (of the moments of thought) arises in continuity the mind can know things. With the present (moment of) *citta,* the mind, the internal element, as the *hetu* (the cause) and with the external object as the *pratyaya* (the condition) there arises the internal unifying cognition (lit. mind-cognition); by means of this internal unifying cognition one can freely know all things, past, present and future. (255a)

It is in this way that the Buddha is said to know all things past, present and future without any impediment. This is a mundane truth and should not be mistaken to stand for the ultimate truth. The knowledge of the past, present and future is pertinent, but pertinent only to the world of the determinate. In the ultimate truth there is neither past nor present nor future. In reference to the ultimate truth of things it has been said that all the three times are of one nature, viz., devoid of any specific nature.[72]

The *Śāstra* observes that it is precisely in order to remove the wrong notion of eternalism in regard to time that the Buddha has used the word "*samaya*" and not "*kāla*" for "time."[72a]

*Samaya* is a derived notion. So it does not give room for misunderstanding (generally). In the teaching of the Buddha mostly *samaya* is used and it is only rarely that *kāla* is used.[73] (66a)

Space and time are not substances. There is nothing like an absolute time which remains as a reality apart from the successive events. Time and space are derived notions, modes of reference. They refer to the arising and perishing of events which constitute the organic, dynamic course of the world of the determinate. We perceive the course of events, give the name "time" to this universal order of succession and draw the distinction of past and future, the remembered and the anticipated, the not any more and the not yet, in contrast with that which is here now, the present. We perceive again the many different contemporaneous events constituting a totality, a togetherness, and give it the name "space," the "container of all' and draw the distinction of directions within it. As the *Śāstra* observes, not only space and time, but in fact all the categories of understanding are derived notions, notions derived from the distinctions perceivable within the composite whole of interrelated events.[73a] The course of events, the conditioned becoming, is fundamental and it is on its basis and as referring to it that these notions are derived. They do not refer to any specific ultimate substances.

### *F. Space: Spatial Directions*

*Spatial directions (dik) as realities:* It has been already noted above that spatial distinctions are of the same nature as temporal ones with regard to being derived names, relational concepts, and not standing for substantial entities. There is not any substance called east or west, even as there is not any substance called long or short, past or present. East and west are references to the ways in which the actual entities or events stand related to one another in the complexes they constitute. And yet the way in which the analysts would conceive things lends itself to the position that east and west, as well as long and short, or even past, present and future are substantial entities which for ever remain in themselves and yet by associating with things give to them spatial and temporal distinctions.

Thus some would urge that *dik* is a reality *(dravya)*, that it is eternal and has its own characters (有相).[74] They would urge:

As (our) *Sūtra* would have it, the direction in which the sun rises is the east and that in which the sun sets is the west, the direction where the sun travels (日行處) is the south and that where the sun does not move (日不行處) is the north. The sun has contact with three parts (日有三分合) viz., before, now and after. The order in its contact with the parts depends on the direction (隨方日分). Its first contact is with the east, (the next contact is with the south, and the last contact is with the west). No part (of the sun) is in contact with that *dik* (viz., the north) in which it does not move (日不行處是無分). (Again) this divides from that, that divides from this (彼間此此間彼)—this is the character of *dik*. If there is no *dik* there is neither "this" nor "that." (Division of) "this" and "that" is the (essential) character of *dik* (彼此是方相).[75] (133b)
To this the *Śāstra* replies:

Now, this is not correct. Sumeru is in the middle of the four regions (四域). The sun turns around Sumeru and illumines all the worlds everywhere. . . . There is no absolute "first" (touch to the sun) anywhere (是實無初). Why? Every direction can be east or south, west or north (in reference to the specific sphere of reference).[76] (133b–c)

The Vaiśeṣikas say that the direction in which the sun rises is the east etc. without any reference to any world. The *Śāstra* observes that it cannot be maintained that there is any direction unconditionally fixed as east or south or west, for each world will have its own east and its own west. Again, the Vaiśeṣikas say that the direction in which the sun has no contact is the north; but on this score, the *Śāstra* observes, they cannot call it a *dik*, for it has not the character of contact with the sun.[77] But here the Vaiśeṣikas would argue that they have mentioned the characters of *dik* in reference only to one country, whereas the critic takes it as referring to the countries on all the four sides and brings an objection, while according to them it does hold that the east has indeed the first contact.[78] On this the *Śāstra* stresses another point, viz., that even if in one country the sun has its contact with the east, this means that the *dik* ends (有邊) at the point where the sun begins. So having an end, *dik* would not be all-pervasive and could not be permanent. Therefore *dik* is only a name, a mode of reference and not any eternal substance.[79]

*Spatial directions as derived names:* As modes of reference spatial directions are in fact held to be supremely important and are called "the great."

(*Dik* is called great in the mundane truth) because it is endless, it is everywhere, it pervades all that is material, it is everlasting (常有) and it benefits the whole world saving people from getting lost in confusion.[80] (288a)

But this does not mean that *dik* is any thing-in-itself. *Dik* is a derived notion. In the system of the composite material entities there hold the distinctions of "this side" and "that side" and it is from these distinctions that the notion of direction is derived. It is a derived name.

(In the world by common consent) the direction in which the sun rises is (called) the east, and that in which the sun sets is called the west. This is the character of *dik*. *Dik* naturally lasts for ever (自然常有). Therefore it is not any specific entity causally produced. It is not any specific entity that was not before but is present now and will cease to be later; therefore it is not anything made. It is not perceptible by the senses (非現前知) and therefore it is most subtle. (288a–b)

Still, it is not anything ultimately real.

It is admitted only in the mundane truth. In the ultimate truth it is denied. (288b)

And here there is no question of falling into the errors of eternalism and negativism. For,

*Dik* is admitted in the mundane truth (as a derived name) and therefore there is no falling into negativism, and it is denied in the ultimate truth and therefore there is no falling into eternalism. (288b)

Clinging to the specific as absolute would create in regard to the spatial and temporal divisions the wrong notions of absolute end and absolute devoidness of end, leading to the errors of negativism and eternalism. The *Śāstra* observes that this would lead the wayfarer to a total abandoning of the attitude of unbounded love and service for all. Suppose the wayfarer traverses helping people of one nation, in one direction, say, in the east, and takes up another in the same direction and thus continues to traverse country after country, in one and the same direction, helping all with his merciful heart. Now if he should give rise to the notion that the direction as well as his faring in it are absolutely endless, then he might give rise to the false notion of absolute endlessness, i.e., eternalism; and if he would think that the direction and his faring in it are exhausted, then he would be a victim to the false notion of absolute end, i.e., negativism. With the rise of these two kinds of wrong notions his loving heart would not be there any more. But through the *śūnyatā* of *dik,* if he would reject his clinging to directions then there would not be these wrong notions of absolute end and absolute endlessness.[81]

For example, in the great ocean, at the time of tide the water reaches the never-ending banks and then returns. And if the fish (that is thrown out in the tide) would not return to the ocean (along with the water flowing back) then it would have to be tossing about on the moist earth (漂在露地) and would be subject to all pain and confusion. But if the fish is wise it will return to the ocean along with the water, and will for ever be in peace and security. The same is the case with the wayfarer. If he will not return along with his mind (to *śūnyatā)* then he will be tossed about in perversion. But if he will return along with his mind (to *śūnyatā)*, then he will not lose his heart of love. This way the great perversions about *dik* are removed in this *śūnyatā* of *dik.* Hence the name great. (288b)

*Space* (*ākāśa*) *as a substance:* If the spatial directions are not substantial, could the space *(ākāśa)* in which the directions are distinguished itself be anything substantial? Even space is only a derived name and not any substance.[82] It stands for the universal possibility of movement. Being nothing in itself it contains all. It is not itself any specific entity. If it were itself a determinate entity with its own nature it would be exclusive of all else and it could not then have been the container of all.[83] It is not an object of sight[84] for it is devoid of form. It is not the blue vault. In fact, when sight is cast at a great distance (where the light emitted from the eyes meets no object) the light returns and thus there is the sight of blue. There is nothing over there which is actually blue. If some one would fly up very high in the sky and examine, he would not see anything there. It is on account of the enormous distance at which the sight is cast that there appears the color blue.[85]

Some would maintain that space *(ākāśa)* is a reality (實有法), a thing-in-itself. They would say that if there were not the element of *ākāśa* as a reality, then the activities like lifting things and laying them down, coming and going, curving and straightening, entering and emerging, etc. would not have been there. For, in the absence of *ākāśa,* there would not be any accommodation for movement (動處).[86]

But, the *Śāstra* observes that if *ākāśa* were a specific, existent entity, then it should have itself a location. For, there cannot be the existence of any specific "spatial" entity without a location. To conceive that space is located in something empty would amount to saying that space is located in space, therefore that is not right. Again, it cannot be taken to be located in some plenum (實), for the plenum is devoid of empty space and hence devoid of accommodation. The stonewall, e.g., being a plenum as accepted by common sense and so having no empty space in it, is devoid of accommodation. Further, if *ākāśa* were a plenum it would not meet the definition of accommodation which is accepted even by those who hold it to be a substance. So even in the plenum which is devoid of accommodation there cannot be the supposed substance, *ākāśa.* So, neither in anything empty nor in the plenum can *ākāśa* which is conceived as a substantial entity be accommodated.[87] Therefore there cannot be any *ākāśa* as a specific entity.

Again, if *ākāśa* were any specific entity, it should have a character of its own. But it cannot be conceived to have any character (無相).

Every specific thing has its specific character (諸法各各有相). When the character is present one understands that the thing is present. For example, earth is hard, water is moist. . . . But *ākāśa* cannot be taken to have any such specific character. Therefore *ākāśa* itself cannot be. (102c)

Now, can it not be that devoidness of form (無色處) is the character of *ākāśa*?[88] It cannot be. Because, "devoidness of form" (無色) simply means the negation of form (破色); there is nothing else that is positive (更無異法) here which can be the unique character of *ākāśa*. The negation of form is comparable to the extinction of flame. Both alike are simply negations; they are not themselves anything positive. So, there is no positive character specific to *ākāśa*.[89] Again, for another reason, *ākāśa* is denied. It is only in contrast with something tangible and full that negation of *rūpa* (色), form and resistance, is conceivable which is now advanced as the character of *ākāśa*. But then, when *rūpa* has not come into existence (色未生時) there can be no character of *ākāśa*.[90]

Again, you say that form is impermanent while *ākāśa* is permanent. In that case, even prior to form, there should be *ākāśa*, for it is permanent. But how can there be "the negation of form" prior to form? In the absence of "the negation of form" there is not the character of *ākāśa*. (And how can there be *ākāśa* without its character?) In the absence of the character, the thing is also absent. Therefore, *ākāśa* is only a name and not any substance.[91] (103a)

*Space as a derived name:* In the mundane truth *ākāśa* is admitted as the necessary condition for movement, as the " container of all." It is capable of containing everything precisely because it is *akiñcana* (無所有故), not itself anything specific; everything dwells in it.

The formed objects have their dwelling place; from them it is known that there is *ākāśa* as their accommodation; the formed objects, being formed, cannot be the container of anything, and so *ākāśa* is known as the principle of accommodation. Formed objects and (formless) *ākāśa* are mutually opposed in character (相違); as formed object is non-accommodative, so it is known that *ākāśa* is the principle of accommodation (受); even as knowledge is known through (or in contrast with) ignorance, pleasure is known through (or in contrast with) pain, just so (in contrast with and) by the absence of formed (and hence resisting) objects, there is said to be *ākāśa,* the principle of accommodation. (426b)

*Śāstra* distinguishes *ākāśa* from the mind and the mental states and says that although in being shapeless (無形), and colourless (無色) there is a certain similarity between them, they are not similar in every respect. While the mind and the mental states are of the nature of feeling and understanding (覺知相), *ākāśa* has for its nature, accommodation; while the former are devoid of accommodation, they are not also totally devoid of specific nature; the mind is known to be of a definite "form" (形) by virtue of mentation *(vikalpa* 分別相). Further, mind and mental states are known to be definitely non-accommodative. For instance the false view does not contain the right view and the right view does not contain the false view. But this is not the case with *ākāśa,* it is the container of all. Again, the mind and the mental states are of the nature of arising and perishing, they can be put an end to. This is not, however, the case with *ākāśa.* Therefore it is said that among all things it is *ākāśa* that is the "container of all." This cannot be said in regard to the mind and the mental states.[92]

But the above consideration should not however lead one to think that *ākāśa* is a reality, substantial and self-being, or even a specific entity with a positive nature of its own. For in truth, accommodation (受相) is but the absence of resistance (無色相). It is the inaccessibility of form (色不到處) or the formlessness that is called *ākāśa;* it is not itself any specific entity.[93] In the case of one who entertains the wrong notion that *ākāśa* is a specific, substantial, entity, there occur all the inconsistencies mentioned above. In the ultimate truth *ākāśa* is of the same nature as Nirvāṇa, which is the universal reality.[94] In being the universal principle of accommodation while not being itself any specific thing, *ākāśa* is the prototype of the ultimate reality.[94] The Great Way is compared to it.

### G. *Substance and Attribute*

*Substance as self-being:* Substance *(svabhāva)* in its general sense of self-being is of the greatest importance to our present treatise, because the one principal idea that runs through its pages is that a determinate entity is not a substance; it is devoid of self-being. In this general sense, substantiality or self-being means ultimacy, unconditionedness, reality. In this general sense character *(lakṣaṇa)* is a synonym of determinate entity as well as its determination or specification.[95] The determinate entities are divisions within the undivided being, determinations within the indeterminate *dharma*. These are held as "entities" only by convention and there is no absoluteness about them with regard to their "own" natures and there is no sharpness of their division from the rest. In this general sense, all that is determinate can be called a "character" which is a representation, a determination by the self-conscious intellect of the reality that it confronts. And of the relation between the determinate characters and the indeterminate *dharma,* their ground, there is no question of any absolute description in terms of identity or difference.

*Substance as substratum of quality:* It is this consideration of the mutual implicatedness and the relativity of determination between the specific "entities" or characters and their ground, that is found even in regard to the limited issue, viz., of the relation between quality and substance. Substance is the substratum *(lakṣya)* in which the quality *(lakṣaṇa)* rests or "inheres." It is the subject of which the character is predicated. The questions are:

Does the quality rest in the qualified or in the not qualified? Between the quality and the substratum, which is earlier and which is later? Or, are they simultaneous? Are substance and quality identical or separate?

Quality does not inhere (不入) in the qualified (相) for in the qualified the quality is already there. Nor does it inhere in the thing devoid of quality for (that which is absolutely devoid of quality is not any thing) and so in it there is no scope for any quality at all. Apart from the qualified and the not qualified, there is no (third) thing in which the quality can inhere.[95a] (549a)

Further, there is nothing absolutely fixed (不定) as the qualifier and the qualified.[96] That which is the qualifier in one situation can itself be the qualified in another and vice versa. Again, it is only in relation to the qualified (substance) that there is the qualifier and it is only in relation to the qualifier that there is the qualified.[97]

Again, between substance and quality there cannot be any conceivable relation of priority or posteriority. Between the two, which comes earlier and which, later? Which of them is found prior to the other depending on which the other can come into existence? Could the character be prior (先有相) and hence existent even when there is not the substance? Or could the thing be prior to quality (先有所相)? Either way the fact that quality and substance are correlative is ignored.[98] Could they be simultaneous? Then, as the *Kārikā* points out, they should be independent of each other.[98a] Further, it is only having found that substance and attribute could not be established as separate, that one entertains the idea of their togetherness. Now, in order to prove their togetherness their separateness is desired. As their separateness has not been proved, their togetherness is also not proved. Moreover, how can they be together, if they are separate? Between substance and attribute there can be neither togetherness nor separateness.[99]

Starting with the completely isolated, self-contained elements, to suppose that they later get related is to fail to provide a basis for their relation. Moreover, even the "one substance," which is to provide the basis for the relation of "the many attributes," itself becomes reduced to one of the many, and stands itself as much in need of a relating principle as the many attributes themselves. That way neither substance nor attributes can be established. And there being neither substance nor attributes, there cannot also be anything existent. In the absence of anything existent, there is also nothing non-existent, and there is also no one who would cognize these.[100] This is the impasse that results from the supposition that substance and quality are things in themselves.

*CHAPTER VIII*

# THE WORLD AND THE INDIVIDUAL

*Section I*

## NON-SUBSTANTIALITY OF THE ELEMENTS OF EXISTENCE

*Correlativity of concepts and non-substantiality of elements:* The correlativity of the concepts that stand for the kinds of mutual relatedness of actual entities or events needs to be distinguished from the non-substantiality of the latter which are the basic elements of existence. Both of these are the different phases of *śūnyatā* or essential conditionedness of the world of the determinate. Events happen in mutual relatedness within which they can be analyzed, distinguished, and designated as different kinds of happening. As each of these events is a unity of its constituent factors, it can be called "one." Again, as these events are constituted of many factors and are themselves in turn constituent factors of further composite entities, they can also be called "many." It is the continuous stream of events that is called one thing. While to the eyes of flesh things appear as indivisible, simple and ultimate, to the eye of wisdom it is clear that they altogether lack substantiality and permanence. Again, while an event or an entity is a concrete, composite "thing" analysable into constituent elements, the factors designated by the correlative concepts like long and short, east and west, past, present and future, are not themselves any "thing." They are simply ways in which the concrete things or their constituent elements stand related mutually. These are also ways in which things are analyzed and unified in understanding. Events or actual entities are the basic elements of existence; they exist; they arise and perish; they constitute streams of being; they have their respective causal factors; they have their distinctive natures according to which they turn out their respective functions. What the correlative concepts designate are the ways in which events happen.

*The essential conditionedness of the elements of existence:* The being of elements lies in their becoming, in their function; and in accordance with the work they turn out they derive their names and are classified into different categories. It is the mission of the Mādhyamika to reveal that the notion of the ultimacy and separateness of these basic elements is not only devoid of ground but is definitely contradicted by the very nature of things. If everything is in fact self-being and unchanging, then, the concrete relatedness and conditioned becoming of things are denied. This is the basic *reductio ad absurdum* of the extreme of eternalism. The same result follows even in the case of the extreme of negativism. The extremes meet in being species of falsification. The Middle Way consists in rising above the level of clinging to existence and non-existence and realizing them as aspects of conditioned becoming, the essential nature of all things, subtle as well as gross. Further, while conditionedness as the mundane truth brings to light the possibility of bringing things into being as well as of terminating them, the way this possibility is harnessed depends on how one understands the significance of life. Not only every event is essentially related to all the rest but every event inasmuch as it is conditioned, owes its being to the unconditioned, undivided ground which alone can provide sufficient reason even for the mutual relatedness of events. That the conditioned as such is not unconditioned is the deeper significance of the teaching of *śūnyatā*. By this understanding one is led to the comprehension of the truly unconditioned, viz., the undivided being *(advaya-dharma)*.

*The compositeness of physical entities:* All elements, physical as well as mental, are *śūnya,* i.e., relative and non-substantial, conditioned and changing.

There are in all two kinds of elements, physical (色法) and non-physical (無色法) (or mental). The physical can be analyzed down to the minute atoms and all that can be seen to scatter and become extinct without any remainder . . . The non-physical (or mental) elements are not cognized by the five (external) senses. Of the internal sense *(citta)* birth, stay and extinction can be (easily) seen; so it is known that it admits of (temporal) division; as *citta* admits of (temporal) divisions it is impermanent. Being impermanent it is non-substantial, *(śūnya)*. Being non-substantial it is not real, not unconditioned. The single instant of a snapping of the finger contains sixty "moments," and in every one of these moments there are phases of birth and death. It is by virtue of the birth of the continuity of these mental elements that it is possible to know that this is the mind of greed, this is the mind of anger etc. The wayfarer comprehends the stream of birth and death of the mental elements like the flow of water or the flame of the lamp. This is known as the door to the comprehension of *śūnyatā* (入空智門). (171a–b)

No existent element ever remains devoid of change. Of the physical elements, if earth, e.g., always remained hard, then it should not under any circumstance give up its hardness. The *Śāstra* observes that there are obvious cases of solid things giving up solidity and becoming liquid. Wax, for instance, and metals like gold, silver, and iron turn into liquid when heated. Similarly liquid becomes solid; for example, water becomes ice when cold. Thus everything gives up its present nature (捨相) and becomes different; there is no absoluteness about it.[1] Further, every element of existence can be analysed and seen to be constituted of several factors without which it would not have its being. Earth, for instance, has its being as the togetherness of color, smell, taste and touch; in the absence of any one of these there would not be the thing called earth as none of these elements can alone constitute it. If, for example, color by itself constituted earth, then it should have been devoid of smell, taste and touch. And the same is the case with all the other elements.[2] Again, it cannot be that earth is just a collection or sum of these elements and that these elements are ever existent by themselves, coming together only under suitable conditions. For, while earth is one and integral, the basic elements are four.

How can one be four and four be one?[2a] (194c)

Therefore it cannot be that earth is just these basic elements themselves (以色爲地) come together under suitable conditions. To imagine so is to miss the original integrity of the thing. But in order to maintain its integrity, should someone imagine that earth is something separate from these elements (離色爲地), he would again miss its true nature.[3] For there is not anything like earth in itself apart from the elements of color, smell, taste and touch.

To suppose that earth stays within these elements or that it arises from these is to suppose their difference from it.

If from these four elements there arises the thing called earth, then it should be that earth is different from these four. For example, from the union of father and mother there is born the child, and the child is different from them. If earth were something different from these four basic elements, as the eye perceives color, the nose perceives smell, the tongue perceives taste, and the bodily sense perceives touch, there should have to be some other sense to perceive earth which is different from these. But as there is no such special organ with a special sense to perceive it, it follows that there is no such (separate) thing called earth.[3a] (194c)

There is no knowing of anything called earth in itself apart from these four elements; it is a figment of imagination. *Abhidharma* holds, the *Śāstra* observes, that earth is the gross matter derived from the four fundamental physical elements. It holds that the subtle atomic element of earth has the character only of hardness, whereas the derived element is the visible gross physical thing which has the characters of all the four elements. But now, if earth is taken as only the visible form, then there would be the difficulty that it should be devoid of taste, smell and touch. Again, as earth is taken as hardness by definition, the merely visible forms which are not impenetrable like the image of the moon in the water, the image of the face in the mirror, the shadow of the tree, have no character of hardness and cannot therefore be classified as *rūpa* (physical). The character of hardness is perceived only through contact with the sense of touch. Moreover, if the upholders of analysis would hold that because the visible matter which is gross is itself the earth and has hardness for its character therefore it must have been matter derived from the basic element of earth (地種) which is the element of hardness, then, the visible matter has in it the characters of moisture and heat too, which should, according to the Ābhidharmika, properly belong to the basic elements of water and fire.[4]

But here the Ābhidharmika would say that these four basic elements are not apart from one another; in the derived earth there is not only the basic element of earth but there are also the basic elements of water, fire and wind. Similarly in each of the other derived forms of physical elements also all the four basic elements are found. Only in earth, the earthy element is more and therefore it is called earth. The same is the case with the other elements too.

But how can he maintain this?

If, e.g., in fire all the four basic elements are present, then all of them should be of the nature of heat. For, there is nothing in fire that is not hot. But if the other three elements are there in fire and yet are not hot, they are not called fire. But if they are not there, then you should admit that these elements give up their self-nature, and the entire thing is called fire. (194c)

Suppose the Ābhidharmika would say that these three are there as such, but they are too subtle to be perceived (細故不可知). Then they are as good as not being there (則與無無異), for we have no ground to speak of them as being there.[5]

It is only if anything is obtained in its gross state then we can reason back to their subtle state (even when unperceived). But if the thing is not perceived in the gross state, there is no way of knowing that it is there in the subtle state (若無麁亦無細). (194c–195a)

The notion that there are in reality subtle, independent elements called earth etc., which are ultimate and substantial while all gross things are *śūnya,* relative and non-substantial is only an imagination that does not hold. All things, physical or mental; gross or subtle are alike *śūnya.*

*Non-ultimacy of atomic elements:* But is it necessary that everything should exist by only depending on the cooperation of causal factors? How about the atomic elements? They are most subtle and are therefore indivisible. Being indivisible they cannot be said to be the results of the combination of causal factors. Of the gross things it can be said that they are produced and destroyed; but how can the atoms which are indivisible be produced and destroyed?[6]

Here the *Śāstra* replies that there is not anything absolutely fixed as the "subtlest"; the name has been simply imposed on certain things. Gross and subtle are relative denominations. It is only depending on the gross that there is the subtle. Moreover, the things that one takes to be subtle would admit of even further analysis into still subtler elements (in the light of which the former would be gross).[7] The subtlest, the atomic element, is a purely conceptual limit which is significant not in itself, but only in relation to the gross.

Further, if the subtle elements are physical, then they are not indivisible (atomic), and if they are indivisible they would lack the character of being physical as they would not have the spatial divisions.[8] Again, the subtle physical elements must have in them as much share of color as of taste, smell and touch. If they have these, then they are not indivisible, but if they do not have these, then they lack these qualities. The divisible is not eternal and the eternal (indivisible) is not physical. The *Śāstra* observes, in truth as the *Sūtra* says, "Whether gross or subtle, internal or external, *rūpa* is found on examination to be devoid of permanence and self-being."[9]

Some may say that they do not admit of the subtle eternal entities called atoms; they just take the visible form as *rūpa* which is there definitely and undeniably. How can this be analysed and demonstrated as *śūnya*?[10] The *Śāstra* says:

Now, even if you do not accept atoms (as subtle, eternal entities), still, the visible *rūpa* that is born out of the togetherness of the four basic elements is also a derived name. For example, when the wind blows the water all over the four sides, there arises the ball of foam (which is not anything substantial). This is the case even with the *rūpa* that is born of the four basic elements.[11] (292a)

If the four basic elements are scattered apart (離散) there is nothing like the physical object of sight. For, in the case of the exclusion of all elements, smell etc., there is no separate physical, entity as such.[12]

When by means of understanding one analyses everything into its component elements, then, one finds that *rūpa* (色) the physical entity is unobtainable as anything substantial. If *rūpa* were a substantial self-existent entity (實有) then even apart from all these elements there should be a separate entity called *rūpa,* but (actually) there is no such separate entity. Therefore the *Sūtra* says, "Whatever *rūpa* is there, all that arises from the cooperation of the four basic elements." As it arises from the cooperation of several causal factors, it is all a derived name. Being a derived name, it can be analysed and scattered (and known to be composite and therefore *śūnya,* non-substantial).[13] (292a)

Further, it may be recalled that the fact that there are names for things should not be taken as the ground for their substantiality. While significant names suggest the possibility of the objects which they stand for, they do not necessarily mean that they are substantial; to suppose that they do so is to fall into the error of eternalism.

*The mental elements: Experience and the object of experience:* Further, objects of experience have no being isolated or disconnected from the experiencing of them; these are inseparable correlatives. An exclusive emphasis on either of them would be only a falsification.

Take, for example, the hardness of earth. Hardness is there only as (an object of experience) perceived by the sense of touch (身根身識) (and interpreted by the sense of *manas)*. If it is not an object of the experience of touch, then there is no (possibility) of (knowing that there is such a thing as) hardness at all. (171a)

Suppose it is said that whether the sense of touch experiences the hardness or not, earth is always hard.

Now, either one has already experienced hardness personally (若先自知) or one has heard of it from another (若從他聞) and has thus come to know that there is such a thing called hardness. If hardness is not at all an object of experience in any way then (there is no knowing of anything like hardness and) it is (as good as) non-existent. (171a)

There is no knowing that the earth is hard even when not experienced. Cognition and objects of cognition are correlative; one cannot be found without the other. The element of cognition for example comes into being only depending on its object; when the object becomes extinct, even the element of cognition ceases to be. When the object is denied even its idea stands denied; the one is not found without the other. All the four kinds of mental elements arise and function only depending on their respective objects. There is no absoluteness about them. They are comparable to fire in respect to their functions:

Fire, for example, receives its name in accordance with the object that it burns and without the object of burning fire cannot be found. With the visual sense as the cause and the color as the object there arises the visual sensation. Independently of the object the sensation cannot be.[14] (292a)

This is true not only of sensation but of all phases of mental life. All mental elements are subject to birth, decay and death. They are impermanent and never remain self-identical even for a moment. All that constitutes the concrete course of life is essentially conditioned; it is a becoming, an event, an arising and perishing. And the supposition of the ultimacy and separateness of the basic elements is spurious.[15]

*Section II*

## THE NOTION OF SELF AS A SUBSTANTIAL ENTITY (SOUL)

*The notion of self as a substantial entity (soul):* Prompted by the sense of "I," under ignorance one imputes unconditionedness to the conditioned, imagines permanence in regard to the impermanent, and clings to the composite entity as incomposite and simple. Hence the false notion of a particular yet permanent entity called "soul," in regard to what is only a composite organism of conditioned events.[15a] The soul is held to be specific, one of the many, and is yet imagined to be permanent and non-relational, individual and yet an eternal substance. In addition to the inherent incongruity of an imagination of this kind, there is a further incongruity in that it makes the individual unrelated to the organic, dynamic course of personal life and deprives the latter of all significance. The imagination is spurious; it is linked at its root with the notion of the ultimacy of difference. What it amounts to is the eternality of the divided. The Vaiśeṣikas as pluralists hold this. The Jainas and Sāṅkhyas, although tending to denying the ultimacy of difference in epistemology and ontology respectively, still hold to the plurality of the individual souls. Thus they all hold a position which is inherently unstable.

*The Buddhists who think that self is a substance:* Of the Buddhists, some seem to have entertained this notion of self or person as a simple, eternal, substance.[16] The Sarvāstivādins deny the reality of self or person; but in their denial they swing to the other extreme of denying personality altogether, thus tending, on the one hand, to a mechanistic conception of personality and, on the other, to a plurality of ultimate elements. Here again extremes meet. A total assertion of personality and a total denial of personality alike result in a purely mechanistic view of life; both alike fail to provide adequate ground for the purposefulness of life and the dynamic, organic nature of personality.

To such of the Buddhists who tend to hold the view that apart from and independent of the *skandhas* there is the individual as a substantial entity, the *Śāstra* would reply that it would amount to tending towards eternalism, an extreme against which the Buddha exhorted so much His disciples to guard themselves. Further, even granting that the individual entity is there apart from the five *skandhas,* how is that entity to be known? It is not there among the objects of the six kinds of sensation. Again, these objects are seen to be impermanent, subject to birth and death and not self-possessed; but the individual as an entity is supposed to be a permanent self-being, not subject to birth and death. Certainly no entity of that kind could be found among the objects of the different kinds of sensation. If there were any such entity, then there should have been an altogether separate sense, a seventh *vijñāna,* to cognize it.[17] But there is no such thing.

*The soul-theory of the non-Buddhists:* The non-Buddhists urge that the soul which is one's own self cannot be denied without stultifying oneself. The self should be recognized as the subject, they argue. Every one has a soul of his own; and the soul of each is a separate, self-identical entity; it is permanent; it is the knower, the doer of deeds and the experiencer of results. They place their view on the following grounds.
(A) The soul as the self of everybody is the object of the notion of "I"; it is the basis of distinction between oneself and another. If within one's body there is not one's own soul, then it should have to be admitted that the sense of "I" arises even without any object. And if even in reference to one's own person the sense of "I" is (devoid of object and hence) false, then why should it not arise in reference to another?
(B) If within the body, there is no soul (as the subject) then, as sensations arise and perish every moment, what other principle is there to distinguish and synthesise them? Without such a principle how can there be any definite knowledge that this is blue and this is red?
(C) Further, if within the body there is no soul, at the end of the present span of life, who follows the deeds and receives their results, good or bad? Who experiences pleasure and pain? And who realizes freedom?[18]

On these grounds, these people hold that soul should be definitely recognized as a real, substantial entity.

### A. *Soul and the Sense of "I"*

(I) *Is soul as the basis of the distinction of "self" and "other"?* As regards the sense of "self" and the sense of "other," the *Śāstra* draws attention to their correlativity as references and observes that there is no rigidness even in regard to their spheres of reference. No rigid line could be drawn between "self" and "other." What is referred to as "self" at one time or in a certain context may be the "other" (or not-self) at another time or in another context so that this question as to why the sense of "I" should not arise in reference to another person could be met with a counter question: If in reference only to another person one holds the sense of "I" (若於他身生計我者),

Then, why does this sense not arise in the case of one's own person? (148b)

Further, this question is based on a supposition of an absolute distinction between self and other, which again presupposes an absolute entity called soul (若有神者可有彼我) as the object of the reference of "self" conceived as independent of and separate from the "other." But it is this very existence of the soul (神) as a separate entity that is in question; when this is itself not settled, how could the further point of the absolute distinctness of "self" and "other" be based on it?

This is like the question being asked about the nature of the hare's horn and the reply being given that it resembles the horn of the horse. (148b)

Further, the objection, why the sense of "I" is not born for one in reference to another, is relevant to the position of the soul-theorist and not of the Mādhyamika. Because, the soul-theorist holds that the soul is all-pervasive and so, there should arise for one the sense of "I" even in reference to another. The *Śāstra* observes that actually there are persons who do give rise to the sense of "self" even in reference to "other" persons as well as in reference to what is usually considered as not-self.

The contemplatives of the non-Buddhist schools, for example, during the course of their contemplation on the all-pervasiveness of elements give rise to the notion "I am the earth, earth is myself." . . . Again, in a state of confusion (顛倒) one might hold the sense of "I" even in reference to other persons.[19] So it cannot be argued that because there are the notions of "self" and "other," therefore there should be the soul as a real, substantial, specific entity.

(II) *Is soul the object of the notion of "I"?* The objector contends that even granting that there is no soul, the sense of "I" is surely there. If there were no soul, this sense should have to be devoid of a definite object. That cannot be.[20] The *Śāstra* observes that the sense of "I" is certainly not devoid of object. The usual object of the sense of "I" is the body-mind complex, the stream of the five *skandhas*. Owing to perversion there arises in one the different kinds of the false sense of self in reference to it. It is this complex of the five *skandhas* that is the object of the sense of "I" and "mine." It is not anything substantial as it is a composite entity; everything in it is causally born, subject to arising and perishing and hence devoid of self-hood. Out of ignorance one imagines it as a substantial entity and clings to it as "I" and "mine." That the sense of self usually arises only in reference to a specific set of five *skandhas* is a matter of deep-rooted habit (習); out of habit one conceives a particular complex of five *skandhas* as one's self.[21] Without this fixedness the world of convention would be a mass of confusion. But this fixedness in reference should not lead one to think that the object of this reference is a real, substantial entity. Again, it may be added, not all self-reference need be one of clinging: there is the non-clinging sense of "I" as well as the clinging sense of "I." Actually the clinging to the complex of the five *skandhas* as "I" and "mine" is purely a case of ignorance and perversion. There is in truth no absoluteness about the sphere of self-reference; one should not seek for an absolute rule in this regard. Further, if the sense of "I" were something absolute and stable, and if it were to refer invariably to a particular substantial entity, then every one should forever be committed to a divided life, which even the soul-theorists would not admit.

(III) *Has soul any definite nature?* Moreover, of this soul that these people imagine as the definite object of the notion of "I," truly, no definite nature can be found. It cannot be held that the soul is absolutely permanent or that it is absolutely impermanent, that it is completely self-possessed or utterly devoid of self-possession, that it is something material or immaterial, etc.

A definite substantial entity must have its own definite nature; a thing devoid of nature is (as good as) non-existent. If the soul is devoid of all nature, it is as good as non-existent.[22] (149a)

The soul, for instance, cannot be held to be eternal; if it were eternal, it should be devoid of death and rebirth; a person should not then be conceived as possible of being killed. An eternal and all-pervasive entity such as soul should not be conceived again as transmigrating, for it should for ever be existent everywhere. So how can there happen birth or death to it? Does not death mean leaving this sphere, and birth, emerging in another? Again, such an eternal soul should be devoid of the experience of pleasure and pain. If the soul became sad with the approach of pain and glad with the approach of pleasure, then it should not be beyond change, and hence not eternal. The soul that is eternal and all-pervasive should be like *ākāśa* which the rains cannot wet and the sun cannot dry; it should then be devoid of the distinctions of this world and the other world; it should not be that it dies here and emerges there. Again, if the soul were eternal, then the sense of "I" should also be for ever there, and there should then be no way of becoming free from it. Again, if there were an eternal soul, as these people conceive, then there should be no question of forgetting anything. Only because there is no such eternal soul, and because *vijñāna,* the principle of intellection, is not a permanent entity, therefore there is the forgetting of things. So it cannot be held that there is any such real, substantial, permanent (常) entity called soul. It cannot also be that the person is as such eternal.[23]

But can the soul (神) be evanescent (無常), or even as impermanent as the ever perishing *skandhas?* To imagine that the self is evanescent is to deny causal continuity, which is again to deny the possibility of sin and merit. This is to fall into the wrong notion of negativism. Then there would be none that would reach the next span of life and receive the results of deeds done in the previous span. If the self as well as the body became wholly extinct, then, to realize Nirvāṇa, there would be no need to cultivate the way and terminate the forces that bind one to error and suffering. So it cannot be that the person is evanescent.[24]

Again, is the soul (神) completely self-possessed (自在) and completely self-willed (自作)? In this case every one should get whatever one wishes even without any effort. Actually this does not happen. In fact, one does not get what one wishes and one gets what one does not wish. Again, if everyone were completely self-possessed, one should not commit sin and fall into evil or inferior states of life. No one delights in pain. If the self were completely self-possessed who would be in this state where, in spite of one's desire for pleasure, what one gets is still more pain? Further, people are often forced to do good deeds only because they fear sin. Now, if the person (人) were completely self-willed where is the question of his fearing sin and being forced to cultivate merit?[24a] That the soul is devoid of complete freedom means that it is devoid of the nature of soul. But is the person completely devoid of self-will? If the person were completely devoid of self-will (不作者),

Then, when the sinner is asked by *Yamarāja* (閻羅王) (the king of death) as to who made him commit the sin, how could he reply, "I have done it myself (是我自作)"? Therefore it should be that the person is not completely devoid of self will (非不自作). (149b)

Some imagine that the soul (神) is something of a determinate shape and size, that it is something formed (physical), and that it has a definite location (spatial). Thus some say the soul is in the heart and is as small as the mustard seed (芥子); it is pure and is called the pure physical body (淨色身). Some others say that the soul is like a corn of maize. Some say that it is like a bean. Some say it is half an inch in measure and some say, one inch in measure. They say that in receiving the body it is the foremost to reach it. Some say that the size of the soul varies with the body it receives. At the time of death, so they hold, the soul is the first to go out of the body. But these views are not proper. For, anything that has a shape and is physical is made of the four fundamental physical elements and is causally born and is not therefore anything permanent or substantial.[25] To imagine on the contrary that the person is utterly impermanent is to entertain the error of negativism.

(IV) *Is soul the subtle body?* Some distinguish between two kinds of body, gross and subtle, and say that while the gross body (麁身) is impermanent, the subtle body (細身) is the same as the soul and that in every span of life, the subtle body emerges out of one gross body and enters into another, thus revolving in the five states of existence.[26] The *Śāstra* observes that, first of all, such a subtle body cannot be found anywhere.

Suppose there is the subtle body as you imagine; it should have a location; actually whether in the five *kośas* or in the four bodies (五藏四體), searching everywhere no (such) subtle body can be found (which can answer to the notion of soul).[26a] (149b)

But these people say that the subtle body is too subtle to be seen; at the time of death it will have already left the previous habitation, and when alive one cannot find it by searching for it. So how can one "see" it? Moreover this subtle body is not an object of the five physical senses; only the sages with extraordinary powers can see it. To this the *Śāstra* replies that a thing which is not an object of experience is as good as non-existent. Further one can add that anything that is a "body" is impermanent and non-substantial. The *Śāstra* observes that in fact what these people are speaking of as subtle body (細身) is simply the complex of the subtle *skandhas* of the intermediary state (中陰), i.e., the state between death and rebirth.[27] The physical element, whether internal or external, subtle or gross, is all impermanent, subject to birth and death. It is not any real substantial entity.[28]

But can the soul be anything non-physical? Of the non-physical, there are on the one hand the four kinds of mental elements, i.e., the four *skandhas,* and on the other, there are the incomposite elements. The mental elements are subject to birth and death; they do not endure even for a moment; they owe their being to causes and conditions and are not self-possessed. So these cannot answer to their notion of soul. Of the incomposite also there is nothing that can answer to their notion of soul, for the incomposite is not anything that could be seized as 'I" or "mine."[29]

In this way between heaven and earth, inside or outside, in any of the three times or any of the ten directions, searching for the soul, one can not find it (求我不可得). (149c)

(V) *Is soul an object of inference?* The existence of soul cannot even be inferred as there are no characteristic signs of its own by which it can be inferred. Anything known as existent is known by virtue of its characteristic sign (有相故則知有). Seeing the smoke and feeling the heat, one can know that there is fire. As there are different kinds of sense-objects one can know that there must be the different senses to perceive them. By reason of the different activities of considering and understanding things, one can know that there are the mind and the mental states. But the soul is devoid of characters and how can it be known that it exists?[30]

The soul-theorists argue: Are there not breathings in and out (出入息)? Can they not serve as the marks of soul? Again, the opening and closing of the eyes (視眴), the duration of life (壽命), the different states of mind like the feeling of pain and pleasure, love and hatred, and effort, all these can serve as the marks of soul (是我相).[31] If there is no soul who has all these? Therefore it should be known that inside the body there is the soul. Because the soul impels from within, the vital principle functions. It is the soul that directs and puts into action even the mind; without a soul it would be like an ox without a driver. If there is no soul who directs the mind? It is the soul that experiences pleasure and pain. Devoid of soul, the body would just be like wood, without the capacity to distinguish things. Although the soul is subtle and cannot therefore be cognized through the five senses, still through these signs of soul one can infer that it exists (因是相故可知爲有). Here the *Śāstra* observes that all these marks mentioned above as the signs of soul are truly the signs of *vijñāna* (皆是識相), the self-conscious principle of intellection, the individual centre of personality.[32] When *vijñāna* is present then there are the activities of breathing in and out, the opening of the eyes to see etc., as well as the duration of life. When *vijñāna* leaves the body, then none of these marks can be found. Further, as these people maintain that the soul is eternal and all-pervasive,[33] and hold that breathing etc. are its characteristic marks, so, even the "dead" person should have the activities of breathing, seeing, etc. In truth, breathing etc., are the physical activities that take place due to the power of the wind which functions according to (the direction it receives from) the *citta* or *vijñāna*. These are truly the marks of *citta* or *vijñāna* and not of any soul (此是識相非我相). Although sometimes there are cases of temporal lapse (暫無) of the explicit sense of self, it is not altogether extinct; it continues even then in a subtle form, but soon after the state of lapse, the element of self-consciousness becomes explicit. This is comparable to a person going out of his house for some time; just because he has been away for some time it cannot be said that the house is devoid of a master. Similarly although sometimes there is a temporary lapse of self-consciousness still it cannot be said that it is totally absent at any time. Even elements like pain and pleasure, love and hatred, and effort belong essentially to *citta;* they have their common object with it, and they function along with it. They are there when *citta* is there; when it is not there even these will not be. Therefore these are the characters of *vijñāna* and are not pertinent to any eternal entity called soul.[34]

(VI) *The substantialist and the organismic views of self:* In the course of the present discussion there has emerged the important point of distinction between what can be described as the substantialist view of self and the organismic, dynamic conception of self. While it is undeniable that the dynamic system of bodily and mental events constituting personality is taken even by the substantialists as a system of conditioned events, they entertain the notion of a separate substantial entity called "soul" as its ground, and consider that as the true object of the sense of "I."

This substantial entity or soul, is thought to be eternal and all-pervasive, while at the same time being many and separate. Not only is each soul separate from the other souls, but each soul is separate also from the complex of bodily and mental events with which it is associated. Still it does deeds, experiences pleasure and pain and transmigrates from one set of bodily and mental elements to another. It is evident that this notion is a mixture of contradictory ideas, and as the Buddhist would hold, it is really an imagination of unconditionedness and permanence in regard to the complex of *skandhas,* which is in truth a determinate system of conditioned events. If this rejection of "soul" were to lead one to the other extreme of imagining that personal life is altogether devoid of a basis, that would be to swing to the error of negativism. Both alike deprive personal life of its significance and deny its very possibility.

The Middle Way consists in the recognition that the complex system of personality is not absolute, that there is no element in it which forever remains the same, as well as that no element in the system of personal life ever perishes totally.

The course of personal life is a continuous organic system of events. But still, what gives it the unique character of being personal is the sense of "I," the fundamental fact of subjectivity, the experiencing of the inner life as "I" and "mine," in other words, the principle of self-determination or self-conscious intellection. But the point about this principle is that it is not any unconditioned, substantial entity. It is essentially a process, a function of experiencing and determining from within itself the course of events which it gives rise to as its self-expressions in response to the basic urge in it, the thirst for the real, and that, in the context of the objective world which it confronts, perceives, understands and interprets. Thus the principle of self-conscious intellection, the empirical subject, is not only relative to the objective world, but more important still, its function is conditioned at root by the sense of the unconditioned which is its basic insight. The fundamental fact about man is his thirst for the real.

What is sought to be brought to light is this essentially conditioned, dynamic, organic nature of the course of personal life and it is demonstrated here that to this conception of personality, the soul of the substantialists is not only devoid of relevance but altogether contradictory.

The farer on the Middle Way will say that all that is of positive significance in the conception of soul is truly relevant to the self-conscious principle of intellection. In fact it is this principle itself that they falsely conceive as "soul."

(Truly) that which you are speaking of as soul (我) is simply (our) *vijñāna;* it is nothing else.[34a] (149b)

All the marks of soul, as stated above, are truly the marks of *vijñāna.* Even the subtle body that these people speak of is but *vijñāna.* It is *vijñāna* itself as the complex of the subtle *skandhas,* as the self-conscious seed of personal life, that "gives up" one state of life and "takes up" another. It is *vijñāna* again that carries out the function of knowing. This takes us to the second main point that the non-Buddhists offer as a ground for entertaining the notion of soul as a real, substantial entity.

### B. *Soul and Knowledge*

*Is soul the necessary condition of knowledge?* The second argument of the substantialists is that while sensations arise and perish every moment, there must be the principle which analyses and unifies them; without it knowledge is impossible.

If there is no soul inside the body how can there be the distinguishing knowledge that this is red and this is blue, that this is yellow and this is white?[35] (148b)

Here the *Śāstra* observes that even if there be a soul it would not be of any help in this matter. For even according to the substantialists the soul by itself cannot do the understanding (不能獨知); it has to depend on the internal principle of *citta* and on the different senses and only thus it can know things.[36]

In that case the soul is really of no use here. The visual sense (grasps the color) and the *citta* understands it as color. When the color element that is born becomes extinct (色生滅) the impression arises (相似生); when (the first) impression comes to an end, there arises in the mind the element called *smṛti* (念). This element of *smṛti* is by nature composite; although (objects themselves) become extinct, still it can know and discriminate things. Even as the sages can know through their power of *prajñā* the things that would happen in the future, similarly *smṛti* (念) can know the past things. As the earlier element of visual sensation (前眼識滅) becomes extinct, there arises in continuation the later element of visual sensation (生後眼識). This latter element of visual sensation will have an enhanced power of grasping (轉利有力). Therefore although the element of color is itself transitory and not stable, by virtue of the sharpness and the powerfulness of *smṛti* (以念力利故) . . . one can distinguishingly know (能分別知) the element of color. (149c)

The objector might argue here that even granting that it is the *citta* that uses the body and performs the act of cognizing things, still there should be the subject, the soul, to use (使) the *citta*. Even as the king employs the commander-in-chief and the commander-in-chief commands the army, so the soul employs the *citta* and the *citta* uses the body.[37] The *Śāstra* observes that this argument would lead to endless regression (是則無窮), for then there should be another soul to employ this soul and thus there should have to be two or even innumerable souls in a body.[38] But if just this one soul can by itself (但我) use the *citta*, even the *citta* can by itself (但心) use the body.[39]

You take the *citta* as belonging to the soul (屬神), and (you hold that) apart from the *citta* the soul has no knowledge. If the soul has no knowledge, how can it use the *citta*? But if the soul has the nature of knowledge, then, of what use again is *citta* to it? Therefore it should be known that *citta* itself being of the nature of (self-)consciousness can use the body, and has no need to depend on a soul at all even as fire can burn things by its very nature, and does not need to depend on man for burning.[40] (200c)

Here the objector argues that although the fire has the capacity to burn, it is not put to use if there is no person to do so (非人不用); similarly although cognizing is the very nature of the *citta,* it is not put to use if there is no soul (非神不使).

Here the *Śāstra* points out that so far as knowledge is concerned, soul is of no use at all. *Citta* or *vijñāna* which is the principle of self-determination is able to put to use and to determine the course of the activity of itself as well as of the elements that belong to it. Even if there were a soul, as it was mentioned above, it would be of no use here. Sometimes fire can burn by itself; it is only in name that the person is said to set the fire to burn. Again the opponent stands defeated on his own ground (論墮負處); the soul is the same as the person; that itself cannot be used as an example to prove its very existence.[41]

### C. *Soul and Deeds*

*Is soul the necessary condition of deeds and moral responsibility?* The third point of the substantialists is that in the absence of a permanent soul, as the present element of *vijñāna* becomes extinct at the time of the termination of the present span of life, the deeds done here would all be lost, for there would be none to follow them and receive their results. Who follows the deeds and who receives the results? Who is the receiver of pain and pleasure? Who realizes freedom?[41a]

To this the *Śāstra* replies that when the true way has not yet been realized by one (未得實道), as one's mind is covered up with *kleśa,* one does deeds which breed for one the next span of life. At the time of one's death, in continuity with the five *skandhas* of the present span of life, there arises the complex of the five *skandhas* of the next span of life. This is like one lamp lighting another. This is again comparable to the birth of the sprout from the seed. Now the birth of the sprout from the seed requires three conditions: soil, water, and seed. Just the same is the case even with the birth of the next span of life from the present one; there is the body, there are the defiled deeds and there are the factors of bondage (結使) like greed etc.; and out of the cooperation of these three conditions there arises the next body. Of these three, the body that is already there and the deeds that are already done cannot be destroyed or abandoned. But there remain the factors of bondage, and these alone can be terminated (但諸結使可斷). Although when these are terminated, the body and the deeds may continue, still one can realize freedom from the cycle of birth and death. This is like the sprouts not arising in the absence of water although the soil and the seeds are there.[42] And so even without the need to suppose a soul it can still be shown how the realization of freedom is possible.

Bondage is through ignorance and freedom is through kowledge; the soul (that you imagine) is useless here (則我無所用). (150a)

Not that there is no person that becomes bound or becomes free. There is no such soul as the substantialists imagine. In truth, it is the complex of bodily and mental elements that is derivedly called the person. The ignorant is bound by the bonds of greed, hatred and stupidity.

But when one realizes the claws (爪) of the undefiled wisdom one tears off (解) all these bonds; then one is said to have become free. It is like the tying (結) and the untying (解) of the rope. The rope itself is the knot; the knot is not something apart from the rope. Still in the world, one speaks of the knotting and the unknotting of the rope. The same is the case with *nāma* and *rūpa*, the bodily and mental elements. It is the complex of bodily and mental elements that is derivedly called the person; the bondage and the body-mind complex are not two separate things. It is only in name that the body-mind complex is said to become bound or become free. (150a)

In common discourse there is the talk of bondage *of* person and freedom *of* person. But this should not lead one to imagine that there is an eternal substantial, separate entity that becomes bound and becomes free and remains all the time unaffected in essence either by bondage or by freedom. Just the same is the case even with the receiving of the results of good and evil deeds. Although there is not any single self-identical entity called soul, still with regard to the composite entity, viz., the body-mind, there is the "receiving" of the results of deeds, good and bad. Still, in the world we say that the person receives them. Hence there is the imagination that there is a separate substantial entity called soul. This is again like the cart containing the load (車載物). There is no real, substantial entity called cart apart from and independent of its different parts. All the same the cart gets the name of containing the load. This is just the case with the person receiving the fruits of sin and merit.[43] What receives merit and sin is the body-mind complex, and this is referred to by the derived name, person. Here it is the unwary that is led to wrong notions.

*Section III*

## THE COURSE OF PERSONAL LIFE

### A. *Person as an organism*

(I) *Person as an organism:* There is no denial here of the fact that the person does deeds and receives the results, good or bad.[44] The deeds are in fact what the self, the self-conscious person, brings to birth as his very way of giving expression to his potencies and aspirations; the deeds constitute his very being. But in regard to this, the soul that the substantialists imagine is of no use. On the contrary it would make the person altogether unrelated to his deeds and his relation to them becomes a mystery.

As the subject, the person is the self-conscious, self-determining principle. He works out a career for himself under the stress of the sense of the unconditioned. He is conditioned by the forces dormant in him. He confronts an objective reality which he perceives, understands and interprets. He works out for himself an organic system of events which is to give expression to the basic urge in him, and he identifies himself with it. As identical with it, the person is an organism, and personality is an organization, a way of being.

(II) *The organism and the constitutent events:* Between oneself and the system of events that one gives rise to, the two aspects of the integral course of personal life, there cannot be any description in terms of absolute identity or absolute difference;[45] one would reduce the self to the terms of its own creations and the other would make it alien to the expressions of its very being. The self is not just the *skandhas,* the bodily and mental elements themselves put together; the person is one and integral, whereas the *skandhas* are distinct and five, many.

> One is not five and five is not one.[46] (369a)

The person continues while the specific elements arise and perish every moment. If the person also perished along with the perishing *skandhas,* then he would be as good as just grass or wood, arising and dying automatically. He would just be an automaton, without any of the implications of selfhood. In that case personal identity and moral obligation would be devoid of sense. Again, the view that the person is completely apart from the *skandhas,* which is the substantialist view, commits all the errors of eternalism. This would be practically to deprive the course of personal life of all its significance, denying the purposiveness of life, denying causal continuity and denying one's connection with one's deeds.[47]

The *Kārikā* compares the person to the fire and the *skandhas* to the fuel, in order to illustrate the nature of the relation between them.[48] If the fire is absolutely the same as the fuel, the agent and the object would be one and the same; if they are absolutely different, the one would be independent of the other. Having started with the notion of their separateness, it is futile to try to establish their relation as mutual dependence. The relation between them is inconceivable in absolute terms. Just the same is the case with self and its constituents—there can be no unconditional description of the relation between them.[49]

But this is not to deny either the self or its constituents. Even with regard to the relation between them, it is always possible to make relative statements from specific standpoints, in a non-clinging way. Personality is not only admitted in the mundane truth, but is essential there. Being essentially conditioned, the individual owes his being to the togetherness of the five *skandhas*. The self is not something purely imaginary like the second head or third hand which are mere names.[49a] What corresponds to the notion of self is the body-mind complex constituted of the elements which the self-conscious principle has itself given rise to by way of giving expression to its deepest urge. This complex of *skandhas* is not anything substantial. Substantiality is simply imposed on it by the ignorant.[50]

The four fundamental physical elements as well as the derived physical elements surround the *ākāśa* and thus there arises the name body (in reference to this complex entity which is the physical basis of personal life). In this there becomes manifest the seed of *vijñāna* (the self-conscious seed of personal life). . . . Endowed with the seed of *vijñāna* and determined by it (the body-mind complex) carries on the diverse deeds, physical and mental. On this essentially conditioned and non-substantial complex of the six basic elements there is imposed the name of man or woman. (206b)

As a stanza puts it,

In bowing down, in looking up, in bending or straightening, in standing and coming and going, in seeing and talking—in none of these there is any substantial entity (called soul). The wind functions according to (the determination of) *vijñāna* and thus there arise all the diverse activities. This *vijñāna* is by nature unstable, becoming extinct every moment. (206c)

This *vijñāna* is not anything substantial; it is a continuous process, an unbroken stream of events that arise and perish every moment; it is these that constitute the course of personal life. While this is so, it is due to ignorance that one gives rise to the false sense of self with regard to it and is thus led to the notion of a substantial soul. It is by the realization of the truth of suffering, its state and its relatedness to its conditions and consequences, that one puts an end to this false sense of self. With the false sense of self put an end to, one realizes that all the constituents of self are impermanent, essentially conditioned and non-substantial. One thus comes to understand the entire network of the factors that constitute and the forces that condition the course of personal life, by giving up one's clinging to the extremes of existence and non-existence. The *Śāstra* says:

Free from these two extremes of existence and non-existence to dwell in the Middle Way, this is the universal truth. The universal truth is itself the Buddha. For it is by virtue of one's realizing the universal truth that one is said to have attained Buddhahood. (747a)

Even the Buddha is not an exception to the mundane truth that individuality is a conditioned being and is derivedly named.

All the virtues of the roots of merit that the Buddha sowed from the start of His mind on the Way are the sources of His bodily features. Even His body is not anything substantial and self-contained; all (that is found there) belongs to the original causes and conditions; all of that has come into being as the result of (His) deeds. Although these causal factors (and their results) stay for long in the world, still by nature they are composite (and conditioned) and so even these should return finally to impermanence (or extinction). When these constituent factors of the Buddha's body are dispersed and destroyed, it is no more there. This is like the arrow shot into the sky by a skilful archer; although the arrow would reach a long distance, still it has to fall to the ground. This is just the case with the Buddha's body; although it is brilliant with all the features and subfeatures, although the merits He achieved (are innumerable) His name and fame are limitless, and the number of people He saved are beyond measure, still even His body had to return to extinction. (747b)

Is the Buddha existent or non-existent after passing away? Thoughts such as these do not fit in the case of Him, who is by nature *śūnya*. This remark holds good both in the case of the mundane and the ultimate nature of the Tathāgata. The Buddha as a person is not any unconditioned being. Buddhahood is an essentially conditioned, continuous course of personal life albeit the highest, the purest, and the best. In His ultimate nature the Buddha is the unconditioned reality itself.

The Tathāgata is the (ultimate) *dharma* devoid of birth and death; how could one seek to know His (ultimate) nature through the *prapañca* (戲論) (conceptual constructions) (of "is" and "is not")? If one seeks (to see) the Tathāgata through *prapañca* then one will not see Him. But if by this one should hold that there is no Tathāgata at all, then one would fall (again) into perversion. Therefore it is not proper to seek (to see) the Tathāgata through the *prapañca* of "is" and "is not."

Whatever is the nature of Tathāgata is also the nature of all things; whatever is the nature of all things is also the nature of Tathāgata. The nature of the Tathāgata is complete *śūnyatā;* that is also the nature of all things.[51] (455a)

### *B. Cycle of Life*

*The cycle of the life of the ignorant:* Of the course of life that the ignorant live the root is ignorance, while of the life that the wise live the root is wisdom; and of both, in fact, of all things, the ultimate root is *dharmatā,* which functions in the mundane truth as the ground and the order of the course of all things and is itself, in the ultimate truth, the universal reality, the Nirvāṇa. That there is orderliness in the course of things holds good in every case of becoming. Conditioned becoming is the very way in which there happen the cultivation of the way to freedom as well as the course of life in bondage, even as concepts, words, are the very means as much for the teaching of the non-contentious way as for clinging, contention and quarrel. What makes the difference is the continuation or the extinction of the perverting force of ignorance.

Under ignorance people seize the determinate as itself the ultimate and cling to things. Thus they give rise to passion and do deeds that lead them to the diverse states of existence. Out of their own deeds they suffer all kinds of pain. They do not know this truth. Having themselves given rise to things they themselves cling to them.[52]

*Links in the cycle of the life of the ignorant:* (I) *Birth as the condition of old age and death:* The bodhisattva who helps all to terminate the root of suffering should analyse and investigate the forces that operate in the life of the ignorant and trace them to their root. Searching for the root of pain (尋苦因緣), he understands that *jāti* "birth" or (clinging to) embodiment is its root (由生故).[53] As the Buddha has taught in His teaching of the twelve links, it is owing to birth or (clinging to) embodiment that there come into being the factors of old age, disease and death.

Common people do not know that it is from "birth" that one suffers pain. When they meet with a painful situation they simply get enraged and hate (other) people; they do not hold themselves responsible for it. At the outset they do not reprove "birth" (which is truly the source of pain). Therefore they only increase the factors that bind them; they multiply (reinforce and enhance) the conditions of "birth." (The common people) do not know the true origin of suffering. (696a)

(II) *The tendency for embodiment as the condition of birth:* The bodhisattva pursues his enquiry further to find the reason for one's birth in the life of bondage (復推生因緣). He finds that the reason for birth is *bhava* (有) the tending to become. This tending is for embodiment in one of the three worlds *(dhātu)*, the sensuous world, the world of fine matter and the incorporeal or immaterial world. (Tending towards and) clinging to (著) life, embodiment or becoming in one of these three spheres, one gives rise to deeds, good and evil.[54] It is this tending, this inclining towards the kinds of embodiment that is the source of birth in bondage.

(III) *Craving and clinging:* But what is the origin of *bhava,* this tending to become?

The origin of *bhava* is the *upādāna* (seizing) of four kinds (四種取), and the source of *upādāna* is *kleśa* headed by *tṛṣṇā* (愛等諸煩惱).[55] (696B)

The *Śāstra* makes out that it is one and the same element that is called craving as well as seizing; when subtle (小) and still unable to produce deeds it is called craving *(tṛṣṇā)* while when developed (增長) and able to produce deeds, it is called seizing (取) *(upādāna)*. The four kinds of seizing are, seizing the objects of sense-desire, seizing views, seizing mere moralism and seizing the "I" under the wrong notion that the individual self is a substantial entity. It is by craving for these four kinds of things and by seizing (取) and clinging (著) to them that one gives rise to the different kinds of deeds that lead one to birth in the different kinds of life in bondage.[56] Craving for, clinging to, and tending towards definite forms of life are but different phases of the one urge, the urge for embodiment, which is the thirst for fulfilment. Such fulfilment yields satisfaction, pleasure, while the state of lack is the state of pain.

(IV) *Senses, sense-contact and the feeling of pleasure and pain:* The craving is a seeking for fulfilment in embodiment, leading to achieving the feeling (受) of pleasure which attends on fulfilment and satisfaction. Negatively, this is the longing to overcome the state of pain; this is the root of craving. The feeling of pleasure depends on touch *(sparśa)* (觸), the contact of the senses with their respective objects. The *Śāstra* observes that the element of touch is the root of all mental elements like feeling etc. (受等心數法根本).[57] Touch comes into being out of the togetherness of the three things, the organ of sense, the element of awareness and the object. The six senses (viz., the five externals and the one internal, the *manas)* are the bases *(āyatana)* for the function of sense and the arising of touch, sensation. Although touch arises from the togetherness of all these three factors, still, it takes the six (internal) bases (六入) i.e., the six senses as its basis; they are the primary factors and hence only they get the name of being the origin of touch.[58]

(V) *The physical and the mental bases of personality and the seed of personal life:* The six bases (六入) of sensation and cognition arise from the *"nāma-rūpa,"* the body-mind complex. *"Nāma"* here stands for the incorporeal or mental and *"rupa"* for the physical aspects of individuality.[59] The two together constitute the "being" of the individual. Although these six "bases" are themselves the *nāma-rūpa,* when the six are developed and distinguished from each other they are called the six bases, and when not developed they are called just *nāma-rūpa*. Of these six bases, all the physical elements arise from the basic physical element "*rūpa*," while all the mental elements arise from the basic mental element, "*nāma*." Thus, of the six bases of cognition, the five physical bases are accomplished by "*rūpa*," and the one internal base is accomplished by "*nāma*."[60] Actually, "*nāma*" and "*rūpa*" are the two phases or aspects distinguishable within the integral organic entity. In the developed, distinguished state, the individual is named after these as *nāma-rūpa*, while in the subtle, undistingusihed state the individual is simply called "*vijñāna*." The undistinguished state is the root of the distinguished; *vijñāna* is the root of *nāma* as well as of *rūpa*.

*Vijñāna*, as we have already seen is the person in the subtle intermediary state (中陰).[61] His proceeding from one span of life to another is prompted by the basic urge in him for self-expression; he is ever seeking to become, to bring to manifestation all that is dormant in him. The constitution of personality ever undergoes a ceaseless change, embodying in numberless ways the original insight and the basic urge. It is the seeking of a new self-expression that prompts the self-determining, self-conscious principle to proceed to a new birth. It is due to the felt need to give form to its basic aspiration that it seeks embodiment. *Vijñāna* in this special state of seeking a new abode may be called the subtle "self-conscious seed of personal life." It is subtle and is in seed-form because it is unexpressed but all expressions proceed from it. It is aware of its present being as its own making as well as of its future possibility which it seeks to realize.

It is the defiled *citta* born from the traces (行) of (the passionate) deeds (of the past) that is the primary source of (the present) embodiment (初身因). Even as the calf recognizes its mother, the *citta*, (the self-conscious person) (in this state of transition) understands his own nature (which is but what has given rise to his present state) and hence the name "*vijñāna*." (自相識故名識) (100b)

The *Śāstra* observes that if *vijñāna* does not enter the womb, the womb rots and becomes destroyed.[62]

> *Vijñāna* is (the complex of) the five (subtle) *skandhas* of the intermediary state.[63] (696b)

The intermediary state is the state between death and rebirth. In this state, the constituent factors of the self-conscious individual are subtle (細), undeveloped, and are therefore simply named after *vijñāna*.[64]

The *Śāstra* gives an account of the rise of the intermediary state:

> At the time of the death of a person, he gives up the five *skandhas* of this span of life and enters the five *skandhas* of the intermediary state. At this time, the present body becomes extinct and he receives the body of the intermediary *skandhas*. This extinction of the present body and this arising of the intermediary state cannot be (said to be) before or after (each other). The time of the extinction is itself the time of (re)-birth (滅時即生). For example, the wax-seal impresses the clay; at the time when there is received the impression in the clay, at that very time, the seal also becomes extinct. Accomplishment (of the new) and the extinction (of the old) are simultaneous (成壞一時); even here, there is no (distinction of) before or after. At this time one receives the complex of the *skandhas* of the intermediary state (受中陰中有). Giving up this intermediary state one receives the state of the next span of life. What you call subtle body is just this complex of the intermediary *skandhas*. The body of the intermediary *skandhas* has neither any going out nor any coming in. It is comparable to the flame of the lamp, a stream of constantly arising and perishing events, neither eternal nor evanescent.[65] (149b)

When it is said that the individual in the subtle, seed-form proceeds to take another birth, it does not mean that there is a substantial entity, a soul, that transmigrates from one abode to another, itself remaining unaffected. The person in the state of this transition is not a substance but an organism. The movement is not as that of a ball in an empty space, but a transition like the moving of the flame from one spot to another. It is a continuous process where particular events arise and perish while the activity with a persistent pattern "moves on" by realizing contact with a different set of elements. It is an unbroken process, a continuous becoming; even the elements are also processes, becomings. The arising of the new span of life after death is comparable to one lamp lighting another. This is again comparable to the sprout arising from the seed.[66]

(VI) *The tendencies dormant in the seed of personal life, and the root of the cycle of life:* What conditions the entering of the womb by *vijñāna,* in order to take on a definite embodiment? The *saṃskāras* (行) condition it. *Saṃskāras* are the impressions, the traces of deeds done in the past and it is the deeds that lead the *vijñāna* into the womb for a (definite) embodiment (業將識入胎).[66a]

When the wind blows and the flame goes out, the flame enters *ākāśa;* at that time it rests on wind. (696b)

Similarly in the intermediary state the *saṃskāras* rest on *vijñāna.*

In the previous span of life, when one was a human being, (one's thirst for) sense-contact was aflame and, at the end of that span of life the deeds done there (came to rest on *vijñāna* as subtle tendencies). It is these deeds that lead the *vijñāna* to the womb.[67] (696b)

The basic thirst takes form and becomes canalized in different ways according to deeds. Deeds are prompted by the forms of thirst which in turn become reinforced by the fresh performances of deeds; they revolve in an endless cycle, each depending on and conditioning the other. Deeds leave their traces which give form to thirst and become tendencies; tendencies lead the person to work out and assume ever new embodiments.

The deeds of the present span of life are called *bhava* (有) as they prepare for (and tend to) the fresh embodiment in the next span of life. But now, the deeds that are already past (and are now in the form of tendencies) are called the *saṃskāras* (行), because, of them only the "*nāma*" (the tendency) remains.[68] (696b)

Is there a further principle that conditions even these tendencies, these forms of thirst that set the lines of embodiment? What is the root of the subtle dormant forces that condition the individual to proceed towards embodiment? What is the source of the *saṃskāras?*

The source of *saṃskāras* is ignorance *(avidyā)*. Although all the *kleśas* are alike the source of past deeds (and thus, of *saṃskāras)*, still, *avidyā* is their root and therefore all these get only the name of *avidyā*. Again, of the forces that condition the individual in the present span, thirst and clinging are the prominent ones, and so (in regard to the present span), they get the name. But in regard to the things of the past as one's attitude is one of doubt and perversion, there, only *avidyā* gets the name. Now the root of all suffering is *(avidyā)*.[69] (696b–c)

And

If one can know ignorance and deeds as the conditions of one's existence in the life of bondage even in regard to one span of life, then one can know this (by extension) with regard to even millions of spans of life. (697a)

For everywhere it is the same basic principles that function.

This is like knowing the nature of the fire of the past or of the future by extending one's knowledge of the fire that is here now. (697a)

But if one would attempt to pursue one's enquiry further even beyond ignorance, seeking to know even its condition (更求其本), this search would be simply an endless repetition. And this endlessness of repetition, when clung to, may easily lead one to the extreme of either total devoidness of all beginning and end or of absolute beinning and absolute end (即墮邊見).[70] Then one would miss the way to truth, and be led to mistake the endlessness of regression to mean the utter devoidness of the root-principle, or the complete absence of orderliness. The wise who are non-clinging in mind do not cling to the extremes of chaos and caprice; so they do not miss the orderliness of the course of conditioned becoming, the true nature of mundane existence.

Endless repetition is everywhere the outcome of clinging, confinement; it is truly the inability to get beyond to another higher level, the level of comprehension; it is the outcome of the forging of limitlessness on the limited, the stubbornness to seize the conditioned as itself the unconditioned; it arises from the lack of the knowledge that conditionedness itself is not unconditioned. All clinging leads to extremes, species of exclusiveness.

To seek the further condition of ignorance and to be thus led to extremes is not the same thing as to seek to know the true nature of ignorance. The one is to regress endlessly within ignorance. The other is to rise to a higher level of comprehension. The search for the ultimate nature of *avidyā* is through realizing it as truly *śūnya.*

In order to put an end to ignorance, the bodhisattva seeks to know its true nature (求無明體相). And in the course of his investigation, he enters the comprehension of complete *śūnyatā.* (697a)

When the bodhisattva thus seeks to understand the true nature of *avidyā,* at that very time (即時) (in that very act) he sees it to be in truth the *prajñā* (是明), the universal reality, itself. Then he sees that all things are in truth comparable to magical creations; he sees that it is out of perversion that people give rise to *kleśas,* do evil deeds and revolve in the five states of existence and suffer the pain of birth and death.[71] (697a)

*Levels of understanding the links in the cycle of life:* (I) *The eyes of flesh:* Common people do not get beyond the surface view of things. Even when they see these links in the cycle of the life of the ignorant, they do not understand them as such. They cling to everything and lend themselves to endless suffering. While what they seek is freedom from pain, what they get is still more pain. They see things only with the eyes of flesh.[72]

(II) *The eye of dharma:* The analysts who lay bare these links understand these as leading to suffering; they strive to put an end to its roots, the afflictions *(kleśas)*, and they cultivate elements of goodness conducive to this end.

They analyse all things by means of the eye of *dharma*. They loath at heart and seek to become free from the suffering of old-age, disease and death. They seek to know the origin of old-age and death. (They understand that these) proceed from birth (the embodiment) that comes from deeds *(karma)* and passion *(kleśa)*. . . . (They understand that) the source of *kleśas* is ignorance. It is due to ignorance that people give up what they should take up and take up what they should abandon. (622a–b)

The ignorant seize the *kleśas* and abandon their cultivation of the moral life which should be earnestly pursued. But the analysts who analyse and see things more clearly and seek to abandon the root of suffering and cultivate the factors of the Way do so only in order to seek freedom for their own sake. Again, they do not press their enquiry further to know the ultimate nature of suffering (不究盡求).[73] They are not interested in comprehending the ultimate nature of things.

The seeking of freedom for one's own sake as well as the absence of the zest to pursue one's enquiry up to the ultimate nature of things have their common root in one's tendency to cling to the specific, the determinate, as itself ultimate. This tendency forbids one from realizing the essential relatedness of oneself with all the rest, as well as from recognizing the undivided being as the ultimate reality. The lack of patience and of firmness of purpose, the lack of the zest to know the ultimate truth of things function as obstacles. Clinging to the determinate as itself the ultimate these people end in the extreme of eternalism. They remain blind to the consequences of their own views by their sheer unwillingness to proceed further. They will indeed put an end to the *kleśas* by the cultivation of the moral life; but they will have failed to attain to the complete comprehension of the ultimate truth. They will have also failed to prove true to the spirit of the teaching of their master, the Buddha, viz., the spirit of unlimited wisdom and unbounded compassion.[74]

(III) *The eye of wisdom:* The bodhisattvas, however, are men of great power and of great wisdom. Being sharp in understanding, these pursue their enquiry in order to know nothing short of the ultimate nature (但求究盡), the root-nature, of the twelve links (十二因緣根本相).[75] They pursue their enquiry to the very end. They do not allow themselves to sink out of grief or fear in the mid-way. In their pursuit they do not seize anything determinate as stable or substantial (不得定相). While the analysts take every one of these twelve links as an ultimate element, as a self-being, a substantial entity, the bodhisattvas analyse and see by the power of their sharp wisdom the essential conditionedness of even these. The analysts (分別諸法相者) for instance would take old-age as a substantial entity, an ultimate element, whereas the bodhisattva pursues his enquiry to the very root and finds that there is no substantial entity called old-age.[76] Old age is a state that is essentially conditioned, rising from the togetherness of the specific causal factors.

All the necessary causal factors gather together and hence, depending on this togetherness, there comes into being the state called old-age (諸法和合假名爲老). (622b)

This is like the cart being there when the necessary factors combine. Cart as a name stands for the complex of several factors, every one of which is also an essentially conditioned element. A cart is not any ultimate entity, not a thing in itself. Old-age or even ignorance is also like this; it is also essentially conditioned; it is also a derived name and is not anything unconditioned, not any thing in itself (假名非實).[77]

The wise who understand the conditionedness of even *avidyā* see that in its true nature *avidyā* is of the same nature as *ākāśa*. In truth, every element is of the same nature as *ākāśa*. In its ultimate nature *avidyā* is *prajñā* itself. The wise understand deeply the conditioned origination of the mundane existence and thus become free from the perversions of extremes (離諸邊顛倒).[78]

*Phases in the cycle of life: Thirst, deed and embodiment:* Speaking broadly one may discern three fundamental phases in the cycle of the life of the ignorant, which may be stated as thirst, deed and embodiment. These three together make the cycle and may be said to be the three basic forces conditioning and constituting the life of the ignorant.

The primary force is thirst conditioned by ignorance and issuing in clinging. While the basic meaning of "ignorance" is misconstruction, in the present context it stands also for all the *kleśas* that are dormant in the individual in a subtle form. Of these *kleśas* ignorance is the root and thirst, the foremost. Ignorance, thirst and clinging can be together considered as the basic forces of prompting or impelling, i.e., impelling the individual to do deeds that issue in his further embodiment. Thirst is for fulfilment; the individual seeks fulfilment in a definite, determinate, embodiment or birth in a particular habitation, in order to give shape to the deepest urge in him. The thirst for the limitless is sought to be fulfilled in limited forms, and the determinate is seized as the ultimate.

Impelled by the thirst for fulfillment, the individual does deeds. While the particular deeds become extinct, their traces or impressions remain, and these become the tendencies, the specific canalizations of the basic urge. While the traces of past deeds have set the lines of present embodiment, the traces of the present deeds proceed to bring about modifications in the being of the individual that determine the kind of his future embodiments. In all cases while the thirst for fulfilment through embodiment constitutes the basic impulsion, what determines the kind of embodiment is the canalizing of the basic thirst issuing in the tendencies. "*Saṃskāra*" and "*bhava,*" as seen above, respectively stand for the traces of the past that determine the present and the traces of the present that determine the future. These two constitute the forces that canalize the basic thirst and determine the lines of embodiment. This is the second phase which includes also the actual putting forth of effort to work out specific embodiments in definite lines. The rest of the links in the cycle may be considered as the actual factors of embodiment. As the thirst is for the limitless, and the specific embodiment is something determinate, finite, the thirst is not fulfilled. Hence the seeking for further formation, a new embodiment. So it is the thirst again that constitutes the impulsion for a new embodiment, following the definite lines now newly set by the fresh deeds of the present, which carry forth the old traces also in a new form. And there ensues the fresh embodiment and in its wake there follows the seeking for yet another new embodiment. Thus the ignorant revolve in the cycle of birth and death.

It seems that it is a consideration of this kind that lies behind Nāgārjuna's analysis of the cycle of the life of the ignorant into three fundamental phases.

Thus the *Śāstra* says:

*Kleśa, karma* and *vastu* succeed one another, making the continuous cycle; it is this (cycle) that is called the twelve-linked (cycle of life). Of these *avidyā, tṛṣṇā,* and *upādāna* constitute *kleśa* (affliction), *saṃskāra* and *bhava* constitute *karma* (deed) and the remaining seven constitute *vastu* (體事) (factors of embodiment).[79] (100b)

The third of the three, "*vastu*" is replaced also by the term *duḥkha* (苦) or suffering perhaps to indicate that the state of embodiment in the case of the ignorant is essentially fraught with restlessness which is the source of suffering. These three, says the *Śāstra*, revolve in a cycle functioning as conditions to one another.

*Kleśa* is the condition of *karma* and *karma* is the condition of *duḥkha* (or *vastu*). *Duḥkha* is the condition of further *duḥkha,* (for) *duḥkha* is the condition of *kleśa.* (Again,) *kleśa* is the condition of *karma* and *karma* is the condition of further *duḥkaha.* This *duḥkha* is the condition for (further *duḥkha*). This is what is meant by these phases revolving in (an endless) cycle. (100b)

There is also the other analysis of the cycle of life, viz., in terms of past, present and future. The *Śāstra* refers to this also. Thus it says:

> Of these twelve links, the first two (初二) (*avidyā* and *saṃskāra*) belong to the past, the last two (後二) (the further state of embodiment and the states of old-age and death that ensue it) belong to the future, and the remaining eight in the middle (中八) belong to the present. (100b)

If we bear in mind that time for the Buddhist is not an entity but a way of comprehending the course of events, it becomes clear that what they mean even in this analysis in terms of time is also the succession itself of the different phases of the course of life, one conditioning another and all together constituting the cycle.

*The basic import in the account of the cycle of life:* What is of major interest in this account of the cycle of life is the basic teaching which it is intended to convey, viz., that it is the thirst functioning under ignorance and issuing in clinging that lies at the root of the life of the ignorant. Error and pain of all kinds are ultimately traceable to their root, viz., clinging, which itself owes its being to the thirst for fulfilment misconstrued and miscarried under the influence of ignorance. The error of misplaced absoluteness, the seizing of the determinate as itself ultimate is the root-error, the root form of all errors It is rooted in the false sense of self, the imagination of unconditionedness in regard to a specific embodiment, the ego, the body-mind complex as itself ultimate. Even the imagination of a substantial entity, a soul, is rooted in the misconstruction of the thirst for the unconditioned, its confinement to the level of the conditioned, and resulting in endless regression in understanding and endless repetition of birth and death. The truth that man is not confined to the level of the determinate, but has in him the possibility of rising above it, that he is the meeting point of the real and the unreal, the conditioned and the unconditioned, is the basic import of the sense of the real in him. It is the ground of all his activities as a self-conscious being. To set free the sense of the real from its moorings in abstractions constitutes the chief-most mission of the farer on the Middle Way.

*Vijñāna, the subtle body and the mahat:* We have seen that the *Śāstra* identifies the subtle body of the non-Buddhists like the Sāṅkhya with the *antarābhava-vijñāna,* the intermediary state, of the Buddhists; it identifies also the *mahat* of the Sāṅkhyas with this *antarābhava.* It seems that a distinction has got to be made between the *antarābhava* which is a composite entity constituted of all the *skandhas,* the constituents of individuality, in the subtle form, and the principle of self-conscious intellection *(vijñāna)* which is their maker, their master, the principal element among them.[80] When *"vijñāna"* is mentioned to be the same as the subtle body it is as the *antarābhava,* the composite entity, the whole personality in the subtle form, that is meant. When it is said to be the same as the *mahat* it is to the principle of intellection that the special reference is made. However, this can be only a relative emphasis. For, on the one hand the *mahat* at the stage of evolution is full with potencies. On the other hand when it is identified with *vijñāna* which is self-conscious intellection it has got to be taken with *ahaṅkāra,* the "I." *Vijñāna* and *mahat* are alike the principles of determination from which there proceed all further determinate entities or categories. They are alike the subtle, i.e., non-specific, undistinguished, seed of all distinct and determinate events. In both alike there lie implicit the lines of future development which become explicit and are made specific. They contain the tendencies which develop and take form, become definite. Both are alike not substances but principles of activity and systems of activities.

But while the Sāṅkhyas tend to take *mahat* as a universal principle, *vijñāna* is here definitely an individual principle. While the drawing of these and other parallels and contrasts that spring from this prolific statement of the *Śāstra* that the *mahat* is the same as *vijñāna* would indeed be fruitful towards the working out of an outline of the relation between the Sāṅkhya and the Buddhist philosophies, it is necessary to note that the intention of the *Śāstra* does not lie in the suggestion of these parallels. It lies in pointing to the fact that the Sāṅkhya conception that *prakṛti* is an ultimate reality is but an imagination, a seizing of the determinate as itself the ultimate. The *Śāstra* points out that the contemplatives, in the course of their remembering their previous spans of life in order to search for their root, stop at the complex of the intermediary *skandhas* in which all is indistinct and from which all the distinct phases of life proceed. Now this complex of the intermediary *skandhas,* in being cognizable as of a definite nature, is something determinate and is therefore not ultimate. Seeing this, the contemplatives seek to place it on an ultimate basis, a completely indefinite principle. So they infer the reality of such a completely indefinite principle and call it *prakṛti*. They seize it as an ultimate principle, but it is not really ultimate. The truly indeterminate, the Mādhyamika would say, which is the unconditioned reality, is nothing short of the undivided being; *prakṛti* is not that.

Thus the *Śāstra* says:

Those who are given to contemplation see by virtue of their power of remembering former spans of life, things of eighty thousand *kalpas;* beyond this they are not able to know anything. They just see the *vijñāna* of the intermediary state which appears in the beginning i.e., prior to gross embodiment. And they think that because this *vijñāna* (being something determinate) cannot be without its causes and conditions therefore it must also have its own causes and conditions. (Giving rise to this thought,) what they fail to understand through the power of knowing the previous spans of life, they simply construct out of imagination and thus conceive that there is an entity called *prakṛti* (世性); they conceive it as beyond the knowledge of the five senses, subtle like an atom. In this *prakṛti* (which is *avyakta,* completely indistinct) there arises first of all the *mahat* (覺), (which is the first determinate principle and is the basic principle of all further determination). This *mahat* is simply the *vijñāna* of the intermediary state. (546c)

The intention of this stricture on the Sāṅkhya is to point out that what they hold to be ultimate is really not so; what they cling to as unconditioned is only the complex of conditioned entities, the five *skandhas*. The truly ultimate is nothing short of the undivided reality (*advayadharma*).

*The ignorant and the wise:* It is essential to note that the cycle of life rooted in the thirst conditioned by ignorance and issuing in clinging is not applicable to all cases of the course of mundane life. It is applicable only to the case of the ignorant. The Buddha takes birth and accepts an intermediary state prior to assuming the specific embodiment as a definite person. But He is not impelled by the thirst for becoming, He is altogether free from ignorance and passion. Wisdom and compassion can as much be operating forces as ignorance and passion in conditioning mundane existence. Again, the things that constitute mundane existence are what the individual himself gives rise to in response to the basic impulse in him, viz., the urge to realize the real. The ignorant, having himself given rise to things, himself clings to them. As with the silkworm, his own constructions become a web to him where he gets caught and becomes subject to suffering. But the wise who know and have no illusions about things do indeed create concepts as well as conventional entities and accept willingly the specific embodiments and yet they are not subject to suffering, because they are free from ignorance and passion. To the non-clinging the world is itself Nirvāṇa, while to the clinging even Nirvāṇa would turn out to be *saṃsāra*. It is the mission of the farer on the Middle Way to enable everyone to destroy ignorance and overcome clinging, to enable everyone to transform the basic forces of the course of life from ignorance and passion to wisdom and compassion.

## CHAPTER IX

# REALITY

### Section I

## THE INDETERMINATE GROUND

*The indeterminate ground of the determinate:* Rightly comprehended, the conditioned entity itself lays bare the truth of its ultimate nature.[1] The realization of this ultimate nature of things clearly belongs to a level which is not confined to the conditioned while at the same time not also completely devoid of the conditioned. Strictly, the undivided is the unutterable; but the unutterable is yet uttered on the mundane level in a non-clinging way. The utterance that in their ultimate nature things are devoid of conditionedness and contingency belongs to this level. This very truth is revealed also by saying that all things ultimately enter the indeterminate *dharma* or that within the heart of every conditioned entity, as its core, as its true essence, as its very real nature, there is the indeterminate *dharma*. While the one expresses the transcendence of the ultimate reality, the other speaks of its immanence. The one says that the ultimate reality is beyond the distinctions that hold only among things in the world of the determinate and the other, that the ultimate reality is not an entity apart and wholly removed from the determinate, but is the real nature of the determinate itself. These are different ways of conveying on the mundane level by means of determinate concepts the basic truth of the ultimate reality. This conveying of the unutterable truth through utterance is necessary for those who are engrossed in the world of concepts and conventional entities under the sway of ignorance and have lost sight of the true nature of the very things which they have themselves given rise to. There is the need to enable one to open one's eye of wisdom, to grow "the claws of wisdom" in order to rend asunder the bonds of ignorance and passion, to realize the true way and get back to one's true essence, the unconditioned reality.

### A. *Tathatā*

*The import of the essential relativity of the determinate:* The precise import of the conditioned is its dependent nature, its deriving its nature from an "other," a "beyond" which is not itself dependent. It is possible to ignore this import but it is impossible to deny it. Unconditioned reality asserts itself in the very denial; for the ground of the denial is just the sense of the undeniable. It is to the unconditioned as the ground of the conditioned that the attention of the wayfarer is directed, for he is the seeker of the ultimate truth. While confinement to the conditioned in one's search for the unconditioned inevitably results in an endless regression, criticism is meant to enable one to rise above this confinement by realizing the essential conditionedness of all that is specific. To cling to the determinate as itself ultimate is not only futile but leading to self-contradiction. It is the laying bare of this self-contradiction that should enable one to cease to cling.

Can it not be that the conditioned is essentially different and therefore completely separate from the unconditioned? Between the things that are essentially different and completely separate there is no relation of essential dependence. The unconditioned is not another entity apart from the conditioned. Nor are the conditioned and the unconditioned as such identical. The unconditioned is relevant to the conditioned precisely as its ground. The one is the real and the other is the unreal; the one ever remains as it is, the other arises and passes away; the one is undivided by time or space, devoid of the divisions of internal and external, while the other is essentially distinct, determinate, admitting of the division of internal and external. The determinate has its being precisely as a determinate form of the indeterminate, a division within the undivided. But of the indeterminate, there is no absolute determination, of the undivided there is no absolute division. In other words, the undivided is the reality and the divided is the appearance. The real is the real nature of all that is; it is the nature that no entity ever leaves; the many unique, distinct entities are different among themselves as many, but as the real, in their real nature, they are undivided.

But as the comprehension that the unconditioned is the ground of the conditioned is one in which there is still the distinction of the one from the other, it is not the comprehension of the ultimate truth; it is still the mundane truth. It belongs to a level which is not confined to the determinate nor wholly exclusive of it. Those who cling to the determinate as well as those who cling to the indeterminate commit the error of exclusiveness; they cling to extremes. To seize the determinate as itself the ultimate is to commit the error of eternalism, while to imagine that the indeterminate is wholly exclusive of the determinate is to commit the error of negativism; the latter view amounts to the imagination that a literal abandoning or even an annihilation of the determinate is the necessary condition to realize the indeterminate. These exclusive views conceive the determinate and the indeterminate as separate from each other. As the two are essentially different, so they think, they should be entirely separate. Actually, in the "essential nature of things" there is the difference of mundane and ultimate. The mundane nature is called the essential nature only by convention. Certainly it is not meant as an absolute truth. To imagine that things are ultimate and self-existent in their unique and distinct natures is to commit the error of eternalism. But this is not to deny the unique and distinct as essential in the mundane truth; it is to deny the imagined ultimacy and absoluteness with regard to them.

(In the ultimate truth) all things are *śūnya,* devoid of their own natures; there is no individual, no "I" and ("mine"). And yet (in the world) conditioned by causal factors, there are the four fundamental physical elements as well as the six senses. And each of these ten elements has its own (nature and) capacity; it can come into birth (as the result of the cooperation of its causal factors) and can bring into birth (in its turn other things, itself functioning as a causal factor for their birth). And everyone of these has its own function, for example, earth can hold things and water can moisten things.—In this way everything has its own (nature and) function.[2] (444b)

While *tathatā* as the mundane truth means such natures of things as impermanence, relativity, non-substantiality, devoidness of selfhood, *tathatā* as their ultimate nature means the unconditioned, unborn *dharma*.

One comprehends that in the universal reality there is nothing that is determinable either as permanent (or as impermanent,) . . . and one abandons even these comprehensions. (In the ultimate realization,) all such modes of intellection come to an end. This is the universal reality, the same as Nirvāṇa, the unborn and the unextinct *dharma*, which ever remains in its true nature and is never subject to birth (and death).

Water, for example, is cold by nature and it becomes hot only when fire is added to it. With the extinction of fire, the heat of the water also becomes extinct and water returns to its original nature and remains cold as before. The mind using all the diverse modes of intellection is like the water getting fire. The extinction of all modes of intellection is like the extinction of fire. The original nature of mind, the *tathatā*, is like the coldness of water. . . . This is *tathatā*. It eternally remains in its fundamental nature (如實常住). For such is the very nature of things. (299a)

Speaking with special reference to the human individual, while the determinate being, the organism worked out by the self-conscious person as the expression of his very being, is a system of events which together constitute his "self," if one imagines that, being determinate, one is essentially other than and therefore completely separate from the indeterminate *dharma*, one would commit the error of misplaced absoluteness, for that would amount to thinking that the determinate self is one's real self, one's ultimate nature. This is to miss the true import of the sense of the unconditioned; this is to make reality altogether irrelevant to man. The wise who rise above exclusive clinging understand the conditioned as well as the unconditioned; they understand also the conditioned as itself in its ultimate nature the unconditioned reality, the Nirvāṇa.

*The kinds of tathatā: Two kinds:* Thus we have broadly two kinds of essential nature; the one is relatively essential which is also essentially relative, and the other is the ultimate essence of all that exists. From the standpoint of the ultimately essential, the relatively essential is so only in name; it is only the mundane truth; but it is false to deny the relatively essential even in the mundane truth. Both these kinds of essential nature, the relative and the ultimate, are admitted as the two kinds of *tathatā* by the farer on the Middle Way. The *Śāstra* calls one the mundane and the other, the transmundane.

The *tathatā* (the true nature) of things is of two kinds, the specific nature (各各相) and the real nature (實相). The specific nature is like the hardness of earth, the moistness of water, the motion of wind, etc.—in this way everything has its own nature. The real nature is that which one finds to be their ultimate nature after an examination of (every one of) these specific natures. This ultimate nature is that which cannot be seized, that which cannot be denied and that which is free from all errors (of imagination). . . . (E.g., the hardness of earth cannot be held to be its unconditioned nature.) Examining earth in the light of unconditionedness, it is found that no specific nature of earth could be found to be unconditioned. In truth earth is *śūnya*. *Śūnyatā* is the ultimate nature of earth. Just the same is the case with the specific nature (別相) of all things.[3] (297b–c)

*Levels of comprehension:* That the true nature of things ever remains unaltered by one's subjective fancies is the basic import of "*tathatā*."[4] And this is true as much of the mundane as of the ultimate nature of things. And a right understanding of the mundane itself reveals, leads to the ultimate truth.

First while analyzing the distinct natures of things the wayfarer understands that apart from *rūpa* there is not another element called birth. This is to deny the ultimate separateness and the self-containedness of elements. This is itself the revelation of their essential nature as becoming, change, relativity and contingency. This is to say that they are *śūnya*. *Śūnyatā* as the mundane truth of things means this nature of change and relativity, and in this nature, things are one, indistinct, undivided, while as specific forms of becoming they are distinct, many, and different. It is this realization of the *śūnya*-nature, the non-substantial and dependent nature of things again that directs the mind to their ground, viz., the indeterminate *dharma,* with which as the ground the many things appear as its phenomenal diversifications, and which they themselves are in their ultimate nature. The ultimate truth of things is the undivided being. It is in this way that the denial that *rūpa* etc. are not anything substantial and self-natured leads one to the further realization that they are themselves the unborn *dharma* in their ultimate nature. It is in this way that *rūpa* itself when truly seen, enters the status of non-duality.[5]

*Rūpa* etc. (色等法) are the objects of the experience of common people while the *tathatā* (如) of things is their ultimately real nature (實相), the reality that is not false and deceptive (不虛誑), and this is the object of the experience of the sages. *Rūpa* etc. are composite things and are therefore unreal. They are the objects in which common people fare through imaginative constructions (凡夫所憶想分別行處). It is therefore that they are unreal (虛妄). They are not as such real (不即是如). It is only when the truly real nature of *rūpa* is comprehended that one is said to know their ultimate reality. But then, it is only in relation to *rūpa* etc., that the name *"tathatā"* "the real nature" is derived (因色等法得如名). It is therefore said that the realization of the indeterminate *dharma* is not apart from the determinate entities. When truly comprehended, the determinate entities, *rupa* etc. enter into *tathatā* (入如中); there all things are of one nature devoid of particular natures (皆一相無異).[6]

*The kinds of tathatā: Three kinds: Śūnyatā* as the rejection of absoluteness in regard to the specific and determinate takes one from the analysis and appreciation of the unique nature and function of every distinguishable element to the realization of its essential relativity. And *śūnyatā* of *śūnyatā* as the rejection of absoluteness in regard to the conditionedness of the conditioned takes one from the comprehension of the relativity and non-substantiality of the specific and determinate to the realization of their ultimate truth as the undivided being. In the light of this consideration one can distinguish three kinds of essential nature, the lower progressively leading to the higher by cancelling the notion of the ultimacy of itself. The first consists of the specific, determinate, distinct nature of everything, the second, of the non-ultimacy of these specific natures, the relativity or the conditionedness of all that is determinate, and the third, of the ultimate truth, the undivided being as the ultimate reality of all that is. The *Śāstra* thus distinguishes three kinds of *tathatā*, the lower (下), the middle (中) and the superior (上).

Drawing this distinction, the *Śāstra* says:

Again, in the world, everything has nine kinds (of characters);

1) Everything has its *vastu* (體), "substance," stuff;

2) Everything has its *dharma* (法), characteristics; e.g., although both the eye and the ear are constituted of the four fundamental physical elements, still, only the eye can do the seeing and not the ear; again, e.g., fire can only burn things and not moisten them;

3) Everything has its own power or capacity (力); e.g., fire has the capacity to burn and water has the capacity to moisten things;

4) Everything has its own cause (因);

5) Everything has its own conditions (緣);

6) Everything has its own consequences (果);

7) Everything has its essence, essential nature (性);

8) Everything has its own limitations (限礙); and

9) Everything has its own way to open up and communicate (開通方便).[7] (298c)

Whenever anything is born, says the *Śāstra*, it has all these nine factors.[8] That every thing in the world has all these factors is called the worldly, inferior *tathatā*. That all these factors ultimately return to change and extinction (終歸變異盡滅), this is the middle *tathatā*. For example, the body, at birth, emerges from impurity; although the body is bathed in perfumes and decked with ornaments, still, ultimately, it returns to impurity. This is the middle *tathatā*. That things are neither existent nor non-existent, neither arising nor perishing, that all things are in their ultimate nature purity itself, where all determinate modes of knowing become extinct, this is the superior *tathatā*.[9] *Tathatā* is the real nature of all things, that nature which is there as it ever has been and has never become different (常如本法).[10] This is *tathatā*.

*The deeper nature of things and the deepening of understanding:* It is necessary to note that the distinction between the mundane and ultimate nature is a distinction of the levels of comprehension. It is not to divide things into mundane and transmundane nor to separate the one from the other; nor is it an exclusion of any of these. It is essentially a deepening of understanding. In the realization of the deeper nature, the surface natures are not destroyed but transformed. And when the surface natures are seen once again, they are seen with a new light, with a deeper meaning. The distinction between the levels of understanding is the one between the eyes of flesh and the eye of wisdom; and in neither is there any denial of anything. *Rūpa* is not denied in the mundane truth; it is seen there as essentially a conditioned becoming. In the ultimate truth again, *rūpa* is not denied; it is seen in its real nature as itself the unconditioned reality, the Nirvāṇa. Speaking of the two levels of understanding, the *Śāstra* says:

(The understanding of) *rūpa* is of two kinds: one is the understanding of *rūpa* as seen with the eyes of flesh by the common people, and this is *rūpa* conceived under false constructions: the other is the comprehension of the true nature of *rūpa* by the sages (free from imaginative constructions). The real nature of *rūpa* (as comprehended by the sages) is the same as Nirvāṇa. *Rūpa* as conceived by the common people is (just) called *rupa;* but when this *rūpa* enters the *tathatā,* (as in the case of the comprehension by the sages), it is never more a thing subject to birth and death; (it is Nirvāṇa itself).[11] (382a)

That *rūpa* enters *tathatā,* that all things enter *tathatā,* is an expression of the basic truth that in their ultimate nature all things are realized to be the unconditioned reality itself.

All the different streams ultimately return to the great ocean; all the small kings live by the support of the great emperor; all the stars derive their light from the sun. (334a)

Even so do all things have their being dependent on the *dharma-dhātu,* live their lives on its support and ultimately return to it.

If the bodhisattva would not conceive that this is *dharma* and this is not *dharma,* (if he would comprehend that) all things blend into one essence, even as all the myriad streams blend and become of one essence in the great ocean, then, indeed, has his cultivation of *prajñāpāramitā* found fulfilment. . . . The indeterminate nature is the true nature of all things. Determinations and divisions are the constructions of imagination. (528a)

*Tathatā* or the "true nature" of things at the different levels, mundane and transmundane, is also called *dharmatā* at two different levels (法性有二種). Thus while the unique nature and capacity of every specific thing which one comes to know through analysis of things with a non-clinging mind can be called the mundane *dharmatā,* the limitless *dharma* (無量法), the ultimate reality may be called the transmundane or the ultimate *dharmatā.*[12] This distinction between the mundane and the transmundane natures of things is also described in terms of *dharma-lakṣaṇa.*[13] Thus the mundane *dharma-lakṣaṇa* (世間法相) means the unique, distinct, natures and capacities of things, their causes and conditions which produce them, and the consequences which follow from them in turn. But when these distinct characters of things are analyzed and examined to the very end, then they are seen to enter the unborn *(anutpāda) dharma* (入無生法中), which is their ultimate nature; there is nothing that exceeds it.[14] The unborn *dharma* is another name for the unconditioned reality, Nirvāṇa (無生名爲涅槃).[15] The mundane *dharma-lakṣaṇa* is also called composite, conditioned, *dharma-lakṣaṇa* (有爲諸法

相) and the transmundane *dharma-lakṣaṇa* is also called the incomposite, the unconditioned, *dharma-lakṣaṇa* (無爲諸法相). The latter is the ultimate self-nature of all things (諸法自性).[16]

*Progressive realization of the real:* It is to be remembered that for the seeker of reality the analysis and appreciation of the distinct natures of the determinate entities is not an end in itself. It is the necessary first step towards a complete comprehension of the ultimate reality not only as the real root, the universal ground of all that is, but as the real nature of every specific entity. The wayfarer would first cultivate the comprehension of the mundane nature of things, viz., that they are (possible) sources of suffering, impermanent, devoid of substantiality. He would then cultivate the comprehension of the ultimate nature of things that they are essentially of the nature of peace, freedom, the unborn *dharma,* devoid of all determinate natures. He would cultivate again, the comprehension of how the cycle of life of the ignorant revolves, with all its links, how there comes into being the huge bundle of suffering. He would cultivate also the comprehension of how the cycle of the life of the ignorant should be terminated by putting an end to all its links one by one, and thus how the entire bundle of suffering comes to an end. All these he would cultivate in the completely non-clinging way (無所得故).[17]

In the case of ordinary people the realization of the truth of things is progressive, gradual. In this progressive realization, the wayfarer would first know, for example, such characters (相) of things, that they are completely devoid of substantiality; then he would know that they are subject to birth and death (生滅), arising when the necessary causal factors are there and passing away when they get scattered. He would know that things when born do not come from anywhere and when extinct do not go anywhere, that they are not any changeless and self-identical substances, but essentially changing and relative. Finally he would know the ultimately true nature (如) of things, that they are neither born nor destroyed, neither coming nor going.[18] Again, in understanding *rūpa,* for instance, one would begin with the sensing of *rūpa* (色) as just the bare object of sight, in which the distinct characters of the thing have not yet been discerned. This is the bare awareness of *rūpa*. Then one would understand such natures or characteristics of *rūpa,* as (that it is hard, formed and colored, etc.,) that it is impermanent, subject to arising and passing away, that it is impure etc. This is the knowledge of the characteristics *(dharma)* of *rūpa* (色法). Then one would know the essential conditionedness and relativity of *rūpa,* its complete devoidness of substantiality; one would know that it is only under ignorance that one takes it as real and substantial. This is the knowledge of the (mundane) nature *(tathatā)* of *rupa* (色如). Finally, one would comprehend the (ultimately) true nature of *rūpa (rūpa-lakṣaṇa* 色相), viz., that it is complete purity, complete *śūnyatā.*[19]

*B. Dharmadhātu and Bhūtakoṭi*

*The real as the immanent as well as the transcendent: Dharmadhātu* is a reference to the ultimate reality, Nirvāṇa, the ultimate nature of all that is conditioned and contingent. In *dharmadhātu "dharma"* stands for Nirvāṇa (法性者法名涅槃).[20] It stands also for *prajñāpāramitā,* which is the ultimate reality, the same as Nirvāṇa.[20a] *"Dhātu"* conveys the sense of the essential, intrinsic, inmost nature, the fundamental, ultimate essence (本分種).[21] The basic, fundamental source (本生處) of all things is what is called *"dhātu"* (性).[22] It is the primary aim of the wayfarer to realize the *dharmadhātu,* the unconditioned reality. Speaking of Nirvāṇa as the ultimately true nature, the inmost essence of all things, the *Śāstra* says:

In the yellow stone, for example, there is the essence (性) of gold and in the white stone there is the essence of silver. In this way, within the heart of everything in the world there is the essence of Nirvāṇa (一切世間法中皆有涅槃性) (which is the inmost essence of all things). The Buddhas and the sages having themselves realized it through the power of wisdom and skill and by the cultivation of moral life and contemplation, teach others also the Way enabling all to realize this *Nirvāṇa-dharma-dhātu.* Those who are sharp in their power of grasping comprehend immediately (即知) that all things are only the *dharma-dhātu* itself, even as those with supernormal powers can (immediately) transform brick and stone into gold. But those who are not sharp in their power of grasping adopt suitable means and seek to realize the *dharma-dhātu* (through long cultivation) and only then will they be able to realize it (方便求之乃得法性). This is like smelting the ore in the great cauldron and then obtaining gold from it.[23] (298b)

For example, within the wall, there is already the empty space (先有空相). Now, if a child were to try to fix a wooden peg there, he would not be able to do it, for he has not the necessary strength. But a grown up man can drive it in, for his strength is great (大力者能入). The same is the case with one's faring (in *prajñāpāramitā)*. Within the heart of everything there is the ultimate reality, (the ever-present) self-being (諸法中自有如實相). But when one's capacity to comprehend is little, one cannot make all things enter *śūnyatā,* (and therefore one cannot realize the ultimately real nature of all things). But those whose power of comprehension is great can comprehend the ultimate truth. (563c–564a)

Again, we have the *Śāstra* saying:

(This *tathatā,* the universal reality, is in all). It is in the Buddha, it is also in the bodhisattva, for it is one (undivided). It is therefore that the bodhisattva is considered to be the same as the Buddha (爲如佛). Apart from and devoid of *tathatā,* there is nothing; there is nothing that does not ultimately enter the *tathatā* . . . (There is no doubt that) even in the beasts there is the *tathatā.* But they have not yet fulfilled the necessary conditions (to realize the ultimate reality in them). They have not yet brought to light the *tathatā* in them. Therefore they are not able to course in *tathatā* and (benefit either themselves or) other beings. They are not able to course in *tathatā* and reach *sarvākārajñatā.* (Therefore they are not said to be the same as the Buddhas.) Therefore the bodhisattva should cultivate this *tathatā-prajñapāramitā* (如般若波羅密). Cultivating the *tathatā-prajñāpāramitā,* the bodhisattva can fulfil the realization of the *tathatā,* (the ultimate essence of all things). (653c)

*The real as the supreme end:* It is to the skilful penetration of the mind into the *dharma-dhātu,* the unconditioned reality, that *"bhūtakoṭi"* refers.

(Skilfully) to enter the dharmadhātu, this is what *bhūtakoṭi* means. (It consists in) the comprehension that it is the universal reality, the immeasurable (無量), the limitless (無邊), the most profound, the most mysterious *dharma* (最爲微妙), that is called the *dharma-dhātu,* excelling which, exceeding which, there is not anything else. (298c–299a)

In the term *"bhūtakoṭi," "bhūta"* (實) stands for the unconditioned reality, the *dharma-dhātu* (法性), and *"koti"* (際) means with mysterious skill to reach the end, the limit, the apex (妙極於此);[24] it also means realization (證故爲際)[25] the point of penetration (入處).[26] *Bhūtakoṭi* is also called the *anutpādakoṭi* (無生際), the (supreme) end, the summit, devoid of birth (and death).[27]

When the diverse characters of things are analysed and investigated to their very end, to their very bottom (推求尋究), (all things are seen) to enter the *anutpāda-dharma,* the dharma devoid of birth, (the *dharma-dhātu);* it is seen that there is not anything that excels this ultimate reality. It is this (entering of all things into the unconditioned reality) that is called the *anutpādakoṭi* (303a)

In *anutpādakoṭi, anutpāda* refers to Nirvāṇa, the unconditioned reality (and *koṭi* means the entering of things, the penetration of the mind, into it). Nirvāṇa is the unborn, unextinct *dharma;* it is the ultimate reality, the supreme end (末後究竟). It is not itself anything born. In truth all things are in their ultimate nature, the Nirvāṇa itself, . . . all things themselves are the *anutpādakoṭi.* (303a)

It is (the real nature itself of) all things that is called the *dharma-dhātu.* . . . For, (ultimately) all things enter the indeterminate, incomposite, reality. It is therefore that the comprehension (學) of the *dharma-dhātu* amounts to the comprehension of all things. (689b)

In the *dharma-dhātu,* the beings get transformed into the *dharma-dhātu* itself. (335c)

(All beings are ultimately identical with the unborn *dharma).* For the thing that is unborn and undestroyed (in its ultimate nature) is the same as the *dharma-dhātu.* The *dharma-dhātu* is itself the *prajñāpāramitā,* (which is the same as the bodhisattva and the Buddha). (335c)

*The thirst for the real in man:* While the *dharma-dhātu* is the ultimate nature of all beings, in man there is immanent the sense of the unconditioned as his true essence. While the limitless *dharma* is immanent in the heart of every determinate entity, it is only the self-conscious individual that is aware of his real nature. But under ignorance the sense of the unconditioned is misconstrued, and hence the sense of lack, the thirst, the restlessness in the heart of man. This is man's thirst for the real. Losing (one's comprehension of) the true nature of things, one sees all things only pervertedly, crookedly. And the meaning of this restlessness lies in realizing one's ultimate nature, getting back to one's real self, one's true essence.[28] With the realization of this ultimate reality the thirst is completely quenched, the heart becomes full and contented, and there is no longer any hankering for anything. Thus, the *Śāstra* says:

Even as it is the very nature of water to flow down (如水性下流) by reason of which all waters return (會歸) to the great ocean, blend and become of one essence, just in the same way all determinate entities, all natures general and particular, return ultimately to *dharma-dhātu,* blend and become of one essence with it. This is *dharma-dhātu.* Even as the diamond which is at the top of the mountain (金剛在山頂) gradually settles down until it reaches its destination, the field of diamonds, and having got there it will have got back to its self-nature (到自性) and only then does it come to a stop, just the same is the case with all things. Through knowledge, through discrimination, (the mind seeks the true nature of things and thus) gets to *tathatā*. From *tathatā,* the mind enters its original nature (入自性), where it remains as it ever was, devoid of birth (and death) and with all imaginative constructions put an end to. This is the meaning of *dharma-dhātu.*

Again, even as the calf (如犢子), alarmed (by the sight of the diverse things) all around, bleats (and runs about in restlessness) and comes to rest only when it has gotten back to its mother, just the same is the case with all beings. Beings are varied and different; their acceptances and rejections vary. But when they reach their inmost nature, then their movement stops. Nothing else is there to reach exceeding this. This is the meaning of *dharma-dhātu.* (298b–c)

(With the realization of this ultimate reality) the heart becomes full and contented (心則滿足); never more has it any desire to seek (a fulfilment) (更不餘求). It is then that the mind has realized (its true nature). For example, the person walking on the road, walks forth every day never stopping. But when he reaches his destination, then indeed he has no more of the mind to walk (無復去心). Just the same is the case with the wayfarer when he gets ultimately established in *bhūta-koṭi*.[28a] (299a)

*Factors conducive to comprehension:* In right understanding, the many things themselves are not denied, nor do they stand apart constituting an impediment to comprehending the ultimate truth; they open up their true nature, reveal their ultimate truth. They "flow into" the ultimate reality, where all things blend and become of one essence. It is in the realization of this ultimate truth that the meaning of the restlessness in the heart of beings consists. The *dharmadhātu*, the ultimate nature of everything, is itself the *prajñāpāramitā*. It is the complete, the perfect, which is immanent in all things. By following up everything in its unique nature and by progressively assimilating it into the limitless, one comprehends that all things enter the *dharma-dhātu*, the fullness, the completeness of being. Everything is led up to its perfection in its own way by a progressive assimilation of that which lies beyond it; it is in truth a gradual realization of the true nature. The *Sūtra* as well as the *Śāstra* bring out this truth of the perfection immanent in everything by declaring that the perfection *(pāramitā)* of everything is *prajñāpāramitā*.[29] That which is the highest in all is the *prajñāpāramitā;* the true essence of every determinate entity and every conceivable character is *prajñāpāramitā*. Thus the perfection *(pāramitā)* of the endless (無邊波羅密) is *prajñāpāramitā*, for it is comparable to *ākāśa*. It is immeasurable like the waters of the great ocean, says the *Śāstra*.[30] Endlessness means limitlessness which is devoidness of an "other." Devoidness of division exemplified in *ākāśa*, when rightly comprehended, would convey the ultimacy of the non-dual *dharma*. "Ends" mean again the extremes of perversion (邪見邊).[30a] Devoidness of ends means to rise above extremes and to fare on the Middle Way, the way of *prajñā*. Whether in the mundane truth or in the ultimate truth, endlessness in its true form is the *prajñā-*

*pāramitā* itself. Similarly sameness, undeniability and devoidness of determinate characters, when rightly comprehended, convey the ultimate truth of the unconditioned *prajñā* as their very perfection, completeness, in which they find their fulfilment. They bear out again the mundane truth, the Middle Way.

Again, with the denial of the self-enclosedness of things and the realization of their essential relativity, the wayfarer perceives that everything tends (趣 *gati)* to everything else.[31] Self-transcendence is seen to be the inherent nature of all things by virtue of which one thing when pursued leads up to another, in fact to all the rest, to the entire universe. This is the essential relatedness of all determinate entities among themselves. But as we have seen, this is not the only import of essential relativity. What is of greater importance to the wayfarer is the further import of the unconditioned as the ground of the conditioned. The essentially relative implies the essentially absolute as its own ground; the essentially determinate is intrinsically derived from and dependent on the indeterminate *dharma*. This is the deeper truth, the profound truth, of *prajñāpāramitā*. The wayfarer that comprehends this profound truth should tend to *sarvākārajñatā,* the knowledge of all forms (當趣一切種智)[32] which is the same as *bodhi,* the ultimate *prajñā,* the unconditioned *dharma*. The bodhisattva realizes that all things enter *prajñā*. Wisdom seeks the true, the real.[33] So the farer on the Way directs all his activities, his entire being, to this one supreme end, viz., the realization of *prajñā*. This realization is not for his own sake, but for the sake of all beings. By his wayfaring he makes the entire world tend to *prajñā*. He functions as the destination and the resting point, the refuge, for the entire world (爲世間趣).[34] This tending to *prajñā* is not a thing that the bodhisattva superimposes on things from outside. By their very nature things are *śūnya,* essentially relative, and hence pointing to the unconditioned as their ground.

It is by keeping oneself in harmony with (the comprehension of) the complete *śūnyatā* (隨順畢竟空) that one keeps oneself in line (順) with the knowledge of all forms. (562a)

As the *Śāstra* observes, the elements, *rūpa* etc. are themselves the knowledge of all forms and the latter is itself all the elements; the *tathatā* of the one is also the *tathatā* of the other.[35]

*Section II*

## THE UNDIVIDED BEING

*The distinction of the determinate and the indeterminate:* Even as the essential conditionedness of things, when rightly comprehended, leads one to the unconditioned as their ground, just in the same way the comprehension that the conditioned entity is itself in its ultimate nature the unconditioned reality leads one to the further comprehension of the ultimate truth that the conditioned and the unconditioned, are not two, not separate. The distinction holds only in the mundane truth where it is a relative distinction and not an absolute division. The highest truth is the undividedness of the conditioned and the unconditioned; there is not even the distinction of the divided and the undivided.

The (ultimate) meaning of *prajñā* should not be conceived as either divided or as undivided; (it is the *dharma)* that is neither existent nor non-existent, neither entering nor emerging, . . . neither *tathatā,* nor not *tathatā,* neither *bhūtakoṭi* nor not *bhūtakoṭi*. (482b)

To conceive that the distinction of the conditioned and the unconditioned is an absolute division is to separate the determinate entities and the indeterminate *dharma;* this is to deny not only the relevance of the unconditioned to the conditioned but also to deny the very possibility of determinate existence. The *Sūtra* says:

If the *koṭi* (extremity) of reality and the *koṭi* (extremity) of the individuals were (ultimately) different (實際衆生際異者) then the bodhisattva could not fare in the *prajñāpāramitā*. Truly the *koṭi* of reality and the *koṭi* of beings are not (ultimately) different; therefore the bodhisattva is able to fare in *prajñāpāramitā* (and realize the *bhūtakoṭi* in order to help all people). (692c)

As an individual, one is different from another; this is the mundane truth where distinctions are essential. But in the ultimate truth, with respect to their ultimate nature, the individuals are not different; for the ultimate nature of one is itself the ultimate nature of all.

(The ultimate nature of Subhūti is the same as the ultimate nature of the Buddha). The ultimately true nature of the Tathāgata is neither going nor coming (如來如相不來不去). The ultimately true nature of Subhūti is also neither going nor coming. Therefore it is that Subhūti is born in the same way as the Buddha (隨佛生). . . . The ultimately true nature of the Tathāgata is the same as the ultimately true nature of all things; the ultimately true nature of all things is itself the ultimately true nature of the Tathāgata (一切法如相即是如來如相). It cannot even be (conceived) that within this ultimate reality there is any other ultimate reality.[36] (563a)

Again, the ultimately true nature of the Tathāgata eternally stays (常住相). The ultimately true nature of even Subhūti eternally stays. The ultimately true nature of the Tathāgata has no change, no division (無異無別) . . . The ultimately true nature of the Tathāgata and the ultimately true nature of all things are in truth but one reality, not two, not divided (一如無二無別). This ultimate reality is unmade (無作); it will never be other than what it always is (終不不如). It is therefore that this ultimate reality is not two, not divided. (The same is the case even with the ultimately true nature of Subhūti and, in fact, of every being). It is altogether devoid of imaginative constructions (無念) and devoid of divisions (無別). (563a)

While one is in the mundane truth where the conditioned and the unconditioned are held relatively distinct, it can be said that the unconditioned reality is within the heart of the conditioned entities. But to take it as an absolute statement is to conceive a total separation between the conditioned and the unconditioned; this is to miss the point that that was a way of expressing the truth that the conditioned is itself in its ultimate nature the unconditioned reality, and to misconceive the nature of the conditioned and of the unconditioned. In the ultimate truth it does not hold that the unconditioned is within the distinct, determinate, entities.

The ultimately real nature (the *tathatālakṣaṇa* 如相), of the Tathāgata is not past or present or future. . . . The ultimately real nature of the Tathāgata is not in the real nature of the past, etc.; the ultimately real nature of the past etc. is not in the ultimately real nature of theTathāgata. The ultimately real nature of the past etc. and the ultimately real nature of the Tathāgata, all this is one reality, not two, not divided (一如無二無別). The ultimately real nature of the "I" (我如) . . . the ultimately real nature of the knowledge of all forms *(sarvākārajñatā)*, the ultimately real nature of the Tathāgata, all this is one reality, not two, not divided. When the bodhisattva realizes this reality *(tathatā)* he is called the Tathāgata (得是如故名如來) (563b)

While the determinate entities are themselves in their ultimate nature the indeterminate *dharma,* it cannot be maintained that the ultimate nature of the determinate is itself anything determinate, that the nature of things in which they are undivided is itself anything divided, and that the determinate entities are subject to birth and death in their ultimate nature. Thus the *Sūtra* says:

The non-dual nature of *rūpa* is not *rūpa* (色不二是非色). . . . All the *rūpa* that there is and the entire non-dual *dharma,* . . . all this is in truth, the one, undivided, ultimate reality, which neither gathers nor scatters, is devoid of color, devoid of shape, devoid of resistance; it is all of one nature, viz., being of no particular nature (一相所謂無相). . . . It is therefore that the non-dual nature of *rūpa* is not *rūpa*. . . . *Rūpa* enters non-duality (入無二法數) . . . (All things enter non-duality. The non-dual, undivided being is the unborn *dharma.) Rūpa* is not different from the unborn *dharma* (色不異無生), the unborn *dharma* is not different from *rūpa*. . . . It is therefore that *rūpa* enters non-duality. (436c)

On this, the *Śāstra* comments:

(Truly) *rūpa* is, by its very nature, ever unborn (色性常自無生). It is not that it is now deprived of the nature of birth through the power of *prajñā*. If one would destroy *rūpa* making it *śūnya* and yet would retain the original thought of (clinging to) *rūpa* (猶存本色想), (that would not be the true comprehension of *śūnyatā*). . . . But if one would comprehend that *rūpa,* by its very nature, has been ever unborn (從本已來常自無生), (that would be the true comprehension of *rūpa* and) then one would not retain any more the thought that clings to *rūpa* (as permanent or impermanent). Therefore it is said that the unborn *dharma* (which is the real nature) of *rūpa* is not *rūpa* (色無生爲非色). . . . The wayfarer, having comprehended the unborn, undying, nature of *rūpa,* might conceive, "Now, *rūpa* has become unborn." (In truth, *rūpa* has always been the unborn *dharma.*) It is therefore said that the unborn nature is itself the non-dual nature.[36a] (437a)

*The ultimate reality as (A) svabhāva-śūnyatā:* The fundamental teaching of the indeterminate, transcendent, non-conceptual nature of the ultimate reality which is yet the ground of determinate existence and of specific conceptual constructions, is conveyed in the *Sūtra* as well as in the *Śāstra* by means of such expressions as *svabhāva-śūnyatā,* complete *śūnyatā, samatā* and purity, and by means of such examples as island and *ākāśa*. Complete *śūnyatā* means complete indeterminateness; that this is the essential nature *(svabhāva)* of the ultimate truth of things is conveyed by *svabhāva-śūnyatā*.

Thus the *Śāstra* says:

The universal reality is just the *svabhāva-śūnyatā* (性空). (697c)

This *svabhāva-śūnya-dharma,* the ultimate reality *(dharma)* that is essentially *(svabhāva)* indeterminate *(śūnya)* should not be conceived either as dual or as non-dual.[37]

The *svabhāva-śūnya-dharma* has truly no abode (無實住處); it does not come from anywhere, nor does it go anywhere. This is the eternal *dharma-lakṣaṇa* (常住法相). The eternal *dharma-lakṣaṇa* is another name for the *svabhāva-śūnyatā*. It is also called the universal reality (諸法實相). In it there is neither birth nor extinction. (697c)

The *svabhāva-śūnya-dharma* should not be clung to even as *śūnya*. To seize the *śunya* nature of the *svabhāva-śūnya-dharma* is to turn *śūnyatā* itself into something determinate, while the reality that is the *svabhāva-śūnya-dharma* is free from all determinations.[37a]

(B) *Samatā:* The ultimate nature of things, the *svabhāva-śūnyatā,* is also called *samatā* to mean the essential sameness of things in their true nature.

The *śūnyatā* of the internal . . . the *śūnyatā* of the external . . . the *śūnyatā* of self-nature, this is the *samatā* of things (等法) which the bodhisattva should cultivate. *Rūpa* is devoid *(śūnya)* of the character of *rūpa* . . . the unexcelled *samyak-sambodhi* (the complete *bodhi* par excellence) is devoid *(śūnya)* of the character of *samyak-sambodhi*. This is the *samatā* of things. The bodhisattva dwelling in this *samatā* of things (住是等法) realizes the *samyak-sambodhi*. (604c)

This essential sameness of all things is comprehensible both in regard to their mundane and to their ultimate nature. In respect to their mundane nature it means their essentially conditioned relative, dependent nature. In regard to their ultimate nature, it means the ultimate reality of the undivided being which is the very real nature of all that is.

The bodhisattva who comprehends the essential sameness of all beings as well as of their constituent elements holds his mind "in balance" (如称) and fares with equanimity (平等) of mind.[38] The *Sūtra* says:

The *samatā* of all things (諸法平等) is not made by anyone . . . not even by the Buddha. Whether there are the Buddhas or there are not the Buddhas, the true nature of all things remains eternally *śūnya*. This *svabhāva-śūnyatā* is itself Nirvāṇa. (728c–729a)

(C) *Purity:* This ultimate *samatā* or the ultimate *śūnyatā* is also called purity, to indicate its complete devoidness of all determinate nature. Purity is another name for the undivided being, the ultimate reality.

It is the ultimate *samatā* of things that I call purity. What is this *samatā?* It is what is called the *tathatā,* the unchanging, the not-false, the *dharma-lakṣaṇa,* the *dharma-dhātu, dharma-sthiti, dharma-sthāna, bhūta-koṭi.* Whether there are the Buddhas or there are not the Buddhas, the *dharmatā* eternally stays. It is this eternal *dharmatā* that is called purity. But even this (name, purity) is mentioned only in the mundane truth *(vyavahāra);* this is not a teaching of the ultimate truth. The ultimate truth transcends all definitions and descriptions, transcends all comments and disputations, transcends all words. (724a)

(D) *Nirvāṇa, the Island:* To indicate that the ultimate, profound nature of all things ever remains unaffected by the imaginative constructions of the ignorant, it is called the island, the central land which the streams of ignorance and passion do not reach. Nirvāṇa, the ultimate nature of things, is thus comparable to an island. Thus the *Sūtra* says:

Whether in a river or in a great ocean, (if in a spot) the water is prevented from flowing in from any of the four sides, the spot comes to be called an island. . . . Such is also the nature of *rūpa* (and all other things when) the prior and the posterior ends are terminated. . . . With the prior and the posterior ends stopped, all things themselves would be (the profound *dharma)* the peace, the most precious jewel, viz., the *śūnya, anupalambha* (無所得), the residueless extinction of thirst, the complete freedom from passion (離欲), the Nirvāṇa. The bodhisattva teaches the world this *dharma,* the most profound *dharma,* the complete peace. (558c)

And the *Śāstra* comments:

Water here refers to the three streams of defiling elements (*āsrava*) (viz., ignorance and passion in regard to things of the world of desire and of the higher worlds) . . . all the *kleśas* and all the deeds and their results. The central principle, the land in the middle, is the *dharma* of complete *śūnyatā,* the utterly unseizable, viz., the Nirvāṇa. This is the island. People get sunk in the waters of the four streams and all the *kleśas,* but the Buddha, with His boat of the Eight-fold Way picks them up and puts (引著) them on the island of Nirvāṇa. (559b)

(E) *The unutterable truth and the wheel of dharma:* In the highest truth, really, there is nothing spoken. For, the ultimate *dharma* being completely *śūnya* and therefore devoid of determinate characters is unutterable.

The *sambohdi* par excellence (this highest truth of non-duality) is most profound, difficult to see, difficult to understand, most incomprehensible. Only he who has realized the subtle profound peace, the *prajñā* (微妙寂滅智), can comprehend this most profound truth. It is difficult for anyone else to (comprehend it and) have faith in it. (In the ultimate truth) the *sambodhi* par excellence is devoid of any obtainer, devoid of any place or time of obtaining. This is the most profound truth, viz., devoidness of duality. (562b–c)

The *Sūtra* observes that it is for this reason that the Buddha, when He realized the truth, at the outset, delighted at heart in keeping silent; He did not like to speak about this *dharma*. For, this *dharma* of the Buddhas, viz., the unexcelled *samyak-sambodhi,* is most profound, difficult to comprehend.[39]

Commenting on the reason for the Buddha's silence the *Śāstra* states that in addition to the incomprehensibility of this profound truth by ordinary minds, there is yet another reason (更說因緣):

*Tathatā* is the truly real nature (眞實相) of all things. For example, whether it is in a palace or in a humble hut, whether it is the sandalwood or just the ordinary wood that is being burnt, in regard to the space *(ākāśa)* in both these places there is no difference. Of all things, when one seeks to know the (ultimately) true nature, (one finds that) all that is just the *tathatā* (the undivided, non-dual *dharma*). (And where all is one and devoid of distinction how can there be any speech?) For this reason, the Buddha delighted at heart in keeping silent, when He first realized the *bodhi* (初成道) He did not like to teach the *dharma.*[40] He knew that it is difficult for ordinary minds to comprehend the profound *dharma.* (563c)

The setting of the wheel of *dharma* in motion is not denied as a mundane truth, but it is not an ultimate truth. The wheel of *dharma* is *prajñā-pāramitā* itself.[41] And in the ultimate truth, the *dharma* is devoid of movement; in their ultimate nature all things are devoid of movement.

*Parjñāpāramitā* does not emerge either for moving forth or for moving back. (516c)

It is necessary to note that the utter unspeakability of things in this ultimate truth does not mean that they cannot even be spoken of in the mundane truth. The undivided being, the indeterminate *dharma,* is non-exclusive; it is this that is the highest reality. It is not exclusive of determinations although it is false to hold them as absolute. In the mundane truth the indeterminate *dharma* is expressed through the determinate modes of thought and speech in a non-clinging way. The question is not one of speaking or not speaking but of clinging or not clinging to the speech and to the things spoken of.

(F) *Comparable to ākāśa:* The ultimate reality is compared to *ākāśā,* the principle of accommodation, which is not anything in particular and is yet the universal possibility of movement depending on which everything lives and moves.

*Ākāśa,* being completely pure, is not anything specific *(akiñcana);* still, depending on *ākāśa* all things get accomplished and fulfilled. All the same, it cannot be said that *ākāśa* itself does anything, nor can it be said that *ākāśa* is devoid of use. (Precisely the same is the case with *prajñā-pāramitā.)*[41a] (507c)

*Ākāśa* is not any determinate entity; it has no specific character that could be spoken about; it is unspeakable and unseizable.[42] Not being anything determinate, *ākāśa* is completely non-obstructing. It is only the determinate that obstructs. The non-dual *dharma* is like *ākāśa* in being completely unobstructive. On it depend all things for their origin, growth and fulfilment. It is in complete harmony with all things. As the *Sūtra* says:

> This *dharma* is in harmony (隨順) with all things; it is in harmony with *prajñpāramitā*, . . . it is in harmony with the knowledge of all forms. This *dharma* is non-obstructing (無礙). It is not an obstruction to *rūpa* . . . It is not an obstruction to the knowledge of all forms. This *dharma* is unobstructing by nature; in this regard, it is of the same nature as *ākāśa*. (563a)

*Śūnyatā* as the principle of comprehension is the true principle of harmony. The harmony worked on the basis of *śūnyatā* is the highest kind (第一相應).

> Of all the ways of (establishing) harmony *(yoga)* this is the best (最第一相應), viz., (establishing) harmony through *śūnyatā*. This harmony excels all other kinds of harmony.[43] (335a)

*Ākāśa* ever remains untouched by dust and darkness. Dust and darkness appear and disappear; they are contingent; but *ākāśa* ever remains as it is. It is not anything that itself arises and perishes, nor does it ever become dirty; not becoming dirty it cannot even be said to have become pure, for it never was impure; in truth it lies beyond the determinate natures of pure and impure. It ever remains untouched by dust and water. Just so does *prajñāpāramitā* remain incapable of being stained by the network of imaginative constructions even though they may be there. Being devoid of any specific form, it cannot be seized. Being unseizable it cannot be tarnished.[44] When one comprehends this nature of the universal reality, one can fare in all the various ways and help all to put an end to error and evil, conflict and suffering.

## *CHAPTER X*

# THE WAY

### *Section I*

## THE WAY OF COMPREHENSION

*The principle of comprehension:* The bodhisattva's realization of the ultimate truth would remain incomplete if he did not take along with him the rest of the beings across the ocean of birth and death, of conflict and suffering. It is the mission of the farer on the Middle Way to return to the world of determinate existence by virtue of his power of skilfulness and his heart of compassion. Again by virtue of this very power of skilfulness, he helps all to overcome ignorance and realize the true nature of their being as well as of all things.[1] It is his aspiration to achieve Buddhahood, the perfection in personality,[2] in order effectively to help all.

Comprehension of determinate existence in the light of the ultimate reality is the essential nature of wayfaring. The dividedness within oneself works for the perpetuation of divisions outside, and that, in spite of one's seeking to realize the undivided being. The rejection of the falsely imagined separateness of the determinate is not an end in itself; its meaning lies in the ever widening integration of all beings, beginning from within oneself and extending ever onwards, based on and inspired by the sense of the real, the sense of the ultimacy of the undivided being. The transformation that the wayfarer seeks to bring about in his own being lies precisely in the integration of his personality by putting an end to ignorance and passion which are the roots of the divided life. Even the division of "within and without" is itself a basic division that he seeks to overcome.

But it is to be remembered that this integration is not something to be forged from outside; nor does it amount to an obliteration of uniqueness and individuality in mundane existence. To think that it is external to things is to imagine that things are not only basically separate but that they are also ultimate in their separateness. And to think that it amounts to an obliteration of uniqueness and individuality is again to imagine that they do not hold even in the mundane truth. The unity that is forged from outside is artificial; it makes only for greater suffering; and the unity that obliterates uniqueness and individuality in the world cancels the very things to be integrated, it ignores personality altogether. Even this makes only for greater suffering.

*The ultimate and the relative:* In the world there is not anything that is not essentially a conditioned becoming; while everything has its own nature and capacity, the "own nature" of anything is not unconditioned. Further, the world of everyone is what one works out for oneself as one's own self-expression, and this, not without the influence of the rest. While every one is essentially related to all the rest and owes his being to them, still everyone has his own unique being, lives his own life; this is the mundane truth. Further, the ultimate meaning of the events that constitute the course of the life of man lies in his urge to realize the real, which is itself the unconditioned ground of the conditioned and the contingent. To work for integration at the mundane level on the basis of and with the full awareness of the ultimate truth is a fundamental aspiration of the bodhisattva. It is his aspiration to enable everyone to realize one's true nature, to put an end completely to forces of ignorance and passion, and to transform these forces wholly into wisdom and compassion.

*Wisdom and compassion as phases of comprehension:* Wisdom and compassion are different phases of the one principle, *prajñā,* the principle of comprehension; they constitute the two-fold way in which the sense of the unconditioned functions in the wise. While the one constitutes insight, knowledge, understanding, the other constitutes feeling, emotion, action.[3] There is no absolute division between intellect on the one hand and feeling on the other. Understanding and activity are essentially related to each other; they are the distinguishable aspects of the integral self, the distinct ways in which the person seeks to realize the values of life. They are also ways in which the wise seek to awaken in everyone the sense of the truly unconditioned. The way of knowledge consists in analysis and criticism, laying bare the distinct and unique natures of things and comprehending their mundane as well as their ultimate truth. It is as truth that the real is sought to be realized in the path of knowledge. The way of compassion consists in effectively widening one's sense of one's kinship, essential bound-up-ness, with all that exists; and this is done through feeling, emotion, work, service. This sense of kinship is deepened by directing attention to the true, abiding essence in every being. The understanding that stops at the surface cannot brighten up permanently the love of man; and the love of man that is not brightened up by deep understanding cannot make for bringing about any permanent good. The ultimate basis of sympathy is the ultimate undividedness of oneself with others. The individual in himself is an abstraction.

*Section II*

## THE GREAT WAY AND THE SMALL WAY

*The Great Way (Mahāyāna) and the Small Way (Hīnayāna):* The *Śāstra* points out that the Great Way is distinguished from the Small Way precisely by virtue of its comprehensiveness: "The big contains the small, while the small cannot contain the big."[4] The farers on the Great Way stress these points to distinguish themselves from the farers on the Small Way:

(I) The Small Way is the way of the "hearers" of truth *(śrāvakas)* and not of those who comprehend it. It is the way of those who cling to difference as ultimate and this amounts to imagining separateness as absolute. Although capable of putting an end to ignorance and passion in themselves, their wayfaring is conditioned by fear of birth and death and not inspired by the ideal of Buddhahood.

(II) Because the "hearers" cling to separateness as ultimate, they do not understand the non-ultimacy *(śūnyatā)* of the basic elements *(dharmāḥ)* and so they do not see these as determinate expressions of the unconditioned. They fall short of comprehending the truly ultimate, the undivided being.

(III) Again, there is a certain self-absorbedness, a certain self-enclosedness, in the farers on the Small Way. They too seek to realize the ultimate good. They, too, fare on the way in order to put an end to passion and gain freedom. But they lack the deep fellow-feeling, the unbounded compassion, which inspires the farers on the Great Way from the very beginning.[5]

*The Great Way is the non-exclusive way:* The way of the hearers takes one straight to the extinction of passion; it involves also an effacement of individuality. But these two are not essentially bound together. The Buddha Himself lived as an individual even after passion and its traces became completely extinct in Him. The farers on the Great Way point out that the "hearers" do not see that individuality can be retained while passion and its traces are overcome. This amounts to imagining that individuality is in itself an evil, something to be done away with; this is their clinging. Extinction of ignorance and passion, when rightly cultivated, results in wisdom and compassion. In fact, the factors of the path of the hearers render their respective functions precisely according to the basic insight that guides them. Insight, wisdom, is the eye, while all other factors of the Way constitute the feet.[6] The basic insight in the Small Way is realization of freedom through extinction of passion; sympathy or compassion is no essential part of it.[7]

Again, the anxiety to efface one's individuality which is accompanied by a lack of the zeal to work for the good of the world must be distinguished from the longing to put an end to ignorance and passion. The farer on the Great Way achieves the extinction of these in his own person only as the necessary means to root out their seeds everywhere. With this he achieves a pure embodiment, free from afflictions; there he is master of himself.[8] He freely assumes embodiments of different kinds, takes birth in hell, walks as man on earth, takes on the life of even an animal, if need be, in order to save even a single being from suffering.

Further, the Great Way is great precisely because it is not exclusive of anyone or of anything; it is the way of all beings as it is not itself any specific way. In this it is comparable to *ākāśa*, the principle of accommodation. This is the way which works for peace and harmony in the world through the rejection of exclusive clinging. Comprehension with its two phases of wisdom and compassion is what characterizes the Great Way. It starts from the realms of determinate existence and its destination is *prajñā*, the knowledge of all forms.[9]

*The Great Way is the way of perfection (pāramitā):* The Great Way is the way that is inspired and guided by *prajñā*, the sense of the undivided, which is basic to wayfaring. It is the *prajñāpāramitā* itself.[10] Actually it is the cultivation of the *prajñāpāramitā* in all its different aspects that is itself distinguished as the different kinds of perfection.

The six *pāramitās* and the *prajñāpāramitā* are one and the same thing and not different.[11] (116b)

*Prajñāpāramitā* contains all elements of merit for it is by obtaining its power of skilfulness that these get into the way of the Buddha.[12] All that is good is contained within the six *pāramitās;*[13] they constitute the body (體) of the Great Way,[14] which is the Buddha's Way.[15] This wayfaring in the light of the sense of the unconditioned is itself distinguished as the phases or aspects of wisdom and merit. It is these phases themselves that are further distinguished as kinds of perfection. Thus the *Śāstra* says:

These two things (merit and wisdom which are the two phases of wayfaring) are cultivated in six different aspects, and these are called the six kinds of perfection *(pāramitā)*.[16] (262c)

Of all the kinds of perfection *(pāramitā)* the perfection of wisdom, insight *(prajñā)* is the foremost.

Without it the other five do not get the name of *pāramitā* at all; they would then be like the blind; *prajñā* is like the eye. The five *pāramitās* without the *prajñā* would be like the unbaked earthen pot filled with water, while *prajñāpāramitā* is like the well-baked earthen pot (holding water); the five *pāramitās* are like the bird without wings while *prajñā-pāramitā* is like the bird with wings.[17] (314b)

*The essential quality of perfection:* A) *Dāna: Charity:* The *Śāstra* observes that the *Sūtra* speaks of five characters (五種相) as constituting the perfection of charity: I) with the thought associated with the knowledge of all forms *(sarvākārajñātā* or *prajñā*), II) one gives away all things, internal and external; III) (having given away all things in charity) and sharing this merit with (共) all beings, IV) one looks back (廻向) to the highest *samyaksambodhi;* and V) (all this one does) with the skilfulness of non-clinging.[18] Commenting on this, the *Śāstra* says:

To associate the thought with *sarvākārajñatā* . . . is to base one's thought (緣) and rely (依) on the Way of the Buddha.[19] (395a)

To aspire to the Way of the Buddha, to saturate one's mind with the thought of the Way of the Buddha, is the foremost condition for one's faring on the way to perfection.

By giving away all things (internal and external) in the light of the Way of the Buddha, one gives up all *kleśas.* (395a)

By virtue of one's heart of great compassion one shares with all being the merit that arises as the fruit of the act of charity. That one "looks back" to the highest *sambodhi* means that by means of the act of charity one seeks only the Way of the Buddha (但求佛道) and not any other fruit.[20] By virtue of his achieving a share in the spirit (氣分) of *prajñāpāramitā,* the true nature of all things, one performs the act of charity in the non-clinging way.[21] Actually the last four of these five characters are subsidiary to the first, viz., devotedness to the way of the Buddha. It is this that is essential. The *Śāstra* observes that because this essential thing is not realized by common people, therefore its meaning has been made clear by means of the other four.[21a] The bodhisattva seeks at heart the knowledge of all forms which is the wisdom that belongs to the Buddha. He makes that his object (作緣), thinks of it (作念) (deeply), fixes his mind (繫心) on it and does acts of charity with the sole aim of realizing this fruit, viz., the wisdom of the Buddha. He does not seek anything else like name or gratitude, nor does he seek to be born in the higher states of existence. He does not seek also to realize complete Nirvāṇa by an effacement of individuality as it is his purpose to help all beings (by retaining it). He seeks only to fulfil the achievement of all the factors of Buddhahood, such as the complete knowledge of all forms, and this, just in order to terminate the suffering of all people. This is what is meant by associating the thought with the knowledge of all forms.[22] That he shares with all beings this merit of his act of charity is like throwing open the granary of a noble family to the use of all. All people find their support in this merit of the bodhisattva even as all birds take their resting place on a tree of good fruits.[23] The merit that the bodhisattva achieves is in harmony with the spirit of the true nature of all things and it is therefore pure with regard to all the three elements, viz., the giver, the receiver, and the object given. With regard to any of these he does not entertain any false notion.[24]

Although the bodhisattva understands the true nature of things he still gives rise to the thought that he should continue to work and does acts of merit (更生心爾作福德); this is because he has for long cultivated the heart of great compassion (久習大悲心). At the time when there arises in him the comprehension of the true nature of things, there shines forth the great compassion too.[25] It is this heart of great compassion that helps him to overcome the temptation to efface his individuality and saves him from rushing to seize the complete Nirvāṇa. The *Śāstra* observes that it is his cultivation of the perfection of effort *(vīryapāramitā)* that helps (助) him in this regard; it enables him to put forth energy to work for the world. The heart of compassion, the thought of service, is thus fortified by the perfection of effort, even as the fire that is about to become extinct is vivified by wind and fuel.[26] The act of charity done in the spirit of non-clinging is free from pride and all other factors of bondage that follow from it. When done with the clinging mind it would no doubt be an act of charity but not its perfection. It would then be a worldly act that binds one and not the transcending act that liberates one. While the cultivation of charity is essential, one's clinging to it is to be rejected.[27]

B) *Śīla: Moral Conduct:* The bodhisattva's cultivation is solely to achieve the Way of the Buddha, and this, in order to help all beings that have sunk in the stream of birth and death. With this mind he cultivates the elements of moral conduct.[28] As a result he is born in a good family, meets good people, gives rise to the right understanding and thereby cultivates all the six kinds of perfection, and obtains the Way of the Budhha.[29] Out of the heart of great compassion does the bodhisattva cultivate his moral conduct and by this cultivation he reaches the Way of the Buddha. It is in this way that his cultivation of moral conduct achieves completeness and by virtue of this it gets the name of perfection.[30] The highest kind of moral conduct, its perfection, consists in the non-clinging way, not clinging to sin or merit as absolute and unconditioned. The bodhisattva that enters deep into the truth of things, cultivating the contemplation of their *śūnya*-nature, beholds with his eye of wisdom that sin and merit are not absolute and unconditioned.[31] The excellence of moral conduct does not permit any attitude of despising the sinner nor any attitiude of taking pride with regard to the merited. It is the non-clinging way imbued with the right understanding of things that gives perfection to morality.

C) *Kṣānti: Forbearance or Endurance:* In the spirit of non-clinging, with the comprehension of the true nature of things and by the heart of great compassion, the bodhisattva cultivates the perfection of *kṣānti* (忍), forbearance, endurance.[32] By the cultivation of forbearance in regard to beings *(sattva)* he achieves unlimited merit, and by the cultivation of endurance in regard to the true nature of elements *(dharma)* he achieves the limitless wisdom. Achieving these two elements of merit and wisdom he accomplishes all that he wishes even as people who have both eyes and feet can go anywhere they wish.[33] If the bodhisattva happens to encounter reviling, he does not avenge himself because he has stamped all things with the three marks of *dharma*,[34] and this gives him the ability to rise above the thought of vengeance. It is this state of mind which arises in him at this time that is called forbearance. By obtaining this forbearing state of mind, his understanding that things should be endured and not given way to becomes reinforced, becomes firm, even as the colour that gets the necessary gum remains firm in the picture.[35]

*Anutpattika-dharma-kṣānti*: By virtue of his understanding of the true nature of things the bodhisattva is able to be non-clinging; he is able to keep free from misconstructions (不作分別) in regard to the senses and their different objects. In their mundane nature they are conditioned, non-substantial and in the ultimate comprehension, they enter the non-dual *dharma*. Although they are not two, they are also not one. By this comprehension the mind gives rise to faith in the truth of things and does not revert (心信不轉). This is the bodhisattva's *dharmakṣānti* (法忍) capacity to sustain the comprehension of the truth of things.[36] It is this capacity to have faith in the purity and the impregnability of the teachings of the Buddha by banishing all wrong notions and gaining the understanding of the truth of things that is called the endurance for *dharma*.[37] As his heart of faith is great, (信心大故), his mind is free from doubt and repentance; as his power of faith is great, his mind can accept and hold firmly the truth of things. This is the endurance for *dharma*.[38] On account of the power of concentration and meditation, the mind becomes soft (柔軟) and pure (清淨); in this state when one hears the teaching of the true nature of things, one responds to it heartily (應心與會), holds it firm in faith (信著) and penetrates deep (深入) into it, remaining free from doubt and repentance. This is the endurance for *dharma*.[39] By means of the power of wisdom one examines everything in various ways and understands that there is not a single thing that can be seized as substantial. By means of his comprehension of this nature of things one is able to endure (能忍), able to sustain (能受). This is one's endurance in regard to the truth of things.[40] By virtue of this endurance for *dharma* the bodhisattva enters the door of wisdom (入智慧門), comprehends (觀) the universal reality and does not revert (不退) or repent

(不悔).[41] Having known the true nature of *prajñāpāramitā,* he does not give rise to imaginative constructions; his mind remains ever free from clinging and thus he has the capacity to forbear, to endure all things.[42]

D) *Vīrya: Effort:* By the non-clinging way the bodhisattva cultivates the perfection of effort. Right effort, putting forth energy in the right way, is fundamental to the cultivation of concentration and meditation as well as of true wisdom (禪定實智慧之根).[43] *Vīrya,* effort (精進) has been also called *chandas* (欲) determination and absence of lassitude *apramāda* (不放逸). Determination comes first; then follows effort, the putting forth of energy; and there is the aspect of the absence of langour which means to keep the effort unfailing.[44] The bodhisattva, with his mind fixed on the Way of the Buddha from the very start, exerts himself in order to cultivate all that is good and thus he gradually achieves the perfection of effort. It is the effort put forth in order to achieve the Way of the Buddha (爲佛道精進) that is called the perfection of effort.[45]

E) *Dhyāna: Concentration and Meditation:* The eternal joy of Nirvāṇa (常樂涅槃) arises from the real wisdom (實智慧), and the real wisdom arises from single-mindedness, concentration and meditation (一心禪定).[46] The *Śāstra* gives here the well-known example of the burning lamp in the windy place. Although the burning lamp has the capacity to emit light still it cannot function fully when it is in the midst of a great wind. When kept in a room undisturbed by wind then its function of emitting light can be complete. Just the same is the case, says the *Śāstra,* with knowledge in the scattered mind. In the case of such a mind even though there may be knowledge it cannot function as fully as in the mind that has become collected and calm by virtue of concentration and meditation.[47] When not saturated with the sense of the unconditioned, when not enlightened by *prajñā, dhyāna* cannot deserve the name of perfection. Again, it is the *dhyāna* followed by the great compassion for all beings and issuing in the oath to help all to realize the joy of contemplation through abandoning the pleasures of sense that gets the name of perfection. It is the spirit of non-clinging that gives the quality of perfection to concentration and meditation. In the non-clinging cultivation of *dhyāna* the bodhisattva does not seize its flavour (不受味), does not seek its result (不求報). He enters *dhyāna* only in order to soften and subdue the mind.[48] He rises from the state of *dhyāna* and enters again the realm of desires (還生欲界) through the skilfulness of *prajñā* (以智慧方便); and this he does in order to help all to cross the stream of birth and death. It is then that *dhyāna* gets the name of perfection.[49] One who has attained the perfection of *dhyāna* does not seize the characteristics of collectedness and disturbedness of mind as absolute and unconditioned, for one has comprehended the true nature of things. The ultimately true nature of the elements that obstruct the mind is also the ultimately true nature of the collected, concentrated, state of mind.[50] The *dhyāna* that is saturated with this comprehension of the ultimate truth has attained its perfection.

F) *Prajñā: Wisdom:*

I) *The nature and kinds of knowledge:* It is to be recalled that while all other factors of the Way practically constitute the "motor-energy," "feet," devoid of *prajñā* they are "blind." It is the knowledge, the insight, the understanding that gives direction to the wayfaring and makes it meaningful. This is the basic principle which governs the entire wayfaring; this is the central truth contained in the teachings of the Buddha. The *Śāstra* cites a *gāthā* to say:

> *Prajñā* is one; the Buddha speaks of it through various names in accordance with the capacity of the person to whom He speaks. For the sake of the different persons (the receivers of His teachings) the Buddha institutes different names to refer to *prajñā*. (190c)

The different kinds of knowledge are the different levels and phases of understanding. All these different levels and phases are alike called *prajñā,* and the entire course of understanding culminates in the complete knowledge of the true nature of things. It is the ideal of this complete knowledge, which is of the Buddha, viz., *sarvākarajñatā,* the knowledge of all forms, that inspires the bodhisattva from the very beginning.

From the very beginning the bodhisattva always seeks the *sarvākārajñatā* (一切種智); in between (starting to achieve and actually achieving it) he (progressively) gains the knowledge of the true nature of things. (190a)

*Prajñāpāramitā* includes all other kinds of knowledge . . . The bodhisattva, the seeker of the Way of the Buddha, should cultivate all *dharmas* and achieve every kind of knowledge, viz., that of the *śrāvakas,* that of the *pratyekabuddhas* as well as that of the Buddhas. (191a)

But still it is the *prajñā* realized by the Buddha that is truly perfect, the true *pāramitā* (實波羅密).

Because it is in order to realize this truly perfect *prajñā* that the bodhisattva cultivates the Way, therefore even the *prajñā* of the bodhisattva is called the *prajñāpāramitā*. . . . In the mind of the Buddha this *prajñāpāramitā* becomes the knowledge of all forms. As the bodhisattva cultivates the way to realize this true *prajñā* and to cross over to the other shore, (his wayfaring in the path of knowledge) is called *pāramitā,* reaching perfection, while in the case of the Buddha who has already crossed over to the other shore, the *prajñā* is called *sarvākārajñatā,* the knowledge of all forms. (190a)

II) *The wisdom of the śrāvakas (hearers) and the pratyekabuddhas:* Unlike the *śrāvakas* whose knowledge is limited and who are just interested in seeking for themselves a liberation from birth and death, the bodhisattvas, the farers on the Great Way, make the great resolve at the very start of their career to help all beings. They possess great love and compassion for all beings everywhere. They seek to attain all the merits of the Buddha and honour and worship all the Buddhas everywhere. They concentrate their attention on the ultimate nature of things, external and internal, and they do not seize and cling to the notions of purity, impurity, etc. The comprehension of the noble is pure everywhere, undeniable and indestructible. This is *prajñāpāramitā.* In the teachings of the *śrāvakas* the emphasis is on impermanence which they seize as an ultimate element, whereas the farers on the Great Way comprehend that birth and death do not constitute the ultimate nature of things; they do not also seize the denial of birth and death as absolute. In the Great Way, it is the extinction of the clinging to specific views and determinate natures that is the ultimate truth.

Briefly, the distaste for the world, the constant thought of Nirvāṇa, the abandoning of the three realms of existence, the extinction of all *kleśas* and the obtaining of the highest *dharma,* viz., Nirvāṇa—it is these that constitute the knowledge of the *śrāvakas.*[51] Although as knowledge this is one in kind with that of the bodhisattvas, the *śrāvakas* do not have the strength of skilfulness. They are devoid of the great resolve, devoid of the great love and compassion. There is not in them the urge to realize the factors of Buddhahood, nor the aspiration for the knowledge of all forms. They simply detest old age, disease and death, put an end to the bonds of passion and tend straight to Nirvana. This is what differentiates the knowledge of the *śrāvakas* from that of the farers on the Great Way.[52] The knowledge of the *pratyekabuddhas* is not substantially different from that of the *śrāvakas;* there are differences only of time (時節), the sharpness of understanding (利根), and the extent of merit (福德).[53] The difference of time refers to the fact that the *pratyekabuddhas* arise only when no Buddhas are born and when the Buddhas' teachings have disappeared in the world. At such a time the *pratyekabuddhas* abandon home-life occasioned even by a small incident and obtain the Way.[54] That their understanding is sharp (利根) does not mean any difference in the quality (相) of their knowledge, but there is a difference in the extent, in the number of elements (法) cognized.[55]

III) *The wisdom of the bodhisattvas and the Buddhas:* The knowledge of the bodhisattva excels that of the *śrāvakas* and the *pratyekabuddhas.* During innumerable spans of life the bodhisattva deeply studies the ultimate nature of all things. His knowledge is supported by and furnished with the other five *pāramitās.* He has the strength of skilfulness; he has the great love and compassion for all beings, and therefore his knowledge is not hindered by perversions. He dwells in the ten stages *(bhūmis)* of the Great Way and therefore his knowledge is powerful and profound. These virtues the 'worthy' *(arahan)* and the *pratyekabuddhas* do not have.[56] Again, while the knowledge of the *śrāvakas* and the *pratyekabuddhas* is *sarvajñatā* (一切智) the all-inclusive understanding which is only rough and gross, *sarvākārajñāta* which is the thorough and detailed knowledge of everything belongs only to the Buddha; the one is brief while the other is comprehensive. But rightly pursued, the former can lead to the latter, i.e., the brief to the comprehensive, the rough and broad to the thorough and the detailed; thus the one may be the cause of the other. The one cancels ignorance only in a general way while the other comprehends in detail everything in every way.[57] The *śrāvakas* and the *pratyekabuddhas* cannot exhaustively know even the details of the life of one individual, such as the sphere of his birth, his virtues and vices, the nature and extent of his deeds, etc., and much less can they know the details of the life of every being. But the Buddha exhaustively knows the general and the specific natures of every distinguishable entity, and therefore His knowledge is called the knowledge of all forms. The *sarvajñatā,* the all-inclusive understanding of the *śrāvakas* and the *pratyekabuddhas* is like the lamp in the picture, which has only its name and not its function.[58]

Again, of the eleven kinds of knowledge (十一智), the first ten, viz., *dharmajñāna* (法智) the knowledge of the constituent elements of things in the world of desire and *anvayajñāna* (比智) knowledge of the constituent elements in the world of fine matter and the immaterial world, the knowledge of the mind and mental states of other persons (他心智), the worldly knowledge (世智), the knowledge of suffering (苦智), its origin (集智), its extinction (滅智) and the way to it (道智), and the knowledge of the final and complete extinction of the roots of suffering (盡智) as well as of their non-origination (無生智), these are common to the *śrāvakas,* the *pratyekabuddhas* and the bodhisattvas, while the knowledge of the true nature of things *(yathārthajñāna* 如實智) belongs only to the Buddha.[59] The last mentioned is the true *prajñā;* it is beyond the scope of the other kinds and it is the knowledge also of these other kinds.

By this true *prajñā* one can understand the distinctive features of knowing (各各相) of these other kinds, their respective objects (各各緣),

their mutual differences (各各別異), and the special mode of each of these (各各有觀法). In (this final kind of knowledge, viz.,) the knowledge of the true nature of all things, there cannot be obtained any character of its own (無相), any object of its own (無縁), any distinctive (無別) determinate nature of its own; in it all the determinate modes of knowing become extinct (滅諸觀法); in it there is not even any knowing (亦不有觀) (as a determinate mode). (234a)

This true knowledge is the ultimate comprehension devoid of all divisions and distinctions; in it knowing and being are not differentiated. It is what can be called the "integral experience." As the all-comprehensive understanding, it contains or is itself the eye of the Buddha.

In the ten kinds of knowledge there are the eyes of wisdom and of *dharma*. But in *yathārthajñāna* (如實智中) the true, ultimate, knowledge, there is only the eye of the Buddha. (234a)

This is the knowledge that only the Buddha has, and so it is the same as the knowledge of all forms. In it all other kinds of knowing find their consummation:

When the ten kinds of knowledge enter the true, ultimate, knowledge, they lose their original names (失本名字). (They merge into it and become of one essence with it.) There remains only the one kind, viz., the true knowledge. This is like all the different streams in all directions entering the great ocean and losing their original names and coming to be called just the ocean itself. (234a)

*Section III*

## THE FACTORS OF THE WAY AND THE GATES OF FREEDOM

*The thirty-seven factors of the Way:* These factors that are emphasized in the way of the hearers are distinguished into seven kinds and these are all centered around the fourfold contemplation on the four different kinds of objects. These are the *smṛtyupasthānas* (念處), the kinds of the application of mindfulness. The application of mindfulness is essentially of the nature of knowledge, insight.[60] This is supported by the *samyak-prahāṇas* which consist of the putting forth of effort to put an end to the forces of ignorance and passion that are already existing and to prevent the ones that have not yet arisen, as well as to retain the elements of wisdom and merit that are already there and to bring into birth the ones that are not yet born.[61] This application of mindfulness is sustained by the *ṛddhipadas,* the elements that make for the growth of concentration and insight, viz., *chandas* (欲) determination, *vīrya* (精進) effort, *citta* (心) thought, idea, and *mīmāṃsā* (思惟) investigation.[62] It may be mentioned that these twelve, viz., the four kinds of the application of mindfulness supported by the four kinds of right effort, *samyak-prahāṇas,* and the four kinds of *ṛddhipadas* practically form the foundation for the entire wayfaring. Among these, the kinds of the application of mindfulness may be said to constitute the pith; right effort and the bases of concentration are centered around these. The faculties *(indriya,* 根) of faith *(śraddhā),* effort *(vīrya),* mindfulness *(smṛti),* concentration *(samādhi)* and insight *(prajñā)* arise in one who cultivates the application of mindfulness *(smyṛtyupasthāna),*[63] and these faculties, when further cultivated, would develop into the kinds of power *(bala,* 力), the powerful forces, that help the wayfarer to move forth.[64] The rest of the thirty-seven are put into two categories the factors of enlightenment (覺分) and the limbs of the way (道分). The latter constitute the well-known eight-fold path consisting of right views, right resolve, right speech, right activity, right kind of living, right kind of initiative and effort, the right kind of mindfulness and the right kind of concentration,[65] while the former, the factors of enlightenment, consist of mindfulness *(smṛti),* analysis and understanding of all things *(dharmapravicaya* 擇法), effort, the sense of joy *(prīti),* the sense of tranquillity or serenity *(praśrabdhi),* the sense of equanimity *(upekṣā)* and concentration.[66] The *Śāstra* points out that it is the first twelve elements themselves that are called the faculties (根, *indriya)* in the case of one whose senses have not yet been sharp, while in the case of one whose senses have become sharp, they are themselves called the kinds of power (力, *bala*). These very factors, the twelve, are called the factors of the Way when the work of their cultivation has not yet been accomplished (事未辦) while they are called the factors of enlightenement when the work has been accomplished and when they are deeply assimilated (事辦思惟修行).[67]

That there is much overlapping in the enumeration of these factors of the way, thirty-seven in all, seems to have been felt even from very early times. These thirty-seven are set forth as an elaboration of the ten basic elements, viz., faith, effort, mindfulness, concentration, knowledge or insight, the sense of joy, serenity and equanimity, determination or will and such elements of the moral life as right speech, right deeds and right kind of living.[68] All these thirty-seven factors of the Way are cultivated by the bodhisattva as the means to comprehending the true nature of things.[69] Application of mindfulness on the different kinds of the basic elements of existence starts with understanding them in their mundane nature as determinate and conditioned, impermanent and sources of suffering. The first form of contemplation is that all things are impure. But it does not stop there. The insight needs to be deepened. The ultimate nature of *rūpa* is not *rūpa;* in its true nature, *rūpa* is devoid of the nature of resistance. Resistance as an activity is not anything unconditioned; and at the root of the phenomenon of resistance there is no substance, no entity which is *rūpa* in itself.[70] All the forms of the cultivation of mindfulness, the application of thought and the process of analysis and criticism serve in the case of the bodhisattva as means for getting at the basic reality, the indeterminate *dharma*.[71] The application of mindfulness is facilitated by the concentration on the impurity of things; but this is not a general rule. Again, the contemplation on the impermanence of things is helpful, but not with all persons. There is the aspect of purity in things as much as impurity; there is again, the aspect of permanence (or endurance or continuity) in things as much as impermanence (arising and perishing).[72] Again, impurity, impermanence, etc. are not the absolute natures of things. It is essential for the farer on the Great Way, which is itself the Middle Way, to analyze, understand and appreciate all the distinguishable aspects of all things; but what is characteristic of the Middle Way is its rising above the extremes by rejecting exclusive clinging. The basic insight is the comprehension of which the symbol is *ākāśa,* which is not anything in particular and is for that very reason capable of accommodating all that is specific and determinate. On *ākāśa* all things depend and thus they live and move and realize their being. *Ākāśa* is the symbol of the Great Way, the Middle Way, the all-comprehensive *prajñā.* The application of mindfulness is essentially in order to achieve this basic comprehension, viz., of the ultimate ground of all things; all else is a means for this.

*The thirty-seven factors and the six kinds of perfection:* It has been seen that of the ten basic elements mentioned above mindfulness is not essentially different from *prajñā* or insight. It can be seen again that joy, serenity and equanimity come under the general category of emotion, feeling; and it can also be seen that effort and will belong together. Thus there are I) faith, II) will, III) emotion, IV) knowledge or insight, V) concentration and VI) factors of moral life. Faith is a very wide term covering insight, effort, emotion, etc. and yet it is emotion and insight that are prominent there. In the scheme of the six kinds of perfection, faith comes under *kṣānti* which stands essentially for the affective side, the side of emotion and feeling, that is enlightened by the sense of the real and is the necessary condition for the putting forth of effort. *Kṣānti* as one of the kinds of perfection means the ability for patient endurance and the capacity to sustain one's unfailing cultivation in the pathway of reality. Will, moral conduct, knowledge or insight, and concentration are each counted as a different kind of perfection. Charity is added to this list and is put as the very first kind. While all these elements can thus be seen as comprised in the different kinds of perfection, what gives them their quality of perfection is, as we have seen, the presence of the insight, the guiding light, the *prajñā,* which is the sense of the real. When these elements get saturated with the sense of the unconditioned and are cultivated in this light, then they gain the name of perfection. Cultivated in the right spirit these lead to the comprehension of the ultimate truth of things.

*The three gates of freedom:* The *Śāstra* observes that one's cultivation of these different factors of the Way should culminate in the comprehension of the truth of things as expressed in the three "Gateways to Nirvāṇa." It is this comprehension that should culminate in one's realization of reality. Thus it says:

The thirty-seven factors constitute the Way that leads to Nirvāṇa; faring on this Way one reaches the city of Nirvāṇa. The city has three gates, viz., *śūnyatā, animittatā* and *apraṇihitatā*.[73] (206a)

*Śūnyatā* (空) is the comprehension of the non-substantiality of things in their mundane nature. *Animittatā* (無相) means to refrain from seizing the determinate natures of things and from making them the occasions *(nimitta)* for the rise of passion and pride. *Apraṇihitatā* (無作) means to abstain from resolving *(praṇidhāna)* to do deeds that spring from passion.

The *Śāstra* further points out that things like the four *dhyānas* (states of contemplation) are "elements that help one in (opening the gates of the city of Nirvāṇa)" (助開門法).[74] Further, depending on (依), dwelling in the states of *dhyāna* and *samādhi* that belong to the realms of form and formlessness, one "tries" (試), experiments with, one's mind through the exercises of the four elements of boundless heart (無量心),[75] the eight exercises of turning away (背捨),[76] the eight exercises of getting "mastery" (勝處),[77] the nine exercises of successive concentration (九次第定),[78] and the ten exercises of all-pervasiveness (十一切處).[79] By experimenting with the mind in these exercises, one will know whether one's mind is softened (柔軟), subdued, under control capable of being put into use according to one's wish (自在隨意). The *Śāstra* compares this with trying a horse before riding.[80] These exercises constitute the expedients or devices by which one seeks to obtain the suitability of mind to comprehend the true nature of things (得解觀). The actual comprehension of truth (實觀) is however what one gains in the thirty-seven factors.[81] Because it is difficult to attain these factors of comprehension directly, therefore, as the means to this attainment, these expedients are set forth; in these one obtains the softness and subduedness of mind, and then it becomes easy to achieve the comprehension of the truth of things through the Way that is constituted of the thirty-seven factors. Thus one gets at the three Gates of Freedom.[82]

These gateways to Nirvāṇa are essentially of the nature of knowledge, wisdom, insight; and yet they are called *samādhi* (states of collectedness of mind) because these three kinds of knowledge will just be cases of confusion (狂慧) if they are not in a collected mind (若不住定中); they would then fall into errors and would be devoid of any use.[83] It is by the cultivation of these three elements that one finally attains to the state of freedom devoid of the residues of passion; the residueless freedom is the real freedom (眞解脱).[84]

These gates of freedom cease to be gates in the case of those who cling to them. *Śūnyatā* for instance has been taught in order to banish one's clinging to the determinate as itself ultimate. But if one clings to *śūnyatā* itself, one again misses the truth of things; one misses the purport of this teaching and thus lapses back into a state of clinging, conflict and suffering. One then gives rise to pride and says, "I have the ability to know the truth of things."[85] This indeed is a perversion. At this time in order to overcome one's clinging, one has to cultivate the door of *animittatā*,[86] which is to refrain from making the determinate characters the occasions for clinging, passion and pride. If one again gives rise to misconstructions in regard to *animittatā*, devoidness of the grounds or occasions for clinging, and misconstrues one's capacity to accomplish this act of realization, then one should consider: "I have indeed gone wrong. Where everything is devoid of absoluteness, devoid of occasions for clinging, how can I seize, cleave to the determinate and give rise to misconstructions?"[87] Then one should fare on the Way keeping oneself in tune with *śūnyatā* and *animittatā* (隨空無相行); one should not give rise to the deeds, bodily, vocal or mental, that are prompted by a seeking (求) for birth in the realms of determinate existence. Then one enters the door of *apraṇihitatā*,[88] by not resolving to do deeds that are prompted by craving and clinging.

The *Śāstra* observes that in Mahāyāna these three doors to freedom are really one and the same principle (是一法) differently expounded for the convenience of cultivation.[89] It further observes that one can enter only through one door at a time.[90] Rightly pursued the one includes the other. If one enters the door free from clinging it will take him straight to the ultimate truth; but if one clings to the door itself, then "the more one pokes in the more will one be daubed with dust and the greater will one's path get blocked (通塗更塞)."[91] In the Mahāyāna, the *Śāstra* observes, all these three doors, which are essentially of the nature of wisdom, insight, have for their ultimate object the universal reality (緣諸法實相). By means of these one beholds that the world is itself Nirvāṇa (觀世間即是涅槃) in its ultimate nature.[92]

*CHAPTER XI*

# CONSUMMATION

*Section I*

## THE BODHISATTVA

*The meaning of the word "bodhisattva":* We have noted above that the bodhisattva, the farer on the Great Way, makes the great resolve at the very start of his career that he shall become the Buddha in order to save all beings from ignorance and passion, error and evil. From the very outset he seeks to realize the wisdom that constitutes Buddhahood, viz., the knowledge of all forms, the knowledge of all the ways of all beings. This is what gives the Buddhas and the advanced bodhisattvas the ability to keep themselves *en rapport* with every situation and render help to each individual in the way suited to him.[1] Speaking of the import of the term *"bodhisattva,"* the *Śāstra* says:

*"Bodhi"* means the way of all the Buddhas (諸佛道), *"sattva"* means the individual (衆生); it also means the great mind (大心). This individual (that is called the bodhisattva) seeks to realize exhaustively all the merits of the Buddha. This thought of his (其心) is unbreakable, indestructible, firm like the diamond-mountain. This is the meaning of great mind. (86a)

As these stanzas put it:

All the factors of Buddhahood, wisdom as well as moral conduct and concentration, can benefit every being; it is this (way of the Buddhas) that is called the *bodhi.*

Of him (who fares on the way to *bodhi)* the *citta* is unshakable; it is capable of enduring (all obstacles) sustaining (the thought of *bodhi)* by and of accomplishing all the factors of the way; it does not give way; it cannot be destroyed. It is this *citta* that is called the *(bodhi)sattva.* (86a) The *Śāstra* continues:

Again, the good *dharma* that is extolled is what is meant by *"sa(t)"* (薩), the essence and character (體相) of the good *dharma* is the meaning of *"tva"* (埵). The *citta* of the bodhisattva benefits itself and benefits others; it helps everyone to cross the stream (of birth and death); it comprehends the true nature of everything; it fares on the way to the highest *sambodhi;* it is extolled by all men of wisdom. Therefore it is this (*citta* or the individual) that is called the bodhisattva.[2] (86a)

Of all the paths, the path of the Buddha is the foremost, the highest. This individual seeks to realize this *dharma* (of the Buddhas) and therefore he is held in high esteem by all the sages. Again, such an individual as this seeks the Way of the Buddha (only) in order to help all beings to become free from (the suffering of) birth, old-age, disease and death; (and so) he is called the bodhisattva. (86a)

There is the great resolve (大誓願), there is the thought that is unshakable and there is the effort that knows no set back; it is by virtue of these three that one is called the bodhisattva.[3]

*The status (nyāma) of the bodhisattva:* The bodhisattva can come to know even at the very first start of his mind on the way that he will become the Buddha;[4] he is completely free from the anxiety to efface his individuality; when he has the temptation to efface it the Buddhas save him from that.[5] His unbounded compassion for all beings is accompanied by the complete comprehension of the truth of things; imbued with great compassion he once again puts forth effort to help all.[6]

The *śrāvakas* loathe and fear (畏惡) the course of birth and death. On hearing that the individual is *śūnya,* devoid of substance, and on hearing the teaching of the four Noble Truths, viz., that all that is composite is impermanent, painful etc., they abstain from giving rise to imaginative constructions in regard to things. Like the deer that is besieged and hit by the poisonous arrow, they just grow anxious and seek quickly to get rid (of all things); they do not entertain any other thought. Even the *pratyekabuddhas* loathe old-age, disease and death, and yet, they can, to some extent, look deeper into the nature of things, and they can also to some extent help other people to cross (the stream of ignorance and passion). They are like the yak caught in the net; although it is hit with the poisonous arrow, it can still look at its cubs with affection and pity. But as to the bodhisattva (the farer on the Great Way), even though he has distaste for old-age, disease and death, he still has the ability to comprehend the true nature of all things; (examining them) to their very bottom, he penetrates deeply into the twelve-linked (chain of causation), enters straight into the comprehension of the non-ultimacy of the basic elements of existence, and enters the limitless *dharma-dhātu.* He is like the elephant of the highest kind (白香), the king of elephants (象王), that has entered the hunter's net. Although it is hit with the arrow, it looks at the hunter with kindness and affection, and remains absolutely free from fear. It has the ability even then to lead its herd to the camp, moving forth in peaceful gait.[7] (295b)

What is it that gives the bodhisattva this strength by which he excels all the rest? It is his capacity to sustain the comprehension of the true nature of things, his capacity to bear with every circumstance devoid of doubt, devoid of fear and anxiety, and his ability to meet every situation with unimpeded insight and unbounded compassion. It is this that is known as the *anutpattika-dharma-kṣānti,* the capacity to endure and to sustain the truth of the unborn *dharma.* By attaining this capacity the wayfarer enters the true status *(nyāma* 位)[8] of the bodhisattva. Thus the *Śāstra* says:

The (true) status of the bodhisattva is the *anutpattika-dharma-kṣānti.* Having achieved this *dharma-kṣānti* (得此法忍), he comprehends the entire world as *śūnya* and remains completely non-clinging at heart. Being (firmly) established in the true nature of all things, he does not any more cling to the world with passion.

Again, the true status of the bodhisattva means the *pratyutpanna-samādhi* (般舟般三昧), the state of meditation (on Buddhahood) in which one feels the constant presence of the Buddhas. Having achieved this state of meditation one feels everywhere the presence of the Buddhas, in all the ten directions; one (constantly) hears the teaching of the *dharma* from them and puts an end to the entire network of doubt. At this time the mind of the bodhisattva remains firm and unshaken. This is the true status of the bodhisattva.

Again, the true status of the bodhisattva means the fulfilment of the cultivation of the six *pāramitās* and giving rise to the expedient *prajñā* (方便智) (by virtue of which) one does not stop (不) even in the true nature of all things. In this state the bodhisattva understands and realizes by himself the real nature of things and does not take the lead of others' words.[9] (262a)

*The irreversible bodhisattva and the strength of skilfulness:* This strength of mind that the bodhisattva thus achieves by his long and single-minded cultivation of the Way of the Buddha keeps him free from all kinds of set back; he knows no reversion.

It is by virtue of this power (which one achieves) by entering the true status of the bodhisattva that one gains the name *avaivarta* (阿鞞跋致), the irreversible, the unshakable.[10] (262a)

Having realized the power of skilfulness, the bodhisattva does not fall back into the lot of common people (凡夫數), the life of ignorance and passion. He is then known as the "realizer of the Way" (得道人). And even if the entire world should attempt to destroy this mind of wisdom and compassion which he has now achieved, no one would be able to shake him from his position.[11]

Thus entering the true status of the bodhisattva, he dwells at the top of all beings (住頂). He is the top-most, the highest of beings. From here he has no fall (不墮). This is the true status of the bodhisattva.[12]

What is it to be the topmost of all beings? What is it to dwell at the top?

It means to have already terminated all hankering for dharma and to keep free from seizing even in regard to this extinction of hankering. (262b)

The bodhisattva of (this superior status) realizes the unparallelled mind (無等等心), and (even then) he does not think high of himself. (For,) he understands the true nature of (even this) mind as really *śūnya;* in him all imaginations of "is" and "is not" (諸有無等戲論) have completely ceased to be.[13] (262b)

By fulfilling the cultivation of four things one obtains entry into the true status of the bodhisattva, viz., the setting forth of the mind, the cultivation of the path, great compassion and (the strength of) skilfulness. (262c)

The mere setting forth of mind is like the mere wish (但有意願) to reach a place while still staying at home; the cultivation of the path is the actual faring on the Way, putting forth effort and turning out the necessary work (造作). Having cultivated the path, viz., of the six *pāramitās* headed by the perfection of wisdom, the bodhisattva comprehends the true nature of all things. With his heart of great compassion he thinks of all beings, viz., that they suffer pain out of ignorance. The power of skilfulness means his ability to remain free from clinging in regard to the true nature of things as well as to his great compassion for all beings.[14]

On account of his fulfilling the cultivation of the perfection of wisdom, he understands things as *śūnya;* on account of his heart of great compassion he has pity for all beings. And in regard to these two, by virtue of his power of skilfulness, he remains completely free from passion and clinging. Although he understands that things are *śūnya,* it is by virtue of this power of skilfulness that he does not abandon beings; and although he does not abandon beings, yet he has the understanding that all things and all beings are truly *śūnya.* He has the equanimity, the balance (等), in regard to both of these. (This is his power of skilfulness and) by this he just enters the (true) status of the bodhisattva. (262c)

The bodhisattva achieves this sense of equanimity by his power of skilfulness, not clinging exclusively either to the *śūnya*-nature of things or to his sense of compassion for all. Clinging to the *śūnya*-nature of things might lead him to the extreme of negativism and clinging to his sense of compassion for all, occasioned by his feeling for their suffering, might lead him to the imagination that this suffering is insurmountable, and that that is the inevitable nature of things. Either way his understanding of things would suffer a set back and along with it his compassion would also die out.[15]

But if one achieves the power of skilfulness one keeps a balance in regard to these two and does not side in with any of them (無偏黨), (does not swing to any of the extremes). The heart of great compassion does not constitute an obstruction (不妨) to his comprehension of the truth of things, and the comprehension of the truth of things does not constitute an obstruction to his great compassion. In this way, by giving rise to this power of skilfulness, (one fares on the Great Way); it is then that one achieves an entry into the true status of the bodhisattva and dwells in the ground of the irreversible. (264a)

Further, the power of skilfulness has also the import of the bodhisattva's ability to equip himself completely with all the factors of Buddhahood, not resting satisfied with only a part of it. It protects him also from the temptation to efface his individuality even before he has fulfilled his original oath, viz., to help all beings to realize the highest reality. When he has the temptation to do so, the Buddhas come and exhort him to think of the time when he first set his mind on the way, the ideal that inspired him from the beginning and the vow that he made at that time. They tell him:

You have just obtained only one (泇始得是一法門) (of the many kinds of things that go to make for Buddhahood); but there are still innumerable kinds of things which you have not yet realized; you should get back (當還) (to the determinate mode of life and once again cultivate the path) in order to collect (集) all (the further) elements of merit. (272a)

They tell him further that although he has understood the true nature of things, other people do not know it, and so it is his mission to help them on the path.[16]

The power of skilfulness lies again in his ability to institute different ways in order to enable all to comprehend the ultimate truth of things[17]. It is by virtue of his power of skilfulness that the bodhisattva enters the determinate modes of existence in the five states (現入五道), experiences the five kinds of objects of sense-pleasure (受五欲) and in that state, he leads all beings to freedom from ignorance and passion.[18]

Cultivating the perfection of wisdom, the bodhisattva sees everywhere all things as *śūnya,* sees that even *śūnyatā* is *sūnya.* At this time all the determinate modes of knowing become extinct and he realizes the unimpeded perfect wisdom. And by virtue of his great compassion and power of skilfulness, he gives rise again (還起) to all deeds of merit, and by virtue of his pure, (non-clinging) deeds (of merit) leaves no wish of his unfulfilled. (314b)

The most distinctive feature of the true status of the bodhisattva is the *anutpattika-dharma-kṣānti.* It is this that gives him the necessary strength of skilfulness. This is the basis of his unbounded compassion. If he does not efface his individuality and does not abandon beings, it is because of his unshakable comprehension of his essential bound-upness, as an individual, with all the rest. The understanding of the *śūnya*-nature of things and the unbounded compassion are only different expressions of one and the same principle, on the planes of knowledge and of feeling and will respectively. This is the characteristic of the irreversible bodhisattva.

He deeply thinks of Nirvāṇa, the unconditioned reality, and in whatever he does, he does not abandon the world. He is like the great dragon (大龍) which keeps its tail in the great ocean and its head in the sky above, and in this way causes the earth to quake, emits lightning and thunder and brings down great shower. (263c)

*Bodhisattva the great being:* Bodhisattva is also called *mahāsattva,* a great being, a being of brave heart; for he can accomplish great tasks, is devoid of any fall, devoid of any set back. On account of his heart that is great and brave (大勇心), he is called a great being. He is the highest of beings; he gives rise to great love and compassion, he establishes the Great Way, has the ability to tread the Great Path, achieves the highest state (最大處) and accomplishes all the features of great men (大人相). He teaches the Way and puts an end even to the strongest elements of passion and pride. He can exhaustively help all beings to cross over to the other shore of peace and joy. Therefore he is called a great being.[19]

Even if one has accomplished all the factors of the Way, the faculties (根), the powers (力), the factors of enlightenment (覺分), the limbs of the way (道分), the six extraordinary powers *(abhijñā)* (六神通), all kinds of concentration and meditation, as well as the power of *prajñā,* still, if one effaces one's individuality only in order to seize the ultimate Nirvāṇa, one would no doubt be deserving the respect of all people, but one would not be held in high esteem by the Buddhas. But in the case of one who is truly on the path of *bodhi,* even though he is still in the state of limitations and afflictions, is still in the womb of ignorance and passion, the womb of the three poisons, and even if one has just set his mind on the Great, unexcelled Way and has not yet done anything to cultivate it, one is nevertheless held in high esteem by all the Buddhas, as one is sure to reach the status of the true bodhisattva by progressively cultivating the six kinds of perfection and by realizing the power of skilfulness. One will then realize the knowledge of all forms, become the Buddha, and help innumerable beings to cross over to the other shore. That way, the lineage of the Buddha, the lineage of the *dharma,* and the lineage of the *saṅgha* do not become extinct.[20]

(Although in the initial stage) the bodhisattva will not have emerged from the shell of ignorance (無明殼), his voice in the teaching of *dharma* excels that of the *śrāvakas* and the *pratyekabuddhas.*[21] (267a)

*Section II*

# THE BODHISATTVA AND THE BUDDHA

## *A. The Ground and the Stages*

*The preliminaries:* The ground that the farer on the Great Way has to cover has been distinguished into several stages. Says the *Śāstra:*

The Mahāyāna is itself the ground; and the ground has ten stages; to move on from the first to the second (and so on), this is the meaning of proceeding (發趣). This is like riding the horse and moving on to the elephant; giving up the horse and mounting the elephant; riding the elephant and moving on to the dragon and giving up the elephant and mounting the dragon.[22] (411a)

As the *Sūtra* puts it, the starting point of the Great Way is the determinate existence in the three realms and the final destination is the knowledge of all forms[23] which is distinctive of Buddhahood. The different stages mark in a very broad way the progressive cultivation and the attainments of the bodhisattva during the course of his wayfaring. He progresses from one stage to another until he reaches the final destination, the attainment of Buddhahood which he accomplishes by achieving all its factors, putting an end to all the traces of *kleśa* and realizing the knowledge of all forms. This consummation he achieves in the tenth stage, which is the final stage. But the wayfaring begins with a deep thought (深心); he thinks deeply of the Way of the Buddha and deeply delights in it.[24] This deep thought, the *Śāstra* says, is really the responding to, the fixing of the mind (應) on the final aim, the *sarvākārajñatā* (薩波若), the knowledge of all forms.[25] That which is characteristic of the wayfarer in the first stage is this deep thought, deeply fixing his mind on the final aim. He develops the sense of equanimity, approaches the teacher, seeks from him the teaching of the good *dharma*, and himself also imparts it to others.[26] The *Śāstra* says that while in the first stage the wayfarer emphasizes the cultivation of charity *(dāna)*, in the second stage he emphasizes the cultivation of purity in moral conduct (*śīla*)[27] which gives him a sense of poise and joy.[28] He cultivates forbearance and compassion and does not abandon any being. He cultivates the sense of gratefulness for all that he gets in the world.[29] In the third stage the wayfarer seeks to achieve wide learning, decks his mind, the field of the Buddha, with the virtues that go to make for Buddhahood; he imparts the pure *dharma* to all; he remains free from pride and cultivates the sense of shame in regard to his own sins.[30] In the fourth stage the wayfarer cultivates the taste for solitude and does not leave it;[31] he becomes a person of few wants, learns to be contented and loathes objects of sense-pleasure and gives away all that he has. His mind does not give rise to thoughts that spring from the sense of duality.[32] Here he cultivates the ascetic practices (dhūta-gunas). The Śāstra observes that the real *dhūtaguna* is the *anutpattika-dharma-kṣānti*, for this is the result of that. The cultivation of *dhūta-guna* leads to moral purity which leads to concentration and meditation which in turn lead to the *anutpattika-dharma-kṣānti*. *Anutpattika-dharma-kṣānti* is itself the true *prajñā*.[33] In the fifth stage the wayfarer keeps away from the company of the house-holders and nuns, and keeps free from the sense of jealousy; he does not indulge in useless talk, and keeps free from pride, anger and lewdness.[34] In the next stage we are told that the wayfarer cultivates all the six *pāramitās* and does not give rise to pride, passion or misconstruction in regard to his cultivation of them; he does not entertain the thought of adopting the path of the *śrāvakas* or the *pratyekabuddhas*.[35]

*The decisive stage:* While the first six stages may be considered as preparatory, the most decisive stage in the career of the bodhisattva is counted as the seventh stage. In this stage his cultivations and attainments could be put under three broad heads. Firstly, this is the stage at which he attains complete freedom from all sense of clinging; he does not cling to "self" or "being"; does not cling to the extremes of existence and non-existence; does not entertain false notions in regard to the causal origination of things; does not cling to the constituents of individuality; remains free from clinging even in regard to the three jewels, the Buddha, the *dharma* and the *saṅgha;* and remains free from clinging even in regard to his own pure conduct. And here he turns back (轉) from all false notions, all imaginative constructions and all *kleśas,* and remains completely free from passion.[36]

Secondly, this is the stage where the bodhisattva realizes the *anutpattika-dharma-kṣānti.*[37] This is the element that is characteristic of the true status of the bodhisattva; it is by virtue of its power that he is called the irreversible,[38] the power by which he is permanently free from falling back into lower aspirations, especially the intentions of adopting the courses of the *śrāvakas* and the *pratyekabuddhas.* It is here that the bodhisattva is susceptible to the temptation to efface his individuality,[39] by overcoming which he gains the true status of the bodhisattva and thereafter he remains irreversible. This is due to the *kṣānti* that he has now realized, i.e., the capacity to sustain the comprehension of the ultimate truth of things, the *dharma* devoid of birth. This *kṣānti* develops here itself into a complete understanding *(jñāna),*[40] and the wayfarer realizes the unimpeded understanding (無礙智) in regard to all things;[41] here he comprehends the ultimately true nature of things (知諸法實相) and rejects the ultimacy of all particular natures (破分別相).[42] Here he achieves in his cultivation a balance between concentration and understanding (等定慧).[43]

Thirdly, we are told, the bodhisattva here abandons his last physical body and obtains the *dharma-kāya,* the body born of *dharmatā.* Thus the *Śāstra* says:

The bodily life in which the bodhisattva achieves the *anutpattika-dharma-kṣānti* and puts an end to all the factors of limitation is his last physical body, the last pure body of flesh. With the ceasing of this he receives the body born of *dharmatā,* unimpeded by factors of limitation. From this state onwards he does not need to be taught the factors of the Way, and even as the boat in the mid-stream of the great river Gaṅgā reaches the ocean of its own accord, without being directed by any boatman (just so does the bodhisattva in this stage reach straight to Buddhahood). (263c)

The bodhisattva even though embodied in the *dharmakāya,* still assumes the body of flesh for the purpose of helping people.[44] He is not bound by the deeds of passion, nor to the realms of determinate existence. He has freely taken on the body born of *dharmatā;* out of compassion for people, he works in the world. Having achieved spontaneity with regard to everything, a bodhisattva such as this seeks to achieve what the Buddhas can accomplish.[45]

Henceforth the bodhisattva has the power *either* to continue in the state of bodhisattva, willingly postponing his own attainment of Buddhahood and preferring to help all to become free from ignorance and passion, conflict and pain, *or,* finding that people would not listen to one who has not the majestic form and the perfection of personality which belong to the Buddhas, to proceed towards Buddhahood and achieve it in the tenth and the final stage, only in order to help all to cross the ocean of birth and death. Thus the *Śāstra* observes that there are bodhisattvas who have fulfilled the cultivation of all the elements of the Way and accomplished all the factors of Buddhahood, and yet do not themselves become Buddhas (而不作佛), but remain for ever helping other people to cross the ocean of birth and death.[46] All the same there are others who proceed towards Buddhahood. With regard to these latter, the *Śāstra* says:

Having achieved the *anutpattika-dharma-kṣānti,* one enters the status of the bodhisattva, enters straight (通達) into the ultimate truth, comprehends the true nature of the Way that is profound, mysterious, devoid of (all determinations like) getting and abandoning. This ultimate truth is not to be seized even by means of the most profound knowledge, much less can it be expressed in words. (At this time) with the heart of great compassion one deeply thinks of all beings. . . . One considers: "If I would straightaway tell them this truth of things (that I have now realized), then they would not believe (me), they would not accept what I say . . . I should now (enhance) my cultivation of the Way of the Buddha, accomplish all the elements of merit and deck my body with the thirty-two features, (only) in order to lead all beings. I should give rise to the unmeasured, limitless power of *abhijñā* (神通力), realize the Way of the Buddha and gain the ability to deal with all beings and all things with spontaneity and freedom. (In that state) even if

I should extol evil things people would readily accept them. How much more readily would they accept if I taught them the true way![46a] (721b)

The *Śāstra* observes that in the case of the bodhisattva who is in the seventh stage although the *kleśas* become extinct, still their *vāsanā*, residual impressions remain. It is by virtue of these impressions that he retains his individuality even when he receives the *dharma-kāya;* he is capable of spontaneously assuming embodiments in physical form; on account of his great compassion for all and on account of his original oath he comes back to the world (還來世間) in order to complete his attainment of the rest of the factors of Buddhahood.[47] He is different from ordinary people as his *kleśas* have become extinct; and as he has still their residual impressions continuing, he is different from the Buddha in whom they are totally extinct. The *Śāstra* observes that it is only in such a state, viz., when the *kleśas* have become extinct and the residual impressions have not yet ceased to be, that the bodhisattva can collect the elements of merit that go to make for Buddhahood.[48] Thus it says:

When the bodhisattva realizes the *anutpattika-dharma-kṣānti* he puts an end to *kleśas* and when he achieves Buddhahood he puts an end to their residual impressions. (262a)

*The consummation:* The bodhisattva's attainments in the eighth stage consist chiefly of two things: firstly, he gains the ability to penetrate into the minds of other people and know their mental constitution; this is very essential for one who wants to help them according to their own capacities and tendencies. Secondly, in this stage, he freely exercises all the *abhijñās,* the elements of extraordinary power and understanding;[49] he realizes the constant presence of the Buddha and beholds Him in His true nature (如實觀佛身).[50] Ever since he set his foot on the path, it has been his deep desire to be in His constant presence and in this he is like the calf that always likes to follow the cow, its mother.[51] And it is by such constant thought of the Buddha that he gets an entry into His way; it is the irreversible bodhisattva that will achieve this ability to be in His constant presence everywhere.[52] The bodhisattva understands that all the various kinds of merits, as well as the limitless wisdom, are achieved only through the help of the Buddhas. It is in the eighth stage of his wayfaring, after gaining the *anutpattika-dharma-kṣānti,* that the bodhisattva truly sees the body of the Buddha. "To see the Buddha (truly) is to see the *dharma-kāya.*"[53] In the ninth stage the bodhisattva realizes the ability to understand the different languages of different kinds of beings and gains also the ability to teach every one in one's own language.[54] In this stage, we are told, he prepares the abode in which he is to take birth, to assume an embodiment, for the final fulfillment, viz., the attainment of Buddhahood.[55]

In the last stage, the bodhisattva becomes verily the same as the Buddha. In this final stage, he subdues the fierce king, Māra, the temptor, the embodiment of temptations, and the Buddhas congratulate him for that. Light emerges from the top of his head. At this time all the merits that he had thus far achieved as a bodhisattva are transformed (變) into those of the Buddha; the residual impressions of his *kleśas* become extinct, he realizes the highest kind of freedom, the unimpeded, immediate freedom (無礙解脱 *ānantaryavimokṣa),* becomes completely equipped with all the factors of Buddhahood such as the ten kinds of power *(bala),* the four kinds of self-confidence *(vaiśāradya),* the four kinds of expertness *(pratisamvit),* and the eighteen kinds of the extraordinary elements *(āveṇika-dharmāḥ),* as well as the great friendliness *(maitrī)* and the great compassion *(karuṇā).* This is the tenth stage. Here he has become the Buddha himself.[56] This stage is called the stage of *dharma*-cloud *(dharma-megha* 法雲地), as the innumerable kinds of the elements *(dharma)* of the Buddha's Way arise in his mind here spontaneously (自然生), even as the great cloud ceaselessly brings down rains.[57]

The *Śāstra* observes that between the bodhisattva in the *dharma-kāya* and the Buddha there is a difference. In regard to their wisdom, while the latter is altogether sharp in understanding, the former is not so. Although even the bodhisattva with the *dharma-kāya* has cultivated all the six *pāramitās* in the true way (如實行), still his cultivation has not yet become complete; he has not yet acquired the ability to penetrate into all the ways of all things. And so he is not called the Buddha. When he has already entered the door of the knowledge of all forms, has comprehended the universal reality and with the instantaneous enlightenment (一念相應智慧) has realized the highest *samyaksambodhi*, by putting an end to all the residual impressions of *kleśas* and by realizing the power of unimpeded, absolute freedom in regard to everything, then he is called the Buddha.[58]

There is a difference between the two. But the difference is slight. It is comparable to the difference between the moon of the fourteenth day and the moon of the fifteenth day. The moon of the fourteenth day is almost complete so that when people see it they are not certain whether it is complete or not; the bodhisattva with the *dharma-kāya* is like this; he has not really reached completion and has not yet become the Buddha. The Buddha is like the full moon; there can be no doubt about His completeness.[59] Although the moon of the fourteenth day is also bright, still its brightness is not equal to that of the fifteenth day.[60] The former cannot raise the tide in the great ocean as high as the latter. In a similar way, although the bodhisattva has the true *prajñā* in its purity, still, he has not yet been able to fulfil all the factors of Buddhahood, he cannot "move" (動) the mind of all the people everywhere. But even as the full moon of the fifteenth day can cause the highest rise of the tide in the great ocean, just so, the bodhisattva, when he becomes the Buddha, can shed light everywhere, can move the minds of all the people in all regions.[61] The difference between the two is that the one is on the move towards (向道) fulfilment, while the other has already achieved fulfilment.[62]

### B. *The Nature and Constitution of the Dfferent Bodies of the Buddha*

*The view of the analysts:* The *Śāstra* deals at length with the nature of Buddhahood as well as of the wayfaring of the bodhisattva as conceived by the Sarvāstivādins, viz., Kātyāyanīputra and his followers. It points out that they do not see the Buddha in His true essence. They lay emphasis on the physical body and they have no conception of the transcendental nature of the Buddha or of the way how the Buddhas and the bodhisattvas spontaneously take on physical forms and yet remain unsullied by ignorance and passion while even living the life of human individuals. Such of the bodily and mental sufferings that the Buddha underwent while in a specific physical form they mistake to have really limited His nature as they think there is nothing further than this particular embodiment to constitute Buddhahood.[63] In other words, the *Śāstra* means to say that the analysts entertain a facile, completely positivistic, one-levelled, conception of Buddhahood; they have no idea of depth. The *Śāstra* points out that in the Great Way it is accepted that even at the very first setting forth of his mind on the path to Buddhahood the bodhisattva knows that he shall become the Buddha by virtue of which he says, "I shall become the Buddha."[64] It points out that the analysts practically limit the possibility of attaining to Buddhahood;[65] they fall short of understanding its universal possibility. They conceive the Buddha as no other than a specific person. They have no conception either of universal principle of Buddhahood or of its true nature. These shortcomings of the analysts are traceable to their basic error, the error of imagining separateness as ultimate. This limits their conception of personality. This deprives them also of an understanding of the basis of limitless wisdom and unbounded compassion. The *Śāstra* observes that they mistake the nature of *prajñāpāramitā* and say that

> The ability to divide the earth . . . into seven parts is *prajñāpāramitā* (92c–93a)

and remarks that this is arithmetic and constitutes a small part of the worldly knowledge; it is not the true *prajñāpāramitā* which consists in the comprehension of the ultimate nature of things as the unconditioned reality, the undivided being.[66]

> The true *prajñāpāramitā* is the mother of all the Buddhas, (for) it can lay bare (示) the ultimate reality of all things. This true *prajñā* (which is the same as the ultimate truth) is beyond all determinations, neither going nor coming. It cannot be obtained anywhere by looking for it. (93a)

*Buddhahood in the Great Way:* A) *The universal presence of the Buddha:* The analysts say that the arising of the Buddhahood depends on time and circumstances, depends on the soil, the race, the place of birth, and the duration of life.[67] But although when the Buddha assumes a specific embodiment He is naturally born under particular circumstances, neither the specific form nor these particular circumstances limit or exhaust the true nature of the Buddha. The *Śāstra* says that in truth the Buddhas are present always (and everywhere).[68] The true body of the Buddha is the body of limitless wisdom and unbounded compassion. The Buddhas always have compassion for every body. Wherever there are old-age, disease and death, wherever there are lewdness, anger and stupidity, there the Buddhas are always born and in the Great Way this truth of the universal presence of the Buddha is taught in various ways.[69] If in spite of it there still prevails suffering everywhere, says the *Śāstra,* it is because the accumulated dirt of the sinful deeds of the ignorant which they have committed since innumerable *kalpas* is too thick, too deep. So people do not see the true merits of the Buddha; they do not see Him. But does this not mean that merit and wisdom are everywhere by themselves and that the freedom of people depends on these? What has the Buddha to do with it? The *Śāstra* answers that although merit and wisdom are universal principles they come to light only through the Buddhas who are in fact their very embodiments. It is thus that the awakening of people to the truth of things depends on them. For instance, although everybody has eyes, when the sun does not arise no one can see anything. And one cannot say "I have my eyes and what have I to do with the sun?"[70]

When one's heart is pure then does one see the Buddha; when one's heart is dirty then one is not able to see Him. (126b)

The Buddha knows the time when one's faculties have matured and then He renders His help. (126c)

B) *The physical body and the dharma-body of the Buddha:* The *Śāstra* strongly remarks that the analysts exaggerate the importance of bodily features and says that there is nothing special about these to say that they are only of the Buddha. They are found even in other great men like the emperor, although in the latter they cannot be said to be complete. In the Buddha, however, they arise as the fruit of the long cultivation of the kinds of perfection, under the guiding light of the perfection of wisdom; only then do these features become complete (具足) and these are specially of the Buddha. The essential point is the cultivation of the wayfaring in the light of the perfection of wisdom. The others cultivate merely the acts of charity etc. devoid of the perfection of wisdom. In them these features have not attained to completeness.[71]

The *Śāstra* observes that in the Great Way the thirty-two bodily features are taught in regard to the path of merit; and the devoidness of features has been taught in regard to the path of wisdom. In regard to the physical body (生身) these features have been taught while the devoidness of features has been taught in regard to the *dharma*-body *(dharmakāya* 法身). The physical body of the Buddha is decked with the thirty-two features and the eighty minor signs, whereas the *dharmakāya* of the Buddha consists of the ten powers (十力), the four elements of self-confidence (無畏), the four elements of expertness (無礙智), and the eighteen extraordinary elements (不共法 *āveṇikadharmāḥ)*.[72] To these there must be added the element of great love and compassion and the six kinds of *abhijñā*, as constituting the *dharmakāya*.[73] The *dharmakāya* is not anything substantial; it is also conditionally originated. It arises as the fruit of long cultivation in the path of wisdom and compassion; it arises from the togetherness of many factors.[74] These elements that constitute the *dharmakāya* being undefiled are truly no occasions for clinging; even these are not anything substantial; these are also conditionally originated and impermanent. In their ultimate nature they are not anything determinate; they are the indeterminate *dharma*, the unconditioned reality itself. In that nature they enter the *tathatā, dharmadhātu, bhūtakoṭi*.[75]

In the world for the sake of those who take delight in seeing the beautiful physical form and through that set their minds on the path, the body of the thirty-two features is manifested. This is the mundane truth, but this is not to deny the ultimate truth of the indeterminate *dharma*, nor the conditionedness of the determinate. The Buddha takes on this embodiment of the thirty-two features and the eighty minor signs only for the sake of those who take delight in beholding Him in that form and this He does as an expedient to create in them an incentive to fare on the Way. Such people do not feel delight in a bodily form which is not comely. "Even the delicious food placed in an unclean pot is something in which people do not take delight." It is like a precious thing tied to a stinking piece of hide.[76]

By means of the bodily features the Buddha benefits the dull in mind, and by means of wisdom He benefits the sharp in mind. By means of the elements that deck the mind, He opens the door to Nirvāṇa, while by means of the elements that deck the body He lays open the door to pleasure in the world of gods and men. By means of the elements that deck the mind He enables people to enter the threefold door of freedom; by means of the elements that deck the body He plucks out all people from the ways of evil (viz., from greed, anger and stupidity). By means of the elements that deck the mind He sets people free from their imprisonment in the three realms of determinate existence.[77]

It is to be noted that the factors that constitute the *dharmakāya* of the Buddha, the elements that "deck the mind," viz., the ten powers etc. are precisely the different forms of wisdom and compassion. The *Śāstra* observes that associated with the great compassion (合大悲) these are taught in the light of the universal reality, the *dharma* that is devoid of birth and death.[78] It further observes that all the ten powers of the Buddha are the powers of wisdom, kinds of knowledge; they are the ten different ways in which the knowledge of the true nature of things functions in Him.[79] By virtue of these ten kinds of knowledge, the Buddha can move the world, assume different bodily forms, save all people and yet can exceed all these acts.[80] Even all the eighteen extraordinary elements (不共法) are only the *prajñā* itself in different forms.[81] The *Śāstra* would say that it is a mistake to think, as the analysts headed by Kātyāyaniputra do, that the love and compassion of the Buddhas are defiled elements. The Buddhas have the ability to keep free from clinging to individuality (離衆生想) and yet help all in the spirit of great compassion.[82] The *Śāstra* points out that the Great Compassion is the root of the Way of the Buddha.[83] The constitutive factors of the *dharmakāya* are the limitless wisdom and the unbounded compassion; these are the different phases, different expressions of the ultimate truth of the undivided being on the plane of mundane life. It is as wisdom and compassion that *paramārtha* is relevant to *vyavahāra,* in regard to wayfaring.

*CHAPTER XII*

# CONCLUSION

*The import of śūnyatā: positive and negative:* It is hoped that it is amply borne out in the present work that *śūnyatā* as negation is a rejection not of *vyavahāra* nor of *paramārtha,* but of one's perversions and clingings with regard to things.[1] The basic perversion is mistaking the unreal for the real, seizing the conditioned as unconditioned, the relative as self-contained; this is the root of clinging. Negation is not an end in itself; its end is the revelation of *tathatā.* With the rejection of the falsely imagined nature, the true nature of things comes to light. As the true nature of things, *śūnyatā* is *tathatā* which is comprehended at different levels, mundane and ultimate. The way that the Mādhyamika employs to reveal the true nature of things is negative; but the truth that is thus revealed is the nature of things as they are. At the level of the mundane truth the error lies in imagining the substantiality of the non-substantial, the self-containedness of the relative and the truth that is revealed by rejecting this false imagination is that all things are essentially relative; the basic elements of existence are not substances, but kinds of conditioned becoming. The error in regard to the ultimate truth consists in imagining conditionedness, relativity, as itself the ultimate nature of things and the truth that is revealed by the rejection of this error is that the conditionedness of the conditioned is not ultimate, that in their ultimate nature, the conditioned and the contingent are themselves the unconditioned reality, the Nirvāṇa. Relativity as mundane truth has its bearing not only in regard to the basic elements of existence, the conventional entities, but also in regard to concepts and conceptual systems. *Śūnyatā* as criticism lays bare the basic truth with regard to all conceptual systems, their origin and their end. These constitute essentially expressions of man's thirst for the real and their end is to enable one to comprehend truly and fully the import of the sense of the real in the context of *vyavahāra*. These are not ends in themselves. Again, as specific systems they are not absolute, not all-inclusive and ultimate. Every system, as a systematic expression of the fundamental nature of things from a specific standpoint, has its own specific constitution and its own function and purpose. It is in this light, with this understanding, that the wise institute devices to convey the truth of things.

The Mādhyamika philosophy is no substitute for any specific system of constructive metaphysics. Its essential purpose is to lay bare the basic truth that underlies all such systems, in fact, of the system-building tendency in man. It is meant to reveal the root of all his activities, theoretic and practical; this root is the thirst for the unconditioned, the sense of the real.[2] The Mādhyamika criticism is in order to enable every one to set free one's basic urge from its moorings in abstractions. It is his intention to reveal the determinate nature of every specific system, by realizing which, one ceases to lay an exclusive claim in regard to one's own way. At the same time there is revealed also the uniqueness and the individuality of every system, its nature, its purpose and function. The Mādhyamika is not only not opposed to system-building, but he would himself institute systems, not as ends in themselves, but as the means to widen one's understanding, deepen one's comprehension. Analysis, synthesis and criticism as well as the different constructive systems have all their respective places and functions in this comprehensive understanding, which is comparable to *ākāśa,* the very principle of accommodation depending on which everything lives and moves and fulfils its being.[2a] It is the revelation of this all-comprehensive nature of true understanding that is the basic meaning of *śūnyatā* in regard to views; this is the underlying idea of the Mādhyamika's rejection of all views and not having any view of his own.

That of the Mādhyamika negative criticism was mistaken even during the lifetime of Nāgārjuna is borne out by the fact that he devotes a whole chapter in the *Kārikā* (ch. XXIV) to say that *śūnyatā* is not mere negation; this we have already seen. Of the Buddhists in his days it was chiefly the Sarvāstivādins that misconstrued *śūnyatā* and of the non-Buddhists the Vaiśeṣikas whose system is in many respects close to the pluralism and the realism of the former joined them. Nyāya accused the Mādhyamika of landing in negativism.[3] It seems that there was a negativism of an extreme kind during the time of Nāgārjuna, and it is to them that the *Kārikā* refers when it says that while *śūnyatā* has been taught as the remedy of all *dṛṣṭis,* those who cling to *śūnyatā* itself are indeed incurable.[3a] It was chiefly the realists who found fault with the Mādhyamika and confused him with the extreme negativist.

*The Mādhyamika and the Advaita Vedānta:* It is possibile that some of the followers of the Mādhyamika line of Buddhist philosophy laid an overemphasis on the negative criticisms which might have led them to tend to minimize the importance of *vyavahāra,* but this is not the case with Śāntideva or Candrakīrti.[4] But on the whole, one can see that by the time of Candrakīrti the import of *śūnyatā* as *tathatā* was getting lost sight of. It is difficult to find in the later Mādhyamika writings anything like the portion in the *Śāstra* (ch. XXXII) which deals with *tathatā, dharmadhātu* and *bhūtakoṭi.* And it seems that it was still the Buddhist philosophers of Mahāyāna that kept the absolutist line of thought alive in India during the early centuries of the Christian era prior to Gauḍapāda, when Vedānta, especially the Advaita, does not seem to have come to the picture.[5] Despite the fact that Gauḍapāda belonged to the Brahmanical tradition, his closeness to the absolutist line of Buddhist Philosophy cannot be doubted.[6] In the light of our text, the *Śāstra,* the picture of the state of Indian philosophy, especially of its absolutistic trend in those centuries, inclusive of even Śaṅkara, takes a different form.

The distinction of *saguṇabrahman* and *nirguṇabrahman* is basic to the philosophy of Śaṅkara. *Saguṇabrahman, brahman* with *māyā,* which is his own power of creation, is the ground of the universe. This *brahman* is spoken of in terms of a personal god, *Īśvara.* He is the creator of the universe; he is its material as well as its efficient cause. He is the all-knowing, all-powerful, the free, eternal being. The entire world proceeds from Him. Although Śaṅkara does accept a personal god, *Īśvara,* as the lord and the creator of the universe, the culmination of his thought did not lie there. For him the account of creation was only a means of realizing the ultimate reality, the *brahman,* as the true nature of all beings as well as of the entire world.[7] *Ātman* is *brahman;* but by this "*ātman*" he did not mean the *ātman* of the Vaiśeṣikas and the Mīmāṃsakas or even of the Sāṅkhyas; for him it meant the true nature, the essential nature *(pāramārthikasvarūpa)* of the individual.[8]

Here we have the meeting point of the Mādhyamika and the Advaita Vedānta, viz., in regard to the ultimate truth, not only in regard to its being devoid of all determinations but in being the very real, essential, nature, the ultimately true nature of all things and of all individuals. The Mādhyamika as well as the Advaita Vedānta speaks of the immanence of the real in man as well as of its transcendence. In regard to the ultimacy of the unconditioned, which is the basic conception of absolutism, there is hardly any difference between the two. In this regard, one can say that the one accepts or denies *ātman* as much as the other; both deny *ātman* as a separate substantial entity inhabiting the body of each individual, and both accept *ātman* in the sense of the essential nature, the *svarūpa* or the *svabhāva,* of the individual as well as of all things. There should be no difficulty in appreciating this, provided one makes a deference for the differences in the traditional usage of these terms. So in regard to the ultimacy of the unconditioned, which is what even the equation, *ātman=brahman* means, there is hardly any difference between the two.[9]

But the Advaita Vedānta as a specific formulation of this basic truth is different from the Mādhyamika. Advaita Vedānta provides a positive constructive system on the pattern of the theistic, personal god, as well as on the subject-object *(viṣaya-viṣayī)* pattern, accepting and emphasizing the immanence of the real in man, as well as its transcendence. But this is only as a means to the realization of the ultimate truth; where all is one and undivided, there is no construction and no metaphysics. Silence is the highest truth.[10] Nāgārjuna does not give us a system of constructive metaphysics; but he lays bare the possibility of different formulations of the basic truth, each of which could function as a basis for a specific conceptual system.[11] The formulation that within the heart of every being as one's very real nature there is the *tathatā,* the unconditioned *dharma,* is for him only a way of expressing the basic truth of the ultimacy of the unconditioned. His fundamental emphasis is on the need to overcome the false sense of the real, the error of misplaced absoluteness, and in this light, for him the specific formulations have all their respective places and functions, while not any of them is absolutely true nor any end in itself. His interest did not consist in offering any system of metaphysics. It lay in bringing to light the basic insight that underlies the construction of all such systems, of any system. In this the Mādhyamika philosophy is on a footing different from the Advaita Vedānta which obviously emphasizes and brings to prominence a specific formulation of the basic truth while not overlooking the all-important truth of the non-ultimacy of such a formulation, viz., that it is a means and not an end in itself. In a similar way the Mādhyamika philosophy is on a footing different even from Vijñānavāda. Vijñānavāda also attempts to formulate a specific metaphysical system, emphasizing the subjective element in cognition and built on the central conception of *ālayavijñāna,* the center and the basis of the course of personal life. But certainly even Vijñānavāda does not overlook the ultimate truth of the undivided being.[12]

*The Mādhyamika in the early Chinese thought:* (I) *Kumārajīva:* It was Kumārajīva who introduced Nāgārjuna to China. Our only source for gathering some idea of his own thought is his correspondence with Hui-yüan now preserved in the Chinese Collection under the title 大乘大義章 (Exposition of the Great Meaning of Mahāyāna).[13] The major part of the correspondence is devoted to an elucidation of the nature of *dharmakāya.* There are also discussed the Sarvāstivāda doctrine of elements, their atomism, the meaning of *tathatā, dharmadhātu* and *bhūtakoṭi,* the nature of the process of cognition and the all-inclusive learning or cultivation (徧學) of the bodhisattva. The main features of Kumārajīva's thought have been set forth by Professor T'ang Yung-t'ung as follows:[14]

(1) Kumārajīva laid special emphasis on the *Prajñāpāramitā-sūtras* and on the works of Nāgārjuna for whom he had great respect; he always looked to these, especially to the *Śāstra* as his source for insight.[15]

(2) He deeply criticised the Sarvāstivāda doctrine of elements. It may be recalled that he was first a student of Sarvāstivāda and later he rejected

it to embrace the Mahāyāna.[16] It is surmised that he did his translation of *Satyasiddhi-śāstra* probably because he felt that this latter text could serve as a stepping stone to Mahāyāna by way of its criticism of the Sarvāstivāda.[17] In regard to Sarvāstivādins the main point of his criticism was that they failed to distinguish clearly between the true and the illusory, the real and the unreal; they clung to the atomic elements as ultimate, whereas in fact there is not even the name of atoms in the teachings of the Buddha.[18]

(3) It was Kumārajīva who for the first time made it very clear in China that the belief in the soul as a substantial entity that passes through states of birth and death while yet remaining itself intact is a basic misunderstanding in regard to the Buddhist doctrine. Prior to Kumārajīva the notion that such a belief in soul formed an integral part of Buddhist philosophy was very prevalent there. The doctrine of *dharmakāya* was understood to mean the eternality of soul. Kumārajīva made it clear that in its ultimate nature the *dharmakāya* is the same as Nirvāṇa, the indeterminate *dharma*.[19]

(4) Kumārajīva's system emphasized complete *śūnyatā*. But he made it clear that this did not mean non-existence, or nothingness, or absolute extinction. He pointed out that *śūnyatā* is in truth neither existence nor non-existence and that in Mahāyāna it has been taught in order to remove the false sense of absolute existence. *Sūnyatā* (as relativity) itself should not be clung to as the ultimate nature of things.[20] While in Hīnayāna impermanence means just the arising and perishing nature of things, in Mahāyāna the teaching of impermanence is intended to bear out the ultimate nature of things as indeterminate, devoid of birth and death. Hīnayāna takes impermanence to mean momentary existence, but this is only to fall back upon the false notion of eternalism, for if a thing can really exist for one moment, it should be that it could exist for all time. The truth is that even when things seem to exist they do not stay, they pass away. It is this passing away of things, which is their peristent nature, that is the true meaning of staying; and it is this awareness of the passing away of things that should awaken one to the ultimate nature of things as completely *śūnya*. In Mahāyāna

complete *śūnyatā* is the ultimate significance, the profound meaning of impermanence.[21]

Again, the ultimate nature of things as indeterminate should be distinguished from utter nihilism. Indeterminateness means the indescribability of the ultimate nature; to give rise to conceptual constructions in regard to this nature and to cling to them is to lose one's comprehension of it.[22] Further, it is this clinging to the determinate as ultimate, it is this seizing the ultimates of analysis as ultimate in reality, that is at the root of the belief in the atomic elements as eternal and uncaused as well as at the root of the belief in the soul as a substantial entity. Both these errors are traceable to the same root, viz., the mistaking of the conditioned as unconditioned, the determinate as ultimate, seizing the imaginary as true. This is like clinging to the moon in the water as the true moon.[23] The ultimately true nature of things, the complete *śūnyatā,* is the same as Nirvāṇa, the inexpressible *dharma.* But this is not to say that it is something apart from and outside the conditioned, contingent entities; it is the very nature of things themselves.[24] As Kumārajīva expressed it in one of the stanzas which he wrote in reply to the query of Hui-yüan, "With the realization of the complete *śūnyatā* (which is the same as Nirvāṇa, the true nature of things), the mind attains the unconditioned joy (which is the true joy)."[25]

(II) *Seng-chao (僧肇):* It can be seen that Kumārajīva was practically setting forth the essentials of Nāgārjuna's philosophy in his correspondence with Hui-yüan. It is necessary to remember that his main sources in this regard were not confined only to the texts that emphasize the negative criticism. It was to the *Śāstra* that he always looked up for inspiration and guidance. The negative side was developed in that line of Chinese Buddhism which emphasized the Three Treatises; but it is interesting that even here the importance of the *Śāstra* was not in any way minimized. Chi-tsang (吉藏), the foremost among those who belonged to this line, always quoted in his works profusely from the *Śāstra* and one of the main things that he emphasized was the skilfulness of non-clinging: Without violating the principle of derived names the wise still teach the ultimate truth of things.[26] Chi-tsang acknowledges his kinship with Seng-chao, one of the two foremost disciples of Kumārajīva.[27] Seng-chao utilizes the negative arguments of the *Kārikā* in order to prove that things do not move, the "Immutability of Things," "the rushing streams do not flow."[28] His purpose is to show that "rest is coincident with motion and that consequently things are immutable."[29] It seems that this involves two points: I) to find peace in activity, to realize Nirvāṇa in *saṃsāra;*[30] and II) that the results of one's deeds are not lost, but preserved.[31] Seng-chao does not seem to have drawn clearly the distinction between eternity or timelessness and the persistence of things in time, especially of the results of deeds done in the past; and it seems that lack of clarity in this regard led him to a position very much like that of the Sarvāstivādins, who hold that everything remains permanently in its own nature, the old and the new ever remain undestroyed.[32] But Seng-chao clarified the meaning of Nirvāṇa and of *prajñā,* showing that *prajñā* of the highest kind is not the same as the ordinary knowledge;[33] yet it is not divorced from things. It is the highest kind of illumination, in which all the traces of the thought of duality and the thought of self are overcome and the traces of passion are extinct. True *prajñā* is void. "Though void, it *(prajñā)* illumines; though it illumines, it is void." Again, "Wisdom knows not, yet it illumines the deepest profundity. . . . Wisdom illumines the Mystery beyond mundane affairs. Yet, though Wisdom lies outside affairs, it never lacks them. Though Spirit lies beyond the world, it stays ever within it."[34]

Nirvāṇa is not apart from *saṃsāra* and The perfect being, free "from illusion, filled with cosmic vision, . . . is able to reach the Root from which all creation sprang, to combine the din of the world with the calm of Nirvāṇa."[35] Again, Nirvāṇa "compasses end and beginning, and leads all creatures to their predestined ends. It nourishes them all, and far as it reaches, it overlooks nothing. Wide as the ocean what does not come from it?"[36] Seng-chao emphasised again the way of "attaining it by not attaining." "It is not attained by 'attaining.' "[37]

(III) *Chi-tsang:* These points on *prajñā* and Nirvāṇa that Seng-chao brought to light, are precisely as they have been set forth in the *Prajñā-*

*pāramitāsūtras* and the *Śāstra*. And it is these, again that Chi-tsang also brought to the fore as the essential points in the philosophy of the Mādhyamika, by drawing attention to the need for non-clinging which is the skilfulness of the wise. His theory of double truth[38] is an extension or an elaboration of the central teaching of the Mādhyamika, viz., of not clinging to existence or to non-existence, not clinging to the *śūnya* or to the *aśūnya*. To cling to the false notion of existence is the error of the common people (and of the Sarvāstivādins) and to cling to *śūnyatā,* which Chi-tsang takes as clinging to Nirvāṇa, is the error of the *śrāvakas* and the *pratyekabuddhas* and to cling to the comprehension of neither existence nor non-existence is the error of the clinging bodhisattva.[39] The comprehension that is truly non-clinging is "neither mundane nor ultimate, neither birth and death nor Nirvāṇa, not even the negation of mundane or ultimate, nor of birth and death, nor of Nirvāṇa." It is this that is the true awakening.[40] Neither birth and death nor Nirvāṇa, this is the ultimate truth of things.[41] But this is really not a rejection of anything.[42] The wise who are skilful do not reject anything. "By not destroying, not violating the truth of derived name, the wise teach the ultimate truth of things." Not moving from the *sambodhi,* they establish everything.[43] In fact nothing is denied, for the things of derived name are themselves in their ultimate nature the unconditioned reality. Here Chi-tsang quotes Seng-chao to the effect that things of the world are neither truly, i.e., absolutely existent nor purely illusory, and so the rejection is not of the things themselves.[44] It is the realization of the nature and distinction of the mundane and the ultimate truths, not clinging to these, that is the Middle Way. Chi-tsang's thought is certainly one of the very best examples of the Mādhyamika Way. His emphasis also is on the negative way, the way by which to reject at different levels the tendency to cling, and to realize the truly ultimate, the undivided reality. The rejection of clinging is the negative import of *śūnyatā* and it is this that is emphasised in the School of the Three Treatises (三論宗).[45]

(IV) *T'ien-t'ai* (天臺) *and Hua-yen* (華嚴): The positive import of *śūnyatā,* viz., the *tathatā* came to be emphasised in the T'ien-t'ai School which takes as its basic texts the works of Nāgārjuna, especially, the *Śāstra* along with the *Saddharmapuṇḍarīka-sūtra*.[46] It is to be noted that the philosophy of Nāgārjuna allows for conceiving the real as the ground of the universe. This is in fact an essential import of *dharmadhātu;* the real is the true root of things; it is the immanent as well as the transcendent; it is within the heart of all beings; it is the ultimate goal of the whole course of life. But with Nāgārjuna this is not the ultimate truth; this is a way of expressing the essential nature of things, viz., that in their ultimate nature they are themselves the unconditioned reality. The conception of *dharmadhātu,* viz., that the real is the ground of the universe, comes to be emphasised in the T'ien-T'ai School, and this is elaborated by the use of the conception of *tathāgatagarbha* as found in *The Awakening of Faith*.[47] There comes to be in it a mixture of Vijñānavāda also.[48] While the distinction of the three characters[49] or natures, viz., the real *(pariniṣpanna* 眞實), the dependent *(paratantra* 依他) and the illusory *(parikalpita* 分别), are framed in terms of Vijñānavāda, the ten kinds of *tathatā* we are told have their basis in the *Saddharmapuṇḍarīka*; these latter bear close relation to the nine kinds of inferior *tathatā* that the *Śāstra* speaks of.[50] The central doctrine of T'ien-t'ai is the "Integration of All Things," i.e., that "all things and events of the phenomenal world, despite their manifold variety, are in a state of harmonious integration (攝), one with another."[51] This is not different from the teaching of the *Prajñāpāramitā-sūtras* when they say that everything "tends" to everything else.[52] We have already seen its place in the Philosophy of Nāgārjuna; it is an essential import of *śūnyatā* as relativity. This is also the synthesis of the real and the phenomenal, as conveyed in the teaching that the real is not anything apart from the world, it is the world itself seen with the eye of wisdom. Again, when the world is seen as distinct from the real the latter is the ground of the former. These ideas come to be developed in T'ien-t'ai. Again, in the true spirit of the Mādhyamika we have the advice, "Only eliminate the ills but not the things. The ills consist in the sensory clingings but not in the great functioning itself."[52a] . . . "we can remain within that world without that fact causing any impediment to ourselves."[53] These features more or less hold good even in the case of Hua-yen.[54] The six characters[55] describe the mundane characters of things as each having its own nature and function and yet being essentially related to all the rest; the ten principles or theories (門)[56] state the dependence of the entire world on the *dharmadhātu,* the true substance, the ground, of which the world is the appearance as well as the indescribability of the relation between the world and its ground in absolute terms. The ruling ideas of both these schools, as Professor Chan puts it, are I) the synthesis of the noumenon and the phenomenon and 2) idealism.[57] Of these one is traceable to the Mādhyamika and the other, to Vijñānavāda.

But it must be noted that in Hua-yen and in T'ien-t'ai one seems to miss a stress on the negative import of *śūnyatā,* which is prominent in the 'School of the Three Treatises' (三論宗). It is the real as the ground of the universe that comes to prominence in T'ien-t'ai and Hua-yen and it is the integration, the synthesis not only among the "ten thousand things" but also of the noumenon and the phenomenon that has come to be emphasised there.

(V) *The Ch'an (Zen)* (禪): That the real is inexpressible, that the fundamental nature of every being is the indeterminate *dharma,* the Nirvāṇa, which is the true Buddhahood, these are essential points in the philosophy of *prajñāpāramitā.* The aspiration of the farer on the Way is to become the Buddha. The wayfarer does indeed cultivate the way; but from another point of view he does not cultivate any way; he "cultivates by not cultivating." Again, he does indeed attain the *bodhi;* but from another point of view he does not attain anything; non-attainment is his attainment. Again, while words, concepts, determinate modes of expression belong to the world of duality, the non-dual *dharma,* the ultimate truth lies beyond concepts; words do not reach there; the mind and all its functionings cease. There is really neither the known nor the knower nor even the act of knowing, in the ultimate truth; it is the utterly inexpressible *dharma.* And yet it is the skilfulness of the wise that they teach the ultimate truth by means of concepts and conventional entities, without violating the true nature of things. As we have seen above, these are some of the salient features in the philosophy of Nāgārjuna. We have here the unconditioned, transcendent nature of the ultimate and the conditioned, contingent nature of the mundane held in harmony. It is in the achieving of this harmony that the skilfulness of the wise consists.

The Ch'an (禪) School[58] laid its emphasis on one of the two sides of these salient points and came to hold more and more to direct transmission than to the written scripture, to the inexpressibility of the ultimate truth rather than to the usefulness of communication by means of words, concepts, conceptual formulations. The Ch'an School accepts the real as the very nature of all; and so in truth it is not anything "attainable." In the last resort nothing is gained; in truth, the way cannot be cultivated, and it is not of any use to rely on the scriptural teachings.[59] It must not be forgotten that in all this Ch'an is speaking of what constitutes the highest truth in the Way the Buddha showed. In this it is directly traceable to the *prajñāpāramitā* and to the philosophy of Nāgārjuna. But it was the negative import of *śūnyatā* in regard to the ultimate truth that the Ch'an chose to take up and develop. Even there it differed from the School of the Three Treatises in so far as it chose the way of direct insight and sudden illumination and did not see any use or meaning in reasoned discourse on the truth of things. It teaches us to abandon words which are "useless furniture."[60] "Simply void your entire mind: this is to have unpolluted wisdom."[61] What the Ch'an means here is the skilfulness of non-clinging; it is the "cultivation through non-cultivation";[62] it is an abandoning not of cultivation but of one's clinging to it. This is to "be amid the phenomenal and yet devoid of the phenomenal."[63] By a way rather different from the other schools Ch'an seeks to reach the same goal of "synthesising the sublime with the common."[64]

*The spirit of the Mādhyamika philosophy:* It is essential to bear in mind that the philosophy of Nāgārjuna has no disdain for *vyavahāra* where it is that thought and language hold. The main purpose of the negative arguments in the *Kārikā* was to expose the self-contradictions inherent in the position of the Sarvāstivādins who clung to the determinate as ultimate, the relative as self-contained. This is the error of misplaced absoluteness. The major function of the negative arguments in the

*Kārikā* is to reveal the relativity of the mundane; the question of the ultimate reality constitutes a minor part. It is the error in regard to the mundane nature of things that needs to be cleared up first. With the revelation of the essentially conditioned, non-substantial, relative nature of things, the tendency to cling might again operate, tending to end in negativism. This is an error in regard to the ultimate nature of things and it is in regard to this error that the *śūnyatā* of *śūnyatā* has been taught. What is sought to be revealed thereby is the non-ultimacy of the relative in their relative nature; the conditionedness of the conditioned is not their ultimate nature. The unconditioned is again not anything apart from the conditioned. The ultimate truth about the conditioned is that it is itself the unconditioned reality, the Nirvāṇa. This is the basic teaching of the Mādhyamika. The very important import of this truth is that to realize the ultimate is not to abandon the mundane but to learn to see it "with the eye of wisdom." To live in the world is itself to realize the Nirvāṇa. What needs to be abandoned is one's perversions and false clingings. It is clear that this applies not only to actual life but to words, concepts, understanding, systems of understanding.

The conditioned is the unconditioned. This is indeed a paradox, but the paradoxical nature of this statement is just as it should be; for in this there is a "confusion," a mixing up of two orders of being. This mixing up is only a reflection of what we ourselves are. Man is at cross roads. He is aware of the unconditioned and knows also the conditioned. With the unconditioned in his aim he has his concourse in the "rounds of birth and death," the world of mundane existence. It is this sense of the unconditioned that acts as the very spring of all his activities, theoretic and practical. It is this that lends meaning to the otherwise mute. The wise do not abandon things saying that these lead them to contradictions and conflict; they preserve these and abandon the roots of conflict, viz., ignorance and passion. Having abandoned these they freely use concepts, construct even conceptual systems if need be in order to root out conflict and suffering. Opposing statements do not land them in conflict for they are free from clinging. Suffering of life does not prompt them to abandon life; they live their lives putting an end to the root of suffering. It is their mission to help all to attain to the

Highest Good. The height to which the Mādhyamika would take us ultimately is one which is the meeting point of all systems. And it is also the meeting point of the root and the branch, the noumenon and the phenomenon. It is an understanding that is non-exclusive. It is a comprehensive attitude where one takes interest in every little thing without being confined anywhere; for here one is aware of the place and function of everything in the grand system as well as of its ultimate meaning. It is this that the *Śāstra* means when it says that not violating the derived name the wise teach the ultimate truth. To use the language of the *Śāstra,* the wise are like the dragon that keeps its tail in the ocean and its head in the sky and brings down showers on earth.[65]

# BIBLIOGRAPHY

I. *The Works of Nāgārjuna* that are (I) available in orginal Sanskrit (II) attributed to him in Chinese and/or Tibetan traditions as well as (III) their restorations and retranslations by modern authors have all been noted on pp. 34–37.

On life and work of Nāgārjuna cp. also 1) Mochizuki Shinkō, *Bukkyō Daijiten,* vol. V, pp. 4995a–4997b and Winternitz, *History of Indian Literature* (Calcutta University, 1933), vol. II, pp. 341–351.

II. *Prajñāpāramitā-sūtras, editions and Chinese translations: 1) Pañcavimśati-sāhasrikā and 2) Aṣṭasāhasrikā:*

1) *Pañcavimsatisāhasrikā-prajñāpāramitā,* ed. Nalinaksha Dutt (Calcutta Oriental Series), London, 1934. This is a rearranged version of the original *Pañcavimśati* to suit to *Abhisamayālaṅkāra* of Maitreya *(abhisamayālaṅkārānusāreṇa samśodhitā).* Still, except for the differences in division that are due to rearrangement, the Skt. text closely follows 摩訶般波若羅密經, T. 223, which is Kumārajīva's translation of *Pañcavimśati.* The text edited by Nalinaksha Dutt is incomplete; only the first *abhisamaya* is published which corresponds up to the end of *prakaraṇa* XXVI (無生品) of T. 223.

There are two complete translations of *Pañcavimśati* in Chinese:

I) Taishō 221 放光般若經, tr. Mokṣala (291 A.D.); see Bagchi, *Le Canon Bouddhique en Chine,* vol. I, p. 121.

II) T. 223, 摩訶般若波羅密經, tr. Kumārajiva (403–404 A.D.); see Bagchi, *op., cit.,* p. 185.

The *Mahā-prajñāpāramitā-śāstra* is a commentary on the original *Pañcavimśati;* both this *Sūtra* and the *Śāstra* were translated by Kumārajiva. The *Śāstra* appears along with the *Sūtra* (T. 223) in T. 1509.

III) T. 222 光讃經 is an incomplete translation of *Pañcavimśati* covering only up to the end of *prakaraṇa* XXIX (穌花品) of T. 223.

2) *Aṣṭasāhsrikā-prajñāpāramitā,* ed. Rajendralala Mitra, Bibliotheca Indica, Calcutta, 1888; the text of *Aṣṭa.* is incorporated in the *Abhisamayālankārāloka,* ed. U Wogihara, Tokyo, 1932–1935; this version is considered to be the earliest version of the Prajñāpārmitā; see N. Dutt, *Aspects,* pp. 39–40. The Sanskrit text of *Aṣṭa.* (ed. R. Mitra) is consulted in the present work specially in regard to that portion of T 223 for which no corresponding Skt portion has been published.

The earliest Chinese translation of *Aṣṭa.* was by Lokakṣema (179 A.D.); 道行般若經 (T. 224); see Bagchi, *op. cit.,* pp. 39–40.

Cp. also:

I) T. 225, 大明度經, tr. Chih-chien (d. 273 A.D.); see Bagchi, *op. cit.*, p. 289;

II) T. 227, 小品般若波羅密經, tr. Kumārajīva (408 A.D.); see Bagchi, *op. cit.*, p. 289;

III) T. 228, 佛說佛母出生三法藏般若波羅密多經 tr. Dānapāla (10th cent. A.D.); see Bagchi, *op. cit.*, vol. II, p. 600. The Taishō edition adduces Skt. parallels in the foot notes, T. 225, 227 and 228 as well as T. 224 are translations of *Aṣṭa.*

For a short account of the different versions of the *Prajñāpāramitā-sūtras,* see Prof. Étienne Lamotte, *Le Traité de la Grande Vertu de Sagesse,* vol. I, pp. vii–ix; Prof. T.R.V. Murti, *The Central Philosophy of Buddhism* (Allen & Unwin, 1955), pp. 83–84.

Prof. Koun Kajiyoshi in his 原始般若經の研究 (山喜房佛書林, 東京, 1944) has tried to trace the original version of the *Prajñāpāramitā-sūtra* by comparing the different versions that are now available.

III. *Editions of the Buddhist Canon in Chinese:*

I) *Taishō-shinshū-daizōkyō* (大正新修大藏經), ed. Professor Takakusu and Professor Watanabe, Tokyo, 1922–1933 (abbreviated in the present work as T.); and

II) *Hsü-t'sang-ching* (續藏經), Supplement to the Kyoto Edition of the Chinese Tripitaka (pub. Zokyo Shoin Tokyo, 1905–1912), reprinted, Commercial Press, 1923.

III) 藏要, publ. 支那內學院 is an excellent annotated edition of selected texts, including 大智度論 (巻 1–34) and 十住毗婆沙論 (巻 1–15).

IV. *Modern Catalogues and Indices:*

1) *Shōwa Hōbō Sō Mokuroku* (昭和法寶總目錄) 大正新修大藏經, 別巻, 1929.

2) *Busshō Kaisetsu Daijiten* (佛書解說大辭典, 大東出版社, 東京, 1931)

3) Nanjō Bunyū, *Catalogue of the Chinese Translation of the Buddhist Tripiṭaka,* Oxford, 1883, rev. ed. Tokyo, 1929;

4) P. C. Bagchi, *Le Canon Bouddhique en Chine,* 2 vols. (Librarie Orientaliste Paul Gunther, Paris, 1927 and 1938);

5) Daijo Tokiwa and Unrai Ogiwara, *Japanese Alphabetical Index of Nanjio's Catalogue of the Buddhist Tripitaka,* Nanjio-Hakushi Kinen Kakkokwai, Tokyo.

6) *Hōbōgirin* (法寶義林), Fascicule Annexe, 1931; and

7) *Fo-tsang tzu-mu yin-te, Combined Indices to the Authors and Titles of Books and Chapters in Four Collections of Buddhist Literature,* Harvard-Yenching Index Series 11, in 3 vols., 1933.

V. *Dictionaries:*

1) *Mahāvyutpatti,* ed. Sakaki Ryosaburo (飜譯名義大集) 2 parts (眞言宗京都大學, pt. I, text, 1916 and pt. II, Index, 1925);

2) *Mahāvyutpatti,* ed., Wogihara Unrai, Tokyo, 1926;

3) Mochizuki Shinkō, *Bukkyō Daijiten* (佛教大辭典發行所, Tokyo, 1954);

4) Ōda Tōkunō, *Bukkyō Daijiten* (大倉書店, Tokyo, 1917); this has a Chinese translation by Ting Fu-pao (丁福保, 佛學大辭典, Shanghai, 1919);

5) *Fa-hsiang tz'u-tien* (朱芾煌, 法相辭典) in 4 vols., Commercial Press, 1939;

6) Soothill W. E. and Levis Hodous, *A Dictionary of Chinese Buddhist Terms* (K. Paul, Trench, Trubner & Co., London, 1937);

7) O. Rosenberg, *Introduction to the study of Buddhism according to Material preserved in China and Japan,* pt. I, Vocabulary (佛教研究名辭集), Tokyo, 1916.

8) *Pali-English Dictionary* by T. W. Rhys Davids and William Steed, Pali Text Society, London.

9) Nyanatiloka, *Buddhist Dictionary,* Island Hermitage Publication No. 1, Frewin & Co. Ltd., Colombo, 1956.

VI. *Studies or Explanatory Notes on the Prajñāpāramitā-śāstra by the ancient Chinese and Japanese Scholars:*

1) Hui-ying 慧影 (6th cent.), 大智度論疏 *(Sub-commentary on the Mahā-prajñāpāramitā-śāstra);* available only in fragments in *Hsü-t'sang-ching,* vols. 74 and 87; contain chs. I, VI, XIV–XV, XVII, XXI and XXIV, the explanatory notes respectively on chs. I, XIX–XXI, XXXII–XXXVI, LIX–LXIV and LXXV-LXXXII of the *Śāstra.*

This work has been referred to by Prof. Demieville in his review of Prof. Lamotte's tr. (vol. II) of the *Śāstra;* see *Journal Asiatique,* Année 1950, fascicule, no. 3 (pp. 375–395), pp. 376–377 and p. 377, n. 1.

On Hui-ying see 續高僧傳 T 2060, p. 630b.

2) Chi-tsang (549–623) has commentaries or explanatory notes on the *Three Treatises,* viz., I) *Madhyamaka-śāstra,* II) *Dvādaśamukha-śāstra* and III) *Śata-śāstra;* these are respectively 中觀論疏 (T 1824), 十二門論疏 (T 1825) and 百論疏 (T 1827). He has also such independent works as

I) 三論玄義 *("The Profound Meaning of the Three Treatises"),*

II) 大乘玄論 *("Exposition of the Profound Meaning of Mahāyāna"),*

III) 二諦義 *("The Meaning of the Two Truths")*

All these works of Chi-tsang have profuse citations from the *Prajnāpāramitā-śāstra,* usually referred to as 釋論, 大論, or 智度論. In the beginning of 二諦義 (T. 1854) he quotes Seng-chao to the effect that although the four treatises (viz., the *Three Treatises* and the *Prajñāpāramitā-śāstra)* differ in their names and in their divisions of subject-matter, still, all of them ultimately return to the Great Truth; by means of the Two Truths they bring to light the Way that is not two, i.e., the Nondual Way (98a).

One would not miss noting this unity of thought especially in regard to the *Kārikā* and the *Śāstra* in the writings of Chi-tsang; although he did not write a separate commentary on the *Śāstra* still his works could as well be taken as so many foot-notes to the different topics in that text.

3) Hui-yüan 慧遠 (523–592), 大乘義章 *(Exposition of the Meaning of Mahāyāna)* (T. 1851). This is a Compendium on Mahāyāna and it is a very useful work. It has arranged the various topics under five headings: A) The Scriptures, B) Their Meaning, C) The Elements of Defilements, viz., (I) *kleśa* (afflictions) and (II) *karma* (deeds), D) The Elements of Purity, viz., (I) *hetu,* the root or the cause and (II) *phala,* the fruit or the effect and E) Miscellaneous topics. The last part E) is

lost. There are in all two hundred and twenty sub-headings for so many topics; in all these, every topic is explained in accordance with *Abhidharma, Satyasiddhi* and *Mahāyāna* and under the last mentioned the *Prajñāpāramitā-śāstra* is quoted throughout, often at great length. This work was of help to me in organizing the materials collected from the *Śāstra*. The Taishō edition bears the notations indicating the references to the chapters (巻) in the respective texts quoted, including the *Śāstra*.

On Hui-yüan, see 續高僧傳 (T 2060) 489c–492b.

4) Ānchō, a Japanese Buddhist monk, has his *Notes* 中論疏記 *on Chi-tsang's Commentary on the Madhyamaka-śāstra* (T. 2225). This was composed in the years 801–806; see Fung Yu-lan, *History of Chinese Philosophy*, vol. II, p. 727.

5) 大智度論類聚標目 (日大本藏經 vol. 27 pp. 457–539) of 日崇 (of 信入院, 前妙蓮寺) (compiled 1668 A.D.) is a useful index to the *Śāstra*.

VII. *Works by Modern Authors:*

1) Étienne Lamotte's *Le Traité de la Grande Vertu de Sagesse de Nāgārjuna* vols. I and II (Bureaux du Museon, Louvain, 1944, 1949).

The two following works contain extracts from the *Śāstra* in English translation on different topics:

2) H. Ui, *The Vaiśeṣika Philosophy* (Oriental Translation Fund, New Series, vol. XXIV, publ. Royal Asiatic Society, London, 1917) and

3) Kimura Ryūkan, *A Historical Study of Hīnayāna and Mahāyāna and the origin of Mahāyāna Buddhism* (Calcutta University, 1927).

The relevant works by modern authors on the general history and philosophy of Buddhism have been referred to in the Introduction and in the Conclusion. Of studies by modern scholars in regard to the general philosophy of the Madhyamika, in addition to the ones mentioned in the present work, these need mention:

1) Yamaguchi, S., *The Controversy of Existence and Non-existence in Buddhism* (佛教に於ける無と有との對論) Kobundo, 1941;

2) Yamaguchi, S., *Essays on Madhyamika Buddhism* (中觀佛教論攷) Kobundo, 1944;

3) Nagao Gadjin, "*The Fundamental Standpoint of the Mādhyamika Philosophy*" (中觀哲學の根本的立場, 哲學研究, nos. 366, 368, 370, 371 of 1947–48);

4) Miyamoto, S., *Thought of the Middle Path and Its Development* (中道思想及びその發達, 法藏館, 東京, 1944) and

5) Miyamoto, S., *The Principal Middleness, Mūla Madhyama and the Voidness, Śūnya* (根本中と空(佛教學の根本問題) 第一書房, 東京, 1943).

# NOTES

*Preface*

1 See Professor Demiéville's review of Professor Lamotte's *Le Traite De La Grande Vertu De Sagesse,* vol. II, *Journal Asiatique,* (Année 1950 pp. 375–395), p. 380.

2 On the life and work of Kumārajīva, see his biographical account in *Kao-seng-chuan,* T. 2059: 330a–333a. Professor T'ang Yung-t'ung has a whole chapter on Kumārajīva and his disciples: *Han Wei Liang-chin Nan-pei-ch'ao Fo-chiao Shih* (漢魏兩晉南北朝佛教史, 中華書局, 北京, 1955), vol. I, pp. 278–340. Cp. also Professor Tsukamoto, *Studies in Chao Lun,* Kyoto, 1954 (肇論研究, 法藏館, 京都市), pp. 130–146; Dr. P. C. Bagchi, *Le Canon Bouddhique en Chine,* I, (Paris, 1927), pp. 178–200; W. Liebenthal, *The Book of Chao,* (肇論) (The Catholic University of Peking, 1948), pp. 1 ff. and p. 67, n. 241. Dr. Bagchi and Professor Liebenthal give translations of extracts from *Kao-seng-chuan.* Professor Demiéville, *op. cit.,* also gives a short account of Kumārajīva.

3 While the generally accepted dates for Kumārajiva and his disciple Seng-chao are 343/44–413 and 383–414 respectively Prof. Tsukamoto *(op. cit.* p. 113) proposes the dates 350–409 and 374–414 respectively.

4 See Liebenthal, *op. cit.,* p. 3.

5 For an account of the translations by Kumārajīva, see Bagchi, *op. cit.,* pp. 185 ff.; see Bibliography for the different translations of the *Aṣṭa* and the *Pañcaviṁśati.*

6 See T'ang Yung-t'ung, *op. cit.,* pp. 301–302.

It is possible that this text bore the titles *Upadeśa* (憂波提舍) as well as *Vyākhyāśāstra* (釋論); see Lionel Giles, D. Litt., *Descriptive Catalogue of the Chinese Manuscripts from Tunhuang in the British Museum* (London, 1957), nos. 4214–4257. The huge number of manuscripts recorded here point to the great popularity that the text enjoyed. For the Tunhuang MS. of the *Śāstra* see also, *An Analytical List of the Tunhuang Manuscripts in the National Library of Peiping* 敦煌刼餘錄 (compiled in Chinese, by Ch'en Yüan, Academia Sinica, Peiping, 1931) Vol. 5, pp. 444–45.

According to Seng-jui, this text must have been of phenomenal proportions. In his Introduction to the *Śāstra* he says that even the abridged version of this text had a hundred thousand verses of thirty-two syllables; Kumārajīva rejected two thirds of it and thus got these hundred scrolls (chüan). And he tells us that Kumārajīva specially abridged the text for the sake of the Chinese who love brevity; otherwise the text would have had a thousand and odd chapters (chüan) (whereas now it is in just a hundred (chüan)). See T. 1509, 57b.

[7] For these, see the Bibliography.

*Chapter I*

[1] Max Walleser, *Life of Nāgārjuna from Tibetan and Chinese Sources. (Asia Major,* Hirth Anniversary Volume, 1923), p. 424.

[2] Cp. *Prasannapadā,* p. 3: *viditāviparīta prajñāpāramitānīteḥ.*

[3] Cp. Asaṅga, 順中論 *(Madhyamakānugama-śāstra)* T. 1565, p. 40a–c.

[4] See K. R. Subramanian, *Buddhist Remains in Andhra* (Diocesan Press, Veprey, Madras, 1932), pp. 53–63.

[5] Our sources for the traditional accounts of the life of Nāgārjuna, many of them short and scrappy, and mostly filled with legends, are these: I) In Sanskrit: A) *Laṅkāvatāra (Sagāthaka)* B) *Mañjuśrīmūlakalpa,* C) Bāṇa's *Harṣacarita* and D) Kalhaṇa's *Rājataraṅgiṇī;* II) In Chinese: A) The *Biography of Nāgārjuna* attributed to Kumārajīva (T. 2047), B) and the biographical account in Hsüan-tsang's *Hsi-yü-chi* (T. 2087), 929a–930a (Watters, *On Yuan chwang,* II, pp. 200–208); III) In Tibetan: A) *The History of the Eighty-four Sorcerers,* B) *Pag-sam-jon-zang,* C) Taranatha's *Hitory of Buddhism;* and to these there can be added D) Buston's *History of Buddhism* (English Translation by E. Obermiller, publ. Heidelberg, 1932). Most of these sources have been considered by Max Walleser in his *Life of Nāgārjuna.* While certainly much discount has got to be made for the legendariness and for the mutual conflict among these accounts as well as for the other fact which goes to explain to some extent their conflicting nature, viz., that the Tibetan sources mix up the two Nāgārjunas, the Mādhyamika philosopher at the beginning of the Christian era and the Siddha Nāgārjuna coming some four hundred years later, it is to be remembered that this case of confusion hardly pertains to the Chinese sources which are earlier. Further, inasmuch as the bare historical accounts singled out from those of the former agree with those of the latter they can be reasonably accepted as pertinent not to the later, but to the earlier Nāgārjuna, the subject of our study; e.g., his connection with the Nāgas and his having brought the *Prajñāpāramitā-sūtras* from them, as well as his friendship with the Śātavāhana king.

[6] As K. R. Subramanian *(op. cit.,* pp. 59–60) observes, in all the inscriptions so far discovered at Amarāvatī, there is no mention of Nāgārjuna. The mention of a Nāgārjunācārya at Jaggayapeta is rather late. This circumstance as well as the circumstance of there having been two Nāgārjunas with their biographical accounts mixed up have led some to doubt and even to deny the first Nāgārjuna's connection with Amarāvatī: see N. Dutt, *Notes on the Nāgārjunīkoṇḍa Inscriptions* (*Ind. Hist. Qly.,* VII, 1931) pp. 633 ff. and K. Gopalachari *Early History of the Andhra Country* (Univ. of Madras, 1941) pp. 125–126, n. 8. For the opposite view, viz., that the philosopher Nāgārjuna himself spent his later days at Bhramaragiri (Śrīparvata) in the monastery built for him by the Śātavāhana king, see P. S. Sastri, *Nāgārjuna and Āryadeva (Ind. Hist. Qly.,* XXXI, 1955 pp. 193–202) and K. R. Subramanian, *op. cit.* It appears that inasmuch as all the available accounts agree in saying that Nāgārjuna was a friend of the Śātavāhana king (Kumārajīva's "South Indian king"), as Hsüan-tsang's description of the monastery agrees with the findings in Nāgārjunikoṇḍa (despite the serious mistakes the Chinese traveller made in

his account of the topography of the area at large) and inasmuch as these accounts of Hsüan-tsang cannot possibly be about the Siddha Nāgārjuna, for the latter can hardly be held to have been the friend of the Śātavāhana king, the tradition that connects the earlier Nāgārjuna with Bhramaragirī can be accepted. On the identification of Bhramaragirī with Śrīparvata as well as on other names connected with Nāgārjuna, see K. R. Subramanian, *op. cit.* and P. S. Sastri, *op. cit.*

[7] Max Walleser, *Life of Nāgārjuna.* p. 427. While the Sarāha of the Tibetan tradition may be the teacher of Siddha Nāgārjuna, one has to take note of the mention by Asaṅga of a Rāhulabhadra as a renowned teacher of the Mādhyamika Philosophy; see 順中論 T. 1565, p. 40b.

[8] T. 2047, 184b, 185c.

[9] *Pag-sam-jon-zang* says that Nāgārjuna began to study Sarvāstivāda in his eighth year under Rāhula and was given initiation; see Sunitikumar Pathak, *Life of Nāgārjuna* (from *Pag-sam-jon-zang*), (*Ind. Hist. Qly.*, XXX, 1954) p. 93; see Max Walleser, *Life of Nāgārjuna* pp. 437–38. It is difficult to say who this Rāhula is and to which Nāgārjuna this refers. It may be recounted that the study of Sarvāstivāda as a preliminary in their career was common to many Mahāyāna teachers; Vasubandhu and Kumārajīva are examples.

[10] T. 2047: 184c, 186a; cp. Max Walleser, *Life of Nāgārjuna, passim.* T. 2047, 1846 speaks of Nāgārjuna's being given the Mahāyāna sūtras by an old *bhikṣu* and later, after speaking of Nāgārjuna's wandering in search of more sūtras, it states (184c) that a Mahānāga took him into the sea, opened up the "*Treasury of Seven Jewels,*" laid before him the case that contained them and gave him to read the Vaipulya-sūtras of measureless subtle doctrines. See also, *ibid.* 185c and 186a.

[11] Max Walleser *Life of Nāgārjuna,* p. 427.

[12] On Deva (Āryadeva), the celebrated disciple of Nāgārjuna and the author of *Catuḥśataka (Śataśāstra)*, see Candrakīrti's introduction to his commentary on this text (ed. Vidhusekhara Bhattacharya, Visvabharati, Santiniketan, 1931); see also *Ind. Hist. Qly.*, VI, pp. 193 ff. For a traditional graphic account of Deva's meeting with Nāgārjuna, see Watters, *op. cit.* pp. 200–201 (T. 2087: 929a–b). The Chinese Tripiṭaka contains a bibliography of Deva, also attributed to Kumārjīva; see T. 2048.

[13] For a slightly different account see Kumārajīva, T. 2047: 185a–b, 186b.

[14] It is necessary to note that the *Śāstra* refers to alchemy and the exchanging of gold coins for copper ones; see *ibid.* 64a, 195c and 298b; cp. Max Walleser, *op. cit.*, p. 427, 430.

[15] T. 2047: 184c, 186a.

[16] Max Walleser, *Life of Nāgārjuna* pp. 431–32.

[17] These are *Suhṛllekhā* (Chin. tr. T. 1672, 1673 and 1674) and *Ratnāvalī* (available in fragments in Sanskrit: chs. I, II and IV, ed. and tr. G. Tucci, JRAS, 1934, pp. 307–325, 1936, pp. 237–252, 423–435). *Suhṛllekhā* was translated by Dr. H. Wenzel from Tibetan into English: *Nāgārjuna's Friendly Epistle* (JPTS, 1886, pp. 6–32). For other translations see Winternitz, *op. cit.*, p. 347, n. 3. T. 1672 was translated into English by S. Beal; see *Ind. Antiq.* 1887, pp. 169 ff.

[18] Cp. Bāṇa's *Harṣacarita,* ch. VIII: *trisamudrādhipataye śātavāhananāmne na-*

*rendrāya suhṛde sa dadau.*

[19] *Epigraphia Indica,* vol. VIII (1905–1906), p. 60: *tisamudatoyapītavāhanasa . . . ekabahmaṇasa.*

[20] See H. C. Raychaudhuri, *Political History of Ancient India* (Calcutta Univ., 1953), p. 491 and *ibid.* n. 1; K. Gopalachari, *op. cit.*, p. 51.

[21] Cp. *ibid.* for Professor Rapson's view.

[22] *History of India,* Pt. I (S. Visvanathan, Madras, 1950), p. 102; K. Gopalachari (*op. cit.* p. 55) assigns to Gautamīputra 82–106 A.D. Professor P. S. Sastri holds that, Hāla, an earlier Śātavāhana king, as well as Vātsyāyana, the author of the commentary on the *Nyāyasūtras* were contemporaries of Nāgārjuna. He also asserts that this Vātsyāyana is identical with the author of the *Kāmasūtras* and that the Kuntala referred to there is the immediate successor of Hāla. Thus he holds that Nāgārjuna was a contemporary of Hāla and Kuntala as well as of Gautamīputra Śātakarṇi. He assigns Gautamīputra to 70 A.D. and Hāla to 10 A.D. (cp. P. S. Sastri, *op. cit.*, p. 202).

[23] H. C. Raychaudhuri, *op. cit.*, pp. 495 ff. See Purushottam Lal Bhargava, *The Śātavāhana Dynasty of Dakṣiṇāpatha* (Ind. Hist. Qly., XXVI, Dec. 1950, pp. 325–329) for a fresh proposal of dates for the Śātavāhana kings; this author assigns to Hāla 46–51 A.D. and to Gautamīputra 106–137 A.D. and tries to show that this chronology is in perfect accord with all the facts of which we are aware.

[24] For a comparative list of the different Purāṇic accounts of the reign-periods of the Śātavāhana kings, see D. R. Mankad, *Purāṇic Chronology* (publ. Gangājala Prakāśana; Charotal Book Stall, Anand, Gujarat), p. 101. Robert Sewell, in his *Historical Inscriptions of Southern India* (Madras University Historical Series, ed. S. K. Aiyangar, Madras, 1932) assigns to Hāla 69 A.D. and to Gautamīputra 113–138 A.D.

[25] Watters, *op. cit.*, II, p. 104.

[26] *Ibid.*, I, p. 245.

[27] *Rājataraṅgiṇī,* I, 173 ff.

[28] The date of Kaniṣka I is still a disputed point, but the generally accepted date of his accession is 78 A. D. For a fresh discussion of Kaniṣka's date see Sudhakara Chattopadhyaya, *Early History of North India* (Progressive Publishers, Calcutta, 1958), pp. 74–81 and 95–97.

[29] See *Śāstra* 70a, 92a, 273a, 341c, 343a. The Chinese Collection has three *Vibhāṣā* texts: T. 1545, T. 1546 and T. 1547. The first two are close to each other but the second is incomplete. The first one is the *Abhidharma-mahāvibhāṣā-śāstra* (tr. Hsüan-tsang). The third, T. 1547, seems to be a different text. While the first two are said to have been compiled by 'five hundred arahats', the third one is attributed to a Shitohanni (Kātyāyanīputra?).

[29a] *Jñānaprasthāna* has two different translations in Chinese: T. 1543 and T. 1544. For a recent retranslation of this text into Sanskrit, see Śāntibhiksu Śāstri, *Jñānaprasthāna-śāstra,* Viśvabharati University, Santiniketan, 1955.

[30] Watters, *op. cit.*, I, pp. 270–278.

[31] T. 2049: 189a–b. Paramārtha worked in China 546–569 A.D.

[32] *Śāstra,* 70a.

[33] While the whole of the present work may be said to be an attempt to lay bare the different meanings of this central, the most basic concept, *śūnyatā,* we may note here roughly its chief imports: 1) In reference to *vyavahāra,* the mundane nature of things, it means basically *naiḥsvābhāvya* which means devoidness of self-being, of uncondi-

tioned nature; this means the relativity, conditionedness *(pratītyasamutpāda)*, the non-substantiality of the elements of existence; this is also conveyed by *upādāya prajñapti,* derived name, which means that the presence of names does not mean the reality of the named; as relativity *śūnyatā* has also the import of the relative, conditioned, non-absolute nature of all specific views. 2) In reference to *paramārtha,* the ultimately true nature of things, *śūnyatā* means the non-conceptual, non-phenomenal, undivided, indeterminate nature of the absolute, ultimate reality, the full, the complete. These two are the principal imports of *śūnyatā* in reference to the true nature of things. 3) *Śūnyatā* means also the awareness or understanding of this truth of things as well as the method of knowledge, viz., criticism, by which it is brought to light; in this sense *śūnyatā* is a synonym of *madhyamā pratipat,* the Middle Way, the way that sees things as they are. 4) *Śūnyatā* means also the fundamental attitude in regard to things which arises as the result of this understanding, viz., *anupalambha,* the skilfulness of non-clinging, not clinging to the determinate as ultimate in its determinate nature nor clinging to the ultimate as anything specific. 5) To these there may be added another important import of *śūnyatā,* viz., the sense of the beyond, the thirst for the real, the thirst for fulfilment, which is the seat and spring of all the activities of man. See below p. 342, n. 84.

[34] Of the available recensions of the *Prajñāpāramitā,* the *Aṣṭasāhasrikā* is the earliest; at the latest it may belong to 1st century B.C.; see N. Dutt, *Aspects,* pp. 39–40 and 328; cp. E. J. Thomas, *History of Buddhist Thought* (2nd ed. Barnes and Noble, N. Y., 1951), p. 212, n. 1.

[35] That Nāgārjuna was not the earliest to interpret the *Prajñāpāramitā-sūtras* is perhaps borne out by such places in the *Śāstra* where it refers to the different opinions in regard to matters like the definition of *prajñā;* cp. *ibid.,* 139c.

[36] See N. Dutt, *op. cit.,* p. 330–331.

[37] For a complete list of citations from the Buddhist Scriptures in the *Śāstra* see Mochizuki Shinkō, *Bukkyō Daijiten,* vol. IV, pp. 3322 ff.; the Nei-hsüeh-yüan edition of the *Śāstra* has noted all citations in regard to chs. I–XXXIV; Prof. Lamotte *op. cit.* has identified many of these in regard to chs. I–XVIII.

[38] Kumārajīva's transl. of this *Sūtra,* T. 475 (vol. 14: 537a–557a); cp. also T. 474 (tr. Chih-chien) and T. 476 (tr. Hsüan-tsang). See especially the section, *Advayadharmadvāra* (T. 475: 550b ff.)

[39] Cp. among other places, 168b, 97b.

[40] Cp. *Kāśyapaparivarta* (Skt. text ed. Stael Holstein) pp. 82 ff.

[41] *Daśabhūmivibhāṣā-śāstra,* T. 1521 (vol. 26, 20a–122b); *ibid.* 21b makes it clear that the text is intended as a commentary on the *Daśabhūmika-sūtra.*

[42] See especially *ibid.,* 28c, 39a–40a, 117a–118b.

[43] Cp. *Śāstra,* among other places (ch. XXXI), 292a–c. Many references to *Āgamas* are found throughout the first thirty-four chapters; these have been noted by the editors of the Nei-hsüeh-yüan edition of this text.

[44] *Śāstra* chs. XII, XIV and LXX have references to the doctrines of Sāṅkhya and Vaiśeṣika; see below, chs. VII and VIII. *Śāstra,* 546c–547a gives a succinct account of the twenty-four *tattvas* of the Sāṅkhya. *Daśabśhūmi-vibhāṣā* mentions a number of non-Buddhist schools; see T. 1521, 31c. Cp. *Ratnāvalī*

(JRAS 1934, p. 321): *Sasāṅkhyaulūkya nirgrantha-pudgalaskandhavādinām; prccha lokam yadi vadaty astināstivyatikramam.*

45 Cp. *Kārikā,* XVI: 3.

46 See below, ch. VIII.

47 Nāgārjuna's *Vigrahavyāvartanī* is a sustained criticism of the Nyāya view of *pramāṇas* (valid means of knowledge); it is to be noted that *ibid.*, verses 21–28 bear out that *pramāṇas* are accepted by the Mādhyamika in the mundane truth. See below, chs. IV and VIII.

48 Cp. *Vigrahavyāvartanī,* 70:

*Prabhavati ca śūnyateyam yasya prabhavanti tasya sarvārthāḥ;*
*prabhavati na tasya kiñcin na prabhavati śūnyatā yasya.*

Cp. also *Kārikā,* XXIV: 14.

49 T. 2047, 184c, 186b.

50 On "*Upadeśa*" being used as a title of the *Śāstra,* see above p. 335, n. 6.

51 Translated into German by Max Walleser (Heidelberg, 1923).

52 *Shōwa Hō-bō Sō Mokuroku* (昭和法寶總目錄, Suppl. Vol. of *Taishō Shinshū Daizōkyō,* 1929) vol. I, No. 4, pp. 697a–c.

53 Cp. *Aksaraśatakam, The Hundred Letters,* a Mādhya mika text by Āryadeva, tr. Vasudev Gokhale, publ. Institut für Buddhismus Kunde, Heidelberg, 1930.

54 Cp. *Mahāyānavimśikā* (ed. Vidhusekhara Bhattacharya, Visvabharati, 1931), pp. 3–4.

55 T. 1616; 864a refers to the *Vijñaptimātratā-siddhi-śāstra; ibid.*, 865a affirms the doctrine that there is only the *vijñāna* and not the external objects; and *ibid.*, 864a and 866a speak of "*ālayavijñāna.*"

56 Cp. *Upāyahṛdaya* (tr. Tucci: *Prediṅnāga Buddhist Texts on Logic,* Gaekwad Oriental Series, vol. XLIX, 1929), intr. p. xi.

57 See T. 1668; 606b ff., 609a, and particularly 611a ff. expound *ālayavijñāna; ibid.*, 608a ff. expound *tathāgata-garbha; ibid.*, 606a cites from *Laṅkāvatāra Sūtra;* and *ibid.*, 595a, 599a and 601a have references to Aśvaghoṣa. This is probably a commentary on *Śraddhotpāda-śāstra.*

58 These are respectively: I) T. 1564 (vol. 30, 1a-39b); II) T. 1566 *(ibid.,* 50c–135c), and III) T. 1567 *(ibid.,* 136a–158c); (I) is translated into German by Max Walleser, *Die Mittlere Lehre* (Heidelberg, 1912). (II) and (III) are translated by me (unpublished).

59 T. 1565 (vol. 30: 39c–50b); see especially the opening section of the text, 39c–40c.

60 T. 1631 (vol. 32: 13b–23a); Tucci translated this text from Chinese and Tibetan *(Prediṅnāga Buddhist Texts on Logic,* GOS, XLIX); the original Sanskrit text with Nāgārjuna's own *vṛtti* was edited by K. P. Jayswal and Rahula Sankrtyayana, App. to JBORS, XXIII. pt. 3. For a revised edition see E. H. Johnston and Arnold Kunst: *The Vigrahavyavartanī of Nāgārjuna* (from Mélanges Chinois et Bouddhiques), The Saint Catherine Press Ltd., Bruges (Belgium), 1951.

61 T. 1521 (vol. 26; 20a–122b); this is perhaps referred to in the *Śāstra* 411b (see *ibid.* with n. 15); this text cites very often verses from the *Bodhisattvapātheya-śāstra=Bodhisambhāra-śāstra* (T. 1660) which is also probably a work of Nāgārjuna; these citations are noted in the Nei-hsüeh-yüan edition of T. 1521.

62 T. 1672 (vol. 32, 745b–748a), T. 1673 *(ibid.,* 748a–751a), and T. 1674 *(ibid.,* 751a–754b) are the translations

of *Suhṛllekhā;* T. 1656 (*ibid.*, 493b–505a) is the translation of *Ratnāvalī.*

63 T. 1654 (vol. 32: 490a–491b); tr. into English by Pt. Aiyaswami Sastri (K. V. Rangaswami Iyengar Comm. Vol., pp. 485–491).

64 T. 1568 (vol. 30: 159a–167c); retranslated into Sanskrit by Pt. Aiyaswami Sastri (Visvabharati, 1955); Pt. Sastri has noted the passages that are quoted here from the *Kārikā*. Chi-tsang tells us that while the verse portion of this text is by Nāgārjuna, the prose portion which is the commentary may have been the work of some later person; see T. 1825: 178a.

65 T. 1574 (vol. 30: 254a–b) retranslated into Sanskrit by Pt. Aiyaswami Sastri: *Bhavasṅkrānti Sūtra and Nāgārjuna's Bhavasaṅkrānti Śāstra* (Adyar Library, Madras, 1938).

66 T. 1575 (vol. 30: 254b–256a); translated from Chinese into German by Phil. Shaeffer, Heidelberg, 1923.

67 T. 1573 (vol. 30: 253a–c); translated into English by Edkins: *Chinese Buddhism*, pp. 302–317; retranslated into Sanskrit by H.R.R. Iyengar, Mys. Univ. Journal, I. 2, 1927.

68 T. 1660 (vol. 32: 517b–541b); the verses are attributed to Nāgārjuna and the prose portion which is the commentary is by a Bhikṣu Tzu-tsai (Īśvara?).

69 T. 1675 (vol. 32: 754b–756b).

70 References here are to *A Comvlete Catalogue of the Buddhist Canon* (ed. by Professor H. Ui and others, Tohoku Imperial University, Japan, 1934).

71 This is not available in Chinese. Buddhapālita and Bhāvaviveka belong to two different traditions (the *Prāsaṅgika* and the *Svātantrika*) of the Mādhyamika School, although the difference between them is still far from clear; Candrakīrti, a follower of the *Prāsaṅgika* tradition, often quotes from Bhāvaviveka and criticises his way of interpreting the *Mādhyamika-kārikā;* see the intr. portion of his *Prasannapadā;* cp. T.R.V. Murti, *The Central Philosophy of Buddhism,* (Allen and Unwin, 1955), pp. 95–98.

72 ed. Louis de la Vallée Poussin, Bibl. Buddhica, IV, St. Pétersbourg, 1915.

73 The commentary on the *Dvādaśamukha* quotes from it; cp. T. 1568: 160a; Candrakīrti very probably refers to this; see *Prasannapadā,* p. 89.

74 See above p. 337, n. 17.

75 *Niraupamya-stava* and *Paramārtha-stava,* ed. and tr. Tucci, JRAS, 1932, pp. 309–325.

76 *Catuḥstava, Ind. Hist. Qly,* 1932: 316–331, 689–705. These four according to Patel constitute the *Catuḥstava;* these obviously do not include *Paramārtha-stava* (Tucci); that must be counted separately and to these there must be added the *Dharmadhātustava* referred to above.

77 *Ind. Hist. Qly.*, 1957, pp. 246–249; cp. *Śāstra,* 100b.

78 Cp. *Bodhicaryāvatāra,* V., 106.

79 For a carefully prepared bibliography of the Mādhyamika works available in Sanskrit as well as those restored or retranslated, see T.R.V. Murti, *op. cit.*, pp. 83–103.

80 See *Śāstra,* 60c–61c. See *ibid.*, 503c where reference is made to the presence of contending schools among the followers of the Buddha during the five hundred years after His passing away when every one clung to his own way and failed to understand Him. This passage has its bearing on the Sarvāstivādins who clung to every specific element as substantial and self-being. Cp. *ibid.*, 319b. That it was one of the great problems of Nāgārjuna to find

and reveal the basic unity in the teachings of the Buddha is clear from such accounts as the four *siddhāntas; see ibid.*, 59b ff., especially 60a; see below, ch. V.

[81] For these terms see below, ch. III.

[82] See *Śāstra*, among other places, 294b, 697a, 720a–b; see below, ch. III.

[83] *Kārikā*, XXIV: 36 and 38:

*Sarvasaṃvyavahārāṃ śca laukikān pratibādhase; yat pratītyasamutpādaśūnyatām pratibādhase.*

*Ajātam aniruddhañ ca kūṭasthañ ca bhaviṣyati; vicitrābhir avasthābhih svabhāve rahitam jagat.*

[84] "Thirst for the real" is also called here "thirst for fulfilment;" "thirst" is my rendering for 求 (*eṣaṇā* seeking, longing). See the very striking passage (*Śāstra* 298b–299a) that describes the mind's thirst for fulfilment which comes to a rest with the realization of reality 心則滿足更不食余求. See a similar expression, *ibid.* 450a: 常得滿足更無所求. See *ibid.* 60b: Even the ignorant seek the pathway to reality. Cp. also 125b, 164a and 192c. *Ibid.* 292a refers to the Buddha's advice to look for reality and not to pursue names. *Ibid.* 562a: "Wisdom seeks, longs for reality." While 求實 or 求法 occurs frequently in the *Sāstra*, we find also expressions like 欲法 and 喜法 (*maratiḥ* and *dharmārāmaḥ*).

*Naiḥsvābhāvya* meaning lacking self-sufficiency, lacking self-possessedness is the basic import of *ṣūnyatā* with regard to the mundane nature of things. A sense of insufficiency in regard to the relative, conditioned and contingent underlies even the critical examination of categories in the *Kārikā*. In the *Śāstra* this sense comes to be emphasized more clearly as the mind's longing for the real.

[85] Determinate = conditioned = conditionally originated; also divided and definite, in the same sense. See below, ch. II.

[86] see below, ch. IX.

[87] *Kārikā*, XXV: 9:

*Ya ājavañjavībhāvaḥ upādāya pratītya vā;*
*so 'pratītyānupādāya nirvāṇam upadiśyate.*

[88] See below, chs. IV and V.

[89] *Kārikā*, XXIV: 14:

*Sarvam ca yujyate tasya śūnyatā yasya yujyate;*
*sarvam na yujyate tasya śūnyam yasya na yujyate.*

[90] *Ibid.* XXIV: 10:

*Vyavahāram anāśritya paramārtho na deśyate;*
*paramārtham anāgamya nirvāṇam nādhigamyate.*

[91] See *Śāstra* 60b.

[92] While *dṛṣṭi* (view) itself could be either wrong *(mithyā)* or right *(samyak)* depending on whether it is clinging or free from clinging, the usual tendency among the Buddhist writers is to use "*dṛṣṭi*" when not qualified by *samyak* to stand for false or wrong view. When the *Kārikā* (XIII: 8) says "*Śūnyatā* has been taught as a remedy for all *dṛṣṭis*, but they indeed are incurable who (cling and) turn *sūnyatā* itself into a *dṛṣṭi*," it is referring to *dṛṣṭi* as dogmatism which seizes the relative as absolute. *Ibid.* XXVII: 30, distinguishes between *dṛṣṭi* and *saddharma*, where the latter is *samyagdṛṣṭi*, the right view of the mundane nature of things, viz., *pratītyasamutpāda*. But *dharma* in this sense is the way and not an end in itself, a raft to be put away and not clung to. Cp. *Majjh.*, i, 135: *kullūpamam mayā dhammo desito nittharaṇatthāya na gahaṇatthāya;* cp. also *Samādhirāja* (q. in *Prasannapadā* p. 135): *madhye'pi*

*sthānam na karoti paṇḍitaḥ.* On right view, see *Śāstra* 312c, 412b and 677c; see below, ch. V.

93 Cp. *Kārikā,* XXV: 24:
*Sarvopalambhopaśamaḥ prapañcopa-śamaḥ śivaḥ; na kvacit kasyacit kaścit dharmo buddhena deśitaḥ.*

94 Cp. Candrakīrti: *Prasannapadā,* p. 57: *paramārtho hyāryāṇāṁ tūṣṇīmbhāvaḥ.*

95 *Ibid.,* p. 494: *kin tu laukikam vyavahāram anabhyupagamya abhidhānābhid-heyajñānajñeyādilakṣaṇam aśakya eva paramārtho deśayitum . . . tasmāt . . . samvṛtir adāv evābhyupeyā bhājanam iva salilārthinā.*

96 On the ultimate meaning of the sense of 'I,' see below, ch. III; see also the author's paper, "The Sense of I" *(Proc. Ind. Phil. Cong.,* 1956, 173–182).

97 Cp. *Vigrahavyāvartanī,* 29–30.

98 Cp. *Sāstra,* 75a, 253b.

99 *Kārikā,* XXIV: 18.

100 *Ibid.,* XIII: 8.

101 *Ibid.,* XXIV: 8.

102 *Ibid.,* XXV: 9.

103 *Ibid.,* X: 16; XXVII: 8.

104 *Ibid.,* XXIV: 14

104a *Śāstra,* 102a ff.

105 *Ibid.,* 191a ff.

106 *Ibid.,* 195c.

107 *Ibid.,* 285b–296b.

108 *Ibid.,* 298b–299a.

109 *Ibid.,* 297b.

110 *Ibid.,* 324b ff.; also *ibid.,* 326b.

111 See e.g., *ibid.,* 256b.

112 *Ibid.,* 347a–351b.

113 See *ibid.,* 563c–564a, also *ibid.,* 653c.

114 *Ibid.,* 692c ff.

115 See especially section 79 of the *Sūtra, ibid.,* 687c, ff.

116 *Kārikā,* XXIV: 10.

117 See the colophon, *Śāstra,* 756c: The first *prakaraṇa* of the *Sūtra* has been explained in the thirty-four chapters and this part is complete; but from the second *prakaraṇa* onwards Kumārajīva abbreviated the text and picked up only the essentials. Cp. T. 2145 出三藏記集, 75b. Hui-yüan is known to have compiled an abridged edition of the *Śāstra;* it is now lost, but the Chinese Collection preserves his Introduction to it; see *ibid.,* 75b–76b.

118 Many of these have been noted in their respective places.

119 See *Śāstra* 288a ff. on the teaching of the non-substantiality of elements *(dharmāḥ),* and 298a ff. on the teaching of *tathatā, dharmadhātu* and *bhūtakoṭi* in the *Āgamas,* the "baskets" of the Sarvāstivādins.

120 See *Ratnāvalī,* IV. 68 ff. (JRAS 1936, pp. 250 ff); cp. *Kimura* Ch. II.

121 *Śāstra* 319b makes an explicit reference to this point: "During the five hundred years after the passing away of the Buddha, the *Saṅgha* was divided into two; some accepted the *dharma-śūnyatā* and some only the *śūnyatā* of the individual *(pudgala);* the latter said that the five *skandhas* are real and that only he who receives the *skandhas* is *śūnya.*" The reference here to *Sarvāstivāda* is obvious.

122 It is necessary to note that the Pāli *Nikāyas* contain some *Suttas* that speak of the *dharmaśūnyatā,* e.g., *Mahāsuñ-ñatā-sutta (Majjh.,* III, 109–118); *Śāstra* (288a) refers to this as contained in the *Samyuktāgama,* the basket of the Sarvāstivādins.

123 *Śāstra,* among other places, 86a, 416a, 650c, 756b.

124 *Majjh.* I, 190–191: *Yo paṭiccasamup-pādaṁ passati so dhammaṁ passati yo dhammaṁ passati so paṭiccasamuppādaṁ passati; Samyu.* II, 17: *Ete te kaccāyana ubho ante anupagamma majjhena Tathāgato dhammaṁ deseti, avijjāpaccayā saṅkhārā, saṅkhārapaccayā viññāṇaṁ* etc.; cp.

also *ibd.* 20; one can consult the whole of *Nidānasamyutta* for the equation *dhamma = majjhimā paṭipat = paṭiccasamuppāda.*

125 Cp. *Kārikā,* XXIV: 18:

*Yah pratītyasamutpādaḥ śūnyatām tām pracakṣmahe;*
*sā prajñaptirupādāya pratipat saiva madhyamā.*

126 *Dhammacakkappavattanasutta; Vinaya (Mahāvagga)* I, 10 ff., *Samyu.* V, 420 ff.; also *Lalitavistara* (ed. Lefmann), I, 416 ff. and *Mahāvastu* (ed. Senart), III, 330 ff.

127 *Majjh.* II, 32; *Dhamman te desessāmi: Imasmiṁ sati idaṁ hoti . . . imasmiṁ asati, idaṁ na hoti. (Cūlasakuludāyisutta).*

128 *Ibid.,* I, 190–191.

129 Cp. *Dhammacakkappavattanasutta.*

130 *Samyu.* II, 17: *Sabbam atthīti kho Kaccāyana ayam eko anto. Sabbam natthīti ayam dutiyo anto. Ete te Kaccāyana ubho ante anupagamma majjhena Tathāgato dhammam deseti; ibid.* 20: *sayankatam dukkhanti . . . sassatam . . . parankataṃ dukkhanti . . . ucchedam;* also *ibid.* 23. Cp. *Kārikā,* XV: 7:

*Kātyāyanāvavāde ca asti nāstīti cobhayam;*
*pratiṣiddham bhagavatā bhāvābhāvavibhāvinā.*

131 *Samyu.* II, 17: *Lokasamudayam kho Kaccāyana yathābhūtaṃ sammappaññāya passato yā loke natthitā sā na hoti* etc. This is virtually what the *Śāstra* (59b ff.) calls the *"prātipakṣika-siddhānta";* see below, ch. V.

132 *Samyu.* IV, 400–401; cp. *Śāstra,* 60a.

133 *Samyu.* II, 60–61.

134 *Dīgha.* II, 66 ff.

135 *Samyu.* III, 113: *rūpam attato samanupassati, rūpavantam vā attānam, attani vā rūpam, rupasmim vā attam.* These very four views when applied to each of the five *skandhas* become the twenty kinds of the false sense of self. Cp. *Vibhāṣā* (T. 1545) 36a ff.

136 *Samyu.* II, 19 ff; cp. *Kārikā,* XII: 1.

137 *Samyu.* III, 46 has this: *ye hi keci bhikkhave samaṇā vā brāhmaṇā vā anekavidham attānam samanupassamānā samanupassanti sabbe te pañcupādānakkhandhe samanupassanti, etesam vā aññataram;* see *Sūtra* 545b ff.

138 *Udāna* (P.T.S.), pp. 66–69. The fourteen questions are called *"avyākṛta"* as the Buddha did not answer these but dismissed them as not fit to answer. These are four sets, all but the last framed in terms of the four extremes of is, is not, both is and is not, and neither is nor is not; the last is conceived only in terms of two extremes, identity and difference: 1) the world is eternal; it is not eternal; it is both eternal and not eternal; it is neither eternal nor not eternal; 2) the world is evanescent; it is not evanescent; it is both evanescent and not evanescent; it is neither evanescent nor not evanescent; 3) the self exists after death; the self does not exist after death, the self both exists and does not exist after death, the self neither exists nor does not exist after death; 4) the individual is the same as the body; the individual is different from the body. These occur in several places in the *Nikāyas: Majjh.* I, 484 ff.; *ibid.,* 426 ff.; *Samyu.* III, 257 ff.; *ibid. (Avyākata Samyuttam)* IV, 374–403. For Nāgārjuna's treatment of these see *Kārikā;* XXVII, which especially treats of the extremes of existence, non-existence, etc., in the case of the self after death and it is clearly brought out that none of the four extremes hold in the case of the stream of personal life which is a continuity of conditioned becoming. *Śāstra* discusses in several places the significance of the Buddha's silence on these matters;

see eg., 74c–75a. See below, ch. V.

139 *Aṅgu.* (ed. Hardy), V, 288: *kammassakā bhikkhave sattā kammadāyādā kammayonī kammabandhū kammappaṭisaraṇā, yam kammam karonti kalyāṇam vā pāpakam vā tassa dāyādā bhavanti;* cp. also *ibid.* 290 ff., and *Dhammapada,* verses 161 and 165.

140 *Samyu.* IV, 179–180: *Evameva kho bhikkhave sace tumhepi na orimantīram upagacchatha, na pārimantīram upagacchatha, na majjhe samsīdassatha . . . evam tumhe bhikkhave nibbāṇaninnā bhavissatha, nibbaṇapoṇā nibbāṇappabhārā. Tam kissa hetu. Nibbāṇaninnā bhikkhave sammā diṭṭhī.*

141 *Udāna.* 80–81.

142 *Udāna.* 33: *bhavena bhavassa vippamokkham āhamsu.*

143 *Ibid. vibhavena bhavassa vippamokkham āhamsu.*

144 *Majjh.*, I, 326: *Avijjāgato vata Bho Bako brahmā . . . yatra hi nāma aniccaṁ yeva samānaṁ niccanti vakkhati* etc.

145 Cp. *Kārikā:* XXV: 9, cited above p. 342, n. 87.

146 *Ibid.*, XXII: 15–16:

*Prapañcayanti ye buddham prapañcātītam avyayam; te prapañcahatāḥ sarve na paśyanti tathāgatam. Tathāgato yatsvabhāvaḥ tatsvabhāvamidam jagat; tathāgato niḥsvabhāvaḥ niḥsvabhāvam idam jagat.*

147 *Majjh.* I, 487–488: *rūpasaṅkhāvimutto kho Vaccha tathāgato gambhīro, appameyyo, duppariyogaho* etc. It may be noted that the *Aggivacchagotta Sutta (ibid.,* pp. 483–489) really falls into two sections: in the first (pp. 483–486) the fourteen questions are asked in reference to the world and the individual: Does the saint exist after death or not? etc. are questions about the continuity of personal life after death; this is about the mundane nature of the individual. But the question, occurring again later, after the Buddha has spoken of deliverance and attachment *(evam vimuttacitto pana bho Gotama bhikku kuhim upapajjatīti)* "Where is he reborn who has attained to this deliverance?" is really regarding the ultimate nature of the Tathāgata, in which nature He is "deep, immeasurable, unfathomable." The case is just the same even with *Kārikā* XXII where we see on the one hand the indescribability of the relation of the *skandhas* to the individual and on the other, the transcendent nature of the Tathāgata described as *prapañcātīta, avyaya.* See below, pp. 234–35.

147a For details see below, ch. IX.

148 *Kārikā,* XXIV: 8–9.

149 *Śāstra* 59b, 59c, 60a.

150 *Ibid.*, 254a; see below, ch. V.

151 This is especially clear in such places as *Śāstra* 59b ff.

152 For the mention of the three "marks of the *dharma,*" as distinctive of the Buddhist doctrine, see *Śāstra,* 222a; cp. also, *ibid.*, 170a. Cp. Yamakami Sogen, *Systems of Buddhist Thought* (Calcutta University., 1912), pp. 7 ff.

153 See below pp. 107–110.

154 For a short account of Councils see E. J. Thomas, *History of Buddhist Thought,* ch. III.

155 While the Pali Chronicles give the Vajjian practices which refer to matters of discipline as the immediate cause of the schism, *Vasumitra's Treatise (Masuda,* p. 15) gives the Five Points of Mahādeva which concern the doctrine. Cp. *Vibhāṣā* 510c–512a. See Et. Lamotte, *The Buddhist Controversy on the Five Propositions, Ind. Hist. Qly.*, June and Sept. 1956, pp. 148 ff. E. J. Thomas observes, "Whether these points were actually discussed at the second Council is not important. The

historical fact is that they were held by the Mahāsāṅghikas along with their buddhological theories." *Op. cit.*, p. 173, n. 2. These Five Points as well as the Ten Practices serve to bear out the way how one party looked upon the other, one considering the other as advocating looseness in discipline, and the other considering the one as immature in understanding.

[156] According to Vasumitra *(Masuda* pp. 15–17) all the schools of the Mahāsāṅghikas shoot out in the second century A. N. and all the schools of the Sthaviras shoot out in the third century A.N. except the Saṅkrāntivādins who emerge at the beginning of the fourth century A.N.

[157] E. J. Thomas observes that the period of the "growth" of Abhidharma is also the period of the "rise" of Mahāyāna; this is the period between Aśoka in the 3rd century B.C. and Kaniṣka in the 1st century A.D. *(op. cit.* p. 158)

[158] *Śāstra* often refers to the two lines of Buddhist philosophy, viz., Mahāyāna and Abhidharma and by the latter it means in this connection the Sarvāstivādins, the full fledged pluralists (see e.g. the final portions of chs. XIX–XXIX); and between the absolutism of Mahāyāna and the pluralism of Sarvāstivāda, there are intermediaries who on the whole share certain important philosophical tenets and these constitute what can be called "the line in between."

[159] *Masuda* VII, pp. 53–57. *Bareau* pp. 114–120.

[160] *Masuda* VIII, p. 57; *Bareau* pp. 121–126. See the author's translation, *Sāmmitīya Nikāya Śāstra, Visvabharati Annals* (Visvibharati University, India), Vol. V, pp. 155–243.

[161] *Masuda* XII, pp. 67–69; *Bareau,* pp. 155–159.

[162] *Ibid.*, pp. 160–166. In the *Vibhāṣā* (T. 1545) the Dārṣṭāntikas figure as a very important group of Buddhist thinkers. We do not have any school of this name in the lists of the early Buddhist schools. It is quite possible that the formation of this school was rather late, some time before the composition of the *Vibhāṣā;* but by the time of its composition they had already become a very important group and they are very frequently mentioned there. There is a tradition that the Dārṣṭāntikas belonged to the same lineage as the Sautrāntikas and were anterior to them. Thus K'uei-chi tells us in his Notes on Siddhi (ch. IV, q. in *Fa Ren*, II, 9b) that the lineage of the Sautrāntikas is to be distinguished into three stages: I) under the leadership of Kumāralāta (100 years A.N.) who is also known as *dṛṣṭānta (dārṣṭāntika)* teacher; II) under Śrīlāta and III) the Sautrāntika proper; the last mentioned have the name Saṅkrāntivādins and they apper 400 years A.N. Cp. also *Fa Ren* III, 46a.

The Dārṣṭāntikas, as it could be gathered in the *Vibhāṣā,* show very clear leanings in the direction of absolutism and even idealism. They hold that the derived, dependent nature of things means their lack of absoluteness (T. 1545, 154b, 479a–c, 760a-b, 797b), that the *pratyayas* are not real and substantial (*ibid.* 283a) and they admit a theory of illusion and say that illusory objects are devoid of reality. (*ibid.* 193b, 390c and 696b).

[163] Both these interpretations are based on the words of the Buddha. The first is based on such statements as "*Sabbam uccati dvādaśāyatanāni*" *(Mahāniddesa)* and the second, on "*Atītam ced*

*bhikṣavo rūpam na abhaviṣyat* etc." *(Saṃyuktāgama* III, 14, q. in *Prasannapadā*, p. 444). Cp. *Vibhāṣā* (T. 1545), 378b–c. See *Kośa* V, verses 25–26 (Stcherbatsky, *Central Conception*, pp. 77–82; also *ibid.* pp. 37–43). *Dharmāḥ*= elements=essences; every element has a self-being unaffected by function, time; see *Vibhasa* chs. LXXVII-LXXVIII; and *ibid.* ch. XXXIX. That the Yoga conception of time and change as contained in Vyāsa's commentary on the *Yoga-sūtras* is patterned in the light of the Sarvāstivāda view has been noted by Stcherbatsky *op. cit.*, pp. 43–47.

164 Cp. *Vibhāṣā* 394b–c.

165 *Ibid.*, 41a, 200a.

166 *Ibid.*, 202c–203a.

167 *Ibid.*, 408a.

168 *Ibid.*, 393a, 394b–c.

169 *Ibid.*, 393a, 393c, 700a.

170 *Ibid.*, 200a, which has also the parallel of *kriyā-parisamāptikālo hyeṣa naḥ kṣaṇah (Kośabhaṣya* II; 46; CCB p. 41, n. 1); cp. also *Vibhāṣā* 703a.

171 *Ibid.*, 702a and 703a.

172 *Ibid.*, 393c–394b.

173 *Ibid.*, 201c.

174 *Ibid.*, 202a.

175 *Ibid.*, 479c.

176 *Ibid.*, 200a, 201c.

177 *Ibid.*, 200b.

178 Cp. *ibid.*, 1002b–1003c; cp. also *ibid.*, 201c.

179 Cp. *Kathāvatthu* I, 6–7 *(Points of Controversy*, pp. 84–101) for the Theravādin's criticism of Sarvāstivāda; for the Sautrāntika's criticism of Sarvāstivāda see *Kośabhāṣya* V: 25–26 (CCB pp. 76–91). In sum, the Sautrāntikas make out that the Sarvāstivādins I) fail to show a criterion to serve as the *raison d'etre* of function; II) fail to distinguish between the essence which they take as non-temporal and the function which is temporal, and consequently fail to distinguish between the composite and the incomposite; III) mistake the continuation of the past to mean its everlastingness and hence its self-being; IV) mistake again the fact-hood of the object of cognition to mean its substantiality and self-being *(svabhāva)* and V) fail to draw a clear line of distinction between existence and non-existence. The Dārṣṭāntikas, again, point out that the Sarvāstivādins fail to provide for negation and error or illusion and mistake relative existence to mean absolute self-being: see *Vibhāṣā* 390c, 479c and 283a–c. For the Sāmmitīyas' criticism of Sarvāstivāda see *Sāmmitīya Nikāya Śāstra* p. 183 and passim.

180 Cp. *Vasumitra's Treatise (Masuda)*, V, 38 ff.; *Bareau*, p. 144; Cp. also Stcherbatsky, *The Soul Theory of the Buddhists* (Bulletin de l'Academie de Sciences de Russie, 1920), pp. 852 ff.

181 *Sāmmitīya Nikāya Śāstra*, p. 187.

182 *Masuda* VII, 2.

183 See above, note 179; cp. *Kośabhāṣya*, V, 25—26 (CCB pp. 82 ff.).

184 *Masuda* I B, 6.

185 *Masuda* III, 5.

186 See *Masuda* VII, 1; XII, 3–5, IX, 12, *Sāmmitiya Nikāya Śāstra* pp. 182–183 and passim.

187 *Sāmmitīya Nikāya Śāstra*, p. 183.

188 *Fa Ren* III 4b–5a; cp. also *Masuda* II.

189 *Fa Ren* III 5b ff.; cp. also *Masuda* III.

190 *Fa Ren* I 39b–40a; cp. also *Masuda* I.

191 *Fa Ren* I 40a–b.

192 *Ibid.*

193 *Ibid.*

194 See E. J. Thomas, *History of Buddhist Thought*, pp. 173–174; also *Masuda* I, 1 ff.; *Bareau*, pp. 57 ff.

195 *Fa Ren* I 40b–41b; *Abhidharma* is here interpreted as the "true principle"

and this again as "the ultimate truth."

196 *Fa Ren* II 43b.

197 *Masuda* I 42–44; *Fa Ren* II 44b; even the Vibhajyavādins maintained this view (see *Vibhāṣā,* T. 1545, 140b); cp. also *Aṅgu.* I, 10: *"pabhassaraṃ idam bhikkhave cittaṃ tañ ca kho āgantukehi upakkilesehi upakkiliṭṭhaṃ."*

198 *Sāṃmitīya Nikāya Śāstra,* pp. 175, 181.

199 See *Fa Ren* III 48a–b.

200 *Saṃyu.* III 120; cp. with this the oft occurring statement of the *Prajñāpāramitās,* "the Buddha is the Bodhi, the Bodhi is the Buddha," etc.

201 E. J. Thomas (*op. cit.,* p. 174) observes that the tendency to emphasize the transmundane nature of the Buddha can be found at work before the period at which Mahāyāna can be called a separate system.

202 *Śāstra* emphasizes in many places the point that analysis of elements is essential for the complete comprehension of the nature of things and is as such cultivated and taught by the bodhisattva, the farer on the Great Way; see *ibid.,* among other places, 192b–c and 293c–94b.

203 *Kārikā,* X: 16.

204 *Ibid.,* XXVII: 8; *Śāstra,* 723c.

205 Cp. *Kimura,* pp. 71–72; he however tends in the earlier part of his book (ch. II) to the view that the Mahāyāna Sūtras were as such taught by the Buddha. For a different view see N. Dutt, *Aspects,* pp. 57 ff.

206 Cp. Et. Lamotte, *The Buddhist Controversy on the Five Propositions, Ind. Hist. Qly.,* June and Sept. 1956, (Gautama Buddha 25th Centenary Special Issue; pp. 148–162), pp. 161–162.

207 On the contribution of Sarvāstivādins to the growth of Mahāyāna see N. Dutt, *Aspects,* pp. 26 ff.; it is however difficult to identify, as Dr. Dutt tends to do here, the original Buddhism with Hīnayāna, nor is it reasonable to hold as Kimura tends to do that the Mahāyāna Sūtras were as such taught by the Buddha. Hīnayāna and Mahāyāna are later denominations for the two different streams of Buddhist philosophy and religion and the seeds of difference must have been there from the very beginning. The idea of *dharma-śūnyatā* seems to have been there with the Mahāsāṅghikas from the earliest times, prompted and supported, presumably, by such *sūtras* as the *Mahāśūnyatā-sūtra.*

208 *Śāstra,* 267c. see below, ch. X.

209 *Śāstra,* 85b–86a; cp. *ibid.,* 487a.

210 *Ibid.,* 295b–c; see below, ch. X.

211 *Śāstra,* 97a–c, 171c–172a; see below, ch. X.

212 *Śāstra,* 258c–260b; see below, ch. X.

213 *Śāstra,* 264b.

214 *Ibid.,* 92a ff. launches a long criticism on the Sarvāstivāda view of the path of bodhisattva and of Buddhahood; cp. also *ibid. (Sūtra)* 464c.

215 Cp. *ibid.,* among other places, 475b ff.; this is an oft-occurring idea in the *Prajñāpāramitā-sūtras.*

216 E. J. Thomas observes that it is in the *Avadānas* of the Sarvāstivādins that we first find the bodhisattva ideal and proceeds to say that while we do not know how the earliest schools of Mahāyāna began, we do know that they "must have begun amongst the Sarvāstivādins" *(History of Buddhist Thought,* pp. 169 ff.). In any case the absolutistic tendencies must have worked very closely on the elements of analysis. The analysts in turn must have felt the need to make room for Buddhahood as the highest of ideals. The *Jñānaprasthāna* as

well as its commentary, the *Abhidharma-mahā-vibhāṣā-śāstra* expound the bodhisattva-way. (See T. 1545, 893 ff.) The point that the *Śāstra* makes out is that the Sarvāstivādins do not properly comprehend and adequately appreciate the nature and value of the path of bodhisattva or of the ideal of Buddhahood; they fall short of true wisdom and compassion.

217 Cp. *Śāstra,* 86a: 諸乘諸道皆入摩訶衍; see below, ch. X.

*Chapter II*

1 For a graphic account of man's thirst for the real, see *Śāstra,* 298b–299a; see below, pp. 264–265.

2 The ultimate object is the unconditioned reality which one realizes by stripping it bare of the veils of convention; see below, Section II, *Modes of Convention.*

3 The factors of the Way are all traced to *prajñā and puṇya,* wisdom and meritorious action; see *Śātra,* 262c. See below, p. 280.

4 It is to be noted that hereafter throughout the work the closely printed passages are translations from the *Śāstra,* unless otherwise indicated; the raised number appearing immediately at the end of the passage refers to the number of the note that appears at the end of this book; the number in the parenthesis that follows the raised number refers to the place where the passage occurs in the Taishō edition of this text, T. 1509; *"Sūtra,"* unless otherwise indicated refers to the *Sūtra* portion in this text.

*bodhisattva:* the full text is *"bodhisattva mahāsattva";* in this compound, hereafter *"mahāsattva"* is omitted for the sake of brevity wherever the sense of the passage is not affected; for the meaning of *mahāsattva,* see ch. XI.

*peacock:* the text has also mandarin ducks (鴛鴦) which is omitted in the present translation.

5 *reflects all things:* lit. there is nothing that he does not see (無不悉見). Cp. *ibid.,* 372b, for the example of *sphaṭika,* the crystal, which, while in itself has not any colour, still appears in different colours according to the things in front of it; see below, p. 96.

6 Cp. *ibid.,* 148a: Beauty and ugliness are in the mind and are not fixed in the thing itself.

6A See below, ch. III.

7 Cp the oft occurring passage: "Whether there is the Buddha or there is not the Buddha, the true nature of things ever remains the same; even the Buddha becomes (or is called) the Buddha by virtue of His having comprehended this true nature of things." See *Śāstra* 548a, 549a, and among other places, 75a, 253b, 516c, 653a–b. See below, chs. III and IX.

8 Convention = *vyavahāra* = *prajñapti; nāma* is an equivalent of *prajñapti, vyavahāra,* also *saṅketa;* cp. *Pancaviṁśati.,* p. 228; also *ibid.,* p. 99: *yac ca tan nāma tat prajñaptimātram* etc.; *nāma-saṅketa* is frequently used in the *Prajñā-pāramitā-sūtras; ibid.,* p. 153 has: *samjñā samajñā prajñaptih vyavahāram* as equivalents; (on these four terms see AAA pp. 69, 257–258).

*Prajñapti* is name as well as concept; it is the means to hold the thing in mind (cp. *prajñaptih tatsaṅketodgrahaṇam,* AAA, pp. 257–258); similar to *nāma,* defined in *Śāstra,* 688b (以名取諸法是故爲名); *saṁjñā* ("idea," sometimes "perception") defined as *nimittodgrahaṇa* (or *lakṣaṇodgrahaṇa* 取相), the picking up of characters, emphasizes the formation of concepts; in *"tena te bālā iti samjñām gacchanti" (Asṭa.*, p. 15), *samjñā* is a synonym of *nāma;* thus *nāma, prajñāpti* and *samjñā* are equivalents meaning not only the verbal expression, the "name," the word that stands for the thing, but also the concept that the word conveys; it is this way that *prajñāpti* is used in *"upādāya prajñapti;"* it is interesting to note that the Chinese translate this term as "derived name," (假名), although in that combination *prajñapti* means notion, idea or concept as well as name.

*Vyavahāra,* the world of convention is an elaboration *(prapañca)* of name (or of *nāma* and *lakṣaṇa); thus vyavahāra* and *prapañca* also serve as synonyms of *nāma* or *prajñapti; Pañcavimśati* (p. 100) has, *"sarva ete prajñaptidharmāḥ . . . yāvad eva nāmamātreṇa vyavahriyante."*

It is to be noted that *prajñapti-dharma* or simply *(upādāya-) prajñapti* means not only the names but also the entities they designate; cp. *Asṭa.* (p. 200), *"vāgvastveva nāmety ucyate;" Pañcavimśati* (p. 105) distinguishes between the object and the name that designates the object in *"tañ ca bodhisattvam tacca bodhisattvanāma."*

The *Śāstra* points out that names are what are fixed by convention or common consent: "The ancient people conventionally established names (假爲立名) as the means to specify or identify things; the later people (use these names and by their means) cognize the things which they designate; in this way everything has (come to have) its own name." *(ibid.,* 246b). Cp. *Pañcavimśati.* (p. 250): *āgantukam etan nāmadheyam prakṣiptam yad uta bodhisattva iti.*

The different meanings of *lakṣaṇa* are discussed in the text below.

8a See *Śāstra* 190b and 651a, on the distinction between the knowledge that is complete and the knowledge that is incomplete; both these passages contain the example of the room lit by a dim light which becomes brighter when lit by a brighter light which goes to show that in the first instance along with light there was darkness.

9 Cp. also *ibid.*, 164a and 292a.

10 Cp. also *ibid.*, 105a–b.

*the creations of the Buddha:* the text has, "all the Buddhas"; in these translations "all" is omitted in this compound for the sake of brevity.

11 Cp. also *ibid.*, 723b, 105b.

12 *Citta = vijñāna =* the self-conscious principle of intellection: the "seed" and the "centre" of personality; in the contexts where *citta* or *vijñāna* is used to mean the person it is improper to translate the term as just consciousness; "mind" would be a better term; in some places the self-conscious principle or person has to be used. See below p. 238. Cp. *Śāstra,* 86a: this *citta* is called *"(bodhi) sattva."* Cp. the note *ibid.*, 383a (confused with the text): *"sattva* (individual) is 心 in Chinese"; *ibid.*, 301b refers to *citta* as the "inner master (内主);" cp. the whole account of *cittasmṛtyupasthāna (ibid.*, 200a–c) which begins with the question: Who is the experiencer of this pleasure? See below, chs. III, VIII and XI.

13 Cp. *Sūtra,* 688b; also *ibid.*, 646b.

14 *Ibid.*, 688b; cp. the definition of *prajñapti* in AAA, pp. 257–258. See above p. 349, n. 8.

15 *Śāstra,* 319c.

16 *Ibid.*, 319b–c.

17 *Nāma and artha:* Note the substitution of *nāma* for *pada.* Here the topic is *padārtha* (句義) *(bodhisattva-padārtha).*

Cp. *Śāstra* 246a–b, where *artha, dharma* and *nirukti* are discussed under the four *vaiśāradyas; ibid.:* "While the hardness of earth is *artha,* the name 'earth' is the *dharma,* and the enunciation of this nature of earth by means of words is *nirukti.* . . . *Artha* stands for the specific as well as the general characters of things while the names that convey these meanings, viz., that hardness is called earth (etc.) is *dharma.*" *Ibid.,* 246b refers also to the inseparability of word and its meaning and the indescribability of their mutual relation as either identity or separateness.

[18] Cp. also *ibid.,* 747a: "Through the grasping of characters there is the name."

[19] *Seizes with a bias* (偏取): this is practically the same as (取相) *lakṣana-grāha;* this is however to be distinguished from *nimittodgrahaṇa,* also 取相, as a definition of *samjñā,* which is by itself ethically neutral. On *grāha* see ch. III.

[20] *Lakṣaṇa* in its second meaning is a synonym of *prakṛti* or *svabhāva* in the sense of nature or essential nature; *tathatā, dharmatā, dharma-lakṣaṇa* are also used in this sense; it is to be noted that the nature or essential nature that is conveyed by these terms admits of the distinction of mundane and ultimate; *bhūta-lakṣaṇa* (實相) however stands only for the ultimate nature of things. For this meaning of *lakṣaṇa,* cp. *Śāstra,* 495b. For details see ch. IX.

[21] *Dhātu* has also the meaning of "source," "origin": cp. *Śāstra,* 644b: "*Dhātu* means 'the origin', 'the source' of the birth of all things (諸法本生處名爲性)." This is one of the senses of "*dhātu*" in *dharmadhātu,* which is also said to be "the root of all things (諸法性是一切法根本)." (*ibid.,* 699b). Cp. also *ibids.* 611c. See below, ch. IX.

[22] Here, "cumulative cultivation (積習) has got perhaps to be rendered as "repeated accumulation" in regard to "earth" with which the question starts.

[22a] On this sense of *lakṣaṇa* see also *ibid.,* 548a, c.

[23] *Seizing the lakṣaṇa: lakṣaṇa-grāha* (取相): this is to seize the relative as absolute, to cling to the determinate as ultimate; this is to fare in duality oblivious of its non-ultimacy. On *grāha* and *vikalpa,* see below, ch. III.

[23a] On 分別憶想 see below, p. 352, n. 4.

[24] *The name fire:* Cp. the lines 22 and 26 on page 358a: there seems to be a confusion between the name fire and the object of this name; but this is no serious difficulty here.

[25] Cp. *Vigrahavyāvartanī,* 9, "*nāma hi nirvastukam nāsti,*" an objection by the Sarvāstivādins *(dharmāvasthāvidaḥ)* and Nāgārjuna's reply, *ibid.,* 57–58.

[26] *Names that arise in a similar way:* the reading 亦如是 of n. 66 is preferred.

[27] On atoms see below, ch. VII.

[28] This whole passage, *Śāstra* 358b-c, constitutes its interpretation of "*nāma-saṅketaprajñaptyām avavādaprajñaptyām dharmaprajñaptyām ca śikṣitavyam,*" *(Pañcavimśati,* p. 102).

*the universal reality* etc.: cp *ibid.,* 195c: "To put the heart of the matter, the universal reality is itself the *prajñāpāramitā.*" Cp. also *ibid.,* 370a.

[29] *Ibid.,* 495b, line 17, 無相 should be just 相. Here 法相 is not to be confused with *dharma-lakṣaṇa* which means the true nature of things; here it is the 法有 of *ibid.,* 147c, referred to above as a mode of determinate being.

*The eyes of flesh etc.,* see below, ch. IV.

*Identical with tathatā etc.:* see below, ch. IX.

[30] *Śāstra,* 548c.

## *Chapter III*

[1] Cp. *Pañcaviṁśati.*, p. 232: *sa cet kāmadhātuḥ . . . avipariṇāmadharmī bhāvo abhaviṣyat nābhāvaḥ naivedam mahāyānam sadevamanuṣāsuram lokam abhibuhūya nirayāsyat.*

[2] The illustrations of illusion occur at several places in the *Prajñāpāramitā-sūtras:* see *Śāstra,* chs. VI, LXXI, LXXXVIII, XCV and XCVI; these are intended to bear out the nature of ignorance by which one gives rise to misconstruction and clinging as well as the wisdom of the wise who understand the unreal as unreal and fare in things with the skilfulness of non-clinging.

[3] See *ibid.*, 296c, 338b and 546c.

[4] Cp. *Pañcaviṁśati.*, p. 147: *Naite Śāriputra dharmāḥ tathā saṁvidyante yathā bālapṛthagjanānām abhiniveśaḥ . . . yathā na saṁvidyante tathā saṁvidyante, evam avidyamānāḥ, tenocyate avidyeti . . . tatra bālāḥ avidyāyāṁ tṛṣṇāyāṁ ca abhiniviṣṭāḥ; tair avidyāṁ tṛṣṇāṁ ca kalpitāṁ kalpayitvā avidyātṛṣṇābhyāṁ abhiniviśya ubhābhyāṁ antābhyāṁ saktāḥ; te ubhav antau na jānanti na paśyanti; yathā dharmāḥ na saṁvidyante, te tān dharmān kalpayitvā namarupe abhiniviṣṭāḥ.* Cp. also *Aṣṭa.*, p. 15.

*They so exist etc.:* The Chinese passage could also be rendered: Things are of such and such nature, things are devoid of such and such nature—this the people do not know and this is ignorance. The Sanskrit parallel of this is not very clear and it has a tendency to identify *avidyā* with the objects of *avidyā (avidyamānā tenocyate avidyeti); Aṣṭa.*, p. 15 has: *tenocyante avidyeti.*

*perversions and imaginative constructions* (妄見分別): also, 想念分別 and 憶想分別: to all these variants of "imaginative construction" the Sanskrit parallel has *"kalpayati"* or *"kalpayitvā"; "vikalpa"* as a synonym of 分別 is usual in this context; 想念分別 is literally *saṁjñāsmṛtivikalpa,* where *smṛti* stands for "thought" (as in *smṛtyupasthāna*), and 憶想分別 is also literally *smṛtisaṁjñāvikalpa* where *smṛti* is memory rather than thought; 念 is also *manyate,* "considers," "thinks," and this, when followed by *abhiniviśate* (著) "clings," stands for wrong thought, an equivalent of (妄見), which is *mithyādṛṣṭi,* misperception, which is also expressed in Sanskrit by *paśyati* or *samanupaśyati* (見) (cp. the opposite, *na samanupaśyati, asamanupaśyan nābhiniviśate* 不見故不著, *Pañca*, p. 38, *Sūtra,* 318a), as well as *upalabhate* (得) which means perceives as well as gets at, seizes, by which one stops (住) *sthāsyati* and does not move on, does not transcend (不出); he who thus stops fares merely in the determinate entities devoid of the comprehension of their true nature, *rūpe carati* (行色), *nimitte carati* (行相) *na carati prajñāpāramitāyām, Pañca,* p. 138; this is also expressed by *lakṣaṇopalambha* or *nimittopalambha* (得相 or 取相) seizing the determinate as itself ultimate, with no proper understanding of the truth of things; such a one stops merely at the determinate (但住相); he is not skilful and so he imagines and clings, *kalpayatyabhiniviśate* (想念分別著); *Pancaviṁsati*, p. 148, *Sūtra* 374b.

*the two dead-ends:* it is under misperception and misconstruction both of which are conveyed by *"dṛṣṭi"* or *"mithyādṛṣṭi"* (妄見), that one mistakes the relative as absolute; the two sides of the natural polarity of thought become sundered and they thus become dead-ends *(anta)*, where there is no getting back to the original unity of the thing or to the ultimate truth of the relative; it is in this sense that *lakṣaṇa* or *nimitta* (相) is identified with *anta* (邊); see *ibid.*, 752a; this seizing of the relative as absolute is engendered by passion that is rooted in ignorance *(avidyātṛṣṇābhyam abhiniviśya ubhābhyām antābhyām saktāḥ)*, for they do not know and do not see, *na jānanti na paśyanti*, that things are not of such nature as they imagine.

*the clinging* (著者): *abhiniviṣṭāḥ*, also *saktāḥ*; *sakti* is *abhiniveśa*, cp. *śūnyeṣu dharmeṣu na saktiḥ kāryā* (自相空法中不應著); *Pañcaviṁśati*, p. 169, *Sūtra*, 381c.

[5] *Ibid.*, 103c, also *ibid.*, 723b.

[6] *Gives rise to perversion* (轉異邪曲): *viparyaya* turning around, upsetting, is exactly 轉 which is perversion, seeing things topsy-turvy, upside down; also, *viparyāsa*, *avidyā-viparyāsa* (無明顚倒), *ibid.*, 723b; this is seeing things as they are not, the real as unreal and the unreal as real; for 顚倒 see *ibid.*, 723a–723c; we have also 變異 (*ibid.*, 298c). To see things pervertedly is to see them different (異) from what they are, which is a false (邪) and crooked (曲) and not straight (不正) way of considering things; cp. *ibid.*, 685c: The Buddha teaches the truth of things to all and He does not pervert it (不轉); cp. also *ibid.*, 689a. *Ibid.*, 572a has: "The irreversible is called so because he has turned away from all sense of clinging" (轉著心故名不轉); note here the difference in the use of 轉; see also *ibid.* 479a.

[7] *Svabhāvaśūnyatā*, the earlier part of this passage has, "The ultimate reality of all things *(sarvadharmabhūtalakṣaṇa)* is itself *svabhāva-śūnyatā*." (697c). See below, ch. IX.

[8] *Sees a man with horns on his head:* this very example appears in *Vibhāṣā* (T. 1545) 194b, where in respect to this dream it is stated that there is no error here; in the waking state, the human body has been seen separately and the horns have been seen separately and in dream these have been mixed up, that is all. It is this very position which must have been in vogue with the Sarvāstivādins that has been expressed in the present passage of the *Śāstra* as the contention of the questioner. *Vibhāṣā*, 193b–194c contains a long account of the nature of dream according to the Vaibhāṣikas.

[9] For the distinction between the right understanding of the wise and the wrong understanding of the common people, see *Śāstra*, 171c, 559b, 609c, 611c, 642b and 726a; see also *ibid.* 101c–105c.

[9a] Cp. *Ibid.*, 726a.

[10] See *ibid.*, 700a.

[11] Cp. the author's paper *"The Sense of I," Proc. Ind. Phil Cong.*, 1956, pp. 173–182; parts of this paper have been utilized in this section of the present chapter.

[12] *The moon is really in the sky* (月實在虛空中): perhaps 實 which has been rendered here as "really" could also mean "real" in the sense of 本 "original" of which the moon in the water is the reflection.

Cp. *Yathādarśam upādāya svamukhapratibimbakam, dṛśyate nāma taccaiva na kiñcid api tattvataḥ; ahaṅkāras tathā skandhān upādāyopalabhyate, na ca kiñcit sa tattvena svamukhapratibimbavat.*

(q. *Prasannapadā*, p. 345); while this stanza says that the reflection in the mirror is of one's own face, it does not say of what the sense of "I" *(ahaṅkāra)* is the reflection in the *skandhas*;

but it is not difficult to see the closeness of this stanza to our passage.

[13] Cp. *ibid.*, 102b.

[14] Cp. *Kārikā* XVIII: 2–4, where the same idea is expressed in the order of extinction of greed etc.

[15] See above, p. 344, note 135.

[16] Cp. *The Sense of I*, p. 177.

[17] *Śāstra* (730a) brings out this truth by saying that the sense of "I" is ethically indeterminate *(avyākṛta* 無記) and flexible *(mṛdu* 柔軟); cp. *The Sense of I*, p. 177.

[18] Cp. *Kārikā*, XXVII: 8: *nāpi nāsty eṣa niścayaḥ:* It cannot also be that the self absolutely is not; this is the truth.

[19] Cp. *Kārikā*, XVIII: 6, for the different kinds in the Buddha's teachings in regard to "I" *(ātman)*.

[20] Cp. also *ibid.*, 697a.

[21] Cp. also *ibid.*, 696c.

[22] Cp. also *ibid.*, 720b. see below, ch. VIII.

[23] See above, p. 344, notes 130, 131; see *Kārikā*, XV: 7; *ibid.*, XV: 11 has,

*Asti yaddhi svabhāvena na tan nāstīti śāśvatam; nāstīdānīm abhūt pūrvam ityucchedah prasajyate.*

[24] Cp. *Ibid.*, XVIII: 4, along with *Prasannapadā* (p. 349). On the sixty-two *dṛṣṭis*, cp. *Brahamajāla-sutta (Dīgha)*; for an exposition of these *dṛṣṭis* in the light of *Kārikā* (ch. XXVII) see N. Dutt, *Ind. Hist. Qly.* (1932) pp. 706 ff. *Parāmarśa* in this context means clinging, attachment; see Nyanatiloka, *Buddhist Dictionary* (Fervin & Co., Ltd., Colombo, 1956), under *parāmāsa* (the Pali equivalent of *parāmarśa)*; in Chinese it is 取. It is the proper understanding of the conditioned origination that is taught as the remedy to all these *dṛṣṭis;* see *Prasannapadā*, p. 571; also *Ārya-śālistamba-sūtra* (q. *Prasannapadā*, pp. 593–594). See below, ch. V.

*Chapter IV*

[1] Cp. *Kārikā*, XXIII: 24–25.

[2] *Śāstra*, 101c ff., 德女經; Professor Lamotte renders this as *Therīsūtra; op. cit.*, p. 361.

[3] It may be noted that when *Kārikā* (XXIII: 15) says

*Yena gṛhṇāti yo grāho grahītā yacca gṛhyate; upaśāntāni sarvāṇi tasmād grāho na vidyate,*

it is to the ultimate truth of things that it refers.

[4] See *Śāstra*, 105b–c; *ibid.*, 105c says: There are things that are the (usual) objects of clinging and there are things that are not so; by means of the latter (the nature of clinging in regard to) the former is brought to light.

[5] Cp. *Vigrahavyāvartanī*, 37: *"nāsti tamaśca jvalane"* = there is no darkness in the light itself.

[6] Cp. also *ibid.*, 543b *(Sūtra):* The mind imbued with passion is in its ultimate nature devoid of passion.

[7] *Ibid.*, 505c; also *ibid.*, 312c: The ultimate nature of the three poisons is itself Nirvāṇa (三毒實相即是涅槃). "Purity" is a synonym of Nirvāṇa; see below, ch. IX.

[8] Cp. *Śāstra* 195c.

[9] This passage is preceded by the example of the great red-hot iron ball, which burns up all that comes into contact with it and yet itself remains intact, without any loss of heat; there is nothing else that can burn this up itself (449b). *Ibid.*, 190c compares *prajñā* to a great flame (大火焰) which cannot be seized from any of the four sides. Cp. also *ibid.*, 139c.

Cp. *ibid.*, 289a: when one puts an end to all imaginations and thought-constructions, when all objects cease (to appear) by virtue of this true *prajñā* devoid of objects (無緣實智) (and hence devoid of distinction) one would not fall into the "lot" of birth and death, one would then realize the eternal peace, the joy of Nirvāṇa.

*Ibid.*, 563c: The *bodhi* par excellence is itself *prajñāpāramitā;* when in the heart of the Buddha it is called *bodhi* while in the heart of the bodhisattva it is called *prajñā.*

9a See below, ch. V.

10 The *prajñā* that *arises from the combination of causal factors* is the functional *prajñā;* it has for its object the ultimate reality as well as the conditioned, contingent entities. Sometimes *Śāstra* distinguishes between *prajñāpāramitā* and 方便 the expedient knowledge; the latter consists in hearing the *Sūtras,* and thinking, weighing, and considering their meaning; the former arises from this latter kind. (See *ibid.*, 196c–197a and 263c). See *ibid.* 162a where 方便智 means the consummating wisdom of skillfulness *(upāya)*; cp. also *ibid.*, 552a where 稱 *tulanā* (weighing) is said to be the knowledge (智慧) that is different from *prajñā.* Referring to the limitlessness of objects, *Śāstra* says: As the objects are unending, so is knowledge too; even as when the vessel is big the lid is big too. (see *ibid.*, 74b–c,124a, 266a). *Ibid.* 125b distinguishes *jnāna* (智) from *vijñāna* (識): *jñāna* "weighs" things and distinguishes between good and bad, while *vijñāna* simply seeks pleasure always and does not enter into the proper and the essential. *Ibid.*, 251a distinguishes between *jñāna* (知) and *darśana* (見): after reading or reciting the scrip tures following other people, to weigh and consider (the meaning of what is read or recited), this is *jñāna;* (thereupon) to realize the truth in one's self (自身得証) is *darśana;* the one is not necessarily free from doubt, whereas the other is the direct personal knowledge, clear understanding free from doubt.

11 *The knowledge of the śrāvakas and the pratyeka-buddhas:* see below, pp. 287–288.

12 *Realizes a permanent fulfilment:* see below, ch. IX.

13 *Sūtra* 347a–351a. Cp. *Pañcaviṁśati.*, *Pañcacakṣuravavāda,* pp. 77–83. The five eyes are (I) *māmsacakṣus* (肉眼), the eyes of flesh; (II) *divyacakṣus* (天眼), the *deva*-eye, the eye of gods, the eye that perceives the arising and passing away of beings in the different spheres of existence; (III) *prajñācakṣus* (慧眼) the eye of wisdom; (IV) *dharmacakṣus* (法眼) the eye of *dharma,* the eye that sees the specific nature and tendency of every individual and perceives the way in which each one can be helped to overcome ignorance and passion; (V) *Buddhacakṣus* (佛眼), the eye of the Buddha that completes and comprehends all the other kinds of "sights."

14 *Ibid.*, 347c.

15 *Ibid.*, 347a.

16 *Ibid.*

17 *Ibid.*, 347c; cp. also *ibid.* 236a, 240b–c and 338a–b. *Śāstra* 347a–b mentions two kinds of *deva* eyes: I) obtained as the result of former deeds, II) obtained by virtue of the cultivation of contemplation and meditation (禪定中).

18 *Ibid.*, 348a.

19 Cp. also *ibid.*, 337c: the eyes of flesh do not see the past and the future.

20 *Ibid.*, 428a.

21 *Ibid.*, 348a.

22 *Ibid.*

22a *Ibid.*, 347a; *ibid.*, 524b has: The sights that the eyes of flesh and the *deva* eye yield are shallow; whereas the sight that the eye of wisdom yields is profound, immeasurable. *Ibid.*, 348b mentions two kinds of the eye of wisdom; one kind perceives the general characters of things like impermanence, non-substantiality etc. and the other perceives the specific characters of things; while the *śrāvakas* and the *pratyeka-buddhas* have only the former, the Buddha has both of these.

23 *Ibid.*, 348a, the very last of the views presented. The *Śāstra* counts here several views in regard to the nature of the eye of wisdom. In cases like this, the view that is stated as the very last of the items is usually the one that is considered as most adequate; cp., e.g., the various definitions of *prajñā, ibid.*, 139c, where, although it is said "some say the last account is the true account," it is obvious there that that is the one which the *Śāstra* considers as the most adequate.

*all the activities of the mind return etc.*, cp. *Kārikā*, XVIII: 7:

*Nivṛttam abhidhātavyam nivṛtte cittagocare; anutpannā aniruddhā hi nirvāṇam iva dharmatā.*

24 On *mārgānvayajñāna*, see ch. X.

25 *Ibid.*, 349a–b.

26 See also *ibid.* 348c–349a for details on the eye of *dharma*.

27 See also *ibid.*, 350b.

28 Cp. *ibid.*, 350c–351a.

29 *Ibid.*, 350b; see *ibid.*, for the mention of the merits of the eye of the Buddha, viz., the knowledge of all forms, the ten powers, the four elements of expertness etc. See below, ch. X.

30 On this see below, ch. X.

*Chapter V*

1 Cp. *Sūtra, ibid.*, 424 ff.: *Mahāyāna* is comparable to *ākāśa; ibid.*, 429 ff.: *Prajñāpāramitā* is not different from *Mahāyāna*. See below, chs. IX and X.

2 This is the last of the views presented in regard to the nature of *prajñāpāramitā* (139a–c).

*the flame that cannot be touched etc.*: cp. *ibid.*, 190c; see above, p. 354, n. 9.

3 Prof. Lamotte observes that 衆義經 (*Śāstra* 60c) and 阿他婆耆經 (*ibid.* 63c) stand for *Arthavargīyusūtra;* see his detailed note, *op. cit.*, p. 39, n. 2.

4 *To know this* etc.: the reading *ibid.* 60c, n. 60 is preferred. *Prapañca* as conceptual elaboration needs to be distinguished from getting entangled in the network of concepts; the latter is the result of clinging to concepts and is also called *prapañca;* for the use of *prapañca* in both senses, see *Kārikā*, XXII: 15:

*Prapañcayanti ye buddham prapañcātītam avyayam; te prapañcahatāḥ sarve na paśyanti tathāgatam.*

4a *Śāstra*, 192c.

5 Cp. *Vigrahavyāvartanī* 30:

*Yadi kiñcid upalabheyam pravartayeyam nivartayeyam vā; pratyakṣādibhir arthaiḥ tadabhāvān me anupālambhaḥ.*

Cp. also *ibid.*, 29.

6 *Śāstra* (125a) cites this as the Buddha's advice to His disciples at the time of His entering *parinirvāṇa; artha* (義) is the meaning and words *(vyañjana)* are what bring it to light. *Artha* is one of the four things on which the disciples of Buddha are exhorted to depend; see *Prasannapadā*, p. 43; cp. Lamotte, *op. cit.*, p. 536, n. 1.

7 Cp. also *Śāstra* 726a.

*words are means*: cp. *Prasannapadā*, p. 24: *na hi śabdāḥ dāṇḍapāśikā iva vaktāram asvatantrayanti;* cp. also *ibid.*, p. 494.

8 Cp. *Śāstra*, 125b; see above, p. 355, n. 10; see also p. 350, n. 12; see below, ch. VIII.

9 Cp. *Majjh.*, I, 135; also Lamotte, *op. cit.*, p. 64 n. 1.

[10] Cp. *Śāstra* 63c.
[11] See above, p. 356 n. 3.
[12] On the mundane right view (世間正見) see *ibid.*, 312c; on the distinction between the mundane right view and the transmundane right view see *ibid.*, 412b. See also *ibid.*, 677c.
[13] Cp. *Kārikā*, XVIII: 6:
*Ātmetyapi prajñapitam anātmetyapi deśitam; buddhair nātmā nacānātmā kaścid ityapi deśitam.*
[14] See above p. 344, n. 131.
[15] *both these teachings are true,* cp. *ibid.*, 59b, 139c, 297c–298a, 338b–c, 424a.
*the ring finger:* 無名指 is a literal translation of *"anāmikā,"* "nameless," a term which is most apt to convey the relatively indeterminate nature, which is the point of the analogy here.
[16] Cp. *ibid.*, 254a; cp. also *ibid.* 424a.
[17] Cp. *ibid.* 254a.
[18] Candrakīrti tells us that Nāgārjuna wrote the *Madhyamaka-śāstra* in order to set forth the distinction between the *Sūtras* of *neyārtha* and those of *nītārtha;* see *Prasannapadā,* p. 41: *ata evedam madhyamakaśāstram praṇītam ācāryeṇa neyanītārthasūtrāntavibhāgopadarśanārtham.*
[19] See *Śāstra* (338c) which cites *Kārikā*, XVIII, 8: *Sarvam tathyam na vā tathyam tathyañ cātathyam eva ca; naivātathyam naiva tathyam etad buddhānuśāsanam.*
[20] Cp. 254b.
[21] The four *siddhāntas* are: (世界) mundane *(laukika)*, (各々爲人) individual *(prātipauruṣika)*, (對治) remedial *(prātipakṣika)* and (第一義) the ultimate *(pāramārthika)*. These renderings are of Prof. Lamotte; cp. Lamotte, op. cit., p. 27, n. 1. For the whole account of the four *siddhāntas*, see *Śāstra*, 59b–61b.
[22] Cp. Lamotte, *op. cit.*, p. 32, n. 2. 破群那經 has another reading 破群邪經 which allows the rendering: "The Sūtra on destroying the Multitude of Heresies."
[23] Cp. *Kārikā* XVIII: 10.
[24] Cp. *Śāstra*, 59c.
[25] Cp. *ibid.*, 60a.
[25a] Cp. *Prasannapadā*, pp. 356–358.
[26] *Śāstra*, 60b–c.
[27] *(there) the sphere of the speakable ceases etc.:* Cp. *Kārikā*, XVIII: 7:
*Nivṛttam abhidhātavyam nivṛtte cittagocare;*
*anutpannā aniruddhā hi nirvāṇam iva dharmatā.*
*Śāstra* (61b) cites *Kārikā* XVIII: 8 as the ultimate truth, while *ibid.* 338c cites it as elucidating that the complete *śūnyatā* does not reject deeds as the conditions of the rounds of birth and death.
[28] Cp. *Kārikā*, XXIV: 10.
[29] The following is a brief exposition of the account of "the three kinds of the gateways to the *dharma* (三種法門)," set forth, *Śāstra*, 192a–194b. Of the names of these three (蜫勒門, 阿毘曇門, 空門) the second and the third are clearly *Abhidharma* and *Śūnyatā*. In regard to 蜫勒 it is to be noted that this term occurs twice in the *Śāstra*, 70a–b and 192b–194b. While in the latter context we are told that it was Mahākātyāyana who composed it during the lifetime of the Buddha in order to explain His teachings, in the former context it is considered as one of the kinds of *Abhidharma*. Lamotte read this word as *Pi le* and rendered it as *Piṭaka* meaning the *Peṭakopadesa* of Mahākātyāyana, considered to be one of the principal sources of *Viśuddhimagga* and *Vimuktimārga;* see *op. cit.*, p. 109 n. 2, and p. 113. Being unable to find a better solution and prompted by the force of the context, I have tentatively taken the word to mean *Vinaya,* while still preserving the reading *Piṭaka*. *Piṭaka* is of

course a very general term.
[30] *Ibid.,* 648b: *Vinaya* does not discuss about the true nature of things (結戒不論實相).
[31] *Piṭaka (Vinaya),* 蜫勒門; see above p. 357, n. 29.
[31a] Cp. the account of the three gates of freedom *(vimokṣadvāra)* in *Śāstra* 207c; see below, ch. X.
[32] The *Śāstra* emphasizes analysis as an essential preliminary for the farer on the Great Way, the way of comprehension: see e.g., *ibid.,* 256b.
[33] *capable of comprehending how all of them enter śūnyatā:* lit. capable of making all things enter *śūnyatā* (能令諸法入...空). Cp. also *ibid.* 293c–294b.
[34] *skilful alchemist,* cp. also *ibid.,* 298b. That Nāgārjuna knew alchemy has been noted by some of his traditional biographies; see Max Walleser, *Life of Nāgārjuna;* cp. above, p. 337. n. 14. It appears that he had at least known of this science.
[35] On *dharma-kṣānti;* see below, ch. X.
[36] See above, p. 344, n. 138. *Śāstra* 75a, 253 b and 321b, c refer to the Buddha's four ways of answering (四種答 or 四種論); cp. *Kārikā* ch. XXVII.
[37] See especially *Śāstra,* 546b and 547b; cp. *ibid., Sūtra* 545b ff.; cp. *Aṣṭa.* pp. 268–270; see above, p. 344, n. 138.
[38] The problem of the Buddha's attitude in regard to these questions (十四難 or 十四事) comes up for consideration several times in the *Śāstra;* see *ibid.,* 74c–75a; 253b–54c; see also 124a, 170a, 321c; also *ibid.,* 545b–546a *(Sūtra)* and 547b–c *(Śāstra).* Of these 74c–75a and 253b–254c are similar and they constitute the most complete account of the *Śāstra* in regard to this problem.
[39] Cp. also *ibid.,* 170b.
[40] *impermanence (would be the first door to śūnyatā):* Cp. *ibid.,* 229b, 287c, 290c. Cp. *Kārikā,* XIII: 1–2, XXIII:13–14.
[41] See below, ch. VI.
[42] Cp. *ibid.,* 253b. Cp. *ibid.,* 75a, where the *Śāstra* records the Buddha's answer to an enquirer: I did not make (the order of things in) the twelve-linked chain; whether there is the Buddha or not, the universal order of things ever remains, but the Buddha is capable of teaching this to people (and bringing it to light).

### *Chapter VI*

[1] This is the famous way of *prasaṅga.* Cp. Candrakīrti, *Prasannapadā,* p. 24 *tathā ca ācāryo bhūyasā prasaṅgāpatti-mukhenaiva parapakṣam nirākaroti sma.*
[2] It is to be noted that this is practically the way in which the various positions of "is" and "is not," "self" and "other," etc. are subjected to examination throughout the *Kārikā;* see below, ch. VII.
[3] *Kārikā,* XV: 11:

*Asti yaddhi svabhāvena na tan-nāstīti śāśvatam.*

[4] *Ibid. Nāstīdanīm abhūt pūrvam ity ucchedah prasajyate.*
[5] While almost the entire *Kārikā* consists of arguments framed in terms of extremes, meant to expose the absurd conclusions to which they naturally lead, it may be noted that the *Śāstra* (as well as the *Sūtra)* consider the four *koṭis* in several places; see *ibid.,* 641c ff, 644a ff, 658c, 662a, 686a, 706b, 707c ff; see also *ibid.,* 170c. See below, ch. VII.
[5a] *Śāstra,* 708b.
[6] Cp. *ibid.,* 170c.
[7] Sañjayabelaṭṭhiputta is known to have maintained, *evam pi me no, tathā ti pi me no, aññathā ti pi me no, no tipi me no.* See *Dīgha.* I, p. 25.
[8] *Śāstra,* 61b–62a.

[9] For a series of "neither—nor—" as descriptive of *prajñā,* see *ibid.,* e.g., 482b; the *Prajñāpāramitā-sūtras* abound in this kind.
[10] See *Śāstra,* 642a–b.
[10a] *Ibid.* 642b.
[11] *Ibid.*
[12] Cp. *ibid.,* 646c.
[12a] *Ibid.,* 649b.
[13] Cp. *ibid.,* 686a.
[14] Cp. *ibid.,* 708b.
[15] *Ibid.,* 585c.
[15a] *Kārikā,* XV: 5.
[16] See above, pp. 94–95.
[17] See above, p. 134.

*Chapter VII*

[1] *Bhāva* or "being" in *"svabhāva"* (self-being) connotes not only the being or "is-ness" of the thing, but also its nature, its essence. This nature, which is unique to the thing, the thing's own, could be either relatively or absolutely its own; the important point in the philosophy of the Middle Way is that while the unique, specific natures of things are their own natures, they are not unconditioned; they owe their "being" to the cooperation of their causes and conditions; and that nature of things which is unconditioned is not anything specific; there all things are of one nature, *ekalakṣaṇa,* viz., of no specific nature, *alakṣaṇa.* That everything has its own nature and function but not unconditioned is accepted by the Mādhyamika as a mundane truth; see *Vigrahavyāvartanī,* 22, with the author's own *vṛtti.* See below, ch. IX.
[2] The *Śāstra* mentions Vaipulyakas as tending to view the world as a baseless illusion—which is a case of clinging to *śūnyatā; ibid.,* 61a–b. *Ibid.,* 193c–194a draws the distinction between the wrong view of the nihilist that denies causal continuity and the effectiveness of deeds and the right view of *śūnyatā* that does not cling to the total denial of things. Cp. *Kārikā,* ch. XXIV; cp. Candrakīrti's *Prasannapadā,* p. 159.
[3] This is the substance of ch. XXIV of *Kārikā.*
[4] *Śāstra,* 171a; cp. the Buddha's teaching to Kātyāyana (*Samyu.* II, 17) cited above p. 344, notes 130–131; cp. *Kārikā,* XV: 7; *Śāstra* 170c cites a *gāthā* to say: When one sees the *dharma* devoid of birth then one becomes free from (clinging to) the born, the conditioned; when one sees the incomposite *dharma* then one becomes free from (clinging to) the composite entities. Cp. above, pp. 139–140, the *prātipakṣikasiddhānta. Kārikā* XV: 9–11 make out that the denial of the extremes of "is" and "is not" is in order to bring to light the nature of things as change *(anyathātva).* Cp. also *ibid.,* XIII: 2–5.
[5] Cp. *Śāstra,* 331a.
[6] *Cling to śūnyatā, etc.:* cp. *Kārikā,* XIII: 8; also XXII: 11; see especially *ibid.,* XXIV: 11. See above, n. 2.
[7] On the criticism and rejection of absolute being and absolute non-being as false in respect to the mundane nature of things, see *Śāstra,* 171a–172a and 207b; cp. also *ibid.,* 292b; cp. *Kārikā,* chs. XV and XIII, also *ibid.,* ch. XXIV.

What follows in this as well as in the following sections of the present chapter on the criticism of categories, is, in each case, a substance of the relevant passages in the *Śāstra,* amplified at times by citations from the *Kārikā.* Such amplifications, however, have been stated as such, wherever they occur. Actually this is the portion where the *Śāstra* practically incorporates here and there, often verbally repeating either in prose or in verse, the entire of *Kārikā*. The negative arguments of the latter occur in the *Śāstra* often with the much needed light on the nature and purpose of criticism; this has been stated clearly at the end of every section in the present chapter.

*if everything has an absolute being of its own:* cp. *Kārikā,* XV: 1:

*Na sambhavaḥ svabhāvasya yuktaḥ pratyayahetubhiḥ;*
*hetupratyayasambhūtaḥ svabhāvaḥ kṛtako bhavet.*

Also *ibid.*, 2:

*Akṛtrimah svabhāvo hi nirapekṣaḥ paratra ca.*

Cp. also *Ekaślokaśāstra* (T. 1573, 253a–c); *ibid.*, 253a says that the purpose of this little text is to reveal the devoidness of permanence and self-being in respect to the elements of existence.

*if non-existence were the true nature of things:* cp. *Kārikā,* XXIV: 7 ff.; cp. *Prasannapadā*, p. 491, *nāstitvam śūnytārtham parikalpayan, . . . abhāvaśabdārtham ca śūnyatārtham ityadhyāropya* etc.

*those who cling to the existence view stand opposed etc.: Kārikā,* XXII: 11, points out that even in respect to *śūnyatā*, the clinging that would turn it into an extreme might lead to the other extreme of *aśūnya*, *"Śūnyam iti na vaktavyam aśūnyam iti vā bhavet."* Clinging to non-existence is *ucchedavāda* which holds the extinction of things as total and thus amounts to a denial of causal continuity. This is especially mentioned in reference to the continuity of life after death, with which the question of the effectiveness of deeds is bound up. The *Śāstra* (254a) mentions two kinds of *ucchedavāda* (斷見); one denies the continuity of life after death, and the other denies all things as "nothing." The latter perhaps refers to the Vaipulyakas (referred to above, p. 359, n. 2); *ibid.*, 193c refers to three kinds of *mithyādṛṣṭi* of which the first two could be compared with the first kind of *uccheda* mentioned *ibid.*, 254a and the third of the former with the second of the latter.

[8] Cp. *Śāstra,* 171a.

[9] *Kārikā*, XIII: 5:

*Tasyaiva nānyathābhāvo nāpy anyasyaiva yujyate.*

Cp. also *ibid.*, 6.

[10] *Ibid.*, XIII: 4; XV: 9.

[11] *Ibid.*, XIII: 3:

*Bhāvanām niḥsvabhāvatvam anyathābhāvadarśanāt.*

[12] *Ibid.* XV: 3–5; *ibid.*, 5 has

*Bhāvasya hy anyathābhāvam abhāvam bruvate janāḥ.*

[13] *Śāstra*, 194b.

[14] Cp. *ibid.*, 171a.

[15] Cp. *ibid.*, 171c; see above, pp. 93 ff.

[16] See below, ch. IX.

[17] Cp. *ibid.*, 171b, 229b, 287c, 290c; see above, p. 358, n. 40.

[18] Cp. *Śāstra,* 193b; cp. also *ibid.*, 170c.

[18a] For the mention and criticism of these views see *ibid.*, 104c; cp. *ibid.*, 296b and *Kārikā*, XX: 1–4.

[19] Cp. *Kārikā*, I: 1:

*Na svato nāpi parato na dvābhyām nāpy ahetutah; utpannā jātu vidyante bhāvāḥ kvacana kecana.*

Cp. also *ibid.*, XXI: 13; XXIII: 20; and XII: 1.

[20] Cp. Candrakīrti: *Prasannapadā*, pp. 210–211.

[21] *Śāstra,* 104c. *Kārikā*, I: 1: *"nāpi parataḥ"*; also *ibid.*, XX: 2, 4. See above, n. 19.

[22] Cp. *Kārikā*, XII: 1:

*Svayam kṛtam parakṛtam dvābhyām kṛtam ahetukam; duhkham ity eka icchanti tacca kāryam na yujyate.*

[23] Cp. *Vibhāṣā* for the Sarvāstivāda account of *hetu* (79a ff.) and *pratyaya*

(108c ff.); cp. Stcherbatsky, *Central Conception,* pp. 30 ff., also p. 81, n. 1 and p. 106.

24 Cp. *Śāstra,* 104c–105a; also *ibid.,* 297b; cp. *Kārikā,* I: 7, 12; and also *ibid.,* XX: 1–4, 16–22.

It is necessary to note that of the two principal accounts of the examination of causal origination found in the *Śāstra* (104b–105a, and 296b–297b); in the latter (296b–c) it puts the substance of *Kārikā,* ch. I in the mouth of the objector who misunderstands the negative arguments to mean that the kinds of condition are totally denied in the *prajñāpāramitā* and who thus gives rise to wrong notions and clinging in regard to their denial. Thereupon, the *Śāstra* (296c ff.) proceeds to give an account of these kinds of conditions as set forth in the *Abhidharma,* after pointing out that what is sought to be rejected in the present context is not the conditions themselves, but one's perversions in regard to them. The account in the *Abhidharma* is what the beginners learn and must not be clung to as an account of the ultimate nature of things. Lastly the *Śāstra* (297b) adds a few more negative arguments obviously as a help towards further removal of perversion and clinging. The force of the whole account cannot be missed, which is to clarify the nature and purpose of criticism. The same conclusion is reached even in the earlier account on pp. 104b–105a, but in a slightly different way. One would not miss this general spirit of the critical examination of categories in the several accounts appearing in the *Śāstra.*

25 *Ibid.,* 296c just has: When things are devoid of occasions *(animitta)* and devoid of objective conditions *(anālambana)* how can one speak of *ālambana-pratyaya?* We find a more complete statement in *Kārikā,* I: 8:

*Anālambana evāyam san dharma upadiśyate; athānālambane dharme kuta ālambanam punaḥ.*

For an adequate understanding of this stanza Candrakīrti's *Prasannapadā* (pp. 84–85) is of great help.

26 *Śāstra,* 296b–c; cp. *Kārikā,* I: 9; cp. *Prasannapadā,* p. 86.

27 Cp. *Kārikā,* XX: 6–7.

28 Cp. *ibid.,* XX: 5.

29 Cp. *ibid.,* XX: 10–11, 15.

30 Cp. *Ibid.,* XX: 7–8, 12–14.

31 This is as *ibid.,* I: 10:

*Bhāvānam niḥsvabhāvānām na sattā vidyate yataḥ; satīdam asmin bhavatīty etan naivopapadyate.*

32 *Śāstra,* 296c, has: "When things do not have anything to belong to, anything to depend on, if all are of the same nature how could one speak of the decisive condition?"

33 Cp. *Kārikā,* I: 4:

*Kriyā na pratyayavatī nāpratyayavatī kriyā; pratyayā nākriyāvantaḥ kriyāvantaś ca santy uta.*

34 Cp. *ibid.,* XX: 21:

*Na cājanayamānasya hetutvam upapadyate.*

35 *Śāstra,* 297b; cp. *Kārikā,* I: 13.

36 For the criticism of motion as set forth in *Kārikā,* ch. II, see *Śāstra,* 205b–c, and 427c–428a; cp. also *Daśabhūmivibhāṣā* (T. 1521) 28a. In *Śāstra* 205b–c the negative arguments conclude by pointing out that the true *prajñā* is itself also the right deed, and he who has the right understanding always does the right deed, never any wrong deed.

37 *Śāstra,* 205b; cp. *Kārikā,* II: 1, 8.

38 *Śāstra,* 205c; cp. *Kārikā,* II: 5, 11.

39 *Śāstra,* 205c; cp. *Kārikā,* II: 6.

40 *Śāstra,* 428a: "Coming and staying

are also like this"; cp. *Kārikā,* VII: 14; *Śāstra,* 205c just says, "In this way, all activities are *śūnya.*"

[41] *Kārikā,* II: 18–20.

[42] *Ibid.,* II: 22–23.

[43] *Ibid.,* II: 21:

*Ekībhāvena vā siddhiḥ nānābhavena vā yayoḥ; na vidyate tayoḥ siddhiḥ katham nu khalu vidyate.*

Cp. also *ibid.,* XXI: 6.

[44] *Ibid.,* II: 15 ff.; *ibid.,* VII; 23.

[45] *Ibid.,* II: 24–25.

[46] *Ibid.,* VII: 14.

[47] See above, p. 57.

[48] *Śāstra* 60b. Cp. *Kārikā,* VII: 1, 3. This is practically the substance of ch. VII of *Kārikā* which includes the stricture on the conception of birth of birth; the rest of the chapter follows closely the examination of motion *ibid.,* ch. II and the arguments are for the most part repetitions.

[49] This is the conception of birth and birth of birth expressed in *Kārikā,* VII: 4–5; this is the view of the Sarvāstivādins: see *Vibhāṣā* (T. 1545) 200c–201a; cp. also *Dvādaśamukha Śāstra* (T. 1568) 162c–163c. Candakīrti tells us in his *Prasannapadā* (p. 148) that this is the view of the Sāmmitīyas.

[50] *Kārikā,* VII: 2.

[51] *Ibid.,* XXI: 8.

[52] *Ibid.,* 14.

[53] *Ibid.,* 18–19.

[54] Cp. *Prasannapadā,* p. 329: It is the false realism that cannot establish activity; it is only the doctrine of non-substantiality *(niḥsva-bhāva)* that makes room for activity: *Sasvabhāvānāmeva vyāpārādarśanaḥ niḥsvābhāvānāmeva vyāpāradarśanāt.*

[55] Cp. *Kārikā,* XI: 1:

*Pūrvā prajñāyate koṭir netyuvāca mahāmuniḥ; saṃsāro' navarāgro hi nāsyādir nāpi paścimam.*

*Kārikā* XI, *"Examination of Prior End,"* institutes the argument that birth cannot be either prior or posterior to or even simultaneous with decay and death; *ibid.,* 3–5.

[55a] *Śāstra,* 291a.

[56] *Ibid.*

[57] *Ibid.,* 291b.

[58] On the nature of the teaching of impermanence, see above, p. 358, n. 40 and p. 360, n. 17.

[59] See above, pp. 82 ff.

[60] The *Śāstra* mentions this as a *gāthā* in the *Kālasūtra;* a stanza somewhat near to this quoted in *Prasannapadā* (p. 386) runs:

*Kālaḥ pacati bhūtāni kālaḥ samharate prajāḥ*
*Kālaḥ supteṣu jāgarti kālo hi duratikramaḥ.*

*Kārikā,* ch. XIX, has three arguments in regard to the different conceptions of time: I) the present and the future are not there either dependently on or independently of the past, and the case is the same with each of the other times in relation to the rest; II) there is no eternal substance called time, different from moment etc. and different also from physical entities etc., that is yet brought to light by these; III) there is no time even as an entity *(bhāva)* dependent on things.

[61] *Śāstra,* 65b; cp. *Vaiśeṣikasūtras* of Kaṇāda, II: ii, 7–9.

[62] *Śāstra,* 65b.

[63] *Ibid.*

[64] *Ibid.,* 65b–c.

[65] This is the view of Sarvāstivādins; see above, pp. 57 ff.

[66] *Śāstra,* 65c.

[67] *Ibid.,* 254c.

[68] *Ibid.*

[69] *Ibid.,* 255a.

[70] *Ibid.*

[71] *Ibid.*
[72] Cp. *ibid.*, 563b, 564b.
[72a] *Ibid.* 65c.
[73] 詭名 . . . 稱: the reading *ibid.* n. 14 is preferred.
[73a] Cp. *ibid.*, 65c–66a; cited above, p. 83.
[74] *Śāstra,* 133b. This is clearly the view of the Vaiśeṣikas; the text *(ibid.)* presents the objectors as saying: Although *(dik)* is not mentioned in your *"Four Collections of Dharma" (catur-dharma-piaṭka)* (四法藏), it is mentioned in our *"Collection of Six Dharmas"* (六法藏); (although) it is not included in your (counting of) elements, viz., *skandha, dhātu* and *āyatana,* it is (no doubt) included in our *"dravyas* (陀羅驃)." The six *dharmas* are the six *padārthas,* the basic categories of the Vaiśeṣikas; cp. *Vaiśeṣika Sūtras* I, i, 4; *dik* is included among the *dravyas,* cp. *ibid.*, I, i, 5.

As for *catur-dharma-piṭaka* (四法藏) see *Śāstra,* 143c where they are mentioned as *Sūtra, Vinaya, Abhidharma* and *Samyukta-piṭaka* (雜藏); cp. also *ibid.*, 412a; *"dharma"* in this compound evidently means doctrine; but we have *ibid.*, 497b mentioning 五種法藏 "collection of five kinds of *dharma" (panca-vidha-dharma-piṭaka)* by which it means the categories of being, kinds of elements, viz., the past, the present, the future, the incomposite and the inexpressible (不可說); the true nature of all of these is said to be illumined in the light of *prajñāpāramitā.* Earlier (61a) the *Śāstra* mentions disapprovingly of the Vātsiputrīyas' inclusion of the empirical self under the category of the inexpressible.
[75] Cp. *Vaiśeṣika Sūtras* II, ii, 10–15; *ibid.* II, ii, 14 mentions only the east being regarded as east on account of its contact with the sun, which may be past, present or future; the next (II, ii, 15) *Sūtra* says that the south, the west and the north are to be distinguished in the same way; we do not have here the details in the definition of the different directions which we find in our text, *Śāstra,* 133b.
[76] *Sumeru is in the middle etc.*: on this cosmology, see Lamotte, op. cit., p. 596, n. 2.
[77] *Śāstra,* 133c.
[78] *Ibid.*
[79] *Ibid.*
[80] *Ibid.*, 288a, says that while according to the *Śrāvakas* "the *śūnyatā* of the great *(mahāśūnyatā)"* means the *śūnyatā* of the basic elements, in Mahāyāna it means the *sūnyatā* of the ten directions *(dik)*—the directions are devoid of the nature of directions; cp. ibid., 288b: "Of the transmundane Nirvāṇa is great, while of the mundane *dik* is great."

"everlasting" evidently means here non-temporal, a nature which all concepts share.
[81] Cp. *ibid.*, 288b.
[82] *Ibid.*, 102b.
[83] *Ibid.*, 424b ff. (含受品), especially 426b; cp. also *ibid.*, 102c.
[84] *Ibid.*, 102b: 非可見法
[85] *Ibid.*, 102b–c.
[86] *Ibid.*, 102c; this is the view of the Sarvāstivādins; see *Vibhāṣā* (T. 1545), 388c; *Vaiśeṣika Sūtras* II, i, 20 presents a view that coming in and going out are the marks of *ākāśa* and rejects it as unsound in II, i, 21; the Vaiśeṣikas themselves take sound as its mark, see *ibid.*, II, i, 27.
[87] *Śāstra,* 102c.
[88] *Ibid.*, 102c–103a; cp. *Vibhāṣā* (T. 1545) 388c.
[89] *Śāstra,* 103a; cp. also *ibid.*, 426b.

90 *Ibid.*, 103a; cp. *Kārikā*, V: 1:
*Nākāśam vidyate kiñcit pūrvam ākāśa-lakṣaṇāt.*
It may be noted that "*rūpa*" is not only "form" but also "resistance" which is the characteristic of the "formed;" it means "physical."
91 *Śāstra*, 426c.
*In the absence of the character etc.*: cp. *Kārikā*, V: 1–2:
*Alakṣaṇam prasajyeta syāt pūrvam yadi lakṣaṇāt; alakṣaṇo na kaścicca bhāvaḥ saṃvidyate kvacit.*
92 *Śāstra*, 426b.
93 *Ibid.*, 426c.
94 *Ibid.*; see below, ch. IX.
95 Cp. *Śāstra*, 548a, c. See above, p. 77.
95a *Quality does not inhere in the qualified etc.*, cp. *Kārikā*, V: 3:
*Nālakṣaṇe lakṣaṇasya pravṛttir na salakṣaṇe; salakṣaṇālakṣaṇābhyām nāpy anyatra pravartate.*
In 相不入相, the second 相 should be 有相, for it clearly stands for *salakṣaṇa*, the qualified.
Cp. also *Daśabhūmivibhāṣā* (T. 1521) 116c–117a.
96 *Śāstra*, 549a.
97 *Ibid.*
98 *Ibid.*; cp. *Kārikā*, VI: 1:
*Rāgād yadi bhavet pūrvam rakto rāga-tiraskṛtaḥ; tam pratītya bhaved rāgo rakte rāgo bhavet sati.*
Cp. also *ibid.*, 2–3.
98a *Ibid.*, 3.
99 Cp. *Ibid.*, 8 ff.
100 Cp. *ibid.*, V: 5–6.

## Chapter VIII

1 *Śāstra*, 171a; cp. also *ibid.*, 294b.
2 *Ibid.*, 194c.
2a Cp. *ibid.* 369a.
3 *Ibid.* 194c.
3a For a similar argument to reject self as a separate entity see *ibid.*, 148b; see below, p. 218.
4 *Śāstra*, 194c.
5 *Ibid.*
6 *Ibid.*, 147c; cp. *ibid.*, 326c. *Ibid.* 104b refers to the theory of atoms in the *Vibhāṣā* (cp. *ibid.*, 702a); the theory of atoms in *Śāstra* (547a) presumably refers to the view of the Vaiśeṣikas.
7 *Ibid.*, 147c; see above p. 84.
8 *Śāstra*, 147c; cp. also *ibid.*, 326c.
9 *Ibid.*, 148a.
10 *Ibid.*, 291c–292a.
11 *ball of foam etc.*: cp. the famous citation from *Saṃyuktāgama* cited in *Prasannapadā*, p. 41: *Phenapiṇḍopamam rūpam vedanā budbudopamā.*
12 *Śāstra*, 292a.
13 *if rūpa were a substantial self-existent entity etc.*, cp. *Kārikā*, IV: 2:
*Rūpakāraṇanirmukte rūpe rūpam prasajyate; ahetukam, na cāsty arthaḥ kaścid āhetukaḥ kvacit.*
14 Cp. *Kārikā*, III: 7, where this view of the dependent origination of the visual sensation is presented as the view of an objector, presumably the Ābhidharmika; what is denied here is the possibility of such a dependent originination on the ground of *sasvabhāvavāda;* here it is also an exposal of the absurd conclusion of having to accept the impossibility of the seer, the seen, the act of seeing etc. The dependent origination that accepts the essential conditionedness of all elements is however not only acceptable to the Mādhyamika, but is the very truth that he intends to reveal through his negative criticism.
15 Of the four-fold cultivation of mindfulness *(smṛtyupasthāna)* the first concerns the physical elements, especially, body, the physical basis of personality, and the other three concern the mind

and the mental elements. The mindfulness that is cultivated is mainly with regard to the conditionedness and non-substantiality of these basic kinds of elements. In the case of the farer on the Great Way, this consummates in the realization that their ultimate nature is the undivided *dharma*. See below, ch. X.

15a In the ensuing discussion "soul" (神 or 我) has been used specially to stand for the individual self in the substantialist view. Individual entity or I-substance perhaps fits better in its place.

16 While it is hard to specify a Buddhist school that did believe in the substantiality and permanence of the individual, it should be noted that the *Kārikā*, ch. XVI: 3 mentions a view of this kind; cp. also the *Sāmmitīyanikāya-śāstra*, pp. 166–173 where this is mentioned as one of the seven views discussed and denounced. This makes it clear that this is not the view of the Sāmmitīyas. Cp. the view of Haimavatas in *Bareau*, p. 113; cp. the view of 六法論 cited in *Vibhāṣā*, 37c.

17 *Śāstra*, 148b; see above, p. 212.

18 *Ibid.*, 148b. Cp. also 200b–c. On (A) see *Vaiśeṣika-Sūtras*, III. ii. 9, *Ahamiti śabdasya vyatirekāt na āgamikam;* see especially *ibid.*, *sūtra* 14: *Ahamiti pratyag ātmani bhāvāt paratrābhāvāt arthāntarāpratyakṣaḥ;* cp. also *ibid.*, *sūtras* 18, 20 and 21; on the multiplicity of souls see *ibid.*, III. ii. 20, 21; see *Sāṅkhyakārikā* (ed. S. S. Sunyanarayana Sastri, University of Madras, 1948), 17 for the proofs for the existence of soul *(puruṣo'sti)* and *ibid.*, 18 for its multiplicity *(puruṣabahutvam)*.

19 *Śāstra*, 148c; cp. *ibid.*, 200c.

20 *Ibid.*

21 *Ibid.*, 148b.

22 Cp. *ibid.*, 200c, 230c.

23 *Ibid.*, 149a; cp. also *ibid.*, 200c and 231a.

24 *Ibid.*

24a *Ibid.*, 149a; *ibid.* l. 25: the 相 after 若神自在 should be 自. Cp. also *ibid.* 200c.

25 *Ibid.*, 149b; cp. also *ibid.*, 547a.

26 *Ibid.*, 149b. On subtle body, see *Sāṅkhyakārikā*, 40–42; *ibid.*, 40 runs:

*Pūrvotpannam asaktam niyatam mahadādisūkṣmaparyantam; saṃsarati nirupabhogam bhāvair adhivāsitam liṅgam.*

But it is to be noted that the Sāṅkhyas do not identify the subtle body with the eternal soul, which for them is *puruṣa;* the subtle body is something created though persistent in the sense that it persists through intermediary dissolutions. See *ibid.*, p. 72.

26a While the five *kośas* (sheaths) very probably refer to the *annamaya* (physical) *kośa* etc. of the *Upaniṣads, (Taittirīya, Ānandavallī)* a conception probably then prominent among the Sāṅkhyas, it is not clear as to what the "four bodies" mean.

27 *Śāstra*, 149b. This identification and the identification of the *mahat* of the Sāṅkhyas with the "intermediary state," of the Buddhists, are considered at the end of this chapter; the "intermediary state" itself is treated below, pp. 238 ff.

28 *Śāstra*, 149b–c.

29 *Ibid.*, 149c.

30 *Ibid.*, 230c.

31 *Ibid.*; cp. *Vaiśeṣka Sūtras*, III. ii, 4: *Prāṇāpāna-nimeṣonmeṣa-jīvana-manogatindriyāntara-vikārāḥ sukhaduḥkhecchādveṣaprayatnāśca (ātmano liṅgāni)*.

32 *Śāstra*, 230c–231a; cp. *Sāṅkhyakārikā*, 46 (p. 78) on *"pratyayasarga,"* creation by intellect *(buddhi)*.

33 Cp. Ui, *Vaiśeṣika Philosophy*, p. 140.

34 *Śāstra*, 231a.

34a The reading *ibid.*, n. 8 is preferred;

六 is omitted.

[35] See also *ibid.*, 149c.

[36] *Ibid.*; cp. *Vaiśeṣikasūtras* III. ii. 1: *Ātmendriyārthasannikarṣe jñānasya bhāvo, bhāvaś ca manaso liṅgam.* For the Sāṅkhyas of course it is the *buddhi* that does the knowing of things, see *Sāṅkhyakārikā*, 35:

*Sāntaḥkaraṇā buddhiḥ sarvam viṣayam avagāhate.*

[37] *Śāstra*, 200b–c; cp. also *ibid.*, 230c; *ibid.*, 454c–455a, the same argument is put forth by a Buddhist in regard to "Tathāgata," which in the context of these arguments is exchangeable for "self" or even "soul;" see *ibid.*, 369a: 我即是如去.

[38] Cp. *Kārikā*, IX: 3:

*Darśanaśravaṇādibhyo vedanādibhya eva ca; yaḥ prāg vyavasthito bhāvaḥ kena prajñāpyate'tha saḥ.*

[39] *Śāstra*, 200c.

[40] Cp. *ibid.*, 454c–455a.

[41] *Ibid.*, 200c.

[41a] *Ibid.*, 149c; see also *ibid.* 149b.

[42] *Ibid.*, 149c–150a; see below, p. 235 ff.

[43] *Śāstra*, 150a.

[44] See especially *ibid.*, 338a–c for a strong criticism of the view that denies the continuation of life after death (身滅便無).

[45] On the examination of the relation between the person and the constituents of personality, see *ibid.*, 368c–369a, 454c–455a, 746c–747a; the last two are practically reproductions of *Kārikā*, ch. XXII, including the mention of "*pancadhā mṛgyamāṇaḥ*" (*ibid.*, 8), as well as "*prapañcayanti ye buddham* etc." (*ibid.*, 15); cp. also *ibid.*, ch. X.

[46] Cp. also *Śāstra*, 454c and 194c.

[47] Cp. *ibid.*, 369a.

[48] See *Kārikā*, ch. X; *ibid.*, 15:

*Agnīndhanābhyām vyākhyātaḥ ātmopādānayoh kramaḥ; sarvo niravaśeṣeṇa sārdham ghaṭapaṭādibhiḥ.*

[49] On the five kinds of examination, "*pañcadhā mṛgyamāṇaḥ*" (五種求) of *Kārikā*, XXII, 8, i.e., of the relation between the person and the *skandhas*, which, in addition to identity and difference consist of the notions that he is in them, they are in him and he possess them, see *Śāstra*, 454c–455a, 746c.

[49a] Cp. *ibid.*, 60a.

[50] Cp. *ibid.*, 319b–c.

[51] Cp. *ibid.*, 746c–747a; cp. *Kārikā*, XXII. 15–16:

*Prapañcayanti ye buddham prapañcātītam avyayam; te prapañcahatāḥ sarve na paśyanti tathāgatam.*

*Tathāgato yatsvabhāvaḥ tatsvabhāvam idam jagat; tathāgato niḥsvabhāvaḥ niḥsvabhāvam idam jagat.*

This holds good not only in the case of Tathāgata but also in the case of every individual; see above, n. 37.

[52] Cp. the example of silk worm, *Śāstra*, 294b, 697a; see above, p. 106.

[53] *Śāstra*, 696a; cp. *ibid.*, 622b, also *Kārikā*, XXVI: 8–9. What ensues here is an account of the different links (stages or phases) in the life of the ignorant; this is what is known as the twelve-spoked wheel of phenomenal existence; this is a specific, although the very important, case of the general principle of conditioned origination. *Śāstra* refers to this topic in several places; see especially 100b–c, 622a–623b, 696a–697a. Cp. *Kārikā*, ch. XXVI; cp. also *Pratītyasamutpāda-hṛdaya-śāstra;* cp. also *Ārya-dharmadhātugarbhavivaraṇa* and *Bhavasaṅkrānti-śāstra.*

[54] *Ibid.*, 696b; cp. *ibid.*, 100b, also *Kārikā*, XXVI: 8. *Kārikā* explains *bhava* as the existence embodied in the five *skandhas* (*pañcaskandhāḥ sa ca bhavaḥ*). In the *Śāstra* (696b) *bhava* is

explained as the deeds of the present span of life as they prepare for the fresh embodiment (爲未來有). The deeds leave their tendencies and these lead to the fresh embodiment in the five *skandhas*. Evidently *bhava* is used to stand for what leads one to birth as well as to what one is led. *Bhava* in the former sense may be taken to connote the tending to become which is the root of deeds. On the distinction between *saṃskāra* and *bhava* see below.

[55] Cp. *Śāstra,* 100b, also *Kārikā,* XXVI: 7.

[56] *Śāstra,* 696b.

[57] *Ibid.*

[58] *Ibid.*

[59] *Ibid.;* cp. *ibid.,* 100b. In 是識共生, 共 is taken as altogether; see *ibid.,* n. 35.

[60] *Ibid.,* 696b.

[61] *Ibid.,* see above, p. 233.

[62] *Ibid.*

[63] On the intermediary state *(antarābhava)*, see *Sāmmitīya-Nikāya Śāstra,* pp. 160–162, 195–205 and 233–235.

[64] *Śāstra,* 696b.

[65] Cp. the long account of this topic in *Prasannapadā,* pp. 543–552.

[66] See above, p. 229.

[66a] *Śāstra,* 696b.

[67] Cp. *Kārikā,* XXVI: 1:

*Punarbhavāya saṃskārān avidyānivṛtah tridhā abhisaṃskurute yān taiḥ gatim gacchati karmabhiḥ.*

[68] Thus *bhava* and *saṃskāra* are of the same nature; the difference is of time; the one leads to a future birth and the other has already led to the present birth.

*Nāma* (名) may just be taken as "name"; but here it is perhaps better to take it in the sense of mental element, i.e., as tendency.

*Śāstra,* 100b has: The deeds that proceed from ignorance have the capacity to produce the result (of taking birth) in the world and so they are called *saṃskāras*.

[69] See above, p. 106.

[70] *Śāstra,* 697a; *ibid.,* 622a refers to the account of the twelve links and says that it is this account of conditioned origination that saves one from falling into the wrong views of extremes.

[71] Cp. *ibid.,* 622a. See above, pp. 000 ff.

[72] Cp. *Śāstra,* 622a; on the different kinds of eyes, see above, pp. 119 ff.

[73] Cp. *Śāstra,* 622b.

[74] See below, ch., X.

[75] *Śāstra,* 622b.

[76] *Ibid.*

[77] *Ibid.*

[78] *Ibid.,* 622c.

[79] Cp. *Pratītyasamutpādahṛdaya* (T. 1654), 490b–c. Cp. also *Ārya-dharma-dhātu-garbha-vivaraṇa;* this text puts *kleśa* and *karma* together and thus makes two groups of five and seven; see above, p. 36.

[80] A similar emphasis has been put on *buddhi* by the Sāṅkhya, see *Sāṅkhyakārikā* 36–37.

### *Chapter IX*

[1] Cp. *Śāstra,* 428a: "The ultimate nature of *rūpa* can be known by the power that is in its very nature (以色相力故可知)."

[2] Cp. *ibid.,* 499c; cp. also *ibid., (Sūtra),* 443a; cp. *Vigrahavyāvartanī,* 22.

[3] On the kinds of *tathatā,* see also *Śāstra,* 303a.

[4] Cp. *ibid.,* 297c: 如本無能敗壞; 298c: 如本不異; cp. *Prasannapadā* p. 41: *"tathatā, avitathatā,"* also *ibid.,* p. 265: *"keyam tathatā, tathābhāvo avikāritvam sadaiva sthāyitā sarvadā anutpādaḥ."*

[5] *Śāstra,* 437a.

[6] *Ibid.,* 566a.

[7] Cp. 妙法蓮華經 *(Saddharmapuṇḍarīka-*

*sūtra)*, T. 262: 5c; the ten items counted there come close to our nine items here.

[8] *Śāstra*, 298c.

[9] *Ibid.*

[10] *Ibid.*; see above, p. 367, n. 4.

[11] Cp. also *Śāstra*, 514b–c.

[12] *Ibid.*, 297c. It would be well to note that while 法性 is an equivalent of *dharmatā* as well as of *dharmadhātu*, the latter in this context stands invariably for the ultimate reality, while *dharmatā* can be the true nature either mundane or ultimate. The corresponding Sanskrit version of the *Sūtra (Pañcaviṁśati*, p. 24) of which this portion of the *Śāstra* is the commentary has *dharmadhātu* in place of 法性.

[13] *Śāstra*, 303a.

[14] *Ibid.*, has *anutpādakoṭi* (無生際) for ultimate reality,

[15] *Ibid.*

[16] *Ibid.*, 479b *(Sūtra)*, also 480c *(Śāstra)*.

[17] *Ibid.*, 442c–423a.

[18] *Ibid.*, 689a.

[19] *Ibid.*, 428a; One would not miss to note the interchange of 如 and 相 in these two passages above.

[20] *Ibid.*, 298b.

[20a] *Ibid.*, 334b has: in 法性, 性 means the universal reality and 法 means *prajñāpāramitā*; cp. also *ibid.*, 335c.

[21] *Ibid.*, 298b; in 本分種 *sa- (or sva-) bhāga-dhātu* 種 is *dhātu*, used as a synonym of the 性 in 法性. cp. also *ibid.* 334a.

[22] *Ibid.*, 644b.

[23] Cp. *Dharmadhātustava* (T. 1675) 754b–c for examples to elucidate the immanence of the ultimate reality in all beings.

*transform brick and stone into gold:* see above, p. 358, n. 34.

[24] *Śāstra*, 299a.

[25] *Śāstra*, 297c; also *ibid.* 298c.

[26] *Ibid.*, 298c.

[27] *Ibid.*, 302c–303a, also 眞際, *ibid.*, 299a.

[28] Cp. *ibid.*, 298c. See above, p. 91.

[28a] *The heart becomes full and contented:* cp. also *Śāstra*, 450a.

[29] This is the main theme of 諸波羅密品: *ibid.*, 518b ff.

[30] *Ibid.*, 518b.

[30a] *Ibid.*, 518c.

[31] Cp. *ibid. (Sūtra)* 559b ff. *ibid.* and *(Śāstra)* 560c ff.

[32] *Ibid.*, 561a; also *ibid.*, 561b.

[33] Cp. *ibid.*, 562a: 智慧欲求實事.

[34] *Ibid.*, 559b; *ibid.*, 561b: 爲一切衆生所歸趣.

[35] *Ibid.*, 562b.

[36] *The ultimately true nature of the Tathāgata* etc.: Cp. *Kārikā*, XXII: 16:

*Tathāgato yatsvabhāvaḥ tatsvabhāvam idam jagat.*

[36a] *Śāstra* 437a, l. 12: the 2nd letter from bottom should be 常.

[37] *Ibid.*, 693c.

[37a] *Ibid.*, 697c; cp. *Kārikā*, XXII, 11: *śūnyam iti na vaktavyam aśūnyam iti vā bhavet.*

[38] *Śāstra*, 606a: like the two ends of a balance.

[39] *Ibid.*, 562b; *delighted at heart in keeping silent:* cp. *Kārikā*, XXIV: 12:

*Ataśca pratyudāvṛttam cittam deśayitum muneḥ; dharmam matvāsya dharmasya mandaiḥ duravagāhatām.*

[40] Cp. *Ibid.*, XVIII: 9: *tattva* is "*prapañcairaprapañcitam.*"

[41] *Śāstra*, 517b.

[41a] Cp. *ibid.*, 245c.

[42] *Ibid.*, 514c: 無所說, 無所得相.

[43] *Ibid.*, 334c; cp. *Pañcaviṁśati*, pp. 58–59: *niruttaro hy eṣa yogaḥ . . . paramayogaḥ yaduta śūnyatāyogaḥ.*

[44] *Śāstra*, 514b.

## *Chapter X*

[1] Cp. *Śāstra,* 187c, 272a, 314b, 417b.
[2] On Buddhahood, see ch. XI.
[3] See *Śāstra,* 172b for the distinction of *prajñā* (智慧), and *puṇya* (福德); see below, p. 280.
[4] Cp. *Śāstra,* 416a, 86a; *ibid.,* 269b–270a gives a fairly complete account of the distinction between the Small Way and the Great Way; cp. also *ibid.,* 197c–198a and 85b–86a.
[5] The above three points are broadly as they have been set forth *ibid.,* 85b–86a.
[6] Cp. *ibid.,* 164b; also *ibid.,* 314b.
[7] Cp. *ibid.,* 262b.
[8] The reference here is to the *dharmakāya* of the bodhisattva; on this, see below, ch. XI.
[9] Cp. *Śāstra,* 419c; cp. *Pañcavimśati,* p. 225: *traidhātukāt niryāsyati, yena-sarvākārajñatā tena sthāsyati.*
[10] Cp. *Śāstra,* 394b; cp. also *ibid.,* 429c ff.
[11] Cp. *ibid.,* 394b–c.
[12] Cp. *ibid.,* 554c; also *ibid.,* 270c.
[13] Cp. *ibid.,* 394c.
[14] Cp. *ibid.,* 395a.
[15] Cp. *ibid.,* 314b; also *ibid.,* 85b.
[16] On merit and wisdom, see *ibid.,* 164b, 172b, 180b–c, 418c, 464a–b.
[17] Cp. *ibid.,* 116b, 269b; also *Sūtra* 555b ff.
[18] *Ibid.,* 395a ff; cp. *Sūtra,* 393b.
[19] Cp. also *Śāstra,* 411b: 應者繫心願我當作佛.
[20] *Ibid.,* 395a, 395b.
[21] *Ibid.,* 395a.
[21a] *Ibid.*
[22] *Ibid.,* 395a–b.
[23] *Ibid.,* 395b.
[24] *Ibid.,* 271c; cp. also *Sūtra* 139a, and *Śāstra, ibid.*
[25] *Ibid.,* 271c–272a.
[26] *Ibid.* 272a.
[27] Cp. *ibid.,* 150a: "It is the intention of the Buddha to enable the wayfarer to cultivate the right way and realize the right fruit."
[28] *Śāstra* (154c) defines *śīla* as "stopping the evil deeds and not committing them any more." *Ibid.,* 154c–162a has a short account of the five elements of moral conduct: viz., to refrain from killing, stealing, lewdness, telling lies and drinking wine; *ibid.,* 162a ff. sets itself to the question: While these constitute *śīla,* what constitutes its perfection. *Ibid.,* 415b has: The cultivation of the twelve ascetic practices *(dhūta-guṇas* 頭陀) (like "wearing clothes made of rags taken from a dust heap," "not possessing more than three robes at a time" etc.) leads to the purity of moral conduct; this facilitates contemplation which in turn leads to wisdom; the true wisdom is *anutpattika-dharma-kṣānti,* one's endurance for the ultimate truth of devoidness of birth. On *"dhūta-guṇas,"* see Hardayal, *The Bodhisattva Doctrine* (Kegan Paul, London, 1932), pp. 134–140.
[29] *Śāstra,* 162b.
[30] *Ibid.*
[31] *Ibid.,* 163c.
[32] *Kṣānti,* forbearance or endurance is with regard to beings *(sattva)* and with regard to the truth of things *(dharma);* cp. *ibid.,* 106c–107a, 164b ff. The latter kind refers also to the teachings *(dharma)* that contain this truth. *Kṣānti* with regard to *dharma (dharmakṣānti)* has thus these meanings: I) the capacity to accept the teachings in faith, II) understand their import and III) sustain one's comprehension of the truth of things that one thus gains, so much so that it is saturated in one's whole being, reflected in one's whole life; see *ibid.,*

171c. This is what has been rendered here as "endurance for *dharma;*" it is not mere acceptance; it is to sustain the *dharma* and apply and reveal it in all that one does. The *Śāstra* distinguishes also between *kṣānti* (忍) and *jñāna* (智) by stating that *kṣānti* is the earlier and gross, and *jñāna,* the later and subtle, meaning thereby that they are basically one and the same principle; see *ibid.,* 417c. However, *kṣānti* in this earlier phase needs to be distinguished from *kṣānti* as a consummating phase of wisdom.

[33] *Ibid.,* 164b.

[34] Cp. *ibid.,* 222a for the marks of *dharma.*

[35] *Ibid.,* 164b.

[36] *Ibid.,* 168b; this is *kṣānti* as a consummating phase of wisdom.

[37] *Ibid.,* 170c.

[38] *Ibid.,* 171c; *ibid.* 417c has: "*Anutpattika-dharma-kṣānti* means to accept in faith the ultimate truth of the devoidness of birth and death of things, to comprehend this truth unimpededly and to sustain this comprehension free from reversion (於無生滅諸法實相中信受通達無礙不退)."

[39] *Ibid.,* 171c.

[40] *Ibid.*

[41] *Ibid.,* 172a.

[42] *Ibid. Kṣānti* as the means is the earlier phase of wisdom. The highest kind of *dharma-kṣānti* is that which springs from one's comprehension of the ultimate truth of things, the truth of the devoidness of birth and death *(anutpattika-dharma-kṣānti);* this import is found in many places in the *Śāstra,* see e.g., *ibid.,* 97b, 168b ff., 415b, 417c. *Gambhīra-dharma-kṣānti* is interpreted so as to bear specially on *kṣaānti* in regard to the mundane truth, viz., the conditioned origination; see *ibid.,* 99a.

[43] *Ibid.,* 172b.

[44] *Ibid.,* 173c. *Ibid.* 174a has: One must have the ability to start (能起發) the thing and should have no question or difficulty about it; one must have the strong will and determination (志意), must be free from the feeling of fatigue, and must see it through to the very end; these five constitute the characteristics of *vīrya.*

[45] *Ibid.,* 174c.

[46] *Ibid.,* 180c. Here we have *cittaikāgratā,* i.e., single-mindedness or one-pointedness of mind, and *samādhi,* and *dhyāna* which have been here translated as concentration and meditation; this rendering of the latter is admittedly very wide. When "*dhyāna*" is used as a technical term to stand for the four states of "fine material sphere" *(rūpa-dhātu)* perhaps it could be best rendered as "trance;" it has been also rendered as "mental absorption;" *samādhi* has the root meaning of the mind being collected and completely fixed in the object which would then be strictly "concentration." *Samādhi* as "meditation" (which has the import of thought, reflection) has its relevance to the three *samādhis,* the "gateways of freedom," at least in the earlier stages; cp. *ibid.,* 206a ff. See below, pp. 293 ff. "*Bhāvanā*" (修行), which is used to form the compound *samādhibhāvanā,* has been rendered as "development;" it could as well be "cultivation" that leads to the development. There is another term "*samāpatti*" which is usually transliterated in Chinese; literally it means well attaining; this term is specially used in the compound *ārūpya-samāpattayaḥ* which stands for the four "trances of the immaterial sphere." On these terms see their Pali equivalents in Nyanatiloka's *Buddhist Dictionary,* besides

Rhys Davids *et. al.*, *The Dictionary of Buddhist Terms* (P.T.S.).

47 *Śāstra,* 180c. *Ibid.,* 181a–187c gives an account of the way, the means, to obtain *dhyāna,* under three headings: I) discarding the five kinds of objects which are the objects of sense-pleasure (却五事) (181a–183c), II) giving up the five elements of hindrance (除五蓋) *(nīvaraṇa),* viz., lust, ill-will, torpor and languor, restlessness and worry, and doubt (183c–185a), and III) cultivating five elements, viz., determination, effort, mindfulness, wisdom and onepointedness of mind (185a ff.). On *nīvaraṇa,* see Nyanatiloka, *op. cit.*

48 *Śāstra,* 187c.

49 *Ibid.*

50 *Ibid.,* 189b, c.

51 For the details on the nature and content of the wisdom of the *śrāvakas* and the *pratyekabuddhas,* see *ibid.*, 262b, 266b, 267c, 269c–270a; also *ibid.*, 295b.

52 *Ibid.,* 266b–c.

53 *Ibid.*

54 Cp. *Kārikā,* XVIII: 12:
*Sambuddhānām anutpāde śrāvakāṇām punaḥ kṣaye; jñānam pratyekabud-dhānām asaṃsargāt pravartate.*

55 *Śāstra,* 266c: 利根名異法相是同; it is possible to punctuate after 異 when it means, their difference is only in name, they are identical in quality.

56 *Ibid.,* 267c: on *bhūmis,* see ch. XI.

57 *Ibid.,* 259a; *Śāstra* sets forth the points of distinction between 一切智 and 一切種智 on 258c–259b; *ibid.,* 137c–138a has: 種 *(ākāra)* means the method of or the way to comprehension (智慧門); by means of the knowledge of all forms one enters into (入), comprehends, all things in all the ways and hence the name, the knowledge of all forms. *Ibid. (Sūtra)*, 257c says that by means of the knowledge of the one way *(mārgajñatā)* the way that leads to Nirvāṇa, one gets the knowledge of the nature of all (the particular) ways *(mārgākārajnatā)*; and *ibid. (Sūtra)*, 258c says that by means of the knowledge of all (the particular) ways one gains the all-inclusive understanding *(sarvajñatā)* and by means of the all-inclusive understanding one gains the knowledge of all forms *(sarvākārajñatā)*.

58 *Ibid.,* 259a.

59 *Ibid.,* 234a; *Śāstra* gives an account of the eleven kinds of knowledge on 232c ff.

60 *Ibid.,* 405c; the four kinds of objects are: the body *(kāya,* 身*)*, feeling *(vedanā,* 受*)*, *citta* (心) and *dharma* (法); by *citta* is meant primarily the principle of intellection and *dharma* comprises here not only the mental states, but also the incomposite elements. For the farer on the Great Way these kinds of contemplation have for their ultimate object, the unconditioned reality, the undivided being; see *ibid.,* 203b–c, 204a, 205a, c.

61 *Ibid.,* 405c; cp. also *ibid.,* 202b–c. These are the "*samyak-prahāṇas*" rendered as 正勤, 正懃 or 精進; probably *prahāṇa* is a corrupt Sanskrit form of *pradhāna;* these are the four kinds of "right effort." On this term, see Hardayal, *op. cit.,* pp. 101 ff.

62 *Rddhipadas* are the bases for increasing concentration. *Śāstra* (202c) states that when understanding and right effort increase, if concentration is weak, the mind gets scattered and confused, and hence the need to cultivate collectedness of mind through concentration; in a state of balance between understanding and concentration one achieves all that one wishes. *Ibid. pada* is taken to mean "enough" like the

food being tasty when with enough salt as one wishes; *ibid.: pada* also means "feet" like the two feet of man by which one reaches wherever one wishes. *Ibid.*, 405c takes *pada* to mean necessary conditions as well as aspects.

[63] Cp. *ibid.*, 405c; cp. also *ibid.*, 202c.

[64] *Ibid.*, 405c; cp. also *ibid.*, 202c.

[65] *Ibid.* 203a distinguishes three aspects in these eight elements; three of them pertain to moral conduct *(śila)*, three of them to concentration *(samādhi)* and two, to wisdom *(prajñā)*.

[66] *Ibid.*; on these terms see Hardayal, *op. cit.*, pp. 149 ff.

[67] *Ibid.*, 405c.

[68] *Ibid.*, 198b; cp. *Abhidharmakośa*, VI: 68–69: "*Saptatrimśattu tatpakṣāḥ, nāmato dravyato daśa.*"

[69] *Śāstra* points out that these thirty-seven factors are not exclusively of the *śrāvakas*, or of the Small Way; see *ibid.*, 197b-c.

[70] Cp. *ibid.*, 203b-204a, where an account of the cultivation of the four *smṛtyupasthānas* according to Mahāyāna is given.

[71] Cp. *ibid.*, 203b-c, 204a, c; see especially *ibid.*, 197c-198a.

[72] Cp. *ibid.*, 60a. See above, pp. 148–150.

[73] On the three "gates of freedom" (解脫門 *vimokṣadvāra)*, see also *Śāstra*, 96c ff. *Ibid.*, 218b has: (the contemplation on) the nine characters (九相) (that concern the impurity of the body) opens up the door of the mindfulness *(smṛtyupasthāna)* in respect to body; this in turn opens up the door of the other three kinds of mindfulness; the mindfulness of the four kinds opens up the door of the thirty-seven factors of the way; these in turn open up the door to Nirvāna.

*Ibid.*, 217-218b draws the points of distinction between the *nine* kinds of contemplation that concern the impurity of the body and the *ten* kinds of contemplation which concern impermanence, pain, devoidness of "I," etc. and points out that all the former nine are included in just one of the latter ten. The purport of the latter, which are headed by the contemplation on impermanence, is to lead one to the comprehension of *sūnyatā*. See *ibid.*, 229b.

On the import of *smṛti* and *saṃjñā* in these contexts see *ibid.*, 229a, where these as well as *jñāna* are noted as different *stages* in one and the same process.

[74] *Ibid.*, 206a.

[75] These are the four "*apramāṇas*," also called *brahma-vihāras*, translated as "sublime abodes": these consist of goodness, compassion, altruistic joy and equanimity. See Nyanatiloka, *op. cit.*, under *brahmavihāra*. See *Śāstra*, 229a.

[76] These are the eight *vimokṣas*; these are usually translated as "deliverance;" turning away from and abandoning — this is what the Chinese equivalent 背捨 means and this form has been kept here. These have been dealt with in detail in the *Sātra*, 215a ff.; of these the last five constitute items 5–9 of the nine "successive abodes" *(anupūrvavihāra-samāpattayaḥ)* of concentration; the first three consist of the perception of corporeal form with and without the thought of corporeality inside, and the thought of the *śubha* (淨), the "beautiful." See Nyanatiloka, *op. cit.*, under *vimokkha*, Pali equivalent of *vimokṣa*.

[77] These are the eight *abhibhvāyatanas* (勝處), translated as stages of "mastery." These constitute different ways of contemplating on physical form. For details, see *Śāstra*, 216a-b; cp. Nyanatiloka, *op. cit.*

[78] These are the nine *anupūrva-vihāra-samāpattayaḥ* "successive abodes," com-

prising the four trances *(dhyāna)* of fine material sphere *(rūpadhātu,* the realm of form), and four "attainments" *(samāpatti)* of the immaterial sphere *(arūpadhātu,* the realm of formlessness), and the ninth one, *nirodha-samāpatti,* a state of suspension of conscious, mental activity. See *Śāstra,* 216c, for details; cp. Nyanatiloka, *op. cit.,* under *anupubba-vihāra, jhāna* and *nirodha samāpatti.*

79 *Ibid.,* 206a. These are the ten *kṛtsnāyatanas,* contemplations in which one of the different elements (counted as ten in all) is accepted as the object of attention and is seen above, below, on all sides, everywhere. See *Śāstra,* 216 ff. for details; cp. Nyanatiloka, *op. cit.,* under *Kasiṇa* (the Pāli name for *Kṛtsna). Śāstra* 215b says that *vimokṣa, abhibhvāyatana* and *kṛtsnāyatana* are but progressive stages in the practice (of contemplation).

80 *Śāstra,* 206a.

81 *Ibid.;* for this distinction see also *ibid.,* 215c.

82 *Ibid.,* 206a.

83 *Ibid.,* 206c.

84 *Ibid.,* 207a.

85 *Ibid.,* 207b.

86 *Ibid.*

87 *Ibid.*

88 *Ibid.,* 207c.

89 *Ibid.*

90 *Ibid.*

91 *Ibid.*

92 *Ibid.*

### *Chapter* XI

1 For the various aspirations of the bodhisattva which he seeks to fulfil by cultivating *prajñāparamitā,* see the introductory part of *Sūtra,* 235a ff. = T. 223: 218c–221a.

2 This is an interesting analysis of the term "bodhisattva" which would thus be: *sato bhāvaḥ sattvam, bodhir eva sattvam yasya saḥ bodhisattvaḥ.*

3 *Śāstra* 86b.

4 *Ibid.,* 92a–b.

5 *Ibid.,* 132a.

6 *Ibid.,* 271c–272a; also *ibid.* 132b.

7 Cp. above, pp. 288 ff.

白香象王: Lit.: white—fragrant—elephant—king.

8 *nyāma:* in this word *"āma"* is really immaturity, it means the passion for *dharma;* cp. *Pañcavimśati,* p. 119: *āma ity āyuṣman . . . bodhisattvasya . . . dharmatṛaṣṇā.* Thus *nyāma* means that state of the bodhisattva where this *āma,* i.e., passion for *dharma,* has become extinct: *nirgataḥ āmaḥ yasmāt saḥ.*

9 *Pratyutpanna-samādhi,* cp. *Mahāvyutpatti,* XXIV: 9: *pratyutpanna-buddha-sammukhāvasthitah.*

*Expedient prajñā,* cp. *Śāstra,* 196c–197a; see above, p. 355, n. 10.

On *anutpattika-dharma-kṣānti* see above, pp. 284–85.

10 *Sūtra* devotes a whole section (55) to set forth the characteristics of the irreversible bodhisattva; see *ibid.,* 570a ff.; see also *ibid.,* section 56 (574c ff.); cp. also the commentary thereof. *Avaivarta* has the more usual form *avinivartanīya;* cp. *Aṣṭa,* p. 323; also *avivarta;* cp. *Mahāvyutpatti* XXI: 12, XXIV: 4 and LXV: 46.

11 *Śāstra,* 262a.

12 *Ibid.,* 262b.

13 unparallelled equanimity of mind *(asamasamacitta),* see *ibid.,* 385a ff.; cp. *Pañcavimśati,* pp. 172–173.

14 *Śāstra,* 262c.

15 *Ibid.,* 264a.

16 *Ibid.,* cp. 132a, also *ibid.,* 272a.

17 Cp. *ibid.,* 263a.

18 *Ibid.,* 85a.

19 *Ibid.,* 94a–b.

20 *Ibid.,* 267a.

[21] *Ibid.* The text gives the example of the bird *kalavinka* (迦羅頻伽).

[22] The scheme of the ten stages *(bhūmis)* in the *Daśabhūmika Sūtra* is different from that in the *Pañcavimśatisāhasrikā* (and the *Śatasāhasrikā) Prajñāpāramitā-sūtras*. We have seen that the former *sūtra* (mentioned in *Śāstra* 411a–b) also has a commentary attributed to Nāgārjuna. It seems he had both the schemes before him. The *Śāstra* tries to reconcile the two by pointing out that the latter is "common to all" (共地) and the former is only of the bodhisattva (但菩薩地); see *ibid.*, 411a. For a short account of the ten *bhūmis*, cp. Hardayal, *op. cit.*, ch. VI; cp. also N. Dutt, *Aspects*, ch. IV.

[23] *Sūtra*, 419c.

[24] *Śāstra*, 411b.

[25] *Ibid.*; cp. also *ibid.*, 410a.

[26] Cp. *ibid.* the ten things (十事) that the bodhisattva cultivates in the first stage, which is the stage of clearing and preparing the ground (修治).

[27] *Ibid.*, 413c. *Ibid.*: Even to entertain the thought of stopping at the levels of the *śrāvakas* and the *pratyekabuddhas* is an impurity in *śīla*.

[28] *Ibid.*, 414a.

[29] See *Sūtra*, 410a, 412c–413a, and *Śāstra*, 413c–415a, for the elements that constitute the second *bhūmi*.

[30] Cp. *ibid.*, 410a, 413a, 415a.

[31] Cp. *ibid.*, 410a, 413a; *Sūtra* (413a) and *Śāstra* (415a–b) interpret this to mean to overcome the intention of adopting the courses of *śrāvakas* and *pratyekabuddhas*.

[32] *Ibid.*, 410a, n. 29, 413b and 415b.

[33] *Ibid.*; on *dhūtaguṇa* see above, p. 369, n. 28.

[34] Cp. *Sūtra*, 410a–b, 413b and *Śāstra*, 415b–416a.

[35] Cp. *Sūtra*, 410b, 413b–c and *Śāstra*, 416a.

[36] Cp. *Sūtra*, 410b–c, 416b–c and *Śāstra*, 417a–418a.

[37] Cp. *Sūtra* 410b, 416c; *Śāstra*, 417c.

[38] Cp. *ibid.*, 262a; cp. also *ibid.* 263c: *Anutpattika-dharmakṣānti* is itself the ground of the irreversible.

[39] *Ibid.*, 132a.

[40] *Ibid.*, 417c.

[41] *Ibid.*, 418a.

[42] *Ibid.*, 417c; 分別相 is here taken as distinguishable or distinct natures; however it may also mean the conceived or imagined characters *kalpita lakṣaṇa)*.

[43] *Ibid.* 417c. observes that in the first three stages the chief element is understanding rather than concentration which grows stronger in the next three stages.

[44] *Ibid.*, 265b.

[45] *Ibid.*, 106b.

[46] *Ibid.*, 130a.

[46a] Cp. also *ibid.*, 303c. On the thirty-two features see below, p. 314.

[47] *Ibid.*, 261c.

[48] *Ibid.*, 262a.

[49] Cp. *Sūtra (ibid.)* 410c, 416c; *Śāstra*, 418a ff.

[50] *Ibid.*, 418b; cp. *ibid.*, 416c. See above, p. 300.

[51] *Śāstra*, 127b.

[52] *Ibid.*, 86c.

[53] *Ibid.*, 418b; cp. the well known line (q. in *Prasannapadā*, p. 448): *"dharmato buddhā draṣṭavyāḥ, dharmakāyā hi nāyakāḥ."*

[54] *Ibid.*, 418c; these are *nirukti* (language) and *pratibhāna* (ready wit), two of the four *pratisamvit* or "the elements of expertness;" on this topic, cp. Hardayal, *op. cit.*, pp. 259–267.

[55] *Śāstra*, 419a.

[56] *Ibid.*, 419b–c.

[57] *Ibid.*, 419b.

[58] *Ibid.*, 719b.
[59] *Ibid.*, 106b–c; this example of the moon occurs in *Śāstra* at three places: 106b–c, 273b, and 719b.
[60] *Ibid.*, 273b.
[61] *Ibid.*, 719b–c.
[62] *Ibid.*, 719c; cp. *Sūtra (ibid.)* 718b.
[63] This is a long discussion occurring in *Sāstra*, ch. IV, where the view of Kātyāyaniputra and his followers is stated *(ibid.,* 86c–91c) and the rest of the chapter (91c ff.) is devoted to the Mahāyāna criticism of this view; cp. also *ibid.*, 273a. For the Sarvāstivāda view of bodhisattva vide *Vibhāṣā* (T. 1545) 886 ff.; the *Sāstra* (92a) makes a reference to the *Bodhisattva-prakaraṇa* in *Abhidharma-vibhāṣā.*
[64] *Śāstra*, 92a.
[65] Cp. *ibid.*, 92b.
[66] *Ibid.*, 93a.
[67] *Ibid.*, 93a-b.
[68] *Ibid.*, 93b, 312a-b.
[69] *Ibid.*, 93b: 摩訶衍論中種種因縁説三世十方佛.
[70] *Ibid.*, 93c–94a; cp. *ibid.*, 126b.
[71] *Ibid.*, 273a, b.
[72] *Ibid.*, 274a.
[73] On the physical features of the Buddha cp. *Mahāvyutpatti*, XVII and XVIII. For a short account of these see Hardayal, *op. cit.*, pp. 299–305. *Śāstra* (chs. XXIV–XXVI) gives an exposition of the different elements of the dharma body; on these cp. *Mahāvyutpatti*, VIII, IX and XIII; for a short account of these see Hardayal, *op. cit.*, pp. 19 ff. and 259 ff.

The *Daśabhumi-vibhāsā* (T. 1621: 71 ff.) counts *āveṇika-dharmas* differently but agrees (39c–40a) with *Śāstra* in criticizing those who emphasize the physical features and holds (65c) with it that the root of even these is *prajñā.*
[74] *Śāstra*, 418b, cp. also *ibid.*, 747b.
[75] *Ibid.*, 274a.
[76] *Ibid.*, 274c.
[77] *Ibid.*, 274–275a.
[78] *Ibid.*, 245c.
[79] *Ibid.*, 236b.
[80] *Ibid.*
[81] *Ibid.*, 256a.
[82] *Ibid.*, 257b.
[83] *Ibid.*, 256c.

*Chapter XII*

[1] It may be noted that *pudgala-śūnyatā* is not among the eighteen kinds; all these latter are in fact species of *dharmaśūnyatā* (cp. *Sūtra, ibid.*, 583a), *dharma* being understood in the sense of both the mundane truth of concepts and conventional entities and the ultimate truth, the Nirvāna, as well as the teachings that embody these truths. All these eighteen kinds are elaborately set forth in *Śāstra* 285b–196b. In the present work, the *śūnyatā* as the non-ultimacy of the conventional entities has been set forth in the chapters, *"Criticism of Categories"* and *"The World and the Individual,"* and *śūnyatā* as indescribability, or the inapplicability of concepts in regard to the ultimate reality, that the real is not any "thing," has been given in the chapter, *"Reality." Śāstra* points out that the number and kinds of *śūnyatā depend* on the number and kinds of things to which people cling (隨本所著多少); see *ibid.*, 630b. Cp. also *ibid.*, 550b–c on the mention of the various ways of driving home the understanding of the *śūnyatā* of all elements. *Ibid.*, 346b: By attaining the two kinds of *śūnyatā*, viz., of *dharma* and *pudgala*, one gradually reaches the ultimate truth *(anupalambha-śūnyatā)*. Cp. also *ibid.*, 584a. References to the clinging *śūnyatā* are found in several places; see, e.g., *ibid.*, 480c–481a, 207b. Cp. *Kārikā*, XIII: 8,

XXII: 11; cp. also *ibid.*, XXIV: 13 ff.
[2] Cp. *Śāstra*, 319a: "*Prajñāpāramitā* is distinguished into two aspects; the state of accomplishedness is called the *bodhi*, and the state of unaccomplishedness is called *śūnyatā*." *Śūnyatā* is here the basic sense of unacomplishedness, of the real as not-yet-realized; in other words, the thirst for the real; this is the spring of all activities of man, the self-conscious individual. See above, pp. 264–65.
[2a] Cp. *ibid.*, 245c, 507c.
[3] We seem to have no indication of the Sāṅkhya criticism of the Mādhyamika in those days; *Sāṅkhyakārikā* has nothing of that kind. A study of the Sāṅkhya in the light of the materials supplied in the present work in chs. VIII and IX and amplified by comparison with later texts that stress the *tathāgatagarbha* would be very worthwhile; also the pluralism of the Vaibhāsikas and the Vaisesikas needs detailed study. Some work is done in the field of Buddhist Logic by Profs. Stcherbatsky and Tucci, but it is hardly adequate.
[3a] *karika*, XIII: 8.
[4] A comprehensive History of Buddhist Thought is a real desideratum. For a brief sketch of the development of the Mādhyamika tradition, see Murti, *op. cit.*, chs. III and IV.
[5] Gauḍapāda is assigned to about 500 A.D. See Vidhusekhara Bhattacarya, *The Agamasāstra of Gaudapāda* (University of Calcutta, 1943), Intr. p. xxvi; Radhakrishnan (*Indian Philosophy*, vol. II, George Allen & Unwin, 1927, p. 452, n. 2) suggested 550 A.D.
[6] On this point see Vidhusekhara Bhattacarya, *op, cit.*, Intr., pp. lxxv ff. and *ibid.*, pp. cxiv ff. where he speaks of the direct influence of Buddhism on Gauḍapāda and for a different view, see T.M.P. Mahadevan, *Gaudapāda, A Study in Early Advaita* (University of Madras, 1954), especially ch. IX.
[7] Śankara's *Comm. on Brahma Sūtras*, I. iv. 4. 14; *sṛṣṭyādiprapañcasya brahmapratipattyarthatām;* cp. also *utpattyādiśrutinām aikātmyāvagamaparavāt* (*ibid.*, IV. iii. 5. 14 cited in Radhakrishnan, *op. cit.*, p. 560, n. 1).
[8] See Śaṅkara *op. cit.*, I. iii. 15. 19; cp. Radhakrishnan, *op. cit.*, p. 598, n. 4; cp. also *ibid.*, pp. 475 ff., and pp. 603 ff.
[9] This is especially so, when one remembers that the *Śastra* speaks not only of *tathatā* as being within the heart of every being, but also of being itself the *prajñā*. Cp. above, ch. IX, ch. IV.
[10] Bādhva's teaching to Bāskali; *upaśānto'yamātmā;* see Śaṅkara *op. cit.*, III. ii. 5. 17; cp. *Prasannapadā*, p. 57; *Paramārtho hy āryāṇām tūṣṇimbhavāḥ.*

It must be noted that the ineffability of the ultimate truth is a major import of the Mādhyamika's claim that truth is unseizable and that he has no position of his own. But at the same time transcendence and immanence as well as identity and difference are acceptable for him as relative ways of conveying the undividedness of the ultimate truth. To convey through concepts what lies beyond concepts and conventional entities is the skilfulness of the wise. This is done by denying exclusiveness, by non-clinging. Non-exclusiveness is the spirit of the Middle Way. This is the other major import of the Madhyamika's claim that he has no position of his own. The Middle Way or the Great Way is the very spirit of accommodation. It is the ineffability of the ultimate truth that Prof. Murti has sought to emphasize in his celebrated work, *The Central Philosophy of Buddhism*. (Vide chs. II, V, & VI.) However, the Mādhyamika criticism, of which the primary purpose is to free the mind from dogmatism, from exclusiveness, has for its other major import accommodativeness, comprehensiveness as the spirit of the Middle Way. (See chs. IV, V & VI of the present work.) This cannot be overlooked.

[11] See above, ch. IX.

[12] Cp. *Triṁśikākārikā* 27–30. It is needless to say that this whole matter needs a fresh and detailed investigation, in the light of the present work. A comprehensive history of Indian Philosophy in the first eight hundred years of the Christian era is a basic need.

[13] T. 1856: 122b–143b; *ibid.*, 122b gives the title 鳩摩羅什法師大義. It is gratifying to note that the group of Japanese scholars who have brought out *Studies in Chao Lun* are also hoping to publish their translation of this text; see *ibid.*, p. 8 (Eng. tr. of Tsukamoto's Intr.). On Hui-yüan see W. Liebenthal, *Shih Hui-yüan's Buddhism as Set Forth in His Writings (Journal of the American Oriental Society,* vol. 70, 1950, pp. 243–259); see also T'ang Yung-t'ung, *op. cit.*, ch. XI.

[14] What follows is a summary of the four points stated *ibid.*, vol. I, pp. 314–323.

[15] Cp. *ibid.*, pp. 314–315; cp. also *Śāstra*, 57a.

[16] Cp. T. 2059: 330b ff.; W. Liebenthal, *The Book of Chao*, p. 67, n. 241. See above, p. 14.

[17] T'ang Yung-t'ung, *op. cit.*, p. 315.

[18] *Ibid.*, p. 316; cp. T. 1856, 132c–133a, 135b, 137b.

[19] T'ang Yung-t'ung, *op. cit.*, pp. 316–318.

[20] *Ibid.*, p. 319; cp. T. 1856, 138a.

[21] T'ang Yung-t'ung, *op. cit.*, p. 319. See above, p. 358, n. 40.

[22] T'ang Yung-t'ung, *op. cit.*, pp. 319–320.

[23] *Ibid.*, p. 320.

[24] *Ibid.*, pp. 320–321.

[25] *Ibid.*, p. 322.

[26] 二諦義, (T. 1854), 92a. 二諦義 is one of the important independent treatises of Chi-tsang (549–623) who wrote his commentaries 疏 on all the Three Treatises (三論), viz., *Madhyamaka-śāstra* (中論), *Dvādaśamukha-śāstra* (十二門論) and *Śata-śāstra* (百論). Other independent treatises of Chi-tsang include 三論玄義 and 大乘玄論, T. 1852 and 1853 respectively. See below, p. 333 for Chi-tsang's works and see below, pp. 324–25 for a brief account of his thought.

[27] T. 1854, 92a. Seng-chao (384–414) and Tao-sheng (360–434) were the two foremost of the disciples of Kumārajīva. On Seng-chao we have two excellent studies: I) W. Liebenthal, *The Book of Chao,* referred to above; this is a complete translation of Seng-chao's writings with critical study and copious notes; II) *Studies in Chao-lun* (in Japanese), ed. by Tsukamoto Zenryu (Kyoto, 1954); this is the result of the long and consorted effort of several Japanese scholars and is a very valuable work. Professor Tsukamoto has himself contributed an article, "The position of Seng-chao in the History of Chinese Buddhist Thought." On Tao-sheng, see Fung Yu-lan, *History of Chinese Philosophy* (Princeton University Press, 1953), vol. II, pp. 270–284; see also Liebenthal, *op. cit.*, p. 88, n. 343.

[28] *Ibid.*, p. 49; cp. T. 1858, 151b.

[29] Liebenthal, *op. cit.*, p 47; cp. T. 1858, 151a. This is the theme of 物不遷論 one of the four books of Seng-chao; the other three are 不眞空論, 般若無知論, and 涅槃無名論, all translated by Pro-

fessor Liebenthal op. cit. respectively under the titles, "On the Immutability of Things," "On Emptiness of the Unreal," "On Prajñā not Cognizant (of Objects)" and "On the Namelessness of Nirvāṇa."

[30] One cannot miss this general spirit in the writings of Seng-chao. Cp. T. 1858, 151a, 151b. Cp. book IV of *Chao-lun*, Liebenthal, *op. cit.*, pp. 111 ff.

[31] See Liebenthal, *op. cit.*, pp 36–37; also *ibid.* p. 54; cp. T. 1858, especially 151c.

[32] Cp. Liebenthal, *op. cit.*, pp. 48 ff., 52–53.

[33] This is the theme of Seng-chao's 般若無知論; cp. Liebenthal, *op. cit.*, pp. 67 ff.

[34] Fung Yu-lan, *op. cit.*, p. 268; Liebenthal, *op. cit.*, pp. 73, 71–72; T. 1858, 153b.

[35] Liebenthal, *op. cit.*, pp. 130–131.

[36] *Ibid.*, p. 145.

[37] *Ibid.*, p. 144.

[38] Fung Yu-lan, *op. cit.*, (pp. 293–299) devotes a section to Chi-tsang where he specially studies this topic of double truth. While this is found in almost all of Chi-tsang's writings this is the special theme of 二諦義, T. 1854; see *ibid.*, 90c ff.

[39] *Ibid.*, 91a.

[40] *Ibid.*, 91a–**b.**

[41] *Ibid.*, 92a.

[42] *Ibid.*, 91c ff.

[43] *Ibid.*, 92a.

[44] *Ibid.*

[45] It is obvious that in these reflections of the Chinese thinkers on Buddhist texts they did bring also things from their own treasure of ancient classics. There is indeed a great need for a comprehensive study, historical and doctrinal, of the Chinese Buddhist philosophy in its relations to ancient Chinese thought and culture. Even now the best known history in this regard is that of Professor T'ang Yung-t'ung, referred to above; even that is available only in Chinese, and is not available for the English reading public.

[46] On T'ien-t'ai see Fung Yu-lan, *op. cit.*, pp. 360–386; for a short account of this school and Hua-yen see Dr. W. T. Chan, *Religious Trends in Modern China* (Columbia University Press, New York, 1953), pp. 95–105; also *ibid.*, p. 63, n. 19 for T'ien-t'ai and p. 64, n. 20 for Hua-yen; cp. also Takakusu, *Essentials of Buddhist Philosophy* (ed. W. T. Chan and C. A. Moore, University of Hawaii, Honolulu, 1947) pp. 126–141. It is simply impossible to state in a few lines the essentials of T'ien-t'ai, and no attempt of that kind is made here; what is given here is a few broad lines on which further studies could be carried out in the light of the present work. The same thing applies also to the other two schools here dealt with, viz., Hua-yen and Ch'an.

[47] *Mahāyāna-śraddhotpāda-śāstra*, tr. from Sanskrit to Chinese by Paramārtha (533 A.D.) and Śikṣānanda (700 A.D.?) T. 1666 and 1667 respectively. Dr. Suzuki translated this into English: *Awakening of Faith* (Open Court Publ. House, Chicago, 1900); see W. T. Chan, *op. cit.*, p. 99, n. 9.

[48] The basic text of Vijnanavada is *Vijñaptimātratā-siddhi* (Fr. tr. by Louis de la Vallee Poussin, Paul Geuthner, Paris, 1928–29) which is a composite commentary on Vasubandhu's *Triṁśikā.* See also his *Viṁśikā* (Eng. tr. *Wei-shih er-shih-lun*, by Hamilton, American Oriental Society, New Haven, 1938). Hsüan-tsang translated these into Chinese (T. 1585 and 1590 respectively).

[49] See Fung Yu-lan, *op. cit.*, pp. 365 ff.

[50] The ten kinds of *tathatā* 十如 are as

they are set forth in 法華經 *(Saddharma-puṇḍarīka-sūtra)*, 方便品 *(Upāyakauśalyaparivarta)* (cp. 妙法蓮華經 T. 262, p. 5c); see 佛教概論 by Chiang Wei-ch'iao (中華書局, 1930), pp. 43–44. See above, p. 257. Cp. W. T. Chan, *op. cit.*, p. 64 (n. 19): the "ten features, ("thus-characterized, thus-natured, thus-substantiated, thus-caused, thus-forced, thus-activated, thus-conditioned, thus-effected, thus-remunerated and thus-completed - from - beginning - to-end").

51 Fung Yu-lan, *op. cit.*, pp. 370–371; see *ibid.*, the whole section, pp. 370 ff.

52 see above, p. 286.

52a cited in Fung Yu-lan, *op. cit.*, p. 378.

53 *Ibid.*

54 On this School which is based on *Avataṃsaka-sūtra* 華嚴經 (cp. T. 278, 279, 293), see W. T. Chan, *op. cit.*, p. 64, n. 20; although nominally founded by Tu-shun 杜順 (557–640) its real founder was Fa-tsang "the great master of Hsien-shou" (643–712). On Hua-yen see Fung-Yu-lan, *op. cit.*, pp. 339–359.

55 These are 總, 別, 同, 異, 成 and 壞; cp. Chiang Wei-ch'iao, *op. cit.*, pp. 58–59 where these are stated to be traced back to 華嚴經; cp. Fung-Yu-lan, *op. cit.*, 355 where these are translated as generalness, speciality, similarity, diversity, integration, disintegration.

56 On these, see Fung Yu-lan, op. cit., pp. 349 ff.

57 W. T. Chan, *op. cit.*, p. 95.

58 This is the Zen (in Japanese), what W. T. Chan calls "The Meditation School," see *op. cit.*, p. 69; see his valuable note (p. 70, n. 35) which puts in a succinct way the principal tenets of this School; cp. Fung Yu-lan, *op. cit.*, p. 390; see *ibid.*, the whole section. pp. 386–406.

Dr. D. T. Suzuki's works on Zen are well known; he has rendered a great service to the cause of Zen. Of his latest works these could be mentioned: I) *Zen Buddhism* (A Doubleday Anchor Book, ed. William Barrett, Doubleday & Co., New York, 1956) and II) *Mysticism, Christian and Buddhist* (World Perspectives, vol. XII, Harper & Brothers, New York, 1957).

59 Cp. Fung Yu-lan, *op. cit.*, pp. 401 ff.; the work traces the Ch'an deprecation of written words to Tao-sheng, one of the foremost disciples of Kumārajīva; see *ibid.*, pp. 271–272; see W. T. Chan, *op. cit.*, pp. 70 ff. on the deterioration of Ch'an in Chinese History.

60 Cp. Fung Yu-lan, *op. cit.*, p. 402.

61 *Ibid.*, p. 403.

62 Cp. *ibid.*, pp. 393 ff.; also *ibid.*, p. 405.

63 *Ibid.*

64 *Ibid.*, p. 406.

65 *Śāstra*, 263c.

# INDEX


*abhāva* 無 (non-existence, non-being); *see* non-existence *cf.* being

*abhāva-dṛṣṭi* 無見 (non-existence-view; the extreme of non-existence); see *dṛṣṭi, extremes*

*abhibhvāyatana* 勝處 (stages or spheres of mastery; exercises in contemplating on, and getting mastery over the physical body), the eight, 294, 372b, 373a

*abhidharma* 阿毘曇, 分別 (analysis, definition and classification, as well as the texts that expound these, of the basic constituent elements of all things), as one of the three doors to *dharma* (truth), 141–46, 357b; as a preliminary to comprehension of *śūnyatā*, 44–45, 86, 143-145; as what the beginners learn 361a; see *dharma*

*abhidharma*, (enquiry into and comprehension of the ultimate nature of thngs), emphasized by the Kaukkuṭikas, 64, 347b–48a

*Abhidharma*, (the Buddhist school that emphasized analysis; one of the two lines of Buddhist philosophy mentioned in the *Śāstra*; Sarvāstivāda), 346a; *see* Sarvāstivāda

*Abhidharma-kośa*, 372a

*Abhidharma-mahā-vibhāsā-śāstra*, (a fundamental text of Sarvāstivāda, a commentary on the *Jñānaprasthāna*); 28, 29, 338b; see *Vibhāṣā*

*Ābhidharmika*, (a follower of the Abhidharma; analyst; Sarvāstivādin), 180, 213, 364b; *see* Sarvāstivāda

*abhijñā* 神通 (elements of extraordinary power and understanding), the six, 304, 309, 314

*abhiniveśa* 著 (the interestedness that issues in clinging; clinging), 352a–53a; see *grāha, sakti*

*abhivyakti* (manifestation), as the Sāṅkhya conception of causation, 179–80; *see* Sāṅkhya

*Abodhabodhaka*, 36

absolute existence and absolute non-existence, as extremes, 81, 152–55; their criticism and rejection, 174–77, 359b–360a

absolute statements, and relative judgements, 160–3

absolute views, versus relative positions, 152–3

absoluteness, imagined in regard to the conditioned, 42, 89-90, 154, 171; misplaced, *see* error

absolutes, alternatives conceived as, 154; the false, 66; *see* error, extremes

absolutist line of Buddhist Philosophy, 46, 62–64; *see* Mahāsāṅghikas

abstract, imagined as ultimate, 187, 188

accommodation, the principle of; see *ākāśa*

*Acintyastava*, 36, 37

activity *(kriyā)* and motion, critical examination of the conceptions of, 185–87; cf. *karma*

*adhipati-pratyaya* 增上緣 (decisive condition), critical examination of, 182, 361b; see *pratyaya*

# INDEX

Advaita Vedānta, the, and the Mādhyamika, 319–21
*advaya-dharma* 無二法, 不二法 (undivided being), as the ultimate reality, 32, 39–40, 267–75; *see* the real
*Advayadharma-dvāra* 不二法門 (a section in *Vimalakīrti-nirdeśa*), 339b
affliction; see *kleśa*
*Āgama* (the Sarvāstivāda Scriptures), often cited in the *Śāstra*, approvingly, 32, 339b, and as containing the teachings of *dharma-śūnyatā, dharma-dhātu* and *bhūta-koṭi*, 343b
*Āgamaśāstra* of Gauḍapāda, 376a; cf. *Gauḍapāda*
*Aggivacchagotta-sutta*, 345a-b
agnosticism, as a form of the fourth extreme, 154; *see* extremes
*ahaṅkāra* (the sense of 'I'), and *mahat* of the Sāṅkhya, compared to *vijñāna* of Buddhism, 248
*ahetuka* 無因 (the position of no-cause; rejecting reason and clinging to chance), as a form of the fourth extreme, 154; *see* extremes
*ākāśa* 虛空 (the principle of accommodation; space), 205–6, 274–75; as a comparison to Mahāyāna, 280, 356a; as a comparison to *prajñāpāramitā*, 127–28, 265, 318; as a comparison to ultimate reality, 92, 206–7, 244–45, 270, 274–75; critical examination of the substantialist conception of, 204–5, 363b
*akiñcana* 無所有 (not anything specific), as the character of *ākāśa*, 205, 274; as the nature of the ultimate truth, 104, 136
*Akṣaraśataka*, 34, 340a
*Akṣayamatiparipṛcchā*, 32
*Akutobhaya-śāstra*, 34
*alakṣaṇa* 無相 (indeterminate, of no particular nature), as an extreme, 88; as the ultimate nature of things, 269, 359a; cf. *lakṣaṇa; see* indeterminate
*ālambana-pratyaya* 緣緣 (object of cognition), as one of the kinds of conditions, 181, 361a–b; see *pratyaya*
*ālayvijñāna* (the *vijñāna* that is the store house of potencies), as conceived in Vijñānavāda, 321, 340a; see *vijñāna*
alchemist, bodhisattva compared to the skilful, 145, 358a
alchemy, referred to in the *Śāstra*, 337b, 358a
alternatives, 160–70; extremes and, 151–70; *see* extremes
*āma* 生 (immaturity, passion for *dharma*, in '*nyāma*'), 373b
*Amarāvatī*, 25, 336b
analysis 分別 (*abhidharma, vibhajana*) and the error of the analyst, 142–43; see *abhidharma*
analyst, the, error of, 142–43, 180–81; *see* error
*anāmikā* 無名指 (the nameless finger, the ring finger), cited in the *Śāstra* to illustrate the relatively indeterminate nature of a concept or conceptual system 54, 134, 357a
*Ānandavallī (Taittirīya)* 365b
*ānantarya-vimokṣa* 無礙解脫 (freedom, unimpeded and immediate; the highest kind of freedom that the bodhisattva achieves in the final stage of his wayfaring), 310; see *bhūmi, dharmamegha*
*animittatā* 無相 (refraining from making things occassions for clinging), as one of the gates to freedom or Nirvāṇa, 294, 295; see *vimokṣadvāra;* cf. *nimitta*
annihilationism; see *ucchedadṛṣṭi*
*anta* 邊 (dead-ends), 38–39; the two, 90, 91, 352a–53a; *see* extremes, also *dṛṣṭi*
*antarābhava* 中有 (the state intermediary between death and rebirth), the rise of, 223, 239, 367a
*antarābhavaskandha* 中(有)陰 (the com-

plex of the subtle *skandhas* in transition) 223, 239

*antarābhava* (*-skandha*)*-vijñāna* 中陰識 (the complex of the subtle *skandhas* in transition; the self-conscious seed of personal life in the state intermediary between death and rebirth; the individual in the subtle form), 223, 237–40, 367a

*anupalambha* 不可得, 無所得 (the non-clinging; that which cannot be seized), as a name for Nirvāṇa, 272; as a name for *prajñāpāramitā*, 127-28; *see* Middle Way; *see also* non-clinging

*anupalambha-śūnyatā* 不可得空 (non-clinging *śūnyatā*, a name for the ultimate truth), 375b; see *śūnyatā*

*anupalambha (-yoga)* 無所得方便 (skilfulness of non-clinging), as forming, with undivided being, the heart of the *Prajñāpāramitā-sūtras*, 31; as one of the basic imports of *śūnyatā*, 339a; as the pervading spirit of the philosophy of the Middle Way, 18; *see* non-clinging

*anupūrvavihāra-samāpatti* 次第定 (successive abodes of contemplation; exercises for testing one's control of the mind), the nine, 294, 372b–73a; see *samāpatti*

*anutpāda-dharma* 無生法 (the ultimate reality devoid of birth), 19, 263; see *dharma*, the real

*anutpāda-koṭi* 無生際 (the summit of the reality that is devoid of birth; Nirvaṇa; and the mind's penetrating into it), 263, 368a; see *bhūtakoṭi*

*anutpattikadharma-kṣānti* 無生法忍 (the ability to endure, to sustain the ultimate truth of devoidness of birth, and to bring that to bear upon every situation), 284–85, 299, 370a; as an end to all afflictions, 309; as itself the ground of the irreversible, 374; as the power of irreversibility realized by the bodhisattva in the seventh *bhūmi*, 307; as the true status of the bodhisattva, 299, 303, 307, 308; as the true wisdom, 369b; see *avaivarta*, *kṣānti*, *nyāma*

*anvayajñāna* 比智 (knowledge by extension), as knowledge of the world of fine matter and immaterial world, 289; see *dhātu*

*anyathābhāva* 變異 (change, becoming); as the meaning of negation, 168; as brought to light by rejecting the extremes of "is" and "is not," 359b; *see* becoming

*anythātva;* see *anyathābhāva*

*aparimitāyur-dhāraṇī* (the magic spell that furnishes one a long life beyond measure), 26

*apramāda* 不放逸 (absence of lassitude), as an apsect of effort, 285; see *chandas* and *vīrya*

*apramāṇa* (boundlessness of heart; exercises with which one tests the maturity of one's mind), the four, 294, 372b

*apraṇihitatā* 無作 (the abstaining from resolving to do deeds that spring from passion), as one of the gates of freedom, 294–96; see *vimokṣa-dvāra*

*arahan* (the worthy, the holy, the highest in the path of the "hearers"), 289; see *śrāvaka*

*artha* 義 (meaning); *see* meaning

*Arthavargīya-sūtra*, 128, 131, 356b

*arūpa-dhātu* 無色界 (the immaterial world orthe realm of formlessness); as one of the three "worlds," 236, 372b–73a; see *dhātu*, *samāpatti*

*ārūpya-dhātu;* see *arūpa-dhātu*

Āryadeva 34, 337b

*Ārya-śālistambha-sūtra*, 354a

*asama-sama-citta* 無等等心 (mind of unparallelled equanimity, an attainment unique to the true bodhisattva), 301, 373b

Asaṅga, 35, 336a, 337a
Aśoka, 346a
*Aspects.,* 338b, 339a, 339b, 348a
*āsava*; see *āsrava*
*āsrava* (streams of defiling elements), the three, 272
*Aṣṭādaśa-śūnyatā-śāstra,* 34, 340a
*Aṣṭa.,* 15, 331–2, 335b, 339a, 349b, 352a, 358a, 373b
Aśvaghoṣa, 28, 29, 340b
*aśūnya* 不空 (the opposite of *śūnya,* held as an extreme), as the clinging to the false notion that existence is absolute, 325; as the extreme to which clinging to *śūnyatā* might lead, 360a; see *śūnyatā*
*A-t'a-p'o-ch'i-ching* 阿他婆耆經 (Chungyi-ching 衆義經, *Arthavargīya-sūtra*), 356b;
*ātman* 我 (the essential, ultimate nature of the individual), in Advaita Vedānta, 320
*ātman* ("I," self); see "I," I-substance, soul; *see also* person, *pudgala*
*ātman* (self-being), of the elements, conceived in Sarvāstivāda, 57; see *dharmātmā*
atoms, as conceived in Sarvāstivāda, 59, 364b; their non-substantiality exposed by the Mādhyamika, 84, 214–15, 364b
*Avadānas,* 348b
*avaivarta* 阿鞞跋致 (also *avinivartanīya,* the irreversible bodhisattva), as the bodhisattva in his true status, 300; as having realized the *anutpattika-dharma-kṣānti,* 303; his strength of skilfulness, 300–04
*avaktavya* (lit. indeterminable; the Jaina doctrine that judgements are non-absolute), compared with the Mādhyamika relativism of judgments, 159; cf. *avyākṛta-vastu*
*Avataṃsaka-sūtra* 華嚴經 379a
*avavāda-prajñapti* 受波羅攝提 (convention in regard to the complex entities in distinction from their subtle constitutents), clinging to, 85–86, 351b; see *prajñapti*
*āveṇika-dharma* 不共法 (extraordinary elements unique to the Buddha), the eighteen, 310, 314–15, 375a
*avidyā; see* ignorance
*avinivartanīya* 不退, 不轉 (the irreversible), 373b; see *avaivarta*
*Avyākata-saṃyuttaṃ,* 344b
*avyākṛta-vastu* (questions unanswered by the Buddha), the fourteen, as cases of extreme and the meaning of the Buddha's silence in regard to them, 49–51, 146–49, 344b–45b, 358a
*avyakta* (lit. undistinguished, indistinct nature; *prakṛti),* as an ultimate principle of the Sāṅkhya), 249; see *prakṛti*
*avyaya* (indestructible), as the ultimate nature of the Tathāgata, 345b
*Awakening of Faith,* 378b; see *Mahāyāna-śradhotpāda-śāstra*
*āyatana* 入 (bases of cognition), the six internal, as a link in the cycle of life, 237; the twelve, as one of the three classifications of the elements existence, 63, 83, 87, 128, 363a; see also *dhātu, skandha*

Bagchi, P.C., 335a
Bahuśrutīyas, 63
*bala* 力 (powers), the five, of the bodhisattva, 291; the ten, of the Buddha, 77, 310, 314; see *indriya*
Balaśrī, 27
Bāṇa, 336a, 337b
Bandhutatta, 14
Bareau, André, 346a, 346b, 347b
Beal, S., 337b
becoming, in the early Buddhist througt, 48, 51-53, 58-60, 60-62, 65-69; critical examination of being, non-being and, 174–77
beginning and end, as absolute con-

cepts, 190–92, 362a-b; as relative notions, 192–94
being, and non-being, as extremes, 81, 155-60, 174–77, 359b-60b; modes of determinate, 82–84; the true, 84-86; *see also* becoming, *svabhāva*
Bhargava, Purushottam Lal, 338a
Bhattacharya, Vidhusekhara, 337b, 340a, 376a
*bhava* 有 (tending to become, tending for embodiment; impressions of deeds done in the present span of life leading to fresh embodiment), as a link in the cycle of life, 236; distinguished from *saṁskāra*, 240–41, 367a
*bhāva* 有 (existence embodied in the five *skandhas*), 366b–67a
*bhāva* 有 (being, essence or nature, in *svabhāva* self-being), meaning of the term, 359a; *see* being, *svabhāva*
*bhāva* 有 (being, existence), modes of determinate, 82-84; as one of the extremes, 155
*bhāvanā* 修行 (cultivation, development), of *samādhi*, 370b
*Bhavasaṅkrānti-sūtra* and *-śāstra*, 341a; see *Mahāyāna-bhavabheda-śāstra*
Bhāvaviveka, 35, 341a
Bhramaragirī (Śrīparvata), 25, 336b, 337a
*bhūmi* 地 (stages in the course of bodhisattva's wayfaring), the ten, 32, 288, 305–11; their different schemes, 374a
*bhūtakoṭi* 實際 (the apex or the summit of reality which all beings reach), *dharmadhātu* and, 261–67; meaning of the term, 263; as the universal reality, 114; *see* the real; cf. *dharmadhātu* and *anutpādakoṭi*
*bhūtalakṣaṇa* 實相 (the true, ultimate nature of things; the ultimate truth; the universal reality), 92, 114, 351a; cf. *lakṣaṇa; see* the real
birth of birth 生生 (*utpādotpāda*, secondary birth, in distinction from the primary birth, as conceived in Sarvāstivāda), critically examined, 188–89, 362a
*bodhi* (enlightenment) as not different from the knowledge of all forms (*sarvākārajñatā*), 266; as the way of all the Buddhas, 297; the factors of, 291; the non-clinging realization of, 131-32, 162–68, 348a; see *bodhisattva, bodhyaṅga, prajñā,* also *sarvākārajñatā*
*bodhi* and *prajñā* as different designations of *prajñāpāramitā,* 355a
*bodhi* and *śūnyatā* as distionctions within *prajñāpāramitā,* 376a
*Bodhicaryāvatāra,* 34, 37, 241b
*bodhipākṣika-dharma* (factors of the way), the thirtyseven, and the gates of freedom (*vimokṣa-dvāra*), 290–96
*Bodhisambhāra-śāstra,* 35, 340b; see *Bodhisattva-pātheya-śāstra*
bodhisattva, and the Buddha, 305–16; his fundamental aspiration, 276, 277; his non-clinging realization of *bodhi,* 78, 108, 131–32, 162–68; his realization of Buddhahood 305–11; his realization of ultimate truth, 143–46, 276–78; his status, 298–300; his wayfaring without a set back, 298–99, 300; his wisdom compared with that of the Buddha, 288–90; see also *avaivarta, bhūmi, bodhi,* Buddha, *mahāsattva, nyāma*
*Bodhisattva-Doctrine,* 369b
*Bodhisattva-pātheya-śāstra,* 37, 340b
*Bodhisattva-prakaraṇa,* (a section in the *Vibhāṣā*), 375a
*bodhyaṅga* 覺分 (factors of enlightenment), the seven, 291
*Brahmajāla-sutta,* 354a
*brahman,* of the Advaita Vedānta, and the ultimate reality in the Mādhyamika, 319–321
*Brahma-sūtras,* the, Śaṅkra's Commentary on, 376b

*brahma-vihāra* (the sublime abodes); see *apramāṇa*
Buddha, the, his bodily features, 234; and the Buddhist Schools, 53–55; comparable to the Sun, 150; dharma body and physical body of, 311–12 (Sarvāstivāda view), 312–16 (Mādhyamika view); Nāgārjuna and, 45–53; his natures, mundane and ultimate, 234–35; his presence, universal, 313; his silence, 146–48, 358a; his way, the Great Way, 280; his ways of answering, 146–50; his ways of teaching, 133–50; his wisdom, 150, 288–90, 358b
*buddha-cakṣus* 佛眼 (Buddha-eye), 124–26; *see* eyes
Buddhahood, as not the ideal of Hīnayāna, 278; as perfection in personality, 276; conventional and transcendental or mundane and ultimate, 68–69, 234–35, 348a; *see* Mahāsāṅghikas
*Buddhamārgālaṅkāra-śāstra,* 34
Buddhapālita, 35; see *Kārikā;* cf. Bhāvaviveka
Buddhayaśas, 14
*buddhi* (intellect, a category of the Sāṅkhya), and the *vijñāna* of the Buddhist, 365b, 366a, 367b; see also *mahat*
Buddhist Councils, 55, 345b
*Buddhist Dictionary,* 370–71a, 372b–73a
Buddhist philosophy, the three broadlines in the early, 55–64, 346a; its two chief lines, Hinayāna and Mahāyāna, 46–47; the two lines referred to in the *Śāstra,* 346a
*Buddhist Remains in Andhra,* 336a
Buddhist Schools, the early, basic ideas common to, 53–55; contention among, 37–38, 341b; Nāgārjuna and, 64–66; the rise of, 53–57, 346a
*Buston's History of Buddhism,* 336a

Candrakīrti, 35, 36, 341a, 343a, 357a, 362a; see *Prasannapadā*
categories of understanding, as derived notions, 83, 200; criticism of, 40, 171–208; *see* critical examination
*Catuḥśataka,* 337b; see Deva *Śataśāstra*
*Catuḥstava,* 341b
*Caturdharma-piṭaka* 四法藏 *(Four Collections of Dharma),* 363a
causal continuity, denied in negativism, 176
causal origination; the two principal accounts of its examination in the *Śāstra,* 361a
causal relation, Sāṅkhya and Vaiśeṣika conceptions critically examined, 178–80, 360b; Sarvāstivāda view, critically examined, 180–83, 360b–61a
*Central Conception of Buddhism, The,* 347a, 347b
*Central Philosophy of Buddhism, The,* 22, 341b, 376b–77a
Ch'an 禪 (Zen), Mādhyamika philosophy and, 327–28
Chan, W.T., 327, 378b, 379a, 379b
chance, clinging to, 154; see *ahetuka; see also* extreme
*chandas* 欲 (determination), as a name for an aspect of effort, 285; see *vīrya*
change; see *anyathābhāva,* becoming
*Chao Lun, Studies in,* 335a; 377a; *see* Seng-chao
*Chao, The Book of,* 335a, 377a
charity, perfection of; see *dāna-pāramitā*
Chattopadhyaya, Sudhakara, 338b
Ch'en Yüan, 335b
Chiang Wei-ch'iao, 379a
*Chinese Buddhism,* 341a
Chi-tsang 吉藏, his commentaries on Mādhyamika treatises, 377b; his exposition of Mādhyamika philosophy, 324–25; his theory of double truth, 378a; his view on *Dvādaśamukha-śāstra,* 341a
*Ch'u-san-ts'ang-chi-chi* 出三藏記集 343b

*citta* 心 (mind), and the soul, 225, 227–29; as the basis, center and seed of personality, 64, 73, 114, 229, 233, 350b, 355a; as constructing all that is in the three worlds, 71; as designating person, 238, 298, 350b; as impermanent, 211; as intellect, cogtion, understanding, 199, 227, 228, 229; meaning of the term, 350b; as object of *smṛtyupasthāna*, 350b, 371b; as principle of self-dtermination, 229; as pure in its ultimate nature, 354b; as self-conscious person, 238, 298; as self-conscious principle of intellection, 64, 73, 114; and the soul, 225, 227–29; see *vijñāna*

*cittaikāgratā* 一心, (one-pointedness of mind), 285, 370b

*citta-smṛtyupsthāna,* (application of mindfulness to the self-conscious principle of intellection), 350b, 371b; see *smṛtyupasthāna*

clinging 著, 取 (*abhiniveśa, grāha, upādāna*), as a link in the cycle of life, 236–37; as the root of conflict and suffering, 38, 129; its root or origin, 48, 99, 106, 236–37, 247; to the act of charity, 283; to the conditioned and the unconditioned, 132, 252; to the conditioned as the unconditioned, 66; to "I" and "not I," 104; to negation, 172; to sin and merit, 283; to the specific as the self-contained, 78; to *śūnyatā,* 110, 146, 172, 325, 342b, 359a, 360a, 375b; to views, 109; the way to bring to light, 354b

cognition, true or false, as not devoid of object, 81, 93–96, 216

*Collection of Six Dharmas* 六法藏 (*Ṣaḍdharma-piṭaka* or *-samuccaya*), of the *Vaiśeṣika,* 363a

*Complete Catalogue of the Buddhist Canon,* 341a

composite elements; see *samskṛta*

comprehension, as the criterion of the Great Way, 68–69, 276–77; factors conducive to, 265–67; knowledge as, 127–50 (especially 143–46); levels of, 255–61; as the Middle Way, 40–41; phases of, 277–78; Way of, 276–78; *see* knowledge, Middle Way

*Conception of Buddhist Nirvana,* 20

concepts 名 (*nāma*), and conventional entities, 70–88 (especially 74–81), 209–10; error in construing, 143; of mutual relation, 195; names or words and, 74–75; non-clinging use of, 148–49; see *nāma* and *lakṣaṇa*

conditioned origination; see *pratītya-samutpāda*

conditions, see *pratyaya*

confusion, the veils of, 84; *see* error

contemplation, of nine kinds, on the nine different characters of the body, 372a-b; of ten kinds, on the ten characters like impermanence etc., 372a-b; see *dhyāna, samādhi;* cf. *krtsnāyatana*

contention (or conflict) and suffering, the root of, 38–39, 128–30; *see* clinging; cf. non-clinging, *madhyamā pratipat*

convention *(prajñapti),* the modes of, 82–88; the nature of, 70–81, 349b–50a; the world of, 72–73; see *prajñapti,* also *nirmāṇa, saṁvṛti, vyavahāra*

conventional entities (相 *lakṣaṇa),* concepts and, 70–88; cf. concepts

Coomaraswamy, Ananda K., 22

Councils, the Buddhist, 55, 345b–46a

craving *(tṛṣṇā);* see *tṛṣṇā*

critical examination, of atomic elements, 214–15; of beginning and end, 190–93; of being, non-being and becoming, 174–77; of birth, decay and death, 187–90; of causes and conditions, 178–84; of elements of existence, 209–16; of I-substance, 217–31; of space, 204–07; of spatial directions, 200–03; of substance, 207–08 of time, 194–200, 361a

criticism, analysis and, 141–146; and the error of the negativist, 143; the principle and purpose of, 151–52, 172–73, 361a; its procedure, 152–53; *cf.* Mādhyamika; *see* negative criticism
*Cūlasakuludāyi-sutta*, 344a
cycle of life, the, basic import of, 247–48; links in, 236–42, 366b–67a; phases in, 245–47; the root of, 240–42

*dāna-pāramitā* (perfection of charity), the five characters of, 281–83; cultivated in the first *bhūmi*, 305; see *pāramitā*
*darśana* 見 (realization), distinguished from *jñāna* (knowledge), 355a
Dārṣṭāntikas, 56; their criticism of Sarvāstivāda, 347b; their main philosophical ideas, 346b
*Daśabhūmika-śāstra*, see *Daśabhūmivibhāṣā-śāstra*
*Daśabhūmika-sūtra*, 32, 339b, 374a
*Daśabhūmi-vibhāṣā-śāstra*, 15, 35, 37, 339b, 364a, 375a
deeds 業 *(karma)*, critical examination of soul and, 222, 229–31; see *karma*
Demiéville, 14, 335a
dependent origination; see *pratītya-samutpāda*
derived name; see *upādāya-prajñapti*
determinate, the, and the indeterminate, 267–70; essential relativity of, 252–55, 342a-b;
determinate being, the three modes of, 82–84
Deva; see Āryadeva
*deva*-eye, the, eyes of flesh and, 120–22; *see* eyes
*Dhammacakka-ppavattana-sutta (Sermon on the Turning of the Wheel of Dhamma)*, 47, 344a
*Dhammapada*, 345a
*dharma* 法 (truth or true nature of things; the Buddha's teaching that embodies the truth, as well as the way he showed), 48, 49, 55, 92, 130, 131, 139, 140, 141, 198, 259, 273, 374, 306, 345b, 363a; as conditioned origination, 48, 49, 370a; as the indeterminate, ultimate reality, 87, 140, 141, 207, 251, 256, 266, 267, 273, 274, 292, 314; the eye of, 123–24, 243–44; non-clinging, 164; non-dual, undivided, 32, 34, 97, 118, 122, 145, 264, 269, 275; the peace, 272; the *śūnya*, 272, 273; the three doors to, 141–42, 357b; the three marks of, 345b; unborn, devoid of birth and death, 18, 140, 235, 254, 259, 263, 299, 307; unconditioned, 88, 115, 118, 122, 128, 259, 266; unspeakable, 140, 141, 273; the wheel of, 47–48, 273–74
*dharma* 法 (name, term), in contrast with *artha* (connotation) and *nirukti* (definition or enunciation), 350b–51a; see *vaiśāradya*
*dharma* 法 (characteristics or ways unique to things), 257; the eye of, 123–24, 243–44; *see* eyes; cf. *lakṣaṇa*
*dharma* 法 (factors of the way), 287; *see* way
*dharma* 法 (elements of existence), 46, 343b; the five kinds, 363a; Sarvāstivādins' view of, 57–58, 84, 86, 87, 346b–7a; the six, the basic categories of the Vaiśeṣikas, 363a; see *dharma-śūnyatā*
*dharma-cakra* 法輪 (the wheel of *dharma*), its content, 47–48; and the unutterable truth, 273–74
*dharma-cakṣus* 法眼 (the dharma-eye), 123–24, 243–44; *see* eyes
*dharma-dhātu* 法性 (the ultimate essence, the fundamental source of all things; the reality), 88, 145, 259, 261–62, 272, 299, 314, 327; and *bhūtakoṭi* (the supreme end, the apex of being), 261–67; meaning of the term, 261, 266, 351a, 368a; cf. *bhūtakoṭi*, *tathatā*; *see* reality

*Dharma-dhātu-stava,* 35, 341b, 368a
*dharmaiṣaṇā* 求法 (seeking, longing, thirst for the real), 18, 342a; *see* thirst
*dharma-jñāna* 法智 (knowledge of elements that constitute the world of desire), 289; cf *anvayajñāna*
*dharma-kāya* 法身 *(dharma*-body, the body born of *dharmatā),* of the bodhisattva, 307–309; of the Buddha, 314–16
*dharma-kṣānti* 法忍 (endurance for *dharma,* the ability to bear the truth), 145; meanings of the term, 369b–70a; see *anutpattika-dharma-kṣānti, gambhīra-dharma-kṣānti*
*dharma-lakṣaṇa* 法相 (the true, essential nature of *dharma),* of the elements, 87; the eternal, 270–71; the mundane and the transmundane, 259–60; see *dharma, lakṣaṇa*
*dharma-megha* 法雲 (lit., *dharma*-cloud; the last stage in the bodhisattva's wayfaring, compared to the great cloud), 310; see *bhūmi*
*dharma-prajñapti* (conventional designation of the subtle constituent elements), 85; see *prajñapti, also* convention
*dharma-pravicaya* 擇法 (analysis and understanding of the constituent elements of all things), 291
*dharmārāmaḥ* 喜法 (delighting in and contemplating on the true nature of things), 342a
*dharma-ratiḥ* 欲法 (intersted in comprehending the true nature of things), 342a
*dharma-sthāna* 法住 (the real nature in which things eternally stay; the eternal nature or abode of things), 115, 272
*dharma-sthiti* 法位 (the real state or the stability of things), 272
*dharma-śūnyatā* 法空 *(śūnyatā* of *dharma),* as the indeterminate nature of the ultimate reality, see *svabhāva-śūnyatā;* as the nonsubstantiality of the basic elements of existence, 57, 62, 84, 86, 87, 210-16, 343b, 348b, 375b–76a; see *dharma, śūnyatā*
*dharmatā* 法性 (true nature, a synonym of *tathatā*), the different levels of, 259; as the origin of *dharma-kāya,* 307; see *tathatā*; cf. *dharma-dhātu*
*dharmātmā* 法我 (the self-being of elements), the basic doctrine of Sarvāstivāda, 57; see *ātman*
*dhātu* 性 (essence), as comparable to *prakṛti* and distinguished from *lakṣaṇa* 相, 77; as the inmost essence, the fundamental nature, 261; see *dharma-dhātu, sabhāga-dhātu*
*dhātu* 性 (source, origin, 本生處), as the ground of all things, 261, 351a; see *dharma-dhātu*
*dhātu* 界, 種 (lineage, a classification of elements), the eighteen, 83, 87, 128; cf. *āyatana, skandha*
*dhātu* 界 (spheres, worlds), the three, 236
*dhūta-guṇa* 頭陀 (ascetic practices), the twelve, their true nature and purpose, 306, 369b
*dhyāna* 禪, 定 (states of meditation, concentration, contemplation), as the four trances of the realm of form, 294; meaning of the term, 370b; their place in the factors of the way, 294; their place in the nine successive abodes, 372b–73a; cf. also *samādhi*
*dhyāna-pāramitā* (perfection of concentration and meditation), 285–86; see *pāramitā*
*Dīghanikāya,* 344a
*dik* 方 (spatial directions), critical examination of the substantialist conception of, 200-201, 363a; as derived names, 201–3; see *mahāśūnyatā*
Dīghanakha, 148
dogmatism, explained, 105–106; see *anta, dṛṣṭi,* error *and* extreme

*dravya* 陀羅驃 (實法, reality, substance), as one of the basic categories of the Vaiśeṣikas), 201, 363a

*dravyasat (vastusat)* 實有 (lit. being a real, an immutable substance) as the substantialist view in regard to time, 195; *see* time

dream, cited to illustrate the limited, relative validity of cognition, 94–95; Vabhāṣikas' interpretation of, 353b

*dṛṣṭi* 見 (view), the term explained and the false, distinguished from the right, 342a-b

*dṛṣṭi* 見 (wrong or false view; extreme), origin of, 105–6, 107–10; kinds of, 108–10, 153–55, 174–75, 354a, 360a-b; *see also* error, extreme; cf. *mithyādṛṣṭi*

*dṛṣṭi-parāmarśa* 取見 (clinging to views), as itself a basic kind of false view, 109; see *parāmarśa*

*duḥkha* 苦 (pain, suffering); *see* suffering

Dutt, Nalinaksha, 336a, 338a, 339a, 339b, 348a-b

*Dvādaśamukha-śāstra,* 15, 35, 36, 341b, 362a, 377b

*Early History of the Andhra Country,* 336b

*Early History of North India,* 338b

earth, 地 *(pṛthvī)*, as exemplifying the non-substantiality of physical entities, 211–13; see *rūpa*

effort; see *vīrya*

*ekalakṣaṇa* 一相 (lit. of one nature; the indeterminate nature of the ultimate reality), 359a

*Ekaśloka-śāstra,* 35, 36, 341a, 360a

Ekavyāvahārikas, and their doctrine of nonsubstantiality of elements, 63

elements of existence; see *dharma*

enlightenment, factors of; see *bodhyaṅga*

*Epigraphia Indica,* 337b

error, and negation, 61; as not devoid object, 93–96; in regard to the mundane truth, 90–91; in regard to the ultimate truth, 91–93

error of false realism *(sasvabhāva-vāda)*, 43; *see* error of misplaeed absolutness

error of misplaced absoluteness *(satkāya-dṛṣṭi, sasvabhāvavāda)*, carried to its completion, 102; Madhyamika rejection of, 42; as misapplied drive toward the real, 38, 43; as rooted in the false sense of self, 171, 247; as the root form of all errors, 93, 247; as the root of dogmatic views, 107; as the root of the tendency to cling, 38, 171; *see* clinging, extremes

*eṣaṇā* 求 (seeking, longing, thirst, in *dharmaiṣaṇā,* thirst for the real), 342a

essential nature *(lakṣaṇa)*, the three grades of, 86–88; see *lakṣaṇa*

*Essentials of Buddhist Philosophy,* 378b

eternalism; see *śāśvata-dṛṣṭi*

existence; see *bhāva,* being

experience, and the object of experience, 215–16; *cf.* cognition

extremes, and alternatives, 150–70 (especially 151–60); and clinging, 48, 49, 151, 171–73; the four, 155–160; the two, 107–10; see *anta, dṛṣṭi*

eye(s), (levels and perpectives of understanding), the five, 119–26, 355b–56a; the three, in regard to the cycle of life, 242–45; the two, 258; of wisdom in regard to sin and merit, 283; see *prajñā*

faith, 信 *(śraddhā)*, as one of the five *indriyas* 291; see *indriyas*

Fa-tsang, 法藏 379a

*Fa Ren,* 346b, 347b, 348a

feeling 受 *(vedanā,* one of the five *skandhas)*, as a link in the cycle of life, 237; as an object of the application of mindfulness, 371b; see *skandhas, smrtyupasthāna*

forbearance *(kṣānti)*; see *kṣānti*

Fung Yu-lan, 377b, 378a, 378b, 379a, 379b

*gambīradharma-kṣānti* 甚深法忍 (forbearance with regard to the profound truth, viz., of the conditioned origination,) 370a; cf. *anutpattikadharma-kṣānti;* see *dharma-kṣānti, kṣānti*
gates of fredom *(vimokṣa-dvāra)*, the three, 293–96, 358a, 373a; *see* way
*gati* 趣 (tending), bodhisattva's, to knowledge of all forms, 266; of everything to everything else, 266
*gati* 趣 (being a destination, resting point, refuge) for the entire world, as a virtue of the bodhisattva, 266
Gauḍapāda, 319, 376a
*Gauḍapāda,* 376b; cf. *Āgamaśāstra*
Gautamīputra Śātakarṇī, 27, 28, 338a
Giles, Lionel, 335b
Gokhale, Vasudev, 340a
Gopalachari, K., 336b, 338a
*grāha* 取, 著 (seizing, clinging); *see* clinging
Great Way (Mahāyāna), and the Small Way, 46–47, 55–56, 66–69, 278–79, 343b; as the non-exclusive way, 279–80; as the way of perfection, 280–81; see Mahāyāna, *pāramitā*

Haimavatas, 365a
Hāla, 28, 30, 338a
Hamilton, 378b
Hardayal, 375a
*Harṣacarita,* 336a, 337b
*hetu-pratyaya* 因緣 (productive conditions), critical examination of, 180–81; see *pratyaya*
Hīnayāna (the Small Way), Mahāyāna and, 46–47, 55–56, 66–69, 278–79, 343b; on the use of the term, 20, 278–79; see also *śrāvaka*
*Historical Inscriptions of Southern India,* 338a
*History of Buddhist Thought;* see Thomas, E.J.
*History of Chinese Philosophy;* see Fung Yu-lan
*History of the Eightyfour Sorcerers,* 336a
*Hsi-yü-chi* 西域記 336a
Hsüan-tsang 玄奘, 28, 336a, 337a, 337b, 378b
Hua-yen 華嚴, its relation to Mādhyamika philosophy, 325–27, 378b, 379a; *see also* T'ien-t'ai
Hui-ying 慧影, 16, 333
Hui-yüan, 慧遠, 15, 323, 343b, 377a

"I," the sense of, and the false sense of self, 100–03; as ethically indeterminate and flexible, 354a; the rise of, 98–100; soul and, 219–27; the unerring, 103–05; cf. *vijñāna*
ideas, birth of, as not the criterion for reality of objects, 81; *see also* cognition
ignorance 無明 *(avidyā)*, 89–110; and knowledge, 111–26; as the origin of the cycle of life, 240–42; as the origin of *kleśas;* 106–07; its nature, 89–90, 111–15, 242, 244–45;its power compared to the power of dream, 91; *see* error; *cf.* knowledge
ignorant, and the wise, 96–97, 250
illusion, the idea conveyed by illustrations of, 89–90, 96, 352a; the view that the world is a baseless, 359a; *see* error, ignorance
illusory objects, the nature of, 95–96
illustration(s), of echo, 95–96; of illusion, *see* illusion; of the image in the mirror, 96; of the image of the moon in water, 98–99
imaginative construction *(vikalpa* 分別), 90, 352a-b
impermanence *(anityatā* 無常), as the door to comprehension of *śūnyatā,* 149, 211, 358a; its teaching as remedial in kind, 192–93; right and wrong understanding of, 149, 322–23
incomposite, (無爲 *asaṁskṛta)*, as viewed by the Mahāsāṅghikas, 64; *see* the real

indeterminate 無相 *(alakṣaṇa)*, the, clinging to, 88, 132; the true comprehension of, 87-88; as distinct from the determinate, 267–70; as the ground of the world, 251–67; as the ultimate nature of all, 87; *see* the real; cf. *dharma-dhātu, bhūta-koṭi*

indeterminateness, of the mundane and of the ultimate, distinguished, 52–53; of judgments, clung to as an extreme, 159; see *avaktavya, avyākṛta*

individual standpoint, the, truth taught from, 139; see *siddhānta*

individuality, wrong notion of, distinguished from the sense of self, 100; Hīnayāna attitude to, 68, 279; its effacement, not necessary for extinction of passion, 279, 304, 315

*indriyas* 根 (faculties), the five, among the factors of the way, 291; cf. *bala*

intellect, self-conscious, as the self, the center of personal life, 98, 99; see *vijñāna;* cf. *buddhi*

intellection, self-conscious, as the sense of "I," and its consequent discriminations, 100, 151, 153; see *citta* and *vijñāna*

intermediary state, between death and rebirth; see *antarābhava*

I-substance; *see* soul

Īśvara, Bhikṣu, 341a

Īśvara, the personal god, in Śaṅkara's philosophy, 319

Iyengar, H.R.R., 341a

Jaggayyapeta, 336b

Jaina non-absolutism or indeterminateness of judgments, 16, 156, 159; see *avaktavya;* cf. *avayākṛta, madhyamā-pratipat*

*jāti* 生 (lit. birth; clinging to embodiment), as a link in the cycle of life, 236; *see* cycle of life

Jayswal, K.P., 340b

*jñāna* 知, 智 (knowledge), distinguished from *darśana,* 355a-b; *kṣānti* and, 307, 370a; distinguished from *vijñāna,* 130–31, 355a; see *prajñā*

Johnston, E. H., 340b

*Jñānaprasthāna-Śastra.* 28, 29, 338b. 348b–49a

Juṣka, 28

*kāla* 迦羅 (time), conceived as a substance (Vaiśeṣika), 195, 362b; cf. *samaya; see* time

Kālāśoka, 29

*Kālasūtra,* 363b

*kalaviṅka* 迦羅頻伽, the bird, used for illustrating the bodhisattva's voice, 373b

Kalhaṇa, 28, 336a

*kalpa* (a measure of time), 249, 313

*Kāma-sūtras,* 338a

*Kaṇāda,* 362b

Kaniṣka I, and Kaniṣka II, 28; date of Kaniṣka 1, 338b, 346a; Nāgārjuna and, 28–30

*Kao-seng-chuan* 高僧傳, 335a

*Kārikā,* its criticism of birth, 362a; of causal production 360b, 361b; its criticism of identity and separatness, 362a; its criticism of substance and quality, 364a; its criticism of *svabhāva,* 360a; of time, 362b; its place in Nāgārjuna's philosophy, 16, 42; the different ways in Buddha's teaching, 354a, 357a; on impermanence, 358a; on I-substance, 33, 366a; on mundane existence, 39, 40, 43; on rejection of extremes, 359b; as replete with negative arguments, 42; on rise of extremes, 354a; on Sarvāstivāda doctrine of elements, 43; and the *Śāstra,* 42–46, 359b–60a; on *śūnyatā,* 40, 43

*karma* 業 (deeds), creations of, 73; critical examination of the different conceptions of, 185–90; as leading the seed of personal life to the womb,

240; as one of the phases in the cycle of life, 245–47, of the right kind, 189–190; *saṁskāra* and *bhava* as distinctions within, 240–41, 245, 367a, 367b

*karuṇā* 悲, 慈悲 (compassion), and wisdom, as phases of comprehension, 68-69, 277–78; as arising with the comprehension of truth, 282; as an essential constitutent of the Buddha's *dharma*-body, 315–16; as an essential element of Buddhahood, 310; as not an essential of Hīnayāna, 68, 279; as the root of the Buddha's way, 315

*Kāśyapa-parivarta*. 32. 339b

*Kathāvatthu*, 347a

Kātyāyana, 359b

Kātyāyanīputra, 28, 29, 311, 315, 338b

Kaukkuṭikas, 63–64

*kāya* 身 (body; a composite, conditioned entity), the physical, contemplation on impurity of, 372a-b; application of mind-fulness on, 371b, 372a-b; cf. *sat-kāya-dṛṣṭi;* see *dharmakāya, rūpa-kāya*

Kimura, 348a

*kleśa* 煩惱 (afflictions), as arising from and headed by ignorance and perversions, 63, 91, 92, 100, 105, 106–107, 243, 245; creations of, 73; as one of the three phases of the cycle of life, 246, 367b

knowledge, and action, 70; and ignorance, 111–26; as the principle of comprehension, 127–50; of the unconditioned reality, 117–19; nature and kinds of, 115–19, 286–87, 289; the notion of its dependence on soul examined, 227–29; the ultimate principle of, 116–17; see *jñāna, prajñā;* see also *yathārthajñāna*

knowledge of all forms; see *sarvakarajñatā*

*kośas* 藏 (sheaths), the notion that the five are a repository of the subtlebody, 223, 365b; *see* soul

*Kośabhāṣya*, 347b

*koti* 際 (the apex; to reach the summit), of reality, 263; see *bhūta-koṭi*

*koṭi* 句 (extremes), the four; *see* extremes

*kṛtsnāyatana* 一切處 (bases of all-pervasiveness; exercises in contemplation), the ten, 294, 372a–72b, 373a

*kṣaṇa* 念 (moments, instants); that the bodhisattva's realization of bodhi is instantaneous 一念, 311; Sarvāstivāda conception of, 58–60; *see* time

*kṣānti* 忍 (forbearance, endurance), distinguished into that in regard to *sattva* and that in regard to *dharma*, 283, 369b–70a; earlier and later phases of, 370a; as what Hīnayāna lacks, 68, 278-79; see *anutpattika-dharmakṣānti, dharma-kṣānti, gambhira-dharma-kṣānti*

*kṣāntipāramitā* (perfection of endurance), 283–84; see *pāramitā*

Kumārajīva, biography of Deva attributed to, 25, 34, 336a; biography of Nāgārjuna attributed to, 337b; his exposition of Mādhyamika philosophy, 321–23; life and work of, 14–16

K'uei-chi 窺基 63, 64, 346b

Kumāralāta, 346b

Kunst, Arnold, 340b

Kuntala, 338a

*lakṣaṇa* 相 (sign, mark), in distinction from *dhātu* 性 (nature), 77; *nāma* (name) and, 75–76; as *nimitta* (occassion), 76

*lakṣaṇa* 相 (essential nature), the three gsades of, 86–88; as a synonym of *prakṛti, svabhāva,* also of *dhātu*, distinguished from sign or mark, 76–77, 351a; see also *dharmalakṣaṇa, dharmatā, tathatā*

*lakṣaṇa* 相 (a specific determinate entity), 77–80, 207

*lakṣaṇa* 相 (conventional entities), *nāma* (concepts) and, 70–88

*lakṣaṇa-grāha* 取相 (the seizing of, clinging to the determinate), 78, 351b; see *grāha*
*lakṣaṇodgrahaṇa* 取相 (the picking up of characters), as the definition of *saṁjñā*, 349b
*lakṣaṇopalambha* 得相 (the seizing of *lakṣaṇa*), 352b, see *lakṣaṇa-grāha*
*Lakṣaṇavinukta-bodhi-hṛdaya-śāstra*, 35
*lakṣya* 所相 (subtratum of quality; substance), critically examined, 207–8
*Lalitavistara*, 344a
Lamotte, Étienne, 13, 335a; 345b; 348a; 354b; 357a; 363b
*Laṅkāvatārasūtra*, 336a, 340b
*laukika-siddhānta* (direct teaching of the mundane truth), 138; cf. *vyavahāra*, *siddhānta*
*Le Cannon Bouddhique en Chine*, 335a
*Les Sectes Bouddhiques du petit Vehicule*, *see* Bareau
*Le Traite de la Grand Vertu de Sagesse*, 13, 335a; *see* Lamotte
Leibenthal, Walter, 335a, 377a, 377b–8a
*Life of Nāgārjuna (from Pag Sam Jon Zang)*, 337a
*Life of Nāgārjuna from Tibetan and Chinese Sources*, 336a
logical entities, 86; see *dharma* (elements)
*Liu-fa-lun* 六法論 *(Ṣaḍdharma-sāstra)*, 365a
*Liu-fa-ts'ang* 六法藏 *(Ṣaḍdharma-piṭaka* or *-samuccaya, Collection of Six Dharmas)*, of the Vaiśeṣika, 363a
*Lokātītastava*, 36, 37; see *Catuḥstava*
Lokottaravādins, 63

*Madhyamakānugama-śāstra* 順中論, 35, 336a, 337a, 340b
*Madhyamaka-śāstra* 中論, 34, 35; see *Mādhyamika-Kārikā*
*madhyamā pratipat* 中道 (the Middle Way) and the doctrine of conditioned origination, 47, 48, 53, 81; as identical with the way of comprehension, 33, 40, 42, 127–33; as non-clinging and rising above extremes, 40–42, 88, 210; as the non-exclusive way, 48–51, 127–50; as the remedial kind of teaching, 163; as revealed by the Buddha's silence, 48–51, 148–49, 163; as seeing things as they are, 32, 50, 88; *see* criticism, *prajñā*, *śūnyatā*; *cf.* clinging, extremes
Mādhyamika (the farer on the Middle Way), the mission of, 41–42, 162, 210, 318, 319; on negativism, 172–73
Mādhyamika philosophy, and the Advaita Vedānta, 319–21, 376a–76b; and the Jaina, 156, 159; and the Nyāya, 33, 318–19, 340a; and the Sāṅkhya, 248–50; and the Vaiśeṣika, 33, 178–80, 195–96, 200–202, 219–25; as not a substitute for any specific system, 318; in the early Chinese Thought, 321–28; the spirit of, 328–30
*Mādhyamika-kārikā (Madhyamaka-śāstra)*, 34; the text and its commentaries, 35–36; see *Kārikā*
magical creation, as an illustration for creation of ignorance, 111–12
Mahādeva, five points of, 55, 345b
Mahadevan, T.M.P., 376b
*Mahākaruṇopāya-śāstra*, 34
Mahākātyāyana, 357b
Mahānāga, 27, 337a
*Mahāniddesa*, 346b–47a
*Mahāprajñāpāramitā-śāstra*; see *Śāstra*
*Mahāpraṇidhanotpāda-gāthā*, 35
*mahāsattva* (the great being), as a title for the bodhisattva, 304
Mahāsāṅghikas, and the Sthaviras, 56, 66–68; their chief philosophical doctrines, 62–64; their contribution to Buddhist absolutism, 56, 64–65; their controversy with the Sarvāstivādins, 56, 65, 66, 67, 68; their relation to Mahāyāna, 66–68

*Mahāsuññatā-sutta (Mahāśūnyatā-sūtra)*, 343b, 348b
*mahāśūnyatā* 大空, as interpreted by the Śrāvaka and by the Mahāyāna, 363b
*mahat* 大, 覺 (or *buddhi* of the Sāṅkhya), compared with *vijñāna* and the subtle body, 248–50
*Mahāvagga*, 344a
*Mahāvastu*, 344a
*Mahāvyutpatti*, 373b, 375a
Mahāyāna, and Hīnayāna, 66–69, 278–79; as not excluding Hīnayāna, 46–47; as one of the two lines in early Buddhism that the *Śāstra* mentions, 346a; its relation to the Mahāsāṅghikas, 67–68; *see* Great Way
*Mahāyāna-bhavabheda-śāstra*, 35; see *Bhavasaṅkrānti-śāstra*
*Mahāyāna-madhyamakadarśana-vyākhyā-śāstra*, 35
*Mahāyaña-śraddhotpāda-śāstra*, 340b, 378b; see *Awakening of Faith*
*Mahāyāna-sūtras*, 67–68, 348a
*Mahāyāna-vimśikā*, 34, 340a
Mahīśāskas, their view on self-hood, 62
*maitrī* (friendliness), the great, as a factor of Buddhahood, 310
*Majjhimanikāya*, 344a, 344b, 345a
Mākandika, 131, 132
*māṁsa-cakṣus* 肉眼 (the eyes of flesh, one of the five kinds of eyes), and the *deva*-eye, 120–22, 242; *see* eyes
man; see person
*manas* 意 (or *mana-indriya* 意根, the internal sense), 215, 237; cf. *citta* and *vijñāna*
*Mañjuśrīmūlakalpa*, 336a
Mankad, D. R., 338a
*māra* (the embodiment of temptations), 310
*mārgajñatā* 道智 (broad and rough understanding of the one way that leads to Nirvāṇa), 371b
*mārgākārajñatā* 道種智 (clear and detailed knowledge of the different ways suited to different individuals), 371b
Masuda, 345b, 346a, 346b, 347b, 348a; cf. Bareau
*māyā* (*Īśvara*'s power of creation), in the Advaita Vedānta, 319
meaning 義 *(artha)*, and its relation to word, 75, 350b–51a, 356b
*Mélanges Chinois et Bouddhiques*, 340b
mental elements, the, nonsubstantiality of, 215–16; the course of birth and death of, 211
Middle Way, as the nonexclusive way, 127–50; see *madhyamā pratipat*
mind; see *citta, manas, vijñāna*
mindfulness, kinds of application; see *smṛtyupasthāna*
*mīmāṁsā* 思惟 (investigation), as one of the four *ṛddhipadas* (bases for increasing concentration), 291
Mīmāmsakas, 320
*mithyādṛṣṭi* 妄見 (misperception, false view), meaning of the term, 352a–b; as the view that things just happen without cause or condition, 109; see also *dṛṣṭi*
Mochizuki Shinkō, 332, 339b
moment (念 *kṣaṇa)*, Sarvāstivāda conception of, 58–60; *see* time
moon, the, used for illustrating rise of the sense of "I," 98, 99; used for illustrating the distinction between the bodhisattva in *dharma-kāya* and the Buddha, 311, 374b–5a
moral code *(Vinaya)*, as one of the three gates to *dharma*, 141–42, 357b; the error of blindly clinging to, 143
moral conduct *(śīla)*, the perfection of, 305–6; see *pāramitā*
moral life, its cultivation as one of the three doors to *dharma*, 141–42
moral responsibility, critical examination of soul as the necessary condition tion of, 229–31
motion and activity, critically examined, 185–87, 361b

Murti, T.R.V., 341b, 376a, 376b–77a
*Mysticism, Christain and Buddhist,* 379b

Nāgas, the, and Nāgārjuna, 27
Nāgārjuna, and the Buddha, 46–53; and the Buddhist schools, 53–54, 64–66; 341b–42a; and Kaniska, 28–30; and the Nāgas, 25–27, 337a, 337b; and the Sātvāhanas, 27–28; basic conceptions in the philosophy of, 37–46; on Hīnayāna and Mahāyāna, 66–69; his sources for the study of Mahāyāna, 30–46
Nāgārjunācārya, 336b; *see* Nāgārjuna
Nāgārjuna (Siddha), 336a, 337a
*Nāgārjuna and Āryadeva,* 336b–37a
*Nāgārijuna's Friendly Epistle,* 337b
Nāgārjunīkoṇḍa, 336b
Nāgārjunagarbha, 36
*Nāgārjuna-pañcavidyā-śāstra,* 35
Nahapāna, Kṣaharāta, 27, 28
*naiḥsvābhāvya* 無自性, 自性空 (devoidness of self-being; non-substantiality; relativity), 42, 338b, 341a; cf. *śūnyatā* and *pratītya-samutpāda*
Nālanda, 26
*nāma* 名 (names, concepts), as conventionally established, 74–81, 349b–50a; *see* convention, *prajñapti, samjñā*
*nāma* 名 (mental elements), in distinction from *rūpa* (the physical), 79, 237–38
*nāma* and *lakṣaṇa* (concepts and conventional entities), 70–88; their interrelatedness, 73, 74, 76, 78; their place and function in the world of the determinate, 73; attitude of the wise and the ignorant in regard to, 72–73; see *nāma, lakṣaṇa*
*nāma-rūpa* 名色 (the body-mind complex, in the subtle form), as a link in the cycle of life, 237–38
*nāmasaṅketa-prajñapti* 名字一 (convention of names and signs), as one of the three kinds of convention, 85–86; see *prajñapti*
names, derived; see *upādāyaprajñapti;* see also *nāma, prajñapti, śūnyatā*
Nasik Edict, 27
nature, essential; see *lakṣaṇa, prakṛti, svabhāva*
negation, of the non-clinging kind, 105; as not an end in itself, 317
negative criticisms, their purpose, 44; their significance, 68–70; *see* criticism
negativism, 172–73, 318–19; see *ucchedadṛṣṭi*
negativist, the, error of, 143, 181
*neyārtha* (indirect, expedient way of teaching) versus *nītārtha* (the direct way), 135–36, 357a
*Nidāna-samyutta,* a section in *Samyutta-nikāya,* 344a
nihilists, as holding to the extreme of total extinction of personality after death, 155, 366a; their view defferentiated from *śūnyatā,* 359a-b; *see also* annihilationism, negativism
*Nikāyas,* 47–48, 51, 52, 343b
*nimitta* 相 (occassions), the determinate entities as, for the rise of ideas and emotions, 76, 294; when seized, become dead-ends, 352b, 353a; cf. *animittatā;* see *lakṣaṇa*
*nimittodgrahaṇa* 取相 (picking up of characters or signs), as a definition of perception *(samjñā),* 349b; as distinguished from *lakṣana-grāha* (seizing of characters), 351a
*nimittopalambha* 得相 (or *lakṣaṇopalambha* seizing of the determinate), 352b
*Niraupamya-stava,* 36, 37, 341b; see *Catuḥstava*
Nirgranthas; *see* Jaina
*nirguṇa-brahman* (the indeterminate *brahman,* the ultimate reality in Advaita Vedānta), 319
*nirmāṇa* 化 (creation, a name for the world of convention), 73
*nirodha* (extinction, i.e., of ignorance and passion), as held by the Mahā-

sāṅghikas, 64 as viewed by Sarvāstivāda, 58; see also Nirvāṇa

*nirodha-samāpatti* (a state of suspension of conscious mental activity), one of the nine "successive abodes" 372b–73a

*nirukti* (definition, enunciation, of the nature of a thing by means of words; language), 350b–51a; as one of the elements of expertness, 374b; see *vaiśāradya*

Nirvāṇa (extinction, i.e., of the root of suffering), as death of clinging, 51, 135; as eternal joy, 51; as not apart from *saṁsāra*, 52, 66, 324, 342b; as the ultimate goal of all beings, 51, 263; the ultimate nature of all things, 272–73; see *dharma-dhātu, bhūtakoṭi*

*niṣprapañca* 無戲論 (non-conceptual, beyond concepts), as the nature of the ultimate reality, 156; *see* the real; cf. *prapañca*

*nītārtha* (the direct way of teaching) *versus neyārtha,* the indirect way, 135, 357a

*nīvaraṇa* 蓋 (hindrances), the five, in regard to concentration of mind, 371a

non-being 無 (abhāva); *see* non-existence; cf. *bhāva*

non-Buddhist schools, referred to in the *Śāstra,* 33

non-clinging (不著, 不取 *anupalambha),* skilfulness of, as arising from non-exclusive understanding, 37, 38, 91; as the consummating phase of wisdom, 355a; as forming, with undivided being, the heart of the *Prajñāpāramitā-sūtras,* 31; as one of the basic meanings of *śūnyatā,* 339a, 375b; as the pervading sprit of the philosophy of the Middle Way, 18; in the Buddha's way of teaching, 133; in the use of concepts, 148–49, 160–63; see *madhyamā pratipat, prajñā, śūnyatā*

non-exclusive, understanding, 37–38, 91; way, 127–33; see *madhyamā-pratipat, prajñā*

non-existence, as a distinguishable aspect of becoming, 48, 137–38; as an extreme, 152–55; *see* negativism; cf. being, *bhāva*

*Notes on the Nagarjunīkoṇḍa Inscriptions,* 336b

*nyāma* 位 (lit. the state of being free from immaturity; the status of the irreversible), as the true status of the bodhisattva, 298–299, 301; meaning of the term, 373b; see *avaivarta*

Nyaṇātiloka, 370b–71a; 372b–73a

Nyāya, accusing the Mādhyamika as a negativist, 318–19; view of knowledge, criticised by the Mādhyamika, 33, 340a; *see also* Vaiśeṣika; see *pramāṇas*

*Nyāyasūtras,* 338a

Obermiller, E., 336a

objective, the, and the subjective, non-ultimacy of the division of, 90

objectivism, Sarvāstivāda as an extreme kind of, 61

*"On the Emptiness of the Unreal,"* 不眞空論, 377b–78a

*"On the Immutability of Things,"* 物不遷論, 377b–78a

*"On the Namelessness of Nirvana,"* 涅槃無名論, 377b–78a

*"On Prajñā Not Congnizant of Objects,"* 般若無知論, 377b–78a

*On Yuan Chwang,* 336a

organism, and the constituent events, 231–35; person as an, 231; *see* person

*padārthas* (basic categories of the Vaiśeṣikas), the six, referred to in the *Śāstra,* 363a; see *Vaiśeṣikas*

*Pag-sam-jon-zang,* 336a, 337a

*pañcavidha-dharma-piṭaka* 五種法藏 (collection of five kinds of ele-

ments), referred to in the *Śāstra,* 363a
*Pañcaviṁśatisāhasrikā-prajñāpāramitā-sūtra,* as an abridgment of the *Śatasahasrikā,* 31; as the original of of which the *Śāstra* is the commentary, 13; its different translations, 331 on the bodhisattva's coursing in the Mahāyāna, and its different stages, 374a; on the bodhisattva's immaturity *(āma),* 373b; on the eyes of five kinds, 355b; on names, 349b-350a; on the start and destination of Mahāyāna, 369a; on *śūnyatā* as the highest kind of harmony *(yoga),* 368b; see *Śāstra*
*parāmarśa* 取 (clinging), 354a; see *dṛṣṭi-parāmarśa, śīlavrataparāmarśa*
Paramārtha, 28, 64, 338b
*paramārtha* 第一義 (the ultimate truth), 316, 317, 339a, 342b, 343a; *see* the real; cf. *vyavahāra*
*pāramārthika-siddhānta* (the direct teaching of the ultimate truth), 140–41, 357a; see *siddhānta*
*paramārtha-svarūpa* (the ultimate nature, i.e., of the individual, in the Advaita Vedānta), 320
*Paramārtha-stava,* 36, 37, 341b
*pāramitā* 波羅密, 度 (perfection), the different kinds of, 280, 288, 300, 306, 310; the essential quality of, 281–83; the way of, 280–81; *see* Mahāyāna
*paratantra* (the dependent; name for the mundane truth in Vijñānavāda), 326
*parikalpita* (the imagined; name for the illusory, in Vijñānavāda), 326
*pariniṣpanna* (the real; name for the ultimate reality in Vijñānavāda), 326
Pārśva, 28
past, present and future, critically examined, 194–95, 196–99; *see* time
Patel, Prabhubhai, 36, 341a
Pathak, Suntikumar, 36, 337a
perfection, see *pāramitā*
person, as an organism, 231–35
personality, the conception of, in early Buddhist thought, 56, 59, 60–62, 63, 64, 65, 66; the constituent elements *(skandhas)* of, 231–33, 366a-b; the physical and mental bases of, 237–40
personal life, the course of, 231–50; the seed of, 237–42; see *vijñāna; see also* cycle of life
*Peṭakopadeśa,* 357b
*Phalguṇa-sūtra,* 137, 357a-b
pluralism, in Buddhist philosophy, 57–60, 318; of the Jaina, 156–7; as the view based on the ultimacy of separateness, 46; *see also* Vaiśeṣikas
*Points of Controversy (Kathāvatthu),* 347a
polarity, relative distinctions within a natural phase of intellection, turned into extremes under clinging, 151, 153, 352b–53a
*Political History of Ancient India,* 337–38a
Poussin, Luis de la Vallée, 341b, 378b
*pradhāna* (effort), 371; see *prahāṇa*
*prahāṇa* (in *samyak-prahāṇa* 正懃, 正勤, right effort), of four kinds, 291, 371b
*prajñā* 般若, 智, 智慧 (knowledge), as the act of knowing as well as the ultimate principle of knowledge, the functional, distinguished from the eternal, 116, 117, 355a; of the expedient kind, 355a, 373b
*prajñā* (also *prajñā-pāramitā,* perfect wisdom), as bringing to light the true nature of things, 183, 184; as cancelling all things while itself remaining undenied, 117; compared to the principle of accommodation, 127, 274, 293; as comprehending the *śūnyatā* of all things as well as their distinct natures, 146, 271, 274, 286; as comprehending the unique as well as the universal natures of all things,

144, 146; as the comprehension of the essential unity of analysis, criticism and moral code, 144; as containing all elements of merit, 280; as giving rise to the different views or perspectives, 127; as including all other kinds of knowledge, 287, 289; as inconceivable in terms of duality, 267, 358b–59a; as itself the *anutpattika-dharma-kṣānti,* 306; as itself the *bodhi* par excellence, 355a; as the mother of all the Buddhas, 312; as non-clinging, 127, 128, 131, 163; as one of the five eyes, 122–23; as the origin of all the five eyes, 120, 170; as purifying the different eyes, 122–23; as putting an end to the entire network of *prapañca,* 128; as spoken by the Buddhas through various names, 286

*prajñā,* the undivided being, as inconceivable in terms of duality, 267, 358b-59a; as the true essence in all, 114, 259, 265; as the ultimate nature of the self-conscious individual, 119; as the universal reality, 86, 118, 263, 265, 351b, 368a; as unstained by imaginative constructions, 274–75

prajñā and *puṇya,* wisdom and merit, as the two basic aspects of wayfaring, 280, 349a, 369a

*prajñāpāramitā,* 般若波羅密 (perfection of wisdom), as the foremost of all kinds of perfection, 281, 293; as itself distinguished into *bodhi* and*śūnyatā,* 342a, 376a; as itself distinguished into the six kinds of perfection, 280

*Prajñāpāramitā-sūtras,* on the five eyes, 119; their illustrations of illusion, 89; as the main scriptural source of Nāgārjuna, 30–31; their main teaching, viz., the ultimacy of undivided being and skilfulness of non-clinging, 31; their overarching concept of *śūnyatā,* 31; on stripping bare the true being, 84–88; on the true nature of the Buddha, 348a

*Prajñāmūla,* 35, 340b

*Prajñāpradīpa,* 35, 340b

*prajñapti* 波羅攝提 (name, concept, as well as the entity that the name designates; also convention), meaning of the term, 349b–50a; modes of, 82–88; *see* convention; see also *nāma, smajñā,* cf. *upādāya prajñapti*

Prajñaptivādins, 62, 63

*prakṛti* 性 (essential nature), 76, 77, 351a-b; see also *dhātu, svabhāva*

*prakṛti* 世性 (an ultimate reality in the Sāṅkhya system), how the Sāṅkhyas arrive at the conception of, 248–50; its relation with its products, 180

*pramāṇa* (vaild means of knowledge), as not denied by the Mādhyamika, 169; Madhyamika criticism of the Nyāya view of, 33, 340a

*praṇidhāna* 作 (resolving) to do deeds 294; see *apraṇihitatā*

*prapañca* 戲論 (conceptual elaboration), as the clinging to words or concepts and as the root of all contentions, 119, 129; as itself the way to freedom when free from extremes, 165; as the means to express and communicate truth, 165; as the network of words or concepts in which one gets entangled when under clinging, 129, 356b

*prapañcātīta* (beyond conception), the ultimate nature of the Tathāgata as, 235, 345b, 356b, 366b

*prasaṅga (reductio ad absurdum),* as the way of exposing the self-contradictions inherent in exclusive views, 34, 151–53, 358b

*prāsaṅgika* (the way of *prasaṅga;* a follower of the way of *prasaṅga),* a Mādhyamika tradition followed by Buddhapālita and Candrakīrti, 341a; cf. *svātantrika*

*Prasannapadā* (Candrakīrti's commentary on the *Kārikā*), 36; on *ālambana-pratyaya*, 361b; on *antarābhava*, 367a; on the Buddha's *dharma-kāya*, 374b; on the doctrine of birth of birth, 362a; on *dṛṣṭi*, 354a; on the meaning of *tathatā*, 367b; on mistaking *śūnyatā* to mean nonexistence, 360a; on the Sarvāstivāda doctrine of elements, 347a; on *śūnyatā* making room for activity, 362a; on the ultimate truth as beyond concepts, 343a, 376b; on the usefulness of words, 356b

*praśrabdhi* (tranquility, serenity), one of the seven factors of enlightenment, 291; see *bodhyaṅga*

*pratibhāna* (ready wit), one of the four elements of expertness, 374b; see *pratisamvit;* cf. *vaiśāradya*

*prātipakṣika-siddhānta* 對治—(remedial kind of teaching), one of the four *siddhāntas,* 139–40, 344a, 357a, 359b; see *siddhānta*

*prātipauruṣika-siddhānta* 各各爲人—(teaching from the individual standpoint), one of the four *siddhāntas,* 139, 357a; see *siddhānta*

*pratisamvit* (expertness), the kinds of, 310, 374b; cf. *vaiśāradya*

*pratītya-samutpāda* (conditioned or dependent origination), as the direct teaching of the mundane truth, 138; as the doctrine of the cycle of life, *see* cycle of life; as the essential relativity of things, 39, 138, 160–62; as revealed by the rejection of the fourteen questions, 148, 149; as a meaning of *śūnyatā*, 338b; as a synonym of *śūnyatā* and of the middle way, 42, 47, 163, 344a; as a system of concepts to set forth the basic course of things, 165–69; as the truth revealed by criticism, 168

*Pratītyasamutpāda-hṛdaya-kārikā,* 36

*Pratītyasamutpāda-śāstra,* 35, 37, 366b

*pratyayas* (conditions), the four, critically examined, 180–83, 361a

*pratyaya-sarga* (creation by intellect), a Sāṅkhya conception, 365b; cf. *vijñāna*

*pratyekabuddha* 獨覺 (one who is interested in achieving Buddhahood just for oneself), his eye of wisdom, 356a; his knowledge, 118, 287–88, 289, 299, 304, 371a; see *śrāvaka;* cf. bodhisattva

*pratyutpanna-samādhi* (a state of meditation in which one feels the constant presence of the Buddha), as a criterion of the true status of the bodhisattva, 300

*Pre-Diṅnāga Buddhist Texts on Logic,* 340a, 340b

*prīti* (sense of joy), as one of the seven factors of enlightenment, 291; see *bodhyaṅga*

*pudgala* (individual), as a substantial entity, examined, 217–18, 365a; *see also* I-substance, soul

*pudgalātmā* (the self-being of the individual), as denied by Sarvāstivāda, 57, 343b; cf., *dharmātmā*

*pudgala-śūnyatā* (non-substantiality, essential relativity, of the individual), 343b; as not included in the eighteen kinds of *śūnyatā,* 375b; cf. *dharma-śūnyatā*

*puṇya* 福德 (merit), as forming, along with *prajñā,* the two basic aspects of wayfaring, 18, 280, 349a, 369a

*Purāṇas,* 28

*Puranic Chronology,* 338a

*puruṣa* (self or soul, as conceived in the Sāṅkhya), 365a

quality 相 *(lakṣaṇa)* and substance critically examined, 207–8, 364a

questions, the fourteen unanswered, 49–51, 146–48, 344b–45a, 358a; see *avyākṛta*

Radhakrishnan, 20, 376a
*rāga* 染 (attachment), as arising from clinging, 106; cf. *kleśa*
Rāhula, 337a
Rāhulabhadra, 26, 337a
*Rājataraṅgiṇī*, 28, 336a, 338b
Rapson, 338a
*Ratnāvalī*, 35, 336a, 338b
Raychaudhuri, H.C., 28, 337–8a
*ṛddhi* 神通 (extraordinary powers), as an aid to convert the minds of the common people, 68; cf. *abhijñā*
*ṛddhi-pada* 如意足 (bases for increasing concentration and insight), the four, 291; meaning of the term, 371b–72a
real, the, as comparable to *ākāśa*, 274–75; as essentially indeterminate, 270–71; as the essential sameness, 271; as immanent as well as transcendent, 261–62; as the indeterminate ground, 251–52; man's thirst for, 264–65; progressive realization of, 84–88, 260–61; as purity 272; as the supreme end, 262–63; as unaffected by imaginative constructions, 272–73; understanding of, 51–53, 116–17, 133–41, 252–61; as the unutterable truth, 273–74; see *advaya-dharma, bhūtakoṭi, dharmatā, tathatā*
reality, 251–75; *see* the real
relational, concepts or terms, 82, 195; entities, 82; modes of being, 83
relative judgements and absolute statements, 160–63
relativism, of judgements, 54, 134, 156; *see* Jaina, Mādhyamika
relativity (or determinateness); see *pratītyasamutpāda, śūnyatā*
*Religious Trends in Modern China*, 378b
remedial (對治 *prātipakṣika*), kind of teaching, as one of the four kinds, 139–40; see *siddhānta*
*rūpa* 色 (form and resistance), the notion that their absence is the character of *ākāśa*, critically examined, 205, 364a; see *ākāśa*
*rūpa* 色 (the physical), and *nāma* (the mental), bases of personality, 237–38; as a physical entity, used for illustrating the essential nature of all entities, 255–56, 258, 260, 267, 290
*rūpa-dhātu* 色界 (fine material sphere), as one of the states of trance, 370b; see *dhātu, dhyāna*

*sa-*(or *sva-) bhāga-dhātu* 本分種 (the fundamental, ultimate essence; the real nature), as a meaning of *dharma-dhātu*, 368a; see *dhātu*
*saddharma* (right doctrine), as a synonym of *samyagdṛṣṭi*, and meaning conditioned origination, 342b
*Saddharmapuṇḍarīka-sūtra*, 32, 326, 368a, 379a
*Sagāthaka* (a section in *Laṅkāvatāra)*, 336a
*saguṇa-brahman, (Īśvara,* in the Advaita Vedānta), 319
*sakti* 著 (interestedness that issues in clinging), as a synonym of *abhiniveśa*, 353a
*samādhi* 定 (collectedness of mind, concentration; meditation), as a means to give rise to real wisdom, 285; as one of the five *indriyas*, 291; as a name for the three gates of freedom, 295, 370b; as purifying the *deva*-eye, 121; meaning of the term, 370b; see also *dhyāna* and *cittaikāgratā*
*samādhi-bhāvanā* (cultivation, development of *samādhi)*, 370b
*Samādhirāja*, 342b
*samanantara-pratyaya* 次第緣, (the immediately preceding condition), critically examined, 181; see *pratyaya*
*samāpatti* 三摩鉢底 (lit. well attaining; contemplation, trance), 370b, 372b–73a; see *ārūpya-samāpatti* and *anupūrva-vihāra-samāpatti*

*samatā* 等法, 平等 (the essential sameness of things), as the equanimity of mind given rise to by its comprehension, 271; as a name for the ultimate reality, 270–72; as a synonym of *śūnyatā*, 271
*samaya* 三摩耶 (time, as a derived notion), distinguished from *kāla* (time, conceived as a substance), 199–200; *see* time
*sambodhi*; see *samyak-sambodhi*
*samjñā* 想 (idea, perception, also name), as forming along with *smṛti* and *jñāna* a stage in the process of knowledge, 372b; as a synonym of *nāma* and *prajñapti*, 349b–50a; defined as the picking up of signs *(nimittodgrahaṇa)*, and distinguished from seizing them *(lakṣaṇagrāha)*, 351a
*Sāmmitīyas*, their alliance with Vātsīputrīyas, Sautrāntikas and Dārṣṭāntikas, 56; their chief philosophical conceptions, 56, 61–62, 64, 362a, 365a, 367a; their criticism of Sarvāstivāda, 56, 62, 347b
*Sāmmitīya-nikāya-śāstra*, 346a, 347b, 348a, 365a, 367a
*saṁsāra* (the course of mundane existence), as itself Nirvāṇa when rightly seen, 52, 66, 116–17, 250, 324; see also *vyavahāra*; *cf.* Nirvāṇa
*saṁskāras* 行 (forces; elements), as formative forces in the life of an individual, 240–41, 367a–b; those originating from ignorance, 111–12, 241–42; as a synonym of *skandhas*, 62; distinguished from *bhava*, 240–41, 367a–b; *see* cycle of life
*saṁskṛta* 有爲 (composite) elements, and the incomposite, in Sarvāstivāda, 58; in the Mahāsāṅghikas, 64
*samyagdṛṣṭi* 正見 (right view), as a name for *prajñā*, 99; as a synonym of *saddharma*, meaning conditioned origination, 342b; see *dṛṣṭi*; cf. *mithyādṛṣṭi*
*samyak-prahāṇa* 正勤 (right effort), of four kinds, among the factors of the way, 291, 371b; see *prahāṇa*
*samyak-sambodhi* (the complete awakening; wisdom par excellence), its incomprehensibility 273; its realization by the bodhisattva, 271, 311; persistently to look back to it is a mark of wayfaring, 281
*samyojanas* 結使 (factors of bondage), and the rise of the sense of 'I' and 'mine', 98–99
*Saṁyuktāgama*, 343b, 347a, 364b
*Samyukta-piṭaka* 363a
*Samyuttanikāya*, 344a, b, 345a, 348a
*samvṛti* (veil), as a name for the world of convention, 73; see *vyavahāra*
*saṅgha* (the community of the Buddha's followers), division within, 47, 55, 343b, 345; the two main stems of, 55–56
Sañjayabelaṭṭhiputta, 358b
Śaṅkara's philosophy, compared with the Mādhyamika, 319–21
Sāṅkhya, the, conception of *buddhi*, 366a, 367b; conception of causal relation, critically examined, 33, 156, 178–80; conception of *kośa*, 365b; conception of multiplicity of souls, 217, 365a; conception of *prakṛti* and *mahat*, 248–50, 376a; distinction of self from subtle body, 365b; *tattva* (categories), mentioned in the *Śāstra*, 339b
Sāṅkhya and Vaiśeṣika, criticism of their basic tenets by the Buddhists, 33
*Sāṅkhya-kārikā*, 365a, 365b, 366a, 376a
Saṅkrāntivādins, 61, 346b; see Sautrāntikas
Śāntideva, 34, 37, 319
*Saptaratna-kośa* 七法藏, 27, 337a
Sarāha, 26; *see* Rāhulabhadra
*sarvajñatā* 一切智 (all-inclusive understanding), as distinguished from

*sarvākārajñatā* (knowledge of all forms), 289, 371a-b
*sarvākārajñatā* 一切種智 (knowledge of all forms), as the complete knowledge which is the Buddha's, 286; as the goal of the bodhisattva's wayfaring, 287, 305; as knowledge yeilded by the Buddha-eye, 126; as not obtained in Hīnayāna, 68; as *prajñāpāramitā* in the Buddha's mind, 287; and *sarvajñatā*, 289, 371a-b
Sarvāstivāda, the, analysis of elements as appraised by the Mahāsāṅghikas, 67; contribution to growth of Mahāyāna, 348a; critically examnined 321–22 (by Kumārajīva), 33, 36, 171 (by the Mādhyamika), 347b (by the Sāmmitīyas), 347a-b (by the Sautrāntika); doctrine of bodhisattva criticized in the *Śāstra*, 348b–49a; doctrine of elements, 57–58, 60, 80, 343b; fundamental texts, 28, 338b; interpretation of conditioned origination, 58–59, 187–89; interpretation of Middle Way and *śūnyatā*, 60; interpretation of time and change, 58–60; referred to in the *Śāstra* as one of the two chief lines of Buddhist philosophy, 343b, 346a; study by Mahāyāna teachers, 337a
*Śāstra*, its authorship, 13–14; its citations from the Buddhist scriptures, 339b; its contents analysed, 44–46; its reference to the two chief lines of Buddhist philosophy (Abhidharma and Mahāyāna), 346a; its *Tun-huang Mss.*, 335b; its view on the composition of *Jñānaprasthāna* and *Vibhāṣā*, 29; for topics, *see* under the respective terms
Śāstri, Aiyaswami, 340b, 341a
Śāstri, K.A.N., 28, 338a
Śāstri, P., S., 336b, 337a, 338a
Śāstri, Śāntibhiksu, 338
*sasvabāvatva*, (self-being; absoluteness) imagined in regard to what is essentially conditioned and relative, 42; *see* error
*sasvabhāva-vāda* (error of misplaced absoluteness, error of false realism), 43; as not providing the basis for conditioned origination, 362a; *see* error
*Śāvśatadṛṣti* (the extreme of eternalism), 48, 49, 109; critically examined, 174–77; cf; *uccheda-dṛṣṭi*
*Śataśāstra*, 15, 337b, 377b
*Śatasāhasrikā-prajñāpāramitā-sūtra*, 374a
Śātavāhanas, the, Nāgārjuna and, 27–28, 30, 336b, 338a
*Śātavāhana Dynasty of Dakṣiṇāpatha*, 338a
*satkārya-vāda* (the view that the effect is contained in the cause, the Sāṅkhya view of causation), critically examined, 179–80
*sat-kāya-dṛṣṭi* 有身見, (the view of absoluteness in regard to what is a composite entity; *sasvabhāva* view with regard to self; false sense of self), as the root of all *dṛṣtis* and afflictions, 105–10; sense of "I" and, 100–103
*sattā* (existence), as not possible in the case of what is utterly devoid of self-nature, 182; *see* being
*sattva* (individual), as a synonym of *citta*, 297; *see* person, *pudgala*, self
*sattva* (the essence and character of the good *dharma*), as a component of the term *bodhi-sattva*, 298
*Satyasiddhiśāstra*, 15, 16, 322
Sautrāntika, the, conception of personality and becoming, 62; their relation to Dārṣṭāntikas and Saṅkrāntivādins, 346b; their criticism of Sarvāstivāda, 347a-b
scepticism, as a form of the fourth extreme, 154; *see* extreme
self, Buddha's teachings in regard to, 48–51, 133–35, 354b; the false sense

of, 98–105, 105–10; as an organism, 231–35; substantialist view of, 217–31; *see* person, "I"; *cf.* soul
self-being, see *ātman, svabhāva*
self-consciousness; see *vijñāna*
self-reference, kinds of, 100–103; *see* "I"
Seng-chao 僧肇, 323–24, 335a, 377b–8a
Seng-jui 僧叡, 14, 335b
senses, sense-contact and the feeling of pleasure and pain, as links in the cycle of life, 237; cf. *āyatana*
sensuous world 欲界 *(kāma-dhātu)*, 236; see *dhātu*
Sewell, Robert, 338a
Shaeffer, Phil. 341a
*Shih-hsiang-lun* 實相論 *(Treatise on the Real Nature of Things)*, 15
*Shih Hui-yuan's Buddhism as set forth in His Writings*, 377a
*Sho-wa Ho-bo So Mokuroku*, 340a
*siddhānta* 悉壇 (teaching), of the four kinds, 136–41, 341b–42a, 357a-b
Śikṣānanda, 378b
*śīla-pāramitā* (perfection of moral conduct), 283, 369b; cultivated by the bodhisattva in the second *bhūmi*, 305–6
*śīlavrata-parāmarśa* (clinging to moral code), 109; see *parāmarśa*
silence, the Buddha's, 48–51, 146–48
silkworm, used as example to elucidate the self-responsibility of the individual, 106, 366b
*skandhas* 陰 (groups of elements), the five, as a major classification of elements of existence, 87; as a name for all composite elements, 85, 87, 146, 239, 249; their relation to the individual they constitute, 49, 138, 232
skilfulness; see *upāya*, see also *anupalambha* and *yoga*
Small Way (Hīnayāna), on the term, 20; its difference from Māhayāna, 66–9, 278–79, 369a; *cf.* Great Way
*smṛti* 憶, 念 (memory), 228
*smṛti* 念 (thought, mindfulness), as one of the seven factors of enlightenment, 291; considered along with *samjñā* and *vikalpa*, 352b; as constituting with *samjñā* and *jñāna*, the process of knowing, 372b; see *smṛtyupasthāna*
*smṛtyupasthāna* 念處 (application of mindfulness), of four kinds, as the pith of the entire wayfaring, 291; as culminating, in Mahāyāna, in the comprehension of the Undivided Being as the ultimate reality, 364b–65a, 371b, 372a
soul (I-substance), the conception critically examined, 219–31; as not the basis of the distinction of self and other, 219–20; as not having any definite nature, 221–23; as not an object of inference, 224–25; as not the object of the sense of "I", 220; as not a necessary condition of knowledge, 227–29; as not necessary for moral responsibility, 229–31; as the self conceived as a substantial entity, 217–18, 225–27; as not the subtle body, 223–24; *see* "I", person, self
*Soul-theory of the Buddhists, The*, 347b
soul-theory of the non-Buddhists, 218
space; see *ākāśa*
*sparśa* 觸 (touch), as the origin of all mental elements, 237
spatial directions; see *dik*
*sphaṭika* '(pure crystal) to illustrate the pure mind, 349; seen as coloured, used as an example for illusion, 96
*śraddhā* 信 (faith), one of the five faculties, and of powers, among the factors of the way, 291; *see* way
*Śraddhotpāda-śāstra*; see *Mahāyāna-śraddhotpada-śāstra*
*śrāvaka* the, and the *pratyekabuddha*, as not interested in *ṛddhi*, 68; as not rising to the level of comprehension, 69; their attitude to individuality,

298–99; their knowledge, distinguished from that of bodhisattvas and the Buddhas, 287–88, 356a, 371a
*śrāvaka-yāna* (the way of the hearers), 32; see Hīnayāna
Śrilāta, 346b
Śriparvata, 25, 27, 336b, 337a
*Stanzas Setting Forth the Meaning of Mahāyāna,* 141
Stcherbatsky, 20, 347b, 376a
*Studies in Chao Lun* 肇論研究, 335a, 377b
*Stutyatīta-stava,* 36, 37; see *Catuḥstava*
*śubha* 淨 (the "beautiful"), as the third of the eight *vimokṣas,* 372b
subjective, and the objective, their division, not ultimate, 90
subjectivism (or subjective idealism), denounced by the Mādhyamika, 72
Subramnian, K.R., 336a, 336b
substance, examination of, 207–8; the Sarvāstivāda notion of, 59, 60; see *dharma, lakṣaṇa, svabhāva*
substantialist view of self, critically examined, 217–31; see I-substance, soul
substantialist view of time, critically examined, 194–97
subtle-body 細身 *(sūkṣma-śarīra),* as not to be misconstrued as soul, 223–4; considered in relation with *vijñāna* and *mahat,* 248–50
suffering *(duḥkha)* as one of the phases in the cycle of life, 246; its eradication, the essence of the four noble truths, 47, 197; origin of, 38, 47–48, 107, 111, 197; *see also* affliction
*Suhṛllekhā,* 35, 37, 337b, 340b
*śūnyatā* 空 (lit. devoidness), kinds of, 44, 375b–76a; meaning of the term, 39, 42, 172–73, 338b–39a, 342a, 375b–76a; negative and positive imports of, 317–19, 325, 326–27; synonyms of, 42
*śūnyatā* 空, as the essential (mundane as well as ultimate) nature *(tathatā)* of things, 145, 172–73, 256–57, 317, 322–23
*śūnyatā* 空, as criticism that lays bare the truth of things, 45, 141–46, 163, 168, 172, 294–95, 317, 319, 325, 342b; as the rejection of clinging and of the error of misplaced absoluteness, 110, 256, 270, 317–18; as a remedy for *dṛṣṭis,* 319, 342b; of the clinging kind, 42, 146, 172, 270, 295, 325, 342b, 359a, 360a, 375b; of the non-clinging kind, 104–5, 135–36, 145, 146, 359b, 362a
*śūnyatā* 空 as non substantiality, nonultimacy, conditionedness, and relativity of things, 40, 42, 43, 143, 145, 172–73, 210–11, 213, 215, 326, 342a, 363b
*śūnyatā* 空, as the indeterminate, unconditioned, undivided unutterable nature of the ultimate reality, 270–71, 273; as *samatā,* ultimate sameness of things, 271; as Nirvāṇa, 271, 272, 273, 323
*śūnyatā* 空, as harmony, integration, non-exclusiveness, 42, 43, 275, 326, 342b
*śūnyatā-śūnyatā* 空空 (nounultimacy of *śūnyatā*), 40, 168, 172–73, 256–57, 270–71, 342b, 359b; see *śūnyatā* (clinging and nonclinging)
*Śūnyatā-saptati,* 36, 37
*Śūraṅgama-samādhi-sūtra,* 15, 32
*Sūtra on the Raft,* 131
*Sūtra on the Ten Bhūmis (Daśabhūmika-sūtra),* 32
*Sūtra-samuccaya,* 36
Suzuki, D.T., 378b, 379b
*svabhāva* 自性, 自有 (lit. self-being; essential nature), meaning of the term, 171; see *dharma, dhātu, prakṛti;* cf. *sasvabhāva-vāda*
*svabhāva-śūnya-dharma* 性空, 性空法 *(svabhāva-śūnyatā,* the reality that is by nature indeterminate), 270–71, 353a

*svarūpa* (essential nature), of the individual, in Advaita Vedānta, 320
*svātantrika,* a Mādhyamika tradition upheld by Bhāvaviveka, 341a-b; cf. *prāsaṅgika*
*Systems of Buddhist Thought,* 345b
*Szu-fa-ts'ang* 四法藏 *(Caturdharma-piṭaka),* 363a

*Ta-ch'eng-ta-yi-chang* 大乘大義章, 15
*Ta-ch'eng-yi-chang* 大乘義章, 15
*Taittirīya (Ānandavallī),* 365b
Takakusu, 378b
T'ang Yung-t'ung, 335a, 335b, 377a, 378b
Tao-an 道安, 15
Tao-sheng 道生, 14, 15, 377b
*Taranatha's History of Buddhism,* 336a
Tathāgata 如來, meaning of the term, 269; his mundane and ultimate natures, 52–53; his nature is also the nature of all things and of all beings, 235, 268; his ultimate nature, 235, 268, 269, 345b; the term, used as a synonym of self, 366a; *see also* Buddha
*tathāgata-garbha* (womb of *tathāgata),* a conception used in T'ien T'ai, 326, 340a, 376a
*tathatā* 如 (the nature of things as they are; the true nature of things), basic import of, 252, 367b; *dharma-dhātu bhūtakoṭi* and, 88, 98, 117, 145, 261–65; *dharmatā* and *dharma-lakṣaṇa* as synonyms of, 259, 351a; kinds of, 255–56 (two kinds), 256–58 (three kinds), 326 (ten kinds); *lakṣaṇa* and *prakṛti* as synonyms of, 351a; see also *prakrti, svabhāva*
*tathatā-lakṣaṇa* 如相 (the ultimately real nature), as the eternal undivided being, 268, 269
*tathatā-prajñāpāramitā,* 如般若波羅密 (perfect knowledge of the universal reality), 262
*tattva* (the ultimate truth), as beyond conception, 368b
*tattvas* (basic categories), the twentyfour, of the Sāṅkhya, cited briefly in the *Śāstra,* 339b
teaching, different ways of Buddha's, 133–50
Theravādins' criticism of Sarvāstivāda, 347a–b
*"Therī-sūtra"* 德女經, 354b
thrist (愛, 求 *tṛṣṇā, eṣaṇā),* as *tṛṣṇā, see* craving; as *eṣaṇā,* man's seeking for the real, longing for fulfilment, 264–45, 339a, 342a, 368b
Thomas, E.J. 339a, 345b, 346a, 347b, 348a, 348b
thought, the mission and the laws of, 142–43; *see* concepts, reason, understanding
*Three Treatises, The* (三論), 323, 377b; *see* Chi-tsang, Seng-chao
T'ien-t'ai 天台 and Hua-yen 華嚴, their relation to the Mādhyamika, 325–27, 378b
time, and change, as conceived by Sarvāstivāda 58–60; as a derived notion, 83, 197–200; substantialist notion of, critically examined, 194–97, 362b
*tṛṣṇā* 愛 (thirst, passion, craving), its place in the cycle of life, 236–246; its residueless extinction, 272; as the root of afflictions and of wrong views, 105; *see* thirst; cf. *eṣaṇā*
truth(s), the four noble, 47–48; as the four *siddhāntas,* 138–41; the two, mundane and ultimate, 136–38, 171–73
Tsukamoto Zenryu, 335a, 377b
Tucci, G. 337b, 340a, 340b, 376a
*tulanā* 稱 (weighing, considering), as distinguished from *prajñā,* 355a
Tu-shun 杜順 379a
*ucchedadṛṣti* (the extreme of annihilationism; negativism; the non-existence

view), arising from the mistaking of extinction, of *śūnyatā* or of nonbeing, 172–73, 176–77, 181, 329; as a basic kind of extreme, 48, 49, 108, 146, 154, 155, 160, 177, 181; critically examined along with eternalism, 48, 49, 174–77; its two kinds, 360a-b; see *dṛṣti*, extremes

Ui, H., 341a, 365b
ultimate truth; see *paramārtha; see also* truth
understanding, levels and perspectives of, 119–26, 242–44, 255–56, 258–60, 260–61; *see* eyes
undivided being *(advaya-dharma)*, as the ultimate reality, 267–75; *see* the real
*upādāna* 取 (seizing), of four kinds, as a link in the cycle of life, 236–37, cf. *grāha*; see clinging
*upādāya-prajñapti* 假名 (derived name), as a synonym of conditioned origination and of *śūnyatā*, 42, 338b–39a; the grade of essential nature designated by, 87–88; the mode of determinate being designated by, 82–83; meaning of the term, 349b, 350a; see *nāma, prajñapti;* cf. also *bhāva, lakṣaṇa*
*Upadeśa*, as one of the classes of works attributed to Nāgārjuna, 34; as a possible title of the *Śāstra*, 34, 335b, 340a
*upalambha* 得, 取 (seizing; contention), 38, 352b; cf. *anupalambha*
*upāya* 方便 *(kauśalya, yoga;* the skilfulness of nonclinging), 355a; *see* nonclinging
*Upāyahṛdaya*, 34, 340a
*Upāyakauśalya-parivarta* (a section in *Saddharmapuṇḍarīku)*, 379a
*upekṣā* (equanimity), as one of the factors of enlightenment, 291; see *bodhyaṅga*

Vacchagotta, 48, 49
Vaibhāṣika (a follower of *Vibhāṣā*, an adherent of Sarvāstivāda); see Sarvāstivāda
*Vaidalya-sūtra* and *-prakaraṇa*, 36, 37
Vaipulyakas, the, as clinging to *śūnyatā*, 155; as viewing the world as a baseless illusion, 359a
*Vaipulya (Mahāyāna) Sūtra*, 27
*vaiśāradya* (self-confidence), its four elements among the factors of Buddhahood, 310, 350b–51a
Vaiśeṣika, the, Buddhist criticisms of the basic conceptions of the Sāṅkhya and, 33; their "Collection of Six Dharmas," 363a; conception of causal relation critically examined, 156, 178–80; conception of time critically examined, 195, 362b; conception of spatial directions *(dik)* critically examined, 201, 363a-b; conception of space *(ākāśa)* critically examined, 204, 363b; conception of atoms referred to in the *Śāstra*, 364b; conception of self critically examined, 218–31, 365a, 365b, 366a; conception of *manas*, 366a; their pluralism and realism close to Sarvāstivāda, 318
*Vaiśeṣika-sūtras*, 362b, 363a, b, 366a
Vajeṣka, 28
Vajjian practices, 345b–6a
*Vajracchedikā-prajñāpāramitā-sūtra*, 15
*varṇa* 字 (the word that designates), as a synonym of *nāma*, 75
*vāsanā* (residual impressions of deeds), of affliction, as extinguished by the bodhisattva in the last *bhūmi*, 309; cf. *saṃskāra*
*vastu* 體, 事 (factors of embodiment), as one of the three phases of the cycle of life, 246
*vastu-sat* or *dravya-sat* 實有 (existent as a substance), as a notion with regard to time, 195
Vasubandhu, 337a, 378b

Vasumitra, 64, 346a
*Vasumitra's Treatise,* 345, 347b; see *Masuda,* also *Bareau*
Vātsiputrīyas, 56, 62, 363a; cf. Sāmmitīyas
Vātsyāyana, 338a
*vedanā* 受 (feeling), as a link in the cycle of life, 237; as an object of the application of mind-fulness, 371b; see *skandhas, smṛtyupasthāna*
Vedānta, the Advaita, and the Mādhyamika, 319–21
Vibhajyavādins, the Sarvāstivāda contentions with, 56; their view on *citta,* 348a
*Vibhāṣā* (a fundamental text of Sarvāstivāda), cited in the *Śāstra,* 28, 338b; its composition 29; the three different texts in the Chinese Collection under this title, 338b
*Vibhāṣā* (T. 1545), on *ākāśa,* 363b; on atomic elements, 59, 347a; on birth of birth, 362a; on the bodhisattva-way, 348b–49; on a Buddhist trend of the substantialist view of self, 365a; on the Dārṣṭāntikas, 56, 346b; on dream, 353a-b; on the false sense of self, 344a-b; on the five points of Mahādeva, 345b; on *hetu* and *pratyaya,* 360b–61a; on the Vibhajyavādins' view of *citta,* 348a
view; see *dṛṣṭi, mithyādṛṣṭi* and *samyagdṛṣṭi*
*Vigrahavyāvartanī,* 35, 36, 340a, b, 343a, 351b, 356b, 359a, 367b
*vijñāna* 識 (sense-experience, sensation, cognition); *see* cognition, idea
*vijñāna* 識 (mind, thought, intellect; self-conscious self-determining principle of intellection), as the basis of personal life, 64, 73, 131, 221, 225, 229, 233, 235, 350b, 355a; as conceived in Vijñānavāda, 340a; as the sense of individuality distinguished from false sense of self, 100; as the subtle seed of personal life in transition, 233, 238, 239, 240; see *citta*
Vijñānavāda, the, and the Mādhyamika, 321; the basic texts of, 378b
*Vijñaptimātratāsiddhi-śāstra,* 34, 340a, 379b
*vikalpa* 分別 (imaginative construction), 90, 352a-b; cf. *samjñā*
*Vimalakīrtinirdeśa,* 15, 32, 339b
*vimokṣa* 背捨 (deliverance or turning away i.e., from attachment to spheres of the determinate), the eight exercises of, 294, 372b, 373a
*vimokṣa-dvāra* 解脱門 (gates of freedom), factors of the way and, 290–96; the three, 293–96, 358a, 373a
*Viṁśikā,* 378b
*Vimuktimārga,* 357b
*Vinaya,* 64, 141, 143, 344a, 357b, 358a, 363a
*viparyāsa* 顛倒 (perversion), 353a; *see* error; cf. *viparyaya*
*viparyaya* 轉 (perversion), 353a; *see* error
*vīrya* 精進 (effort), as one of the four *ṛddhipadas,* 291; its five characterstics, 370b
*vīrya-pāramitā* (perfection of effot), 282, 285; see *pāramitā*
*viṣaya-viṣayī* (subject-object) pattern adopted in the Advaita Vedānta, 320
*Visuddhimagga,* 357b
*Vyākhyā-śāstra,* as one of the possible titles of the *Śāstra,* 335b
*vyañjana* (the means to bring to light the meaning, i.e., words), in contrast with the meaning *(artha)* itself, 356b; *cf.* meaning
*vyavahāra* 世間, 世界 (the world of convention; mundane life; mundane truth), direct teaching of, 138; import of *śūnyatā* on, 338b–39a; synonyms of the term, 73, 349b–50a; its distinction from and relation to *paramārtha,* 51–53, 138–41, 316; see *paramārtha, śūnyatā;* see also *prapañca*

Walleser, Max, 336a, 337a, 337b, 340a, 340b
Watters, 336a, 337b
way, the, 276–96; factors of, 290–96; the Great, and the Small, 278–90; *see* Mahāyāna, Hīnayāna; *see also* Middle Way
wayfaring, stages in the bodhisattva's, 305–11; see *bhūmi*
ways of answering, the Buddha's, 146–50; 344b, 358a
ways of teaching, the Buddha's, 133; the direct and the expedient, 135–36; see *siddhānta*
*Wei-shih-er-shih-lun* 唯識二十論 *(Vimśatikā* or *Vimśikā)*, 378b
Wenzel, H., 337b
wheel of *dharma;* see *dharma-cakra*
wisdom; see *prajñā*
world, and individual, 209–50; of con-convention, see *vyavahāra*
words, and their meanings 75, 130–31, 351a, 356b; see *nāma, varṇa*

Yamakami Sogen, 345b
*yāna(s)* 乘 (ways, vehicles), the two, 20, 46–47; *see* Hīnayāna, and Mahāyāna
Yao-hsing, the Emperor, 14
*yathārtha-jñāna* 如實智 (knowledge of things as they are; knowledge also of all other kinds of knowledge; the true *prajñā* belonging to the Buddha), as the highest of the eleven kinds of knowledge, 289–90; see *jñāna, prajñā*
*yoga* 相應 (harmony), as the nature of *śūnyatā,* 275, 368
Yoga, the, conception of time and change as close to Sarvāstivāda, 347a
*Yoga-sūtras,* 347a
Yogācāra, *see* Vijñānavāda
*Yuktiṣaṣṭikā,* 35, 36, 37

Zen 禪 (Ch'an), the, the Mādhyamika and, 327–28; modern studies in, 379b
*Zen Buddhism,* 379b